REASONABLY SIMPLE ECONOMICS

WHY THE WORLD WORKS THE WAY IT DOES

Evan Osborne

Apr

ISBN-13 (pbk): 978-1-4302-5941-1

ISBN-13 (electronic): 978-1-4302-5942-8

President and Publisher: Paul Manning
Acquisitions Editor: Jeff Olson
Editorial Board: Steve Anglin, Mark Beckner, Ewan Buckingham, Gary Cornell,
    Louise Corrigan, Morgan Ertel, Jonathan Gennick, Jonathan Hassell,
    Robert Hutchinson, Michelle Lowman, James Markham, Matthew Moodie,
    Jeff Olson, Jeffrey Pepper, Douglas Pundick, Ben Renow-Clarke,
    Dominic Shakeshaft, Gwenan Spearing, Matt Wade, Tom Welsh
Coordinating Editor: Rita Fernando
Copy Editor: Corbin Collins
Compositor: SPi Global
Indexer: SPi Global
Cover Designer: Anna Ishchenko

Distributed to the book trade worldwide by Springer Science+Business Media New York, 233 Spring Street, 6th Floor, New York, NY 10013. Phone 1-800-SPRINGER, fax (201) 348-4505, e-mail orders-ny@springer-sbm.com, or visit www.springeronline.com. Apress Media, LLC is a California LLC and the sole member (owner) is Springer Science + Business Media Finance Inc (SSBM Finance Inc). SSBM Finance Inc is a Delaware corporation.

For information on translations, please e-mail rights@apress.com, or visit www.apress.com.

Apress and friends of ED books may be purchased in bulk for academic, corporate, or promotional use. eBook versions and licenses are also available for most titles. For more information, reference our Special Bulk Sales–eBook Licensing web page at www.apress.com/bulk-sales.

Any source code or other supplementary materials referenced by the author in this text is available to readers at www.apress.com. For detailed information about how to locate your book's source code, go to www.apress.com/source-code/.

Apress Business: The Unbiased Source of Business Information

Apress business books provide essential information and practical advice, each written for practitioners by recognized experts. Busy managers and professionals in all areas of the business world—and at all levels of technical sophistication—look to our books for the actionable ideas and tools they need to solve problems, update and enhance their professional skills, make their work lives easier, and capitalize on opportunity.

Whatever the topic on the business spectrum—entrepreneurship, finance, sales, marketing, management, regulation, information technology, among others—Apress has been praised for providing the objective information and unbiased advice you need to excel in your daily work life. Our authors have no axes to grind; they understand they have one job only—to deliver up-to-date, accurate information simply, concisely, and with deep insight that addresses the real needs of our readers.

It is increasingly hard to find information—whether in the news media, on the Internet, and now all too often in books—that is even-handed and has your best interests at heart. We therefore hope that you enjoy this book, which has been carefully crafted to meet our standards of quality and unbiased coverage.

We are always interested in your feedback or ideas for new titles. Perhaps you'd even like to write a book yourself. Whatever the case, reach out to us at editorial@apress.com and an editor will respond swiftly. Incidentally, at the back of this book, you will find a list of useful related titles. Please visit us at www.apress.com to sign up for newsletters and discounts on future purchases.

The Apress Business Team

To my students, past, present, and future

Contents

About the Author

Evan Osborne is professor of economics at Wright State University. He has taught principles of economics for 20 years and has used economics to write about a wide array of topics. His current research interests involve the economics of sports and of ancient and contemporary China, and the history of individual liberty. But he is interested in everything.

Acknowledgments

First and foremost, I owe a great deal of gratitude to those students who ask the most interesting questions and challenge me to back up what I claim. Much of what I have learned about how to teach is due to learning from them. In addition, teaching and learning do not end at the classroom door, and so I have also been very lucky to have two demanding children, the ever-curious Weymar and the ever-skeptical Victoria, neither of whom will ever settle for a lazy answer. I am blessed every day to be able to watch and help you grow and to prepare to direct the grand journey of your lives.

Writing a book is a pleasure, but the writer's ego is far too powerful a force to allow him to properly scrutinize his own writing. I thus also owe a lot to Jeff Olson and Corbin Collins, whose meticulous attention to every word made all those words taken together easier on the reader.

Preface

This is a book originally written for students in the general-education course on economics at Wright State University, but my editor at Apress, Jeff Olson, told me that it might be helpful for those in the general public who wanted to understand economics better. It is not designed for the person who plans to major in economics in college, although I would be gratified if such students, and readers generally, also found it of use. It is also not written as a standard textbook, with a lot of text boxes, mathematicized problem sets, and fancy graphics (although there are some simple graphs for discussing supply and demand, because I use them in class). It is rather designed to emphasize the fundamentals that, I have noticed over the years, some students tend not to remember at exam time, perhaps because of the overall volume of material. Much of economics seems easy, obvious even, when you learn how to use it, but unless you constantly remind yourself about the essentials, it is equally easy to forget how to do so. This text, I hope, provides some of the fundamentals of economic thinking as I teach it.

I include some questions in the text, with the answers at the end of each chapter. These are not questions about solving supply/demand intersections, calculating the optimal amount of output, or doing the other sorts of exercises that clog standard undergraduate textbooks. They are usually just extensions of what I am discussing in the text, or ways to get students in the habit of applying economic reasoning outside its normal domain. There are also questions concerning readings that that I have found over the years to be vivid illustrations of some of the principles discussed in each chapter (though the reader is supposed to figure out why).

This book has been a lot of fun to write. It has also been a relief to get my increasingly chaotically edited notes down on record. I must also note forcefully that there is no engaged teaching without engaged students, and I have been blessed to have many of those over the years. In addition, I have drawn on the wisdom of many others. The thing about being a teacher of college economics is that one both makes up and picks up many good stories over the years that can be used to illustrate economic ideas. However, with the passage of time, it is hard to remember what one came up with on one's own and what one got from elsewhere. So, know that I have been influenced in particular by Paul Heyne's *The Economic Way of Thinking* (Prentice Hall), particularly the long out-of-print eighth edition, Thomas Sowell's *Basic Economics* (Basic Books, 2010), Steven E. Landsburg's *The Armchair Economist: Economics and Everyday Life* (Free Press, 2012), and the many insightful posts and stories at Don Boudreaux's and Russ Roberts' terrific Café Hayek blog. I have tried to credit these authors and others whenever I know

I have taken a story or example from them, but it is possible but I have missed some. If so, I apologize.

As a final note, I have one compositional eccentricity. I do not believe in using "he or she," "s/he," or "they" when what is called for is a singular pronoun. I follow the lead of the writer Charles Murray, who believes that sentences calling for a singular pronoun ought to have one, and for convenience's sake that that pronoun should just have the same sex as the writer. So when I use "he," I am making no statements about the roles of men and women in economic theory, or in society.

Anyone with comments—approving, dismissive, argumentative, error-flagging (including dead web links), curious, or other—is welcome to contact me at evan.osborne@wright.edu.

Introduction

The Value of Economics in Daily Life

You may be reading this because you have enrolled in an economic principles class, or you may be simply curious about basic economics. In buying it, you probably thought you were signing up for a discussion of inflation, unemployment, interest rates, whether the standard of living is going up or down, outsourcing, the gyrations of the stock market, and other topics that seem somehow to be related to "economics" and often find their way into the news.

All in good time. But before gaining any further understanding on these matters, we have to start from the foundation of the economic way of thinking. For that is what economics is—not a list of specific topics, but a systematic way of *thinking* about all topics. The list of concepts to which the economic way of thinking can be applied vastly exceeds the short list just mentioned. To tackle those things without mastering the economic way of thinking about them is to put the cart before the horse. This way of thinking has taken several centuries to develop and has proven its usefulness in addressing one social problem after another. But it is not the only way to think about society and how it works. As you read this, try to fit what you learn about economics into what else you have learned about the world and how to think about it—history, philosophy, psychology, and even literature all have useful things to say about human decision making and the society that results from it.

The Foundation of Modern Economics: The Idea of Scarcity

Consider the following questions, which might seem far removed from the seemingly "core" economic topics in the first paragraph:

- **Q1.1** Look at a photograph of a public scene—on a street, in a baseball stadium—or a private one like this party for college freshmen[1] at Rice University in the early 1970s. In addition to somewhat different standards of dress, one thing obvious from the party picture is that people were much thinner then. Why have people in the United States gotten so much heavier over the years? Before you answer, realize that this is a phenomenon that is occurring not just in the U.S. but in countries all over the world.

- **Q1.2** Much commentary in recent years has focused on rising inequality of income in the U.S. Despite that, a phenomenon associated with previous centuries of inequality has almost disappeared: the personal servant. Noble families in Europe might easily have had dozens of household servants. Yet even the wealthiest now get by with relatively few; it is hard to imagine Bill Gates having the kind of massive household staff that the typical English manor in the mid-1800s might have. What changed? (See Arnold Kling's blog post "Where Are the Servants?"[2] for a few suggestions.)

- **Q1.3** Why are people in small towns generally friendlier than people in big cities?

- **Q1.4** The last 50 years have seen the introduction of an incredible wave of time-saving machinery, plus an increase in wealth that allows almost everyone in prosperous countries such as the U.S. to obtain what used to be considered the basic necessities of life. And yet, according to survey data, people report that they are pressed for time and money. (You may feel the same way, despite having much more disposable income than your grandparents did.) Why?

---

[1] http://ricehistorycorner.files.wordpress.com/2012/01/1972-freshman-reception-3.jpg
[2] http://econlog.econlib.org/archives/2011/10/where_are_the_s.html

- **Q1.5** In a photo[3] bouncing around the Internet, supposedly taken of Northeast Asia at night, one can see clearly
  the massive, busy, nocturnal civilization going on in the
  Pacific coast of Japan and in South Korea. The photo also
  shows North Korea, which basically has no light at all.
  This is an indication that South Korea is a much wealthier
  country than North Korea, despite the fact that South
  Korea was dirt poor at the end of the Korean War in the
  early 1950s—poorer in fact than the North (because the
  South inherited fewer factories built under the Japanese
  colonial occupation). Since the end of the war, in the
  North, famine has occurred more than once, even as
  South Korea has built one of the most technologically
  advanced societies in the world. Given that they share a
  common language and more or less a common culture,
  what explains this difference?

Clearly these questions concern different topics, yet a single method can be
used to try to answer all of them.[4] The foundation for this method is called
scarcity. The word is a little unfortunate, because most people take it to mean
"the state of being rare." A better word would be *finiteness*, but *scarcity* is the
word that, thanks to the history of economic writing, we are stuck with.

The foundational assumption of scarcity, which defines how economists
think about everything, has only two very large bricks: our desire to have
more of what we want is infinite, but our means of satisfying our wants are
finite. The first assumption, which is commonly misunderstood, simply says
that as long as we don't have to give up anything else, more money is better than less. Four cars are better than three (assuming that "as long as we
don't have to give up anything else" means we won't run out of driveway
space). And more leisure time is better than less. So this assumption that
our desire for more is infinite is very defensible. Even Mother Theresa and
Albert Schweitzer had infinite desires—they surely believed that if one more
poor person could be helped without cost, he[5] should be.

Invoking scarcity is not synonymous with saying that people have limitless
greed for material things. Many people derive satisfaction in life from sources
that go far beyond such things and so might easily decide that two cars, two
children, or two bedrooms in the house are enough. People routinely pursue

---

[3]http://www.globalsecurity.org/military/world/dprk/dprk-dark.htm
[4]All questions asked in the text are answered, to the best of my ability, at the end of
 each chapter.
[5]Please see the preface for an explanation as to why I use the pronoun *he* throughout
 the book.

objectives that don't revolve around material goods. They sacrifice wealth to care for their children; they take care of the world's most desperate poor or provide financial, technical, or other kinds of literacy to people who need it; they get out of the rat race at an early age and retire to fish and read philosophy even though if they had waited ten years they would have had a lot more money to retire on; they major in French or classics instead of accounting or engineering just for the sheer joy of it.

But these are only arguments about what their wants are, not about their not having unlimited wants. If someone had given Mother Theresa enough money to take care of one more beggar on the streets of Calcutta for one year without strings attached, she would have taken it. If the student who majors in philosophy but has even a minimal interest in engineering could magically absorb information about the latter while he slept, without distracting him from his other course work, he would do so. Life is about more than money, and nothing in the economic way of thinking suggests otherwise. That is because it is defined around *goals*, not material things. Further, *each goal is unique to the person who has it.*

And so in economics we do in fact assume that scarcity is a problem that is always with us—no matter how much you have, more is better. If Bill Gates is walking down the street and sees a $100 bill on the sidewalk, does he pick it up? Surely he does, despite the billions he already possesses. All that is required in the economic way of thinking is that those billions plus $100 are better than those billions without the $100. Bill Gates can find some use for the money that justifies the cost of his bending over to pick it up (which, in light of his and his wife's extensive charitable activities, almost certainly does not involve him buying some material possession for himself). Limitless desires, properly defined, apply to everyone.

▨ **Note**   In principle, we all have limitless desires. But the ability to attain them is limited by finite means.

The second brick of scarcity's foundation is that we cannot have more of what we want without paying some kind of cost. Every choice, in other words, has consequences. There are undoubtedly people who are currently not giving money to Mother Teresa's organization but would be willing to do so if asked. How does the organization find them? And how much are they willing to donate, given that they have other uses for their money? Such knowledge does not fall freely from the sky, and the more resources the organization spends trying to find gain that information, the fewer it has to actually help the poor (or to help them right now, anyway). To major in one field is to forgo majoring in another. To go on vacation on the spur of the moment may mean having less money set aside for retirement; it certainly means having less money available for something. To have a child (and indeed to have a first) means giving up time and money that could be spent on other things. If you want something of value, you must give up something else that you also value. The most common way economists speak about this phenomenon is so widely used that it has become an abbreviation, particularly on the Internet—TNSTAAFL (*there's no such thing as a free lunch*).

The lack of a free lunch is true at the social level as well. To make a college education or health care "free" is to do the impossible. There will be a cost. The only question is who will bear it. This insight in fact does not just apply to "standard" economic questions like why oil is so expensive or the unemployment rate is so high. In fact, it applies to almost the entire spectrum of human activities.

The combination of limitless wants and limited possibilities means that choices must be made. And this is what economics is about—the need to make decisions in an environment of scarcity. If no one can have everything they want, some procedures will be found to decide who gets what.

Rules and Freedom

Some years ago, the Danish town of Christiansfeld launched what must be reckoned an extraordinary experiment.[6] In the center of town, the city fathers got rid of all traffic lights and warning signs and turned the central district into a zone where cars, bicycles, pedestrians and even buses and trucks could all move through without rules of any sort. The policy was called "ambiguity and urban legibility," which does not sound like a promising formula to regulate the flow of traffic, an environment where one would suppose ambiguity— uncertainty about who has what obligations to whom, who has to follow what rules—to be the enemy of safety. Everybody was thrown together in a single space, and it was left only to the discipline of each participant, whether in a car, on a bike, or on foot, to avoid colliding with others.

Remarkably, the accident rate fell dramatically, to a level of zero over three years.[7] Even travel time fell, despite the fact that the only traffic discipline was self-discipline. Travelers used hand and eye signals and their own instincts to get through the shared space more safely and more quickly. A similar experiment was also successful in Bohmte, Germany,[8] despite the presence of a major highway in that city.

---

[6]http://www.wired.com/wired/archive/12.12/traffic.html
[7]http://cityrenewal.blogspot.com/2009/04/post-modernism-transport-planning.html
[8]http://www.csmonitor.com/World/Europe/2008/0912/p07s03-woeu.html

How could it be that traffic interaction without rules, where the only things one could rely on were just one's own self-control and the self-control of others, outperformed the system we have grown accustomed to, where everybody has rules they must follow in order to prevent dangerous choices? The reason is that traffic accidents are a thing that people want to avoid, even as they also want to get where they are going as expeditiously as possible. Allowing everyone to rely on his own self-interest leads to a system that functions not perfectly—the naïve pursuit of perfection has been known to ruin many a government policy—but *as effectively as possible*. No driver gives much thought to the interests of the other drivers, only to his own; and yet everybody's interest is served simply by relying on each individual to pursue his own.

The flow of traffic is like human society in miniature. There is a fixed amount of space that all travelers must share; space, in other words, is scarce. And in these towns there is no central coordination of who is entitled to be in what space when. Yet the space is quickly and efficiently allocated, despite the fact that nobody knows, or cares about, where everybody else is going. Could such a thing work in a big city, with huge volumes of traffic and people desperate to get somewhere quickly? But in a sense it *does* work there as well! In fact, on freeways in particular, one of the reasons the traffic flows so smoothly with remarkably few accidents is precisely because when we want to change lanes, we rely on the rational self-interest of others not to aggressively grab the space. Through this process of uncoordinated but nonetheless actual cooperation, traffic flows.

There are, of course, traffic laws in Los Angeles and Atlanta (although they are often observed mostly in the breach), but on any given road at any given time traffic is flowing in an undirected way yet efficient way, where people get where they are going as effectively as possible by relying on the willingness of other drivers to look after their own self-interest. So too it is with the broader society: there are only so many workers, so much land, so much oil, so many hours in the day, so much money saved up, yet some way has to be found to decide how, precisely, each of these scarce things should be used. And through a coordination process that we will investigate more thoroughly, those resources end up being used for some purposes and not others through the peaceful cooperation that we will call the *market*.

I do not know whether the traffic engineers of northwestern Europe have read it, but in the year 1776 (a momentous year for other reasons, too) a Scotsman named Adam Smith wrote a book that argued in particular that often the same principle that motivated the design of the open traffic spaces in these towns should also underlie the way we decide how resources get used—the way we decide who gets what.

The book was called *An Inquiry into the Nature and Causes of the Wealth of Nations*. It was written at a time when economics was beginning to mature as a distinct area of intellectual inquiry. He was actually known then as a "political economist," because much controversy, then as now, was attached to the relation between things the government did and people's material quality of life. It is a remarkable book that touches on a wide variety of subjects, but what is of interest here is two contentions about human nature and human society:

> In civilized society he [man] stands at all times in need of the cooperation and assistance of great multitudes, while his whole life is scarce sufficient to gain the friendship of a few persons. In almost every other race of animals each individual, when it is grown up to maturity, is entirely independent, and in its natural state has occasion for the assistance of no other living creature. But man has almost constant occasion for the help of his brethren, and it is in vain for him to expect it from their benevolence only. He will be more likely to prevail if he can interest their self-love in his favour, and show them that it is for their own advantage to do for him what he requires of them. Whoever offers to another a bargain of any kind, proposes to do this. Give me that which I want, and you shall have this which you want, is the meaning of every such offer; and it is in this manner that we obtain from one another the far greater part of those good offices which we stand in need of. It is not from the benevolence of the butcher, the brewer, or the baker, that we expect our dinner, but from their regard to their own interest. We address ourselves, not to their humanity but to their self-love, and never talk to them of our own necessities but of their advantages.[9]

The language of course is somewhat archaic, but the passage essentially means that we get that which we desire by relying on the pursuit by others of their own self-interest and not of ours, with the result nonetheless that we all simultaneously do better. Why does the guy we hire to fix our leaky pipe or the merchant we patronize to sell us lettuce generally try to do right by us? Because his business depends on it. At this level the idea is blindingly obvious, but people often ignore or even deny that people generally seek to follow their self-interest, and sometimes go so far as to assert that a society built on "selfishness" simply cannot succeed.

In contrast, the economist assumes that human behavior and human society are best understood by assuming that people always pursue their self-interest as they see it. In the words of the economist Steven Landsburg, evoking the legendary Jewish philosopher Hillel's clever remark: "Most of economics can be summarized in four words: 'People respond to incentives.' The rest is commentary."[10] In other words, *people do things when the benefits exceed the costs, and don't do them when the costs exceed the benefits.* So already we began to get some insight

---

[9]Adam Smith, *An Inquiry into the Nature and Causes of the Wealth of Nations*, Book 1, chapter 2, paragraph 2.

[10]Hillel was supposedly asked to summarize (http://forward.com/articles/14250/the-rest-of-the-rest-is-commentary-/) the Torah, the Old Testament portion of the Bible, in the time he could stand on one leg. The answer? "That which is hateful to you, do not unto another: This is the whole Torah. The rest is commentary—[and now] go study."

into the questions raised at the beginning of the chapter, although I'm not ready to answer them just yet. In each case, the economist would say that the changes have occurred because the incentives have changed—in other words, because the costs and benefits of various actions have changed. If people are becoming heavier, for example, the benefits to doing things that make one heavier must have risen and/or the cost of being heavier must have declined for the average person. To think economically, *always think in terms of benefits and costs.*

▨ **Tip** To think as an economist would, *always* think in terms of benefits and costs.

Remarkably, it is usually true that allowing everyone to pursue his own self-interest leads to a sort of coordination whereby we are as well-off as we can be.[11] Of course, nothing in a market system is literally *coordinated* if that word means someone giving explicit commands that others must obey. But coordination nonetheless happens; goods and services are produced and distributed to people, and those people in turn are able to support themselves. This happens because the process of *market exchange*—people going to work, buying and selling on mutually agreeable terms (or refusing to buy and sell on other terms)—knits us all together and gives us a reason to work together for mutual benefit. People may think they are working for themselves, but in a sense they are actually working for everyone else. Adam Smith's butcher's main social function is to provide meat for his customers, and by giving him a reason to do so (a reason that involves rewards and not punishment) everyone is more likely to have good meat at a good price. In other words, when we let people do what is best for them alone, society as a whole benefits because everybody is given an *incentive* to work together, given that we can't have everything that we want. Much of this book is devoted to exploring why that happens.

The Wealth of Nations is a long, complicated, historically important book. There is far more in it than the excerpts above, and there are some things in it that indicate suspicion of self-interest. For example, elsewhere in the book Smith argues very strongly that relying only on individual pursuit of self-interest can be a mistake, as in the case of businesses that try to fix prices. He also argues that government is essential to provide "certain public works and certain

---

[11]The argument being made here—that letting everybody pursue his self-interest is also in the best interest of the entire society—is sometimes called the *invisible hand*, which is supposed to lead everybody do the right thing for society in the course of doing what is right for them individually. Adam Smith created the phrase in *The Wealth of Nations*, although as noted earlier the book is more nuanced on the broader question of the proper scope of government, and of trade, in promoting the broader social good. However, given the prevailing environment of late-1700s Britain, which was rife with special government privileges for big business and extensive restrictions on foreign trade, all imposed in the belief that the government could control resource use for this broader good, this was a radical statement.

public institutions, which it can never be the interest of any individual or small number of individuals to erect and maintain." However, the book introduced the world to the idea of organizing society the way Bohmte organizes traffic: allow people to interact freely, and you be will more likely to like the results. This process is often called "spontaneous order" or "spontaneous adjustment," because we rely on individuals to change their economic behavior in response to changed circumstances, in contrast to trying to impose order from above.

This idea—that the best rules are often no rules—is sometimes difficult to accept. We see a world in which many problems appear to be unsolved and feel that if we could organize resources in some other way, there would be less poverty, things that seem unfair wouldn't happen, etc. But the basic argument made here is that in fact these things are the result of scarcity. "Solving" them through nonmarket means in the face of scarcity often creates other problems that are worse. Relying on chaos and the free interplay of individuals generally does a better job of solving such problems, with some limited exceptions outlined in Chapter 10.

Rules amid the Chaos

And yet I pulled a fast one in describing the rules of Bohmte and Christiansfeld as "no rules." If you and I were driving our cars in the central space, and I suddenly decided to ram yours, I would be charged with violation of a rule. So too would I be if I decided to drive through the town square carefully, but in your car instead of mine. The fact that we are allowed to interact freely doesn't give me the right to take what is yours, or to damage what is yours. And so we are introduced to the idea of *property rights*. The law vests us with rights to what is ours, which means that there are indeed rules that define what is mine and what is yours. My car is mine, and you can't drive or damage it without my permission. Burglary and pickpocketing are crimes, as is violence outside of self-defense. But we only call these things "rules" because someone is empowered to force the person who breaks them to pay consequences.

In most modern societies that "someone" is the government, and Adam Smith's vision—a pursuit of self-interest generally serving the common good—assumes a government that can enforce people's rights to property, including the right to sell their property to someone else on whatever terms the two parties can agree to. Because societies have discovered historically that such a system works reasonably well, a group of individuals called "the government" generally possesses the power to enforce laws against theft and violence, and often against many other things as well. We could not harness the self-interest of the "brewer, butcher, or the baker" for the greater good of society unless the brewer, butcher, and baker could do business securely, confident they can keep much of the money they make and that their property is safe from vandalism or seizure not just by thieves on the street but by petty government officials too. And so it falls to government to, at a minimum, enforce property rights and make prosperity achievable through the pursuit of self-interest, while at the same time not becoming a source of problems itself.

It is also worth thinking why Bohmte and Christiansfeld have roads to begin with. They are old cities, and their history is not one likely to be repeated in a modern country. (Christiansfeld was apparently founded thanks to a gift from the King of Denmark, who exempted its citizens from trade taxes and paid for the town's founding.) In modern societies, many public services, including roads, are generally paid for not through voluntary trade but by the government assessing taxes (and punishing people who don't pay them!) to pay directly for their construction. Roads are built not by asking people for contributions the way an apricot farmer would ask people if they want to buy his fruit, but by telling people they have to contribute in the form of taxes and fining or imprisoning them if they don't pay.

Roads are socially valuable without question (although they are socially costly too), but government is a tricky thing. Even when democratically selected, it depends on the imposition or threatened imposition of force to get what it wants. If the government needs your property to build a school or military base, the penalties for failing to hand it over are likely to be severe. If the government wants to spend some money on something or other, those who don't pay are punished. If the government tells businesses that they may not hire workers for less than $7.50 an hour, any business that does so faces legal sanction, and it doesn't matter that it can find workers happy to work at that wage.

Government force is a tool that must be used with care. Human history is replete with instances in which the application of force on a large scale by governments has resulted in untold human misery. In the 20th century, much of this horrendous violence was done explicitly to achieve better social outcomes—for example, societies where workers and not "capitalists" ran factories, where poverty was abolished, etc. In addition, particularly in modern democratic societies, there is a tendency to mistake what is good for me with what is good for everyone, and to ignore the consequences for the goals, dreams, and ambitions of other people of using the government instead of the market to get what we want. For these reasons, this application of force—the overriding of the relations humans have organized on their own by the imposition of laws and punishments for not complying with the relations dictated by the government—is something that should be done with care, as Chapter 5 discusses in detail.

▩ **Note**   Government "force" must be used with care—the totalitarian states of the 20th century are testament to the damage excessive force can do to society.

To summarize, economics is based on the idea that we have unlimited wants but limited means to satisfy them. This requires that we make choices. There are many ways to make those choices. One way is to send people out into the market and trade on the basis of their self-interest. We assume that those people will do that which is best for them, and if the incentives they face change, their behavior will change too. Another way is to regiment society—to have a king, the Party, elected representatives, or bureaucrats make the decisions about whether and if so how to build factories, how to regulate the terms of exchange and the prices that people may charge for things, or how to take resources and the opportunities they create from some people and give them to others (the poor, companies that produce "green technology," the elderly, people who have given campaign donations to the politicians currently in office, and so on).

Throughout this book, I compare these two ways of deciding how to solve the fundamental problem of scarcity.

Answers to In-Text Questions

1.1. *Why have people in the United States gotten so much heavier over the years?* Economics focuses a lot on prices and preferences. Here the most sensible answer seems to involve prices—it seems unlikely that people subject to millions of years of evolution have suddenly in the last few decades developed a taste, so to speak, for eating large amounts of food generally or fattening foods in particular. Since changes in weight are a function of changes in calories in minus calories out, I would look for an answer that is based on the idea that the price of expending calories has gone up (for example, because people have chosen to live so far from work that they choose to use motorized transportation to get there, even as the cost of being away from work to go to the gym has also gone up), and the price of consuming it has gone down. That's because the money price of food as a share of total income earned has gone continuously down, because Styrofoam boxes make it easy to take home incredible amounts of restaurant leftovers, because food-storage technology including refrigerators and boxes that can hold Twinkies for long periods of time without the contents spoiling also leaves large amounts of food easily available at easy reach in the home, etc. Improved medical care—pills and surgery—have also made being overweight less costly, although some of these advances were probably themselves driven by the rising rates of obesity. Economic growth and the greater affordability of food that it generates it are phenomena seen not just in the United States but worldwide.

1.2. *Why have personal servants largely disappeared from our society?* As we will see in the next chapter, if one chooses to be a personal servant, as with any job, one must give up some other activity that is also valuable, including but not limited to other kinds of work. Salaries have risen immensely over the years, meaning that what people have to give up to be a personal servant has also risen in value. There was an ample supply of people with few alternatives in the days of the large manor, and so the number of people who were eager to get that work, which might make the difference between being able to support yourself or not, was correspondingly large. Not so anymore. The increasing difficulty of persuading people to be servants because they have more options than they used to is what has made the number of servants fewer.

1.3. *Why are people in small towns generally friendlier than people in big cities?* I would say that the cost of getting to know about people is lower in a small town because you run into them more frequently, it's more likely that you have common friends, and for other reasons. When we don't know someone, we may for safety reasons have to assume the worst about whether or not they are honest and safe to be around. In the big city, we're surrounded by people we don't know anything about. In the small town, we're surrounded by people we have had plenty of opportunity to get to know, by running into them repeatedly (which makes us more willing to engage them) or by introduction or reputation. It is easier to be friendly to people you know a lot about, provided that what you know is good.

1.4. *Why, despite the increase in wealth and time-saving machinery, do people often feel short of time and money?* Time-saving machinery has obviously released a great deal of time from uses that used to claim it, but it has also opened up many other possibilities for using time. What one gives up by sitting around doing very little has grown spectacularly (new entertainment options, new travel possibilities, etc.), and so the attractiveness of sitting around doing nothing *relative to the alternatives* has declined. "Free" time is not really free. People who used to spend tremendous amounts of time doing household chores or farming the fields don't have to do that anymore. Instead they take yoga classes or do market work to earn money that enables them to buy new things. So all the hours in the day still get consumed, along with other things made possible by having more money.

1.5. *Why has South Korea flourished compared to North Korea?*
The ability to use scarce resources more effectively in the
South, because the government enacts policies that encourage resources to be used effectively, makes South Korea
wealthier. The North, in contrast, as an economic dicta-
torship, has policies that almost guarantee that resources
will be used ineffectively. The difference in the two sets of
policies is a big part of what this book is about.

Economics Out There[12]

1.1. A story in the *Telegraph*[13] explains that Danes are frustrated because police give them traffic tickets but won't
tell them why. Why might the self-interest of the people
who run a government lie in having ambiguous laws?
(As always in economics, this is about someone's self-
interest.)

1.2. This Café Hayek[14] article points out how unions are
paying low wages and benefits to people whom they
hire to picket for them, while punishing them for excessive breaks. What self-interest is the union able to pursue
more effectively by hiring cheaper workers and demanding that they work harder? (The answer is *not* simply
"lower costs." It is what they are able to do more of by
lowering the costs of picketing.) What self-interest are
the companies a union negotiates with able to pursue
by successfully turning away union demands? Is there a
moral difference between the two situations?

---

[12]These and others in following chapters are examples of economic principles in action in
the real world.
[13]http://www.telegraph.co.uk/news/worldnews/europe/denmark/7931243/
Danish-drivers-stumped-by-secret-rules.html
[14]http://cafehayek.com/2006/02/getting_more_do.html

Supply and Demand, Considered Separately

Why Red-Eye Flights Are Always Full Now and Other Puzzles Explained

Asked what something costs, your reply will almost surely be in the form of a number, expressed in dollars if you are an American. But why is the number what it is? Why does a sandwich cost $3.50, a gallon of gas $4.00, some books $20, others $40, a new car $20,000? Probably you have some sense of the answer, which involves the costs for the things needed to make these items. Sandwiches need meat and bread, and books need paper and ink. Cars need rubber, several kinds of metals, upholstering, and all manner of other resources. All of these things cost money, as does the time of workers hired.

Opportunity Cost

But that just kicks the can down the road a bit. Why do *these* things cost what they cost? In fact, the way economists think about cost does not directly lead to a number, although a number may sometimes be used to represent it. But the number per se is uninformative. Say you learn that a company in the country of Fredonia plans to export its new smartphone to the U.S., and right now the company is selling it in Fredonia for twelve doubloons (the currency in Fredonia). All that tells you nothing. But translating that price to dollars is informative not because they're dollars, but because expressing it in dollars tells you what sacrifice you have to bear to buy one when they are sold here, compared perhaps to the sacrifice required to obtain an existing smartphone. Cost is therefore not an absolute. Rather, it only makes sense in the context of *comparisons to something else*. The numbers we sometimes attach to costs are merely reflections of this. Knowing something costs $1,000 is meaningless until you know what else $1,000 will buy. Everything in economics is about *relative* analysis—that is, comparisons. The classic example is a comparison of benefits and costs when thinking about an action.

It must also be noted that *things* do not really have costs. Rather, *actions* have costs. College students naturally wonder why the cost of college is so high, and I will return to that shortly. But in the meantime, we must differentiate between the cost of *acquiring* a college education and the cost of *providing* one, which are two different things. In each action mentioned here, I will talk about its cost as its *opportunity cost*, which means *the value of what must be given up to take the action*.

Sometimes a choice is easy to analyze. A student sleeps in and skips his economics class when he expects that the opportunity cost of doing so—the value of what he expects to learn in the class—will be low enough to justify staying home. Note that tricky word *value*. There is clearly a cost to sleeping in and missing a day's worth of material. Is that a monetary cost? Can one attach a dollar value to it? In principle yes, but practically no. The value of the material to some other classmate who really enjoys economics, or who needs to get a very high grade in the class for some reason, may well be higher than it is to some other student for whom these conditions are not true. So value, and therefore the opportunity cost of an action, is *context-dependent*. Value depends not just on the action, but on the person thinking about taking it, and in particular on the value *he* attaches to the alternative *he* is contemplating giving up in order to take that action.

Note also that we need consider only one alternative. Say our student has multiple choices if he doesn't go to class: sleeping in, watching television, or cleaning up the dishes left over from the night before. If sleeping in is what he will in fact choose if he doesn't go to class, the other choices are irrelevant. Only the value to him of sleeping in is the true opportunity cost of going to class.

So what then is the opportunity cost of the action of acquiring a college education? (I mean acquiring a full degree, not one day's worth of material in one class.) If we think of cost only as a number, we think of the money spent on tuition and books and stop. But money is just a number, an index. It doesn't really tell us what was sacrificed. Money (at least American money) is just green pieces of paper in one sense (more about this in Chapter 11) and only acquires value insofar as it can be exchanged for other things. If tuition is $3,000 a quarter, we need to think (perhaps, in light of actual college tuition,[1] after counting our blessings) about what that money would have been spent on—putting money aside for a house, maybe, which reduces the time and money one has to spend to live in an apartment, or buying a car that would otherwise be unaffordable.

But even this omits what is perhaps the most substantial cost of college. Everyone who is not a slave, a child, or incarcerated has command over one key resource: his time. What is the opportunity cost of being in college for four years? The value of whatever that time would have otherwise been used for. For almost every student, this would have been time in the labor force. According to U.S. government data, which are not available for those under 25, the median annual earnings of someone with only a high school degree were about $28,000 in 2008. So that is what on average must be given up every year one attends college.[2]

What about the cost of providing college? This is obviously a different action, taken by different people. If the school is a typical private university, it is run as a kind of nonprofit corporation. The people who run it hire a certain number of faculty. Faculty are not enough to make the university run by itself; it also requires staff to run the offices and supervise and operate units of the university (secretaries, deans, custodians, a president, vice presidents, librarians). Each of these people has an opportunity cost of time, and it is in fact society that bears the cost of their working at the university. Why? Because these people are not doing what they otherwise would be doing, because the university is paying them a salary that persuades them to work there. What society gives up when people work at a university instead of doing something else is obviously a hard and often impossible thing to nail down because it is context-dependent for each individual, but the fact that these costs exist is often critical when we judge whether or not it is worthwhile to rely on markets to make these decisions. The costs of any activity ought to be taken account of when deciding whether it should be taken, and so the degree to which markets take account of these costs is a central issue.

---

[1] http://nces.ed.gov/fastfacts/display.asp?id=76

[2] Technically, it is the value of what the dollars would have been used for, although it is often convenient to summarize this way as long as we remember what the dollars really stand for.

Most universities also possess land. The land is already paid for, so should it be considered costless? It should not. The people who run the university are choosing not to close it down and sell that land off to some other party who would do something else with it—build houses, tear everything down except the football stadium and use that to attract an NFL team, turn it into a wildlife preserve, whatever. Whichever party would be willing to pay the most for the land (and that depends on how much value that party attaches to the alternate use) doesn't get that chance, and so for society that has to be counted as part of the opportunity cost of operating a university there.

In fact, all the resources that the university uses in its operation must be counted—the computers provided to students, the exercise equipment in the fitness center, all the way down to the paperclips used in every office. All of these things are used by the university instead of being used by others in society, and so have to be counted as part of the cost of *providing* the services of that university. So the cost of running a university is actually borne by the rest of us, who are deprived of other things because the university, by trading in the marketplace, has acquired control over a set of resources that are then not used to produce other things. This point is fundamental: the cost of producing is a cost *to society* (technically to specific but unknown people in society) which is deprived of other things of value when this thing of value—a university education—is produced.

▓ **Question 2.1** Why do universities these days often spend so much money on facilities like apartments—which more and more are replacing old-fashioned dormitories—and state-of-the-art exercise facilities?

And so it is with any activity, in particular commercial activities. (I'm using *commercial* here to mean something that is provided in exchange for money, even if the university itself is nonprofit, and not simply for-profit activity.) Any activity requires *claiming resources that have opportunity costs because they are scarce*. As a result, we will eventually want to know whether the benefits from the activity justify those costs. And we have to think beyond the opportunity cost as simply, for example, "workers." We must think instead in terms of what those workers would otherwise be doing. We also want to avoid thinking about cost as a number, except as a measure of the actual cost, which is a thing or things given up.

▓ **Question 2.2** Analyze the opportunity costs, worker and otherwise, of the following actions:

a. Manufacturing iPads in the U.S.

b. Manufacturing iPads in China

c. Publishing a newspaper online

d. Publishing a print edition of the same newspaper

e. Designing video games

f. Manufacturing video games

g. Producing and selling a textbook on your own, by selling it as an e-book

h. Producing and selling a textbook using a textbook company that produces print and e-editions

i. Raising a child

Sunk vs. Marginal Costs

My example about the opportunity cost of going to college is a little incomplete, because many students work while they are in college, which changes the calculations. Note first that the work students do is likely to be work that is quite different from what they would be doing had they not decided to go to college. If a student graduates high school and decide not to enroll in college, the chances are excellent that he will search for work that has some kind of long-term payoff, that serves as the foundation for a career. The work that students do in college, in contrast, is often part-time. It provides little in the way of long-term training that will raise future earnings (there are exceptions, of course), although done well it does signal to future employers that the student has a record of working responsibly. So the student would have to subtract his part-time earnings from what he would earn if he went straight into the labor force, including the value of the training he is getting in his full-time career-based job. But even if we assumed that the value of this training were zero, and that the income from the part-time work is 20 hours a week times $15 an hour times 50 weeks a year (and each student has to decide if this is a realistic estimate or not), that comes to $15,000 a year, meaning that the *marginal* opportunity cost for a student with that amount of part-time working of going to college must include $28,000 (the amount not earned by not working full-time but with only a high-school degree) minus $15,000 (the amount earned working part-time). That equals $13,000, which is nonetheless more than the explicit money spent on tuition.

But I smuggled a word in there: *marginal*. What does that mean? In economics, *marginal* generally has the meaning of "extra" or "additional." It is true that by going to college you are forgoing, using these numbers, $28,000 in annual salary, but you will still earn $15,000 of that in your part-time work. So the net forgone[3] income is the marginal cost, which is only $13,000.

The decision to work has other marginal costs too—costs that still lie in front of you. If you decide to work in the third year of college, it may be that this will extend your time until graduation by a year. Is it worth it? Well, you'll incur (by our earlier numbers) 3 quarters × $3,000/quarter = $9,000 in marginal tuition expense (assuming you pay the same regardless of how many classes you take), but you'll offset that with $15,000 in income. But wait! By deferring graduation, you also defer a chance to earn a *college graduate's* first-year salary, which according to the government for those aged 25–29 is $42,000. That number minus $15,000 equals $27,000, which is the marginal salary forgone. So really, the monetary value of the full opportunity cost is $9,000 (dollars spent on tuition) + $27,000 (dollars not earned because you're not working full-time with a college degree) = $36,000. Thus, extending the time until you graduate is, at least by these numbers, quite costly.

To take a different problem, suppose instead that you decide after your sophomore year to change majors from computer science to petroleum engineering, because you find that the starting salary of a computer programmer right now is $40,000 instead of the $70,000 you expected, whereas the starting salary of a petroleum engineer is $60,000 instead of the $45,000 you expected. (I just made the numbers up.) But it will take you an extra year to graduate. What should count as cost? This time assume, to make it easy, that the student's parents have chosen to pay his college costs. Time out of the labor force would count, as before, but how much time? If you don't change majors and wait two years to graduate, you give up the high-school salary of $28,000 for each of the two years still to go, but you were doing that anyway. Let's further assume that while in college you don't work part-time. So that's not marginal, given the decision you are considering (graduating in two years or three). You *do* have to give up what you expect to be $40,000 (the actual number may turn out, because of market changes, to be higher or lower) in computer-science salary in your fifth year, plus $9,000 in tuition. In exchange, you will earn $70,000 in the first year and more (presumably) every year after. So, assuming you have no intrinsic enjoyment for either job (that is, you are just considering money),[4] the benefits will, at least in expectation, exceed the costs.

---

[3]Note that that word *forgone* shows up a lot in discussion of opportunity cost, because you have to forgo some action to take some other action.

[4]Which, frankly, is often a mistake, because you will be spending so much time at work that enjoyment of it is also an important consideration.

▨ **Note** The only costs that matter are the costs you can still control—that is, marginal costs.

Here is another problem to think about. Think about an airline deciding whether to discontinue a flight. A writer on a blog in 2007 wrote the following:

> Time was, red-eye flights were half empty, or more. You could often spread out on two or even three adjacent seats, and it really was like a little in-flight hotel room. But that time has passed, and red-eyes, as most of the fights, are now full or close to full.[5]

This raises a couple of questions. First, why would an airline ever choose to send a plane out half empty? Planes are expensive, after all. But most of the costs related to paying for the plane, even if the airline had borrowed to buy them, are not marginal but *sunk*. Sunk costs *are costs that involve no opportunity for choice because they are in the past.* So the airline wants to know whether running that flight will incur more in extra (marginal) costs than it will yield marginal benefits. And to be sure there are marginal costs—the crew has to be paid instead of staying at home, extra food and drinks have to be ordered, there is extra wear and tear on the airplane, and there is fuel used instead of paying to store the plane overnight at the airport. As long as there are enough passengers to pay off these marginal costs, including the cost of storing the plane overnight, the plane should fly.

But that raises the second question: what happened? Why, in other words, are red-eyes full now when they were not before? One marginal cost, fuel, is significantly more expensive than it used to be. The airline presumably wants to run fewer flights to save on fuel-buying costs, and some of those red-eye flights no longer make the cut. The ones that remain are therefore fuller. So again, the economically relevant comparison is to compare costs you still have control over with benefits you still have control over. In other words, you want to compare marginal costs and marginal benefits. So, modify the rule in Chapter 1—that actions should be taken when benefits exceed costs—accordingly; it is really *marginal* benefits and costs that matter.

So in sum: costs relate to actions, not goods (although buying a good is an action). They are the value to the person taking the action of what he is giving up to take it, and the costs that matter are marginal.

---

[5]http://staringatemptypages.blogspot.com/2007/08/children-on-red-eye-flights.html

Costs and Supply

You are probably familiar with the term *supply and demand* and may even have some knowledge of it. If giant new oil fields are discovered, we expect gasoline prices to decline. If we suddenly have large amounts of immigration, we expect the locals who compete with those workers to see their wages decline. (This is why natives competing against immigrants in the labor market are the most likely to oppose such immigration) If war disrupts oil production, we expect oil to be harder to come by and its price to go up.

But what is "supply" of, for instance, gasoline? The first thing to recognize is that it is not the amount or quantity supplied at any given moment in time. That is merely something called *quantity supplied*. Instead, supply is a *functional relation* between a hypothetical price obtained and the amount producers of something are willing to offer, based on whatever conditions prevail, other than price, that affect the capacity to produce gasoline. For example, for a given number of oil wells, a given technology for getting oil out of the ground, and a given set of alternative demands on the resources needed to extract oil, refine it into gasoline, and bring that gasoline to market, we can imagine a relation between the price society might offer companies that produce oil and the amount the companies are willing to produce. One can imagine taking a survey of one oil producer (if it is that company's *personal supply curve*, which is perfectly reasonable to analyze) or all possible producers (since their so-called *market supply curve* can just as reasonably be investigated) and asking, "At $90.00 a barrel, how many barrels will you supply? What about at $90.01? At $90.02?" and so on down the line. If we do that, we have a relation that tells us at any price how much oil will be available for consumers to buy.

Well, what will that relation be like? To think about that, we need to think a little bit about the *action* of supplying. To recapitulate, producers need to stake claims to resources to supply things of value, because it takes resources— natural resources, worker time, certain kinds of talents, land, paper clips in the various offices of the oil company, and so on—to make a good that consumers will buy. If we are thinking about the production of gasoline, we need, among many other things, the natural resource oil. If we left it to oil producers to decide where to produce it, to make as much money as possible naturally they would go first to places where it could be extracted very cheaply, as they would first try to get all the resources they wanted from the lowest-cost source. So, if they only got a relatively low price for each unit of the good or service they were selling, producers could still find resources at low enough cost to produce some. But as they are asked to produce more and more, they need to get control of resources with higher and higher opportunity costs, which means the price they need to get to make it worthwhile to buy the rights to those resources gets higher and higher. The initial oil to make gasoline (or plastics, or heating oil) can be had very cheaply in some place like Saudi Arabia where huge amounts of it can be drilled for at very low cost.

Likewise, if we want to grow grain, one of the resources we need is land, and plenty of high-quality land can be had at low costs in thinly populated parts of the Great Plains.

But if we wanted companies that produce gasoline to bring more of it to market, the easy oil would be used up quickly, and we would have to start looking in places like thousands of feet under the sea, or in seams in beds of shale under the ground, where extraction itself requires more costly resources. Greater oil production would also require more workers, more machinery, etc., and these resources also get costlier as they get scarcer. So the price the companies need to cover costs per unit of oil produced will continue to get higher. So too with corn. One supposes that the land under Denver (which actually sits not in the Rocky Mountains but at the edge of the Great Plains) or Kansas City or suburban Chicago would also be suitable for grain production in a strict horticultural sense, as would the land near where those cities end. But the land in the center of the big cities has a very high opportunity cost, because a lot of activity that people find valuable is already going on in the city itself, and would have to be abandoned if crops were grown there. That would be the last land used, one supposes, in the supplying of American-grown corn, and the price required to persuade owners of buildings in Denver and Chicago to tear them down and start growing corn would be very high.

We now have reasoned out the relation between the amount produced and the price producers would need to get to supply that amount—they are positively related. Another way of saying this is that there is a *supply curve*, and it is positively sloped (see Figure 2-1).

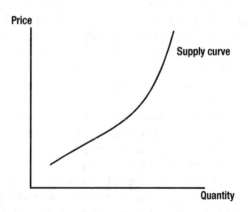

Figure 2-1. The supply curve

Note that this could be the supply curve for anything: lollipops, gasoline from the station at the corner of 5th and Main, the global supply of iPads, the supply of people teaching at universities, the supply of strawberries from California's Central Valley, whatever. All of them are subject to this basic implication of scarcity on the one hand and pursuit of self-interest (profit, in this case) by producers on the other: *because producers will naturally first seek resources at the lowest cost, producing more requires that they be paid more for their output in compensation for having to use progressively higher-cost resources.*

Demand

A supply curve to this point is only a theoretical exercise, the hypothetical consequences of resources becoming progressively scarcer. To find out how markets actually make decisions, we need to match supply with demand. To think about demand, we ask how the number of times an individual worker will eat out as the price of doing so changes, or how many napkins Americans will collectively buy as the price changes. Assuming that people are acting in their rational self-interest, then as we ask them to make greater sacrifices to take the same action (in particular, to consume the same good), they should be less willing to do so, so that the quantity demanded should fall. Thus, the relation between price and quantity in a hypothetical survey of consumers is the opposite of that in our survey of producers, which we can summarize in the *law of demand: as the price consumers face goes up (down), the quantity they are willing to purchase goes down (up).* The demand curve, in other words, is negatively sloped.

Law is of course a pretty strong word. It implies this relationship is always negative. Is that true? The most commonly raised objection is that of luxury or brand-name goods. A pair of warm-up pants with the name Adidas or Nike on it might sell for considerably more than an otherwise identical pair with no recognizable brand name. When getting off the exit ramp after a day of driving, one may be willing to pay more for a brand-name hotel room than for another room at Joe's Inn, which may or may not be of identical quality. But in the first example, one is arguably not simply buying a pair of pants or shoes as much as buying the brand name itself, which lends a certain prestige to the wearer. You are obtaining, in addition to the actual value the pair of pants will render by covering your legs, the value to you of other people seeing you wearing it, the latter service being something the no-brand pair does not offer. In the second case, by adding the phrase "may or may not be," I have glossed over a cost that is often very important: the cost of search. When you check into a Holiday Inn or Hilton, you know pretty much what you will get, because the companies that own those names have spent years investing resources in standardizing the product they offer and in making the public aware of the exact nature of that product. When you check into a non-brand-name hotel, you are flying blind. You save money, but you don't necessarily know the quality of what you're getting. (You could of course have looked up the hotel's ratings online, but ignore this possibility.) To find out, you would actually have to go investigate a room, which requires you to spend time, which is also a cost. All things considered, the brand-name hotel saves you on these costs, and that is reflected in its higher money price.[6] We are confident that this idea of incentives affecting behavior is quite robust: when you raise the price of an action, people will take it less, and lowering the price of an action increases the amount of it we would expect to see. When Professor Landsburg says, "People respond to incentives," this is a big part of what he means. It is conceptually simple, but the trick often lies in remembering always to apply it.

Note finally that willingness to pay, which determines demand and is determined by the available substitutes, is context-dependent. Week-old French bread is more valuable to someone who hasn't eaten in a week (or someone who has a hankering for bread salad) than to others. Some people value wearing nice clothes, some value the comfort of shorts and a T-shirt. And when we speak of market demand, we are speaking of the aggregation of all these individuals in all their particular circumstances.

■ **Tip**   Remember that demand and supply are functions, that is, *relations* between quantity and price. If we speak of shifts in supply or demand, we are speaking of shifts in that entire relation; if we speak of the amount of a good or service hypothetically supplied or demanded at a *particular* price, that is known as *quantity supplied or demanded* (depending on which relation we are talking about).

Elasticity of Demand

Another aspect of demand of interest is how sensitive the quantity demanded is to changes in price. Consider the two demand curves shown in Figure 2-2.

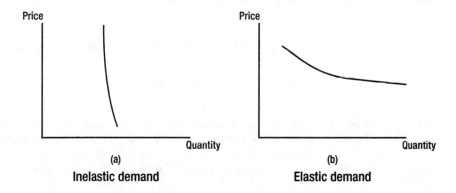

(a)
Inelastic demand

(b)
Elastic demand

Figure 2-2. Inelastic and elastic demand

---

[6] I consider in more detail the problem of costly information in Chapter 4.

At any given price, the curve in (a) is considerably steeper than the curve in (b). This means that quantity is considerably more sensitive to price in figure (b) than in figure (a). In economic language, we say that demand in figure (b) is more *elastic* than demand in figure (a). The definition of *elasticity of demand* is *the sensitivity of quantity demanded to changes in price*.[7] When demand is very elastic, a small increase (decrease) in price by sellers will lead to consumers buying far less (more) of the product, and when demand is very inelastic a big increase (decrease) in price leads to a small decrease (increase) and in the amount consumers buy. The same logic holds for big and small decreases in price by sellers.

What determines whether demand is elastic or inelastic? Think about some actual examples. If the price of gasoline went up significantly, do you think quantity demanded would fall by a little or by a lot? As always, the question is context-dependent. Some individuals are more dependent on their cars than others. And we might not even be talking about individual demand, we might be talking about demand in a particular jurisdiction, or even demand for gasoline across the planet. Once we have defined what market we are talking about, we have to think about what alternatives consumers have to not consuming this product. For someone who lives 50 miles from work in an area with poor mass transit, there are substitutes available for getting to work—he could buy a more fuel-efficient car, he could move closer to work, he could search for people to carpool with so as to share expenses, he could even ride a bicycle. But these are relatively poor substitutes, especially the latter. (Actually, consistent with the idea of opportunity cost as the single best alternative given up, we really need only consider the next best alternative.) If he is on the misanthropic side, carpooling will be a lousy option like all the others, and so we would predict that while he will be a little more careful about the trips he makes, the quantity of gasoline he buys will not drop much in response to the higher price, which means his demand for gasoline is relatively inelastic.

▓ **Question 2.3** Do you think your personal demand for purchasing gasoline is very elastic or very inelastic?

---

[7]There is a strict mathematical definition of elastic versus inelastic demand. The formula for calculating the numerical value of elasticity over some interval of the demand curve in which we study the effect of a price change from P_0 to P_1 is $\left| \dfrac{\frac{Q_1 - Q_0}{Q_0}}{\frac{P_1 - P_0}{P_0}} \right|$, which just means the absolute value of the percentage change in quantity divided by the percentage change in price. If this number is greater than 1, we say that demand is *elastic*, that is, quantity demanded is relatively sensitive to changes in price; if it is less than 1, we say that demand is *inelastic*, that is, quantity demanded is relatively insensitive to changes in price. If by some strange coincidence elasticity of demand were exactly equal to 1, demand would be *unit-elastic*.

Question 2.4 Is the demand for purchasing gasoline by an individual driver likely to be more elastic in the short run, say over the span of a few weeks, or in the long run, after the driver has had time to make major lifestyle changes if he needs to?

On the other hand, think about the demand for gasoline at a particular gasoline station that is one of four at some freeway exit off the interstate. If everybody else is charging $3.50 a gallon, and one bold station owner decides out of the blue to raise his price to $3.60, what should happen to the amount of gasoline he sells? Gasoline is pretty much gasoline, chemically identical from one seller to the next (marketing hype to the contrary), and so one brand of gasoline is an excellent substitute for any other. The only extra cost incurred from changing from one station to another one is that one turns right instead of left, or drives a little farther down the street, and these are practically no costs at all. We would thus predict that elasticity of demand at a particular station is quite elastic. In other words, if that station adjusts its price *holding the behavior of all its competitors constant*, quantity demanded should fall by a lot.

This gets at the general principle governing elasticity of demand: *demand is more elastic the more and better the substitutes are.* When there are high-quality substitutes readily available, it doesn't take much of a price hike for consumers to be willing to consume something else that is almost as good. By the same token, if they are currently consumers of those substitutes, the producer of this good doesn't have to drop his price much to lure large numbers of consumers his way. On the other hand, if we are talking about a life-saving medicine, the only gasoline station for 100 square miles, or other products for which substitutes are few and poor, demand should be less elastic. (Note that "less elastic" is the same thing as "more inelastic," and "more elastic" is the same thing as "less inelastic.")

Finally, we can also talk in principle about elasticity of supply. Elastic supply means that the amount producers are willing to supply increases (decreases) a lot when the price they are offered only increases (decreases) a little. Inelastic supply means that big price hikes (cuts) elicit little increase (decrease) in quantity supplied. What determines elasticity of supply is the number and closeness of alternative uses for the resources needed to supply this particular good. If people who know how to run well-drilling equipment are hard to come by, then the rate at which workers get more expensive will also be high as the quantity of oil produced increases, so the supply curve should be steep. If extra resources are easy to get, then the supply curve should be relatively flat. Elasticity of supply seems not to come up as much as elasticity of demand, so we spend less time on it, but it is just as meaningful a concept economically as elasticity of demand.

Question 2.5 Is the elasticity of supply for gasoline likely to be higher in the short or long run?

Answers to In-Text Questions

2.1. *Why do universities these days often spend so much money on facilities like apartments and state-of-the-art exercise facilities?* I can think of two possibilities. Colleges may have an interest in their students being more comfortable (hence the nice apartments) and healthy (hence the gyms). Once upon a time this attitude of colleges toward their students was known as *in loco parentis*, or taking the role of parents when parents aren't around. But many colleges since the 1960s have abandoned this goal, so I suspect this is not the case. It is more likely that students want these things, and so colleges find it in their interest to provide them. The same argument may apply to big-time college sports, which on their own (without taking account of their effect on enrollment) often lose money.

2.2. a–b. *What are the opportunity costs, worker and otherwise, of making iPads in the U.S. or in a foreign country?* Regardless of where the iPads are produced, the possible resources available to produce them are close to the same in each country. Obviously these include employees to run the assembly lines, different employees to manage the factories (one could even say the time of both kinds workers), the land on which the factory sits, the various metals and chemicals that have to be used to run the assembly lines and have to be put into the iPads, the paper clips needed to hold office memos together, any vehicles needed to transport them from the factory to the port, and so on. The opportunity cost of these resources may well differ in the two countries, which means that the resources may be used in different combinations. In China, they might use more workers and fewer machines, for example. But even after that, it will probably also mean that the iPads can be produced at lower social opportunity cost in only one of the two countries, and judging by where they are made now that country is likely to be China.

c. *What are the opportunity costs of publishing an online newspaper?* Time of reporters and other staff, any costs that must be incurred to acquire the server or cloud space to hold content, probably the acquisition of at least some office space, etc.

d. *What are the opportunity costs of publishing a print newspaper?* Reporter and staff time again, plus more space for the physical production facilities, transportation equipment to get the papers from the printing press to where they are purchased, etc. Is it any wonder— without even considering that a virtual newspaper can hold much more content than a paper one—that paper newspapers are rapidly disappearing in the age of the Internet?

e. *What are the opportunity costs of designing video games?* Probably the most important input is the time, and highly skilled time at that, of the people who come up with video game concepts.

f. *What are the opportunity costs of manufacturing video games?* Assuming the game comes on a CD or other disk format and is not accessed purely online, land and workers and the other kinds of things from parts (a)–(b), which also involve factory production, must be acquired to manufacture these discs. I would guess that this kind of work can be done by many more people, so it will not be as pricey as acquiring the time of the people who design the games.

g. *What are the opportunity costs of producing and selling a textbook on your own and then selling it as an e-book?* The primary input is probably the time of the author. Once the book is uploaded, the opportunity cost of the storage space is practically zero. Indeed, once the book has been written, the author's time becomes a sunk cost, so that the marginal costs of another copy of the book are infinitesimal. This helps explain why e-books are becoming more and more popular.

h. *What are the opportunity costs of producing and selling a textbook published traditionally?* Now the costs of all the workers who work at the publishing company that specializes in finding markets for the book, workers who clean the office building, workers who arrange the president's schedule and keep unwanted people out of his office, etc., must be paid. The benefit, which is why we still observe such companies existing, is that people have an incentive to acquire expert knowledge in how best to market books.

    i. *What are the opportunity costs of raising a child?* The time of the parents and anyone else who helps raise the child and the alternative uses of all the money that must be spent providing for the child.

2.3. *Is your personal demand for purchasing gasoline very elastic or very inelastic?* This depends on you of course. What are the next-best alternatives to your using your car for the things you use it for? The better your alternatives, the more elastic your demand for gasoline will be.

2.4. *Is the demand for purchasing gasoline by an individual driver likely to be more elastic in the short run, say over the span of a few weeks, or in the long run, after the driver has had time to make major lifestyle changes if he needs to?* I would say demand is more likely to be more elastic in the short run. The reason is that in a longer period of time people have more possibilities to make substitutions—they can move closer to the places they go, they can buy a more fuel-efficient car, they can seek out carpool partners, etc. I would go so far as to say that short-term demand is almost always more inelastic than long-term demand for the same action.

2.5. *Is the elasticity of supply for gasoline likely to be higher in the short or long run?* Same answer, for almost the same reason. Over the long term, people in a position to supply something have more possibilities for making alternative arrangements when their short-run plans face new obstacles. If a revolution happens in the Middle East, taking oil off the market, or if the government imposes dramatic new regulations that make crude oil much costlier to drill for, in the short run the producers have little choice but to sit there and take it. In the long run they can discover new kinds of production technologies, find other locations to drill for oil at lower cost, etc.

Economics Out There

2.1. Here's an interesting story[8] from the *Australian*, headlined "$20,000 cash artwork sells for $21,350." Why would someone ever pay $21,350 for $20,000 in cash? How much is $20,000 in cash assembled by an artist worth to you? To an art collector? To someone speculating on the future reputation of the artist who made this artwork?

2.2. This story at the *Examiner*[9] claims that solar panels are in some sense "free" for homeowners, thanks to a tax break for installing them. What is the cost to homeowners of taking the action of installing solar panels with these tax breaks? What is the cost to society of providing the solar panels? Is the latter "free"?

---

[8]http://www.theaustralian.com.au/arts/visual-arts/cash-artwork-sells-for-21350/story-fn9d3avm-1226126777761
[9]http://www.examiner.com/article/city-federal-incentives-make-installing-a-solar-panel-a-zero-dollar-investment

Supply and Demand, Considered Together

Why Gasoline Is $4 a Gallon—or Isn't

To repeat: we live in a world of scarcity, so no one can have everything he wants. Some procedures have to be found to decide how resources will be used and who will get how much of the resulting output. One way to do that is the market, to whose workings I now turn.

Equilibrium

It is first necessary to take our two curves, supply and demand, and place them in the same space, as shown in Figure 3-1.

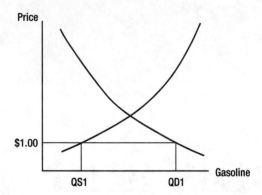

Figure 3-1. Price below equilibrium

The supply of and demand for actions in Figure 3-1 are those for the buying and selling of gasoline. The more gasoline we ask producers to produce, the progressively more costly it gets at the margin as resources become scarcer, so we have the positively sloped supply curve. As the hypothetical price consumers (which includes all users of gasoline, not just drivers of private cars) may face gets lower (higher), gasoline becomes more (less) desirable relative to its alternatives, and so we have the negatively sloped demand curve.

Without for now wondering why, suppose oil companies really had no idea what price to charge. And so just to see what happened, on a particular day they decided to charge a price of $1.00 a gallon. At that relatively low price, they are willing to secure control over enough resources (oil-field workers, refinery workers, land, tanker capacity, paper clips, and so on) to produce, and do in fact produce, the amount noted on the chart as QS1 (with QS standing for quantity supplied). Unfortunately, at that price consumers are very keen to buy gasoline. The amount they're willing to buy, in fact, extends all the way to QD1 (quantity demanded), which of course vastly exceeds QS1. So by 10 in the morning, all the gasoline is gone, and consumers collectively still want QD1–QS1, which the producers are unwilling to supply. Thus many consumers show up at the station and leave frustrated, with their tanks having as little gas as when they got there.

In economics, this situation has a particular name: a *shortage*, meaning that *at the prevailing market price* quantity supplied is less than quantity demanded. Note what it does not mean: the fact that I want a new BMW but don't have one does not indicate a shortage of BMWs, because I could get one if I were willing to pay the price the BMW dealer is offering. In the example shown in Figure 3-1, a lot of people are willing to pay a dollar a gallon for gas, but there is not enough gas to satisfy them all.

This sounds like a pretty unfortunate state of affairs. But the good news is that if the price increases above $1.00 a gallon, sellers will be willing and able to bring more to market, and although the amount of gas consumers want at that price will still be higher than this new amount, the shortfall will be less than it was before. Gasoline producers can produce more and still sell everything they produce at a price that covers even the most expensive of all the new resources they need to acquire. Thus they will make more money than if they turned those consumers away. So producers are still willing to secure more resources and increase production, meaning that this problem tends to eliminate itself. What we call *excess demand*, in other words, is a signal to gasoline producers to bring more to market.

Now consider the opposite problem, shown in Figure 3-2.

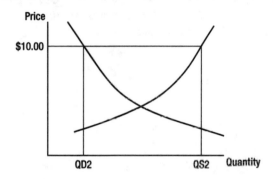

Figure 3-2. Price above equilibrium

Suppose that oil companies' initial reaction to the shortage is to guess that they should increase the price from $1.00 a gallon to $10.00 a gallon. Then society now faces the opposite problem—there is more gas produced (QS2) than consumers want (QD2). At that price, if it persists, individual consumers make major shifts in their behavior. In the short run, they may carpool, work from home if they can, combine trips, give up the marginal vacation over Labor Day that has less value (but perhaps still take the big driving trip at Thanksgiving), etc. Over a longer time horizon,[1] they may buy more fuel-efficient cars, move closer to work, even retire if they are old enough. But one thing they do not do immediately is buy as much gasoline as producers produce. They demand QD2, while at that high price, sellers offer QS2. Gasoline piles up unsold, and over the long term that is no way to run a profitable business, since unsold gasoline would back up throughout the system and take up costly storage space. So prices come down, and this means resources are released to earn their opportunity costs in other industries. Oil gets used for something besides gasoline (and the oil that is the most expensive to extract

---

[1] Remember the question from the last chapter about the ability to adjust toward substitutes over longer time horizons.

actually stays in the ground), workers working the high-cost fields must find other work, some wells are capped, some of the paperclips that the company would have bought for their office when they expected to sell at $10.00 a gallon are not bought and are thus available for others to use, and so on. There is a natural social pressure to decrease an activity (gasoline production) that is not valuable enough to consumers to justify the $10.00 price necessary to produce it in that quantity. In other words, the excess supply that results from the $10.00 price signals producers to produce less.

The moral of the story may be coming into focus at this point. There is only one price that elicits a change in neither quantity supplied nor quantity demanded, and that ensures that the amount produced is exactly equal to the amount desired. That price is where the supply curve crosses the demand curve, say at $4.00 a gallon (Figure 3-3).

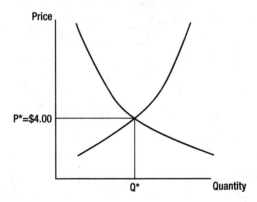

Figure 3-3. Equilibrium

The equilibrium quantity is denoted by Q*; if we are looking at individual demand, the number might be 10 gallons per week. If it were demand in Dayton, Ohio, or in the United States, or by left-handers in Texas, or in any market we might want to inspect, it would be some considerably larger number. As economists generally do, I denote this equilibrium price and quantity—the price and quantity that stabilize this market—with asterisks.

It is important to realize what we have just done here. We have built a *model* of some market for gasoline. What, in economics, is a model? It is not an exact description, because to describe a thing exactly would require that we duplicate the thing exactly—in this case people producing and buying gasoline. A completely accurate model of the gasoline market would be an exact duplicate of the gasoline market, and thus of no use in analyzing the real one. The same problem haunts mapmaking. The more detailed the map you want, the bigger it must be, and an exact map would have to be the same size as the thing you want a map of, rendering the map useless.

In using models like the one for gasoline, we are trying to describe approximately how markets decide who gets what. Is it a good model? Sometimes it doesn't work; after the September 11 attacks, gasoline pumps really did run out of gas for a few days, and car makers sometimes underestimate (and sometimes overestimate)[2] how many cars of a new model they will sell. But overall, we seldom observe consumers unable to get their hands on pencils, cars, houses, a college education, and indeed most things, *provided only they are willing to pay the prevailing* price. That, of course, is different from saying that anyone who wants a thing (health care, a college education, a particular job) can get it on the terms they want. Overall, our little model seems to give us a good understanding of how markets make decisions. We will see shortly that it also helps us understand the reaction to economic change.

But before going on to that, it is worth investigating what is going on behind the market equilibrium. As hinted at earlier, the market is simply a system for deciding what will get made and what won't, and who will get how much of what is made. The market is the system of reliance on self-interest and on people using their resources as they see fit (and not having them taken away without their consent, for example through taxation or regulation, which limits the use of some resources) to allocate resources. This is like a form of cooperation. No, strike that—it *is* cooperation. There is gasoline because oil companies have gone to the ends of the earth looking for crude oil and have paid workers to extract it. They have purchased oil tankers and hired workers to staff them. They have rented space at ports (if the oil is imported) to unload it and have transported it in trucks to a refinery. That refinery was built on land acquired by the oil company, and the gasoline that emerges from it is shipped to thousands of stations that exist because small business owners have negotiated franchise agreements with Shell, BP, and others. And these franchise owners have their own employees, their own negotiations with purveyors of junk food, playing cards, and the other ephemera found in the convenience stores that have so efficiently attached to gasoline stations.[3]

None of this happens because it has been designed. Rather, it all happens one bargain at a time. And the result is that all the gas that we are willing to use, and no more, is there when we want it. It is a sort of un-conducted symphony,

---

[2] http://www.cbsnews.com/8301-505145_162-57390448/chevy-volt-a-bad-sign-for-electric-car-sales/

[3] Once upon a time, gas stations had car-repair bays and mechanics but nothing to eat or drink that didn't come out of a soda machine. Competition has long since pushed car repair to shops that specialize in that, and the service garages in gas stations have been replaced by convenience stores. Why? Because it is a more efficient use of space—a use that creates more value after taking account of the cost of providing it.

an extraordinary thing to watch, as much an aesthetic achievement as a commercial or material one.[4]

■ **Tip**   Remember that "the market" is simply one way of reconciling conflicting individual interests and deciding how scarce resources get used. Prices perform a critical function of giving people guidance about how to act in a market setting, given that others have their own goals too.

To help you think about how it works, here's something to consider that may not have occurred to you. In recent years, the economies of China and India have been rising rapidly, although both countries are still very poor. One byproduct is that a lot of young Chinese and Indians are studying extremely hard, trying to get into good schools and believing that their hard work will pay off in far better jobs than their parents could have imagined were possible. But young people needing to do their homework and practice for exams has caused demand for pencils to increase extraordinarily. More and more young people who used to quit school at a very young age (if they went at all) to start working, especially on farms, are staying in school later and studying harder. So pencils are, seemingly, scarcer.

But have we noticed this in the office supply stores in the U.S.? Probably not. Every time we want a pencil, we need only go to the local store and the shelves are full of them. So a significant social change has occurred, a modification in the value humanity collectively attaches to pencils. There is a greater demand for pencils than there was before, and markets have responded by prompting pencil companies to bid for more resources, figure out ways to either get production costs down (for example, by moving pencil production to places where the cost of acquiring resources, like worker time, is lower), or charge more by making the pencils more valuable (for example, through the development of ever-more sophisticated mechanical pencils). As a result, people who desire pencils get them at a price most are willing to pay. No one gives it any thought, but it happens anyway, without any guiding hand, just like the drivers in Christiansfeld.

Pencils of course are individually negligible, and even collectively are small in the grand scheme of human affairs, but pencilmaking is also a vast industry whose production and distribution is part of a global system. They are really no different from anything whose production and delivery we unfortunately

---

[4] I have written elsewhere (http://www.independent.org/publications/tir/article.asp?a=690) about commerce as an aesthetic achievement and not just something practical, although the article involves a lot of philosophical theory.

take for granted. The lesson, to which we will return, is that the market does not really *allocate* things in the sense of consciously making decisions, although we often use that term as shorthand. Rather, the market is the mechanism by which people pursue their interests cooperatively by using resources in conjunction with others to get things done. It is *individuals* who are consciously making decisions, using only their power to persuade based on the offers they are willing to make. It is a different way of deciding what gets used to do what than a bureaucrat or president ordering people to do things under penalty of law. And the constant delivery of these things under the market mechanism—in the presence also of constant change—is something that our supply-and-demand model can help us understand better.

Changes in Supply and Demand

Remember first the distinctions between supply and quantity supplied, and demand and quantity demanded. When I talk about a "change in supply" or "change in demand," I'm talking about something that shifts the entire supply curve or demand curve in one direction or another. The equilibrium quantity—"quantity supplied"—will also change, but that is something we can think about *only after we think about which curve shifts which way*. And here are the first rules in trying to decide which curve to shift:

1. Supply curves shift if and only if something changes to affect the difficulty of getting the necessary resources to produce the good at any price. This is a change that affects producers primarily—it only indirectly affects consumers after the supply curve has shifted.

2. Demand curves shift if and only if something changes to affect consumers' willingness to pay for the product at any price. Producers are affected only secondarily after the demand curve has shifted.

The most common thing that shifts a supply curve is *technological progress*. I do not mean progress in the product itself—for example, a cell phone with new capabilities. Instead I mean progress that allows producers to produce the good while needing to procure fewer resources. Perhaps the single most powerful example of this in modern times was the creation of the assembly line, which allowed workers to concentrate on particular tasks rather than produce an entire product on their own from start to finish. The assembly line made it much easier—in other words, possible at much lower resource cost—to produce large numbers of standardized products. In 1876, Philadelphia held a grand Centennial Exposition, one of whose exhibits involved leather workers making saddles individually, finishing one every two days. By the time of the Panama Pacific International Exposition in San Francisco in 1915, Ford workers were making one Ford car every half hour on their specially constructed assembly line. Figure 3-4 shows what such technological progress (applied to one particular good, like autos in 1890 versus autos in 1920) looks like in a supply-demand diagram.

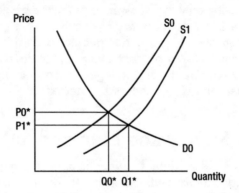

Figure 3-4. Supply shifts right (for example, through technological progress)

Technological progress means that to produce the same quantity, whatever that quantity is, now requires incurring lower resource costs than before. So any quantity can be produced at lower price compared to before, and the entire supply curve shifts to the right,[5] from the curve labeled S0 to that labeled S1. The fundamental value of the product to the consumer at any price does not change in any way, so the demand curve stays the same. The result is that equilibrium price falls, from P0* to P1*, and equilibrium quantity goes up, from Q0* to Q1*. (By convention, in this book a 0 indicates the situation before the change, and 1 is the situation after. In this exercise, the supply curve shifts, but the demand curve does not; if either curve shifts, the *equilibrium* P and Q must both change.) And this is what *should* happen. The fact that we can produce something of value to consumers at lower opportunity cost than before means we should expect to see more of it produced, and we should expect to see its price fall.

This kind of technological progress is actually a continuous story in human civilization, especially in the last 300 years. We can now obtain climate control, calories, transportation, and information at far lower cost than prior generations could, and so our consumption of these things has gone up. Although

---

[5]Note that it is confusing to say "supply shifts down," since this is easy to confuse with the statement that "quantity supplied shifts down," when it actually goes up, from Q0* to Q1*. I prefer to talk about supply curves shifting to the left or to the right, and to be consistent I will use the same language for demand.

we tend to focus on things that seem to be getting more expensive, such as health care (which is actually available in much better quantity and quality to more people around the world than at any other time in history) and higher education (ditto), the overwhelming fact of modern life is our ability to obtain more of the things we want at lower cost than before. The reason for this is explored in detail in Chapter 9.

Another possible change is that a resource becomes harder to get, perhaps because of greater competition for it or disruption in supply. Figure 3-5 shows what the situation would look like in the supply-demand model.

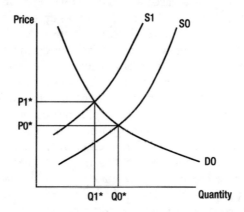

Figure 3-5. Supply curve shifts left/constriction of supply (for example, through embargo, war, or new competition for resources)

When a big new factory opens in town, there is greater competition for employees, land, etc. (When a big factory closes, of course, the effect is the opposite.) Land rents go up, and finding workers may become harder, so it becomes more expensive to operate *other* businesses. The supply curve *for other nearby businesses that compete for the same resources* should shift left. When New York City is booming and there is a lot of new demand for office space, a landlord who owns many apartment buildings will find it harder to turn down higher offers for his property. Many such landowners will choose to convert their land from residential use to commercial use—office towers, shopping centers, and so forth. So the land gets reallocated from lower-priority uses to higher-priority ones. Housing becomes scarcer and more expensive. Naturally, people who lose their apartments when landlords sell these properties are not happy about it. But the opportunity cost of allowing them to stay would be that businesses that can also do things of value for their customers by locating in New York City will be unable to do so. So again, the market is simply a way of prioritizing.

Note that the same effect just illustrated can occur when supplies are cut off because of bad weather, war, or political decisions. A classic example was the embargo on oil exports imposed by Arab countries from October 1973 to March 1974 because of U.S. support for Israel during the war that began in the former month. This made gasoline, which relies on oil as a key resource, costlier to produce and should have caused gasoline prices to go up in the U.S. Indeed it did, although not as much as it should have, for reasons I discuss later. The Chinese government has for some time now limited exports of so-called rare earth metals,[6] which are used in computer screens, computer chips, and environmentally friendly energy production such as wind power, among other things, and this should serve to make these things costlier outside of China.[7]

Note that in each of these cases, we are observing more intense competition for certain resources, which serves to drive up their price and therefore the price of goods that use the resources. In some cases this is because new demanders enter the market (such as the factory opening and seeking workers and land), and in other cases it is because sellers take resources off the market (the oil embargo, a military blockade, the Chinese rare-earth policies). Changes in the terms of competition will again shift supply or demand (it is the supply curve that will shift in the examples discussed so far in this section) and thus cause society to make changes in what gets made. And this again is how markets make decisions. If the Chinese rare-earth limits continue, I would predict that at least in the short term, goods that are made with these elements will become more expensive, and in the long term I would predict that alternatives to these metals would be found, that other ways besides relying on these now more expensive resources for manufacturing would be developed. I would expect, in other words, people to respond to incentives.

Demand curves can also shift as well. Recall that the things that shift demand curves are different from the things that shift supply curves. Demand curves shift because the value of the product to consumers had changed, whereas supply curves shift when the ease with which suppliers can get resources changes.

In Figure 3-6, demand has shifted to the right. We can think, for example, about the product becoming more useful to someone. As the marginal reward for having a college degree goes up, people find they are more willing to pay for it than before. At least in the short term, with the number of available college seats relatively fixed, there is nothing to do but move up along the existing supply curve. More people—professors, secretaries, deans, librarians, tech-support experts, to mention just a few—have to be lured away from alternative activity and paid at least their opportunity cost. And if new buildings

---

[6]http://news.bbc.co.uk/2/hi/8689547.stm

[7]As I write this, this policy is currently being challenged by other countries at the World Trade Organization, which sets rules for member nations about import and export restraints. We will revisit this situation in Problem 9.4.

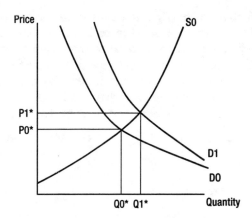

Figure 3-6. Demand shifts right (because, for example, substitute vanishes, product becomes more desirable)

have to be built and new equipment purchased, these resources become more costly, because the supply curve is positively sloped after all, and so tuition goes up.

This reveals an often underappreciated aspect of supply/demand thinking: *the cause of higher prices often can be traced back to the demand side.* In the case of rapidly escalating college costs, much criticism has focused on rising expenses for some elements of a university education, from the salaries of university presidents[8] to academic journal subscription fees.[9] Defensive university officials, when asked about why tuition is rising so fast, invariably point to higher costs. But that simply raises another question: *why* are these costs higher? I would suggest that the rising demand for a college degree is partly responsible for this. This is especially compelling given that new colleges of the traditional form rarely open, so the number of seats can only be expanded modestly in the short run. Supply, in other words, is inelastic in the short run, so rising demand causes price to escalate significantly.[10]

■ Q3.1   Self-check for the reader: What is "the marginal reward to having a college degree"?

---

[8]http://chronicle.com/article/Income-Gap-Widens/129980/
[9]http://www.guardian.co.uk/commentisfree/2011/aug/29/academic-publishers-murdoch-socialist
[10]One entrepreneurial response to this is the rising number of for-profit colleges and the placing—at considerably diminished expense—of courses from elite universities like Stanford and MIT online; it remains to be seen how desirable these will be as substitutes.

Demand can also shift to the right if a substitute for the good disappears. In that case, I would also expect demand to become less elastic. We see this when one grocery store closes in an area that used to have two, or when laws are passed restricting consumers' ability to buy foreign products, and they must turn to domestic ones. In general, *anything* that increases consumer willingness to pay for the product, whether the product is better or because alternatives become fewer or worse, should shift demand to the right.

The last possible type of curve shift is the demand curve shifting to the left (Figure 3-7).

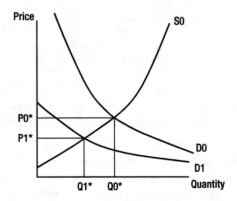

Figure 3-7. Demand shifts left (for example, because a substitute is introduced)

If demand shifting to the right reflects higher willingness to pay, it stands to reason that shifting to the left means lower willingness to pay. The primary reason for this is the introduction of a substitute, which can also be phrased as *increased competition.* (Products seldom become *intrinsically* less valuable, only less valuable relative to the alternatives.) A second restaurant in town should cause demand at the first to go down, so it sells fewer meals and charges less (or increases portions at the existing price). At a much greater level, the intro-duction of cell phones appears to have dramatically lowered the demand for landline phones, and presumably for phone wiring and employees of landline phone services.

The good news about all this is that we always have a way forward. When change happens, markets provide a way, mediated by changes in prices, of transferring resources through competition to minimize adjustment costs. The invention of digital photography and later the insertion of digital cameras in cell phones dealt a near-death blow to film and film cameras, and factories that made them were closed. As a result, land and workers were released, and investment funds were transferred to other uses. Note particularly in the case of workers that many of the workers are *future* workers, who no longer take jobs at Kodak at the age of 20 and are thus employed in industries with brighter futures. In reality, because of a constant flow of innovation, some activities are constantly staking claims to more resources, and others constantly releasing them. Although the graphs so far in this chapter illustrate simple one-time adjustments, the economy is constantly in flux, with resources gradually moving to where they are in greatest demand at the moment because consumers are willing to pay more for those goods than for others that use the same resources.

Prices in this system play a critical role, in particular as a way of making people take account of the consequences for everyone else of their choices. When the price, because of a shortage, goes up, it tells consumers that if they want to continue to buy a good, they will be imposing greater social costs because resources are diverted to this industry from their best alternate use; they will only buy if the value to *them* justifies paying that price. Similarly, producers are told, as the price of what they sell goes up, that in fact society does value more of their goods to an extent sufficient to justify their acquiring those resources. (The opposite reasoning holds true when prices decline in response to a surplus.) If prices are not allowed to freely move up or down, bad things happen because people do not have to face all of these consequences.

This is often not how prices are seen. Prices are often viewed not as a device for coordinating the resolution of conflicting desires over scarce resources, but as acts of will, especially when they are too high, and as the result of "sinful" conduct by one party or another. Following the term coined by Thomas Sowell, *volitional pricing*, I refer to this belief as the *fallacy of volition*— the contention that prices are what they are because sellers or buyers with substantial degree of freedom over what the price will be choose them to be very high or very low.

In fact, our model suggests that the reason prices are what they are is that those are the terms given to us by supply and demand. In my experience, there are few markets more subject to the fallacy of volition than that of gasoline, with 2012 polling data indicating,[11] for example, that the most widely shared reason among the American public for high gasoline prices (when they are high) is "oil companies that want to make too much profit." It would be an interesting experiment, when gas prices are low, to discover how many people credit "oil companies that want to forgo high profits in the public interest." In the meantime, one can only note that oil companies in the long term are not a particularly high-profit industry. And consider the chart shown in Figure 3-8.

---

[11] http://www.reuters.com/article/2012/03/27/us-usa-campaign-poll-idUSBRE82Q19Z20120327

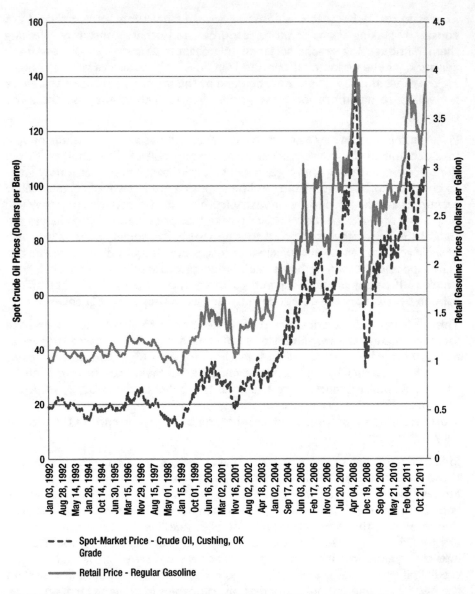

Figure 3-8. Oil and gasoline prices, 1992–2001 (*source: U.S. Energy Information Administration*)

Figure 3-8 is based on government data. The bottom curve, measured on the axis on the left, reflects the prices of crude oil (in particular, of the Cushing, Oklahoma grade sold on the market for oil), resulting from the actions of many thousands of traders buying and selling independently and thus not subject to the will of any one person. The top curve, measured on the axis on the right, reflects the retail price of gasoline. (Since the two axes are different, it is not true that a gallon of gasoline costs more than a barrel of oil, even though the oil curve lies above the gasoline curve as the curves actually work out.) The two curves consistently move almost exactly together. If one focuses in on any short-term portion of the graph, which admittedly covers a very long period of time, one gets the same basic pattern, as shown in Figure 3-9 for the years 2009–2010.

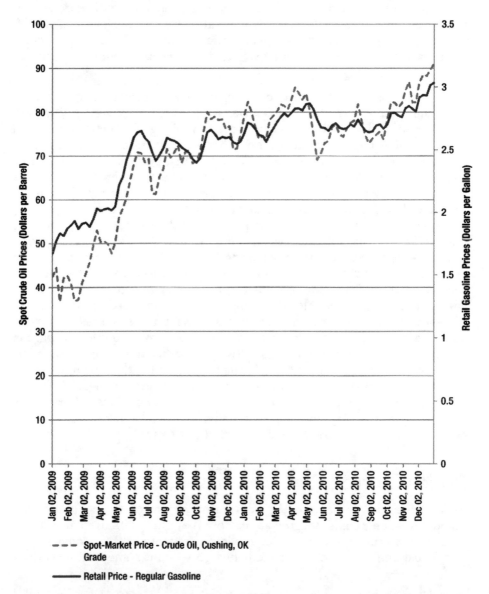

Figure 3-9. Crude oil prices and retail regular gasoline prices, 2009–2010 (*source: U.S. Energy Information Administration*)

So the primary determinant of gasoline prices seems to be oil prices. Oil companies are not unusually greedy when gasoline prices go up, just as they are not unusually benevolent when they go down (which, from time to time, they do, as Figure 3-8 shows). Oil companies are trying to make as much money as possible—pursuing their self-interest—by providing gasoline to consumers, for whom buying it is in *their* self-interest. The existence of a market for gasoline allows both oil companies (including their shareholders and workers) and the people who want to drive (or fly, for that matter, although jet fuel is a different product) to cooperatively pursue their interests. *This* is fundamentally what markets are about: they are a way to get everyone to work together to enable us to do things.

So why the eagerness to blame oil companies when prices go up? There is little understanding of the complex network these companies have woven together to drill for oil in far-flung places by hiring workers, building and running refineries, contracting with other companies to buy equipment, and organizing transport networks all over the globe, in order to get gasoline to the pump. It is an amazingly complex problem, and its cost fluctuates wildly, especially because of changes in beliefs about the scarcity of crude oil. That such beliefs and the resulting changes in oil prices would be the primary determinant of what we pay at the pump is really not such an outrageous thing to believe. But pointing fingers, in the manner of those who charge that prices are high because people are being "ripped off," starts from a different premise, which is that prices could be changed without any significant consequences other than someone not earning money that they don't deserve anyway. But the same people who complain about the greed of others when it means they are not getting the terms they want, the same people unwilling to believe that prices reflect scarcity and value, may be quick to engage in exactly the same behavior when they are on the other side of the transaction, as when labor unions who agitate for higher wages for their own members pay people low wages and no benefits to do the union's own work.[12] (Recall that this was the topic of Economics Out There reading 1.2) But if prices are set because of scarcity and competition, altering them by force of law cannot but have negative consequences, as we are about to see.

Price Controls

As noted earlier, prices are the key mechanism markets use to allocate resources when people disagree about how they should be used. But sometimes prices cause disquiet. Health services cost so much that some people who could benefit immensely nonetheless go without some health services.

---

[12]http://reason.org/blog/show/when-unions-do-the-exploiting

The downside of Manhattan being, in some respects, the center of American if not global business and media is that lots of people want to use the very limited amount of land on that tiny island. And so if one wants to live in an apartment there, one must pay a price (rent) sufficient to compensate the owners for the opportunity cost of not using the land for some other purpose.

Prices that are "too high" (or "too low" when, for example, small farmers go bankrupt because the revenue from their farming cannot support the costs they face, or when workers earn wages that are less than what it takes for them to buy things seen as the minimum marks of a decent life) thus draw public concern. And occasionally this concern leads to passing laws that limit the freedom to charge or pay certain prices, especially via the imposition of legally mandated maximum or minimum prices. By general convention, economists refer to these measures as *price controls*.

The supply/demand model allows us to think about what happens under such measures, and why. Refer back to Figure 3-1. At the time, the figure represented only a temporary situation in the market, before the adjustment to equilibrium had been carried out. Left to its own devices, as we saw, the price would drift up to its equilibrium level P* ($4.00), quantity demanded would decline from QD1 to Q*, and quantity supplied would increase from QS1 to Q*.

Now, if the law imposes a maximum ceiling on prices at $1.00 a gallon, what happens? Proponents of the law, or at least of price controls in general, believe that the primary consequence is that people who cannot afford the good— gasoline, apartments in Manhattan, health care, whatever—will simply get what they need when before, because of the greed of sellers, they couldn't. But everything about that belief is wrong. First, "need" is not a word with an objective meaning; there are only tradeoffs. Second, the reason that at the low price only QS1 is supplied is because the marginal cost of supplying more is constantly increasing—in other words, the supply curve is positively sloped. If we cap the price that can be charged at $1.00 a gallon, what was a temporary situation now becomes a permanent one. Unfortunately, the amount that consumers want at that price, QD1, significantly exceeds the amount that producers are willing to offer them. We have scarcity just like before, but we are no longer allowed to use price to change behavior on both the selling and buying sides of the market.

The scarcity is still there, however; there is still a gap between the amount consumers want and the amount producers will offer them. If price cannot do the job, *some other way will be found to allocate something scarce among the people who are competing for it.* If people are not allowed to bid money, in other words, they will have to bid something else to get their hands on this valuable good. In the case of gasoline in particular, along with a great many other goods, one alternate rationing method is time. You can see what that looks like in a scene[13] from the country of Nigeria. It is one of the largest oil producers in the world, and yet people frequently wait hours and even days in line for gas. Asked why they must endure this, people might blame some proximate cause like the lack of investment in infrastructure or of delivery trucks or refining capacity in their country. But this simply begs the question of *why* is there inadequate investment in such things?

Through a variety of limits on the ability of producers to earn more revenue by selling gasoline, Nigeria, like China, Iran, and other countries, provides insufficient incentive to invest in such infrastructure. If price were the only rationing device, the price of gasoline in Nigeria would be much higher, people would correspondingly consume less, but every time they wanted it, it would be there. But if price is limited as a rationing device, then waiting in line for gas (until it runs out, at which point one must wait for the next delivery) becomes another cost of acquiring gasoline. In the U.S., to get gasoline one pays P* and one is done, while in other countries one must pay a small monetary price but a huge time price. People who are willing to wait to get gasoline get it, and people who are not, don't. (Of course, someone who is not willing to wait to get gasoline can pay someone to wait in line for him, which is another common consequence of price ceilings of this kind. Society must then pay the cost of whatever else the person waiting would have been doing.)

Well, you may say, these are the kinds of things that happen in Nigeria and China, but they couldn't happen here because the U.S. is a more advanced country. But they *did* happen in the U.S. Because of inflation in the early 1970s, Congress gave the administration of President Richard Nixon the power to control prices of many goods, including crude oil, the key ingredient in gasoline. Beginning in 1972, lines began to appear at U.S. gas stations. As noted above, after the U.S. supported Israel against several Arab countries in its 1973 war, the latter countries retaliated by refusing to sell oil (that is, by embargoing oil) to the U.S., substantially exacerbating the problem.

Remarkably, in response, more power was granted to the president to direct the allocation of oil in addition to its price by the creation of the Federal Energy Administration, which developed a mathematical formula for deciding how much oil went not to each driver, as sellers in a free market would do, but to each *state*. Bureaucrats in Washington, instead of oil companies responding to the supply, demand, and prices they faced while trying to make money, decided where gasoline should be allocated. The result was that gasoline stations routinely ran out of gas; this was what motivated people to get in line very early to begin with. (Back in those days, gasoline stations had no convenience stores and were not open 24 hours.)

---

[13]http://www.wright.edu/~evan.osborne/gas3.jpg

Lines dissipated somewhat with the ending of the embargo, but returned with a vengeance in 1979, partly due to political instability in Iran, a major oil exporter to the U.S. Although by this time the deregulation of oil prices had been planned, it had yet to take effect, and at one point during this time crude oil prices in the U.S. secondary market (the market for people who had bought barrels of oil and wanted to sell them) were in some contexts limited to $6 a barrel while the global price at which oil was trading was $30 a barrel. In January, 1981, all price controls on crude oil production ended, and gas lines have essentially been unknown in the U.S. since that time. (Their absence after the Iraq invasion of Kuwait in 1991 and, after a few days had passed, after the September 11, 2001 terrorist attacks is telling.) Instead, prices are used to ration supplies.

I argued earlier that this system of letting supply and/or demand to adjust allows society to most easily accommodate changed circumstances, and that is in fact what has happened in recent years. The rapid development of populous countries such as China, India, and Brazil has led to demand for oil in those places and others to increase rapidly. That increased demand has been transmitted as higher prices, and Americans have made marginal adjustments in their driving habits to accommodate this rise.[14]

Other kinds of price controls have analogous effects. New York City introduced sharp limits on apartment rents and the rate at which they could increase during World War II, and many of those restrictions remain even today. Unsurprisingly, New York City (and other cities where apartment rentals are subject to legal maximums) is a very difficult place to find an apartment. If you are a landowner, why should you use that land to provide relatively low-rent housing when the government of the city of New York is prepared to limit your ability to earn income—and while using the land for other purposes by not building the apartments to begin with is not subject to such restrictions?

In another example of the effects of preventing prices from doing their job of resolving competing demand for scarce goods, in 2010 a senator from New York, using the persuasive space that is often available more to politicians than to others (in the form of a press that loves to cover everything politicians say), got airlines to promise not to charge for overhead-bin space. (So far, they may charge for checked bags without incurring any senator's wrath.) Since that time, the scramble for such space has deteriorated, as passengers ignore the pleas of airline crews and fill the space as fast as they can, often with luggage

---

[14]Note also that an oil embargo, which was so traumatic under price controls in 1973, was also imposed by Arab countries during the previous 1967 Arab-Israeli war, but there were no price controls in effect then, and not coincidentally no gas lines either.

that takes up large amounts of bin space. Were the airlines allowed to charge a price for the space that reflected its value, it would be used more wisely (and passengers would pack more sparingly).

Note also that price-control laws can establish legal minimum prices as well as legal maximum prices. In that case, we would start from the position depicted in Figure 3-2. There is an initial price above the market-clearing (that is, equilibrium) price, which ordinarily induces consumers to buy less and producers to produce less, therefore releasing resources to earn their opportunity cost in some other activity whose output consumers are willing to buy at prevailing prices. The analysis is similar to the case of legal maximum prices, in the sense that an adjustment that would ordinarily happen due to competition now does not, or at least happens in a very costly way. Because producers are given the signal that the price they will get for their output is very high ($10.00 in the figure), they continue to produce very high levels of that output, while consumers facing that price are not willing to buy as much. And so we have a permanent surplus, the mirror image of the permanent shortage when there is a legal maximum price.

So what happens? A more costly form of reaction to the prevailing incentives. Because of widespread sympathy for farmers as a repository of traditional values, a reluctance to import food from other countries in the belief that such supplies are unreliable, and the political power of farmers' lobbyists, many countries guarantee their farmers minimum prices for their output. If those prices were below the equilibrium price it would not matter, but because the goal is to keep farmers who would otherwise exit the industry employed producing agricultural products, that of course seldom happens. In India, the government as of this writing uses a classic price-support scheme in which it buys various kinds of beans and grains, cotton, and crops used for cooking oil from farmers at an announced minimum price if the market price of these goods falls below the minimum. Unsurprisingly, despite India's poverty, huge amounts of surpluses are generated, some of which was actually exported in the 2000s because prices were higher overseas. In addition, the highest-quality grain is often sold by farmers to grain traders, meaning the government gets crops more prone to spoilage.[15]

The governments of the U.S. and the European Union, historically among the world's greatest sinners with regard to giving direct price supports to farmers, have changed their policies and now support farmers not by buying up surpluses at great expense[16] but by giving them crop insurance at below-market rates (U.S.) or loans to buy equipment, again at below-market

---

[15]Shikha Jha, P.V. Srinivasan, and Maurice Landes, "Indian Wheat and Rice Sector Policies and the Implications of Reform," U.S. Department of Agriculture. Available online at www.ers.usda.gov/publications/err41/err41.pdf.

[16]During the days of direct price supports for dairy products, the government (that is, taxpayers) had to pay for storage of immense amounts of surplus cheese and butter.

rates (Europe). These policies continue to generate large amounts of agricultural surplus, which is frequently disposed of by selling it to very poor countries at a price that is above the marginal cost of continued storage but below the marginal cost of production in those countries, so that development of local agricultural capacity which would otherwise make sense is deterred.

Another oft-cited example of minimum prices is the minimum wage. Many countries, including the U.S., have minimum-wage laws. Many American states also have higher minimum wages than the federal minimum. Under such laws, if an employer offers a wage, and an employee is willing to accept it, the two parties are nonetheless prohibited from striking a bargain if the wage agreed to falls below the legal minimum. The result is that jobs demanded exceed jobs supplied, permanently.

Most economists tend to discuss the effect of such laws on the ability of people to get jobs (about which I say more later in this chapter). But the primary effect is actually the output not produced because production costs are higher. After the disastrous 2004 tsunami that killed over 100,000 people in countries bordering the Indian Ocean, for example, relief groups immediately set to work clearing debris and bodies, and in Indonesia paid the prevailing local wage of just over three dollars a day.[17] This illustrates two aspects of supply and demand that are often neglected.

First of all, from the point of view of the entire society, jobs are a means to an end and not the end itself. Again, we like to think that we work for ourselves, but in some sense we actually work for everybody else, providing things that they value. The market for labor, like the market for everything else, is simply a way of tying us together for mutual gain. (See the discussion of cost here for a reminder.)

And this raises the second point, which is that from the point of view of a business and from society, employees are actually a cost. Employees must be paid salaries and benefits, and there's no reason to do that unless the benefits to the employer of doing so exceed these costs. But the amount of money an employee earns is in part dependent on the opportunity cost of the worker's time, which means that to hire a person, society gives up that worker's next-best alternative use of time. Businesses, to the surprise of many, are not in business to provide jobs, and so it is somewhat misleading to refer to them as "employers." They are in business to make money, and typically the primary way they do this is by selling a good product at a good price. Jobs are simply one of many costs incurred in the process of doing that, and when we raise those costs, for example via a minimum wage, we must have less of the things that that business was producing before. In the case of the Indonesian

---

[17]http://www.nytimes.com/2005/01/10/international/worldspecial4/10indo.html?_r=1&

example, had the charities described in the article been required to pay the Western idea of a "living wage," not only would far fewer people have been hired, but the cleanup work would have been much more costly and taken much longer.

▨ **Note** Businesses do not exist to provide jobs. Employee costs are but one of the costs a business, and hence society, incurs on the road to making a profit. Businesses exist to advance their owners' interests, which is generally done by producing things that people want to buy.

But of course a price floor for labor has effects on those who are willing to offer their labor in the market—employees or workers, in other words—as well. Note first that minimum-wage laws do not affect everyone; they are only operative for people whose productivity is not high enough to allow them to command a wage above the minimum. (I discuss the economics of compensation more thoroughly in Chapter 6). However, the flip side of this is that the people who are unable to find work are precisely those whose productivity is *below* the minimum, who one might suppose are those most in need of accumulating work experience. What is more, the existence of minimum wages allows employers to be choosy in ways that they could not in its absence. They may indulge discriminatory tastes to weed out workers that do not differ in terms of productivity from the ones hired, but whose sex, race, sexual orientation, and so on make the employer uncomfortable. Those workers might then find it harder to find a job. Among other places, research has demonstrated that this effect exists in Canada, where minimum-wage laws tend to cause substitution away from younger workers (who are more of a gamble for an employer) toward older ones (who have more of a record that the employer can use to estimate how productive they are likely to be), and for women workers in Japan.[18]

The bottom line with price controls is that the fundamental problem they are meant to address is scarcity, and prices are simply a way of bringing the news—they are not the news itself. Relying on price to allocate scarce resources is of course only one way of solving that problem. But other methods of adjustments bring social costs that reliance on price does not. The most important is *deadweight costs*, which Paul Heyne defines with beautiful simplicity as "costs to the purchaser that are not simultaneously benefits to the seller."[19] Time is

---

[18]For Canada, see Tony Fang and Morley Gunderson, "Minimum Wage Impacts on Older Workers: Longitudinal Estimates from Canada," *British Journal of Industrial Relations* 47 (2) (June 2009): 371–387. For Japan, see Daiji Kawaguchi and Kenji Yamada, "The Impact of the Minimum Wage on Female Employment in Japan," *Contemporary Economic Policy* 25 (1) (January 2007): 107–118.

[19]Paul Heyne, *The Economic Way of Thinking,* Ninth Edition (Upper Saddle River, NJ: Prentice Hall, 2000): 83.

the most obvious example. The hours that Nigerians must stand in line waiting to buy gasoline are without question a cost to them. But unlike the money costs they must shoulder, time costs do not benefit sellers, and therefore do not motivate them to bring more gasoline to market.

In the case of rent control, an entire industry has arisen that helps people find the very small number of apartments that become available. These apartment brokers are a completely unnecessary cost; the dollars that would-be tenants pay for their services is a very real social cost, but to the extent that tenants pay fees to the brokers rather than to landlords, landlords again receive no signal that society would value the provision of more apartments given the social opportunity cost of doing so. If rent control disappeared tomorrow, some apartment brokers would still exist, but they would (much like real-estate brokers in the uncontrolled market for home sales) charge not tenants but landlords, who would be paying to inform potential tenants that apart-ments are available. The supply of apartments would go up, and people in New York would do what people in cities without rent control do—spend a day or two looking at a few apartments, and then rent one.

▓ **Tip** Recall the old saying about not shooting the messenger. Prices are messages about the consequences of particular choices, and people or companies that post them are merely messengers.

Note also that sometimes people actually manage to evade price controls, but only by generating other deadweight losses. Landlords often adopt a require-ment that tenants put up thousands of dollars in *key money*, which is not a deposit but basically a one-time fee to start living in the apartment, on top of their monthly rent. This requires that potential tenants either borrow money or save money for months or years, money that they would otherwise spend on other things. In short, this creates an unnecessary extra step to obtaining a scarce good. In addition, the problem of revenues being too low to cover the cost of the action of providing apartments can also be abated by getting cost down—for example, by refusing to maintain building quality at a level that would prevail if tenants were allowed to use money to express their willing-ness to pay for the extra upkeep.

Another form of deadweight loss occurs because the scarce resources do not end up in the hands of those who value them the most. An elderly widower who has been living in a spacious rent-controlled apartment since the 1940s and raised his children there could now get by on less space, if the choices of elderly people in non-price-controlled environments who move into smaller spaces once they retire are any guide. But because he is paying an artificially limited rent, he is earning a huge surplus by getting to live in a large space in

Manhattan. This has the social cost of preventing someone who values the space more—a family with three children that looks just like the widower's did once upon a time, for example—from using it.

When prices can adjust freely, people whose willingness to pay is at least as high as the posted price get things. People without that same willingness don't get them. When prices are not allowed to do this work (and assuming some method like key money or bribery is not found to duplicate, albeit with deadweight costs, the market price), scarce resources are basically allocated by luck. Some people who want apartments cannot get them and thus fail to come to New York City to pursue their goals, or else live farther away and incur deadweight transport and other costs. Even those who find apartments often wish they could pay more for a bigger one, but the rent lottery leaves them unable to.

And sometimes luck's got nothin' to do with it. It emerged several years ago that the powerful New York City Congressman Charles Rangel had four rent-controlled apartments in a single Manhattan building,[20] using three as a residence and a fourth as an office. Although there is no way of knowing the impact for sure, Congressmen often by the very nature of their job build up useful connections with local movers and shakers and certainly have a measure of power to restrict the trading possibilities of ordinary citizens, which may have had a role in this particular allocation of these particular scarce resources. As a consequence, Congressman Rangel gets four apartments, and three people who might have used these apartments to pursue their dreams of a career in acting, finance, or web design—or who could have come to Manhattan to take care of a sick relative—get none.

But 'twas ever thus. There have been price controls for as long as there have been governments to set them. The Code of Hammurabi, which was promulgated in approximately the 18th century B.C. in Babylon by the king of the same name, is most famous for its requirement of the "eye for an eye, tooth for a tooth" punishment. But in fact much of the code is devoted (as in the early Roman legal code known as the Twelve Tables[21]) to setting prices on goods and services. The historical record is not extensive enough to allow us to know whether the predicted shortages developed, but we do know that around the time of the promulgation of this code, many Babylonian business organizations disappeared. Sometimes we know that the controls are ineffective because of the extreme penalties for merchants who violate them—which historically was often death. Such

---

[20]http://online.wsj.com/article/SB122126309241530485.html
[21]http://en.wikipedia.org/wiki/Twelve_Tables

was the case in the Golden Age of Athens, where a prosecutor made the following plea to the jury:

> But it is necessary, gentlemen of the jury, to chastise them [businessmen charging prices above what was allowed] not only for the sake of the past, but also as an example for the future; where as things now are, they will hardly be endurable in the future. And consider that in consequence of this vocation, very many have already stood trial for their lives; and so great are the emoluments which they are able to derive from it that they prefer to risk their life every day, rather than cease to draw from you, the public, their improper profits… If then, you shall condemn them, you shall act justly and you will buy grain cheaper; otherwise the price will be much more.[22]

And yet much more the price continued to be, judging by the continuing need after this anonymous speech to put merchants on trial for their lives. Note the something-for-nothing promise of capital punishment allowing the public to "buy grain cheaper"; such promises are common features of competition among politicians for public favor. Price controls in the Roman Republic in the first century B.C. resulted in farmers no longer bringing food from the countryside to the city. In 301 A.D., during the Roman Empire, the Emperor Diocletian issued a sweeping edict controlling the price of foodstuffs, clothing, and other goods, with the usual remedy of capital punishment for violators. The result was that far fewer goods were brought to market, and the prices of those that did arrive were often, precisely because of the effect of the controls, much higher than the price permitted by law.

During and after the Black Death in England, which killed perhaps a third of that country's population, labor shortages increased competition for workers and hence their wages, and this time it was employers rather than consumers who were upset with the news prices were delivering, leading the Crown to impose a law against "the malice of laborers," which controlled their wages and prevented them from leaving employment. Laborers unsurprisingly hated the measures and went from town to town looking for the highest wages they could get, disrupting production. This was ultimately followed by an uprising known as Wat Tyler's Rebellion, in which a peasant army of 50,000 to 100,000 people marched into London and killed, among many others, the Archbishop of Canterbury and the uncle of King Richard II. Although the proximate cause was a tax introduced shortly before by the King, earlier restrictions on labor may have had much to do with the economic collapse that made the tax necessary. In any event, as usual, the wage control failed to have its desired effect of allowing people to magically acquire more of what they wanted (in this case, the services of labor) at a lower price. Limits on wages and prices during the French Revolution generated hoarding by merchants for personal

---

[22]Cited in Robert L. Schuettinger, *Forty Years of Wage and Price Controls: How Not to Fight Inflation* (Ludwig von Mises Institute, 2009): 16.

use or for the (deadweight-cost–generating) black market, and so too did price controls on oil and gasoline in the United States in the 1970s fail to have their intended effect.

Prices are telling us things. An action that a person or group of people or society might take is like a box, which we can open or not. Some boxes have nasty surprises inside—famines, crops rotting in the field, green companies producing things that no one wants to buy before going bankrupt and throwing valuable assets into the trash[23])—others have wonderful contents like cars that get us from point A to point B in style, dream homes, food to feed our families, and the other products of the spontaneous order. Prices are like labels on these boxes, giving us a guide to what's inside and thus whether these actions are actions we want to take.

▩ **Note**   Never forget that prices communicate something important to us all—they guide us toward, or away from, actions we might take.

When we allow prices to transmit information about the consequences of choices people might make, resources go to those who are willing to pay the most, including those who are willing to pay the most because they have the most money as well as those who attach intrinsically high value to the good. This is true for all things—housing (mobile home versus mansion or studio apartment), cars (10-year-old used car versus high-end SUV), food (Hamburger Helper and rice versus organic food), and anything else that is scarce. As we will see in Chapter 9, reliance on the spontaneous order and prices (the same thing, really) means that the quality of all goods for all people, rich and poor alike, rises dramatically over time. But additional benefits are that resources gravitate to their most valued uses, and we avoid the social waste of dead-weight costs as well as the incentive to resort ever more to political intervention to solve the problems created by the last political intervention.[24]

And ultimately the greatest benefit of all of letting prices run free is that we are given a way to accommodate as easily as possible the unending tide of social change that occurs in a society characterized by hard work and the desire to move up in the world. This is why the removal of comprehensively choking price controls in postwar Germany[25] (imposed ironically by American occupation authorities lamentably ignorant of the function of prices) was a big

---

[23]http://sanfrancisco.cbslocal.com/2012/01/19/bankrupt-solyndra-caught-destroying-brand-new-parts/

[24]For example, the funneling of money through tax breaks to real estate developers to create more affordable housing, the shortage of which was created by price controls restricting the income those same developers could earn by charging market rents for apartments.

[25]http://www.cato.org/publications/commentary/german-miracle-another-look

part of the reason why the German postwar economic miracle took place, which completely transformed a nation devastated by bombing and invasion into a prosperous, peaceful society.

The lesson, and this is not the last time you will hear it, is that inefficiency—the inability to use scarce resources for greater social value—is not a trivial matter. It involves entire neighborhoods that are not renovated for lack of incentives (many cities around the world are full of run-down buildings that would be renovated if only the owners could capture the value to society doing so), the appalling waste of time and money that could be used to do more socially useful things, and even the frustration of dreams for all of those who have grand plans for scarce resources but who find themselves unable to obtain them.

That fundamentally is what economics is about—the shifting of curves on a diagram reflects far more profound realities about allowing us to live to our potential by relying on markets and prices as the system for moving scarce resources to the best of their various competing uses.

Answers to In-Text Question

3.1. The marginal reward for a college degree is the *extra* income received from adding a college degree to one's educational achievements. (This is the marginal reward in terms of monetary compensation alone, of course; to the extent that you value the knowledge and the social experiences you have, the marginal reward is actually greater.)

Economics Out There

3.1. This *New York Times* article[26] concerns price gouging in Florida after a nasty storm. If price gouging were prohibited (and, critically, if this prohibition could be enforced), what would the effect be on the amount of ice brought to the area? Would the available ice be used in the way that is most valuable?

---

[26]http://www.nytimes.com/2004/08/18/national/ 18scams.html?pagewanted=all

3.2.   These three articles are to be read together:

- Sex Is Cheap[27]
- China Tries to Stop Women Marrying for Money[28]
- Why More and More Intelligent Women Are Being Forced to 'Marry Down'[29]

Is it fair to say there is a market for relationships and marriage? If not, why not? If so, what is being traded for what? How do the circumstances of supply and demand differ in each country, thus leading to different equilibrium quantities and price? (It may help to know that because of a decades-old policy limiting most families in China to one child, combined with a deep cultural preference by parents for boys over girls, there are now significantly more marriage-age men than women in China.)

3.3.   According to a survey by Rasmussen Reports in 2011, 64% of Americans think the primary purpose of business is to create jobs. If this is so, is society better off if farmers get rid of their tractors and other machinery and replace them with unemployed workers? What would that do to the social cost of growing crops? In general, is hiring a worker a social cost as well as a social benefit? What are the primary social benefits business provides?

---

[27]http://www.slate.com/articles/double_x/doublex/2011/02/ sex_is_cheap.html
[28]http://www.telegraph.co.uk/news/worldnews/asia/china/8714097/China-tries-to-stop-women-marrying-for-money-rather-than-love.html
[29]http://www.dailymail.co.uk/femail/article-2058127/Intelligent-women-forced-dumb-educated-man-marry.html

The Economics of Information or Knowledge

We All Want to Know What You Know

What do the following have in common: the surprising difficulty of making a rubber band, a car warranty, the questions a car salesperson asks you shortly after meeting you, and the rise and fall of the Sony Corporation? Unless you have an unusual gift for the economics of information, you may say *nothing*, at least on first reading. But it turns out they are all implications of information being scarce and therefore costly. That information is costly follows immediately from the fact that it has value and requires the expenditure of resources to acquire. But this simple fact has powerful implications for the behavior of people seeking it, the behavior of people trying to take advantage of it, and the best way to organize society to harvest this costly but incredibly valuable resource.

First, a few words on the concept of *information*. Economists often use this word interchangeably with the word *knowledge*. I will do so as well. The two terms throughout this book refer to exactly the same thing. And what is that? It is not the conventional idea of book knowledge—for example, such things as Boyle's Law ($pV = k$), the capital of Norway (Oslo), or the definition of opportunity cost (you're on your own). In economics, information or knowledge is *valuable data about a particular economic environment*. It is awareness of unexploited opportunities (actually all opportunities are, by definition, unexploited), of the cost of particular choices, and of tradeoffs and consequences. One of the most accomplished economists of the 20th century, Friedrich Hayek, writing in a research article written for other economists who would know what he meant, called it "knowledge of the particular circumstances of time and place." He went on to offer the following examples:

> To know of and put to use a machine not fully employed, or somebody's skill which could be better utilized, or to be aware of a surplus stock which can be drawn upon during an interruption of supplies, is socially quite as useful as the knowledge of better alternative techniques. And the shipper who earns his living from using otherwise empty or half-filled journeys of tramp-steamers, or the estate agent [here he means real-estate agent] whose whole knowledge is almost exclusively one of temporary opportunities, or the arbitrageur who gains from local differences of commodity prices, are all performing eminently useful functions based on special knowledge of circumstances of the fleeting moment not known to others.[1]

All of these things represent knowledge of opportunities, knowledge that perhaps only one or a few individuals have. Let us elaborate a little on the economic importance of what would happen if these little pieces of economic knowledge—because they were too costly to learn—went unlearned by anyone. A machine not fully employed means that more goods could be produced if only it were. If oil supplies were interrupted because of an embargo or strike by workers somewhere up the line, and if millions of barrels of oil sat idly in storage facilities because no one knew they were there, people would be forced to give up perhaps very important trips because of unnecessarily higher prices. A steamer (or an 18-wheeler, nowadays) that goes out half empty every night is using almost the same amount of fuel to deliver less cargo than it could. If real estate agents *don't* know about houses for sale that buyers will like at that price, people will be prevented from consummating mutually beneficial exchanges. Even the behavior of the arbitrageur (someone who buys something at a low price and sells it at a higher one) has this function of preventing waste, although you will have to wait until later in the chapter to get a thorough understanding of why. And if it seems unlikely to you that real estate agents would not know about such opportunities, or that a shipper would routinely send out trucks half full, that is testimony to the way we have given people proper incentives to put their knowledge to use for the greater gain of everyone else (for compensation, of course). That too is laid out later in this chapter.

---

[1]Friedrich A. Hayek, "The Uses of Knowledge in Society," *American Economic Review* 35 (4) (September 1945): 524.

Decentralized Knowledge and the Spontaneous Order

Imagine you are in an unfamiliar city—Tokyo, say—and you have a goal: to get to a particular place, a restaurant in a particular neighborhood—Harajuku, say. (The neighborhood may be obscure to you, which serves to illustrate how little economic actors know.) It's a foreign city where you have no experience, and you don't speak the language. If all you had to work with was a map of the Asian continent, it would be as if you knew nothing at all.

This problem actually bears some resemblance to that of someone trying to impose a particular economic vision on society. Standing in a legislative chamber or bureaucratic office somewhere, writing laws and rules, you do not actually know the trade-offs that individual decision makers face when they decide to use their resources in ways that are different from those you want to achieve through your rules. If you impose the rules anyway, bad things are probably going to happen—resources will be used inefficiently, there will be unintended (bad) consequences, and the goals that you seek to achieve will probably not come to pass. This task is like trying to navigate through Harajuku with only a map of Asia, or a crude view of Asia from a satellite orbiting the earth, to guide you.[2]

The reason for the problem of trying to guide an economy by laws rather than relying on individuals trading in the market has to do with the fact that information is scarce. No one can know everything. But lots of little pieces of information are known by individuals, and if we could get that information out to the public, then resources could be used more efficiently. And we do, in fact, do that in a market system. People who think they see opportunities can make money by exploiting them. But opportunity is simply a circumstance that no one else has seen—information that is possessed by the person taking the action, and not possessed by other people.

▓ **Note** *Opportunity* is simply a circumstance no one else has seen. Individuals on the ground who will be rewarded for discovering valuable opportunities are much more likely to uncover them than officials in government office buildings.

Examples of things that can be known locally abound, in addition to those Hayek uses earlier. Where is the best location for that factory? Is this the best use of that space in that strip mall? Should that computer have that feature or

---

[2]In saying this I recognize that the mapping software in smartphones is a considerable improvement over old paper maps, but even is not perfect, owing to the existence of very small stores and the constant turnover in businesses.

not? Should I start my business in this town or that, manufacture my product in this country or that one over there? Should I change my restaurant menu from high cuisine to casual, or change my produce supplier? All of these things are costly to discover, and the farther away you are from the scene, and the less you personally have a stake in getting the decision right, the more your map looks like Asia and the less it looks like Harajuku (which is still not, and can't be, an exact duplicate of the neighborhood). That some people see grand things that no one else can see is obvious from the great entrepreneurial experiments in history. John D. Rockefeller became the world's first billionaire because he saw a way, even if he only saw it one step at a time as his business expanded, to improve upon a cumbersome, underdeveloped oil production and distribution system. His insights didn't just change the way oil was taken out of the ground and transported, they also—by making it cheaper to obtain—made it rational to use oil in ways that no one had thought to use it before. A compelling example is the creation of plastics, themselves key ingredients in many modern machines and consumer goods whose uses neither Rockefeller nor anyone else could have predicted at the time.

But the modern, global oil-distribution system, which is built on the foundation Rockefeller laid, is an extraordinarily complicated system. Oil is extracted from under the ground or ocean before being transported great distances to large refineries, which transform the oil into products that will heat buildings, power vehicles, and so forth. Rockefeller saw farther than anyone in laying down the basics of this system, from his first days refining oil for Standard Oil (which would eventually become the largest company in the world) in Cleveland. He and his employees and partners were also visionaries in figuring out refining techniques that wasted less oil, and in using refining byproducts for such useful products as gasoline, pavement tar, petroleum jelly, and paraffin. Standard Oil employed hundreds of chemists to figure out ways to refine more oil at lower cost and to find new uses for what came out of the refining process. Rockefeller also anticipated a development often credited to Henry Ford by paying his workers far more than market conditions suggested he needed to in the belief that this was the way to retain quality employees and prevent labor unrest, thus lowering long-run costs. The proof of the wisdom of this tactic was the rarity with which he faced labor unrest.[3]

Rockefeller was handsomely compensated to be sure for his innovation, becoming the world's first billionaire and, in inflation-adjusted terms, one of the wealthiest people who ever lived. But this compensation was a reward for the value of what he thought he knew, which turned out to be true: crude oil—seen as a useless by-product of salt mining until a chemist at Yale saw how it could be chemically transformed and used to heat indoor spaces more

---

[3]The preceding description is based on Burt Folsom, Ron Robinson, and Forrest McDonald, *The Myth of the Robber Barons* (Young America's Foundation, 1991), especially Chapter 5.

effectively than increasingly expensive whale oil—could be turned into heating oil and therefore transform the way we live. By making nighttime illumination affordable, it made nighttime entertainment in general and reading in the evening (the only part of the day when time to read was available) accessible not just to the wealthy, who could afford whale oil, but to all. Crude oil enabled much of the industrial innovation that took place after 1860, including the profoundly liberating technologies of the automobile[4] and the modern airplane. Rockefeller saw farther than others, and the market—members of society, in other words, in their role as buyers of products made from refined oil—rewarded him for it.

▓ **Note** Entrepreneurs who spot huge opportunities often, if they are correct, amass huge fortunes to match them. And they deserve them precisely because the value of their discoveries is so high to the rest of us.

Even small-scale knowledge that fails to produce these revolutionary effects is rewarded. The company that masters a more efficient transportation route from point A to point B or figures out how to better transport goods by changing vehicle types is also able to do more for less, and this knowledge too is rewarded. Many of the complicated systems that characterize modern society—including those for transportation, communication, distribution, selling, and others too numerous to mention—were built spontaneously by entrepreneurs taking risks, and by sellers selling and buyers buying.

And this is where the virtues of the market come into sharpest focus. None of these systems, in the sense of networks of exchange, were built by a central designer issuing orders from high. Even when, say, roads are built by the government, the decisions about how many and what kind of trucks to put on them, where they come from and go to, and what should be in them, which is the true essence of a transportation system, are made by risk-takers with skin in the game. Even Rockefeller's Standard Oil was only one of several oil companies at the time, each with its own refinery network, each negotiating separate contracts as needed with transporters and retailers. The entire way that oil, and what it can become, gets from underground and into gas tanks as fuel and machines as lubricants and onto roads as asphalt and into appliances as electric power and chemically woven into plastics and into the soil as fertilizers to increase our ability to feed more people at lower cost—all this has happened because people have spied opportunities and built little pieces of the system. It is impossible to design anything like that in total from a central plan conceived on high.

---

[4]http://futureuncertain.blogspot.com/2007/06/in-defense-of-automobile.html

Countries have tried, such as the Soviet Union from 1917 to the late 1980s, China from 1949 to 1980, Italy from 1922 to 1943, and Cuba from 1959 to the present day. All are examples of societies that believed the way to use resources most effectively was to plan their uses from inside the walls of a large government office building, giving orders that so much oil be shipped here and fertilizer be shipped there, so that the "waste" of competition and profit would not inhibit society from using scarce resources to their greatest benefit. But Thomas Sowell describes the phenomenon in the former Soviet Union of rotting fields of wheat just a short distance from an urban center with huge lines of people wanting to buy bread. If someone both knew these things *and* had the ability to capitalize on what he knew, by cutting wheat on time in one place and delivering the bread to the other, this breathtakingly large waste of resources would not occur. But that person did not exist among the endless rows of bureaucrats in faraway Moscow calculating prices and quantities and deciding how many workers this farm should have and how much fertilizer it should get. Those bureaucrats could not succeed without knowing the information that prices communicate to profit-seeking merchants about the value of different uses of and sources for scarce resources.

Modern human society is a phenomenally complex thing, and its construction reflects the embedded knowledge that the shipping center functions best here, the retail store ought to be located there, strawberries should be grown on this land instead of wheat (or instead of putting houses on it), and a million other little bits of knowledge that people have discovered through trial and error. The more local the place, the harder the knowledge is to get from on high. It is common in modern cities for planning commissions to decide, using zoning rules and other exercises of raw power, what kinds of buildings can be built where, and so the members of these commissions, secure in their advanced training, might argue for example that cul-de-sacs encourage isolation from the broader community and are thus antisocial—without realizing what homebuilders learned when they put their own money on the line. Homebuilders know that cul-de-sacs deter crime by making it difficult and risky[5] for ill-intentioned outsiders to get into and out of the neighborhood. Similarly, controlling growth by limiting the types of homes that can be built limits the ability of developers to try different kinds of real estate experiments. In particular it makes construction of not just homes but all buildings more expensive generally, so that extensive land-use restrictions yield the unintended and unexpected consequences[6] of cities that are too expensive for families to live in, such as San Francisco. In addition, zoning allows special interests—for example, very wealthy existing homeowners—to become expert in how the process works and then manipulate it to prevent undesirable people and the undesirable

---

[5] http://reason.com/archives/2005/02/01/crime-friendly-neighborhoods/
singlepage
[6] http://www.nytimes.com/2005/03/24/national/24childless.html

(and cheaper) properties they would build from "ruining the neighborhood." That this shuts off opportunity for people of more modest means of securing their dream is not in the self-interest of these current residents.

Houston, in contrast, rejects most zoning and restrictions on how landowners can use their land,[7] with the result that housing is among the cheapest in the country and business startup rates tend to be high, simply because people are free to look for opportunity where they find it. This lack of rules in lieu of reliance on self-interest means that residences are usually nonetheless surrounded by other residences and not loud bars, while loud bars are surrounded by other loud bars and not residences, all in defiance of the predictions of what should happen without zoning. Houston relies on the *self-regulating spontaneous order*, in which people looking to open a bar have the freedom to decide what the best place for it is, while people who seek to build housing developments put them where they are likely to make the most money selling to aspiring homeowners.

▨ **Note**   Houston's lack of zoning and land restrictions has resulted in low housing prices and high rates of business formation.

When people are free to organize their resources according to the knowledge they possess and to seek out the goods that best meet their needs, the process ensures that local knowledge—what buyers want and what it costs to bring it to them—is harvested to the greatest extent possible. In a planned city or a planned economy, in contrast, there is no way to discover the costs and benefits of different resource uses from the central planning authority, with the result that tremendous waste and frustration occurs. A useful contrast to the flexible housing markets in Houston would be the planned housing developments in Chicago and St. Louis built in the 1950s and 1960s, which resulted not in the paradise for the poor that was envisioned but in nightmarish housing projects with completely unexpected problems. That's because no one had a real incentive to make money avoiding such problems or eliminating them quickly once they appeared. These projects eventually had to be destroyed.[8]

The distance of government planners from the knowledge needed to arrange resources intelligently (not to mention the fact that planners are often spending other people's money rather than their own) means that much knowledge is lost along the way. Planners, in other words, even if they have the incentive to use resources for greatest social benefit (and if they are simply trying to

---

[7]http://www.fee.org/the_freeman/detail/houston-says-no-to-zoning/#axzz2QwCcPWOe
[8]http://pjmedia.com/richardfernandez/2011/03/03/saving-the-village-in-order-to-destroy-it/

preserve or maintain power, that is doubtful) do not have the means to seek out the costly information that the pursuit of profit creates.

The Indian subsidiary of the giant consumer-products firm Unilever[9] got poor people in India to begin washing their hands frequently, thus preventing the transmission of diarrheal diseases and saving many lives. They did so by hiring locals in pairs to go into villages and tell parents in their native language how hand-washing could prevent infections in their children. In so doing, their sales of hygiene products, and hence their profits, increased. The effective marketing strategy—it is better to say the *discovery*, at some cost, of *knowledge* about an effective marketing strategy—was driven by their desire to make money.[10]

This is the spontaneous order in action: the adaptation of resource uses and behavior to local circumstances. It determines how many Chinese restaurants a city will have—Tupelo, Mississippi, has a few, but not as many as Jacksonville, Florida, which has fewer than Los Angeles. How did this get decided? It did not, in the sense of a formal decision. Instead, people seek out locations for Chinese restaurants and are more likely to build them when they discover a place where the benefits are likely to exceed the costs. Naturally, bigger cities have a larger number of restaurants (and a wider variety, probably because of greater variety of population and hence greater variety in tastes), and indeed a larger variety of food of all sorts. This seems obvious, but has happened without a central plan.

Food is not ordered by any central authority, yet grocery stores in big cities and small towns are chock full of food of every variety. How did it get there? People who grow crops negotiated with people who ship them to grocery stores, and the stores are put in places where the people who own them expect to make the most money, and those places in turn are the locations that are the most convenient for the greatest number of shoppers. Such questions as "What kind of food should we sell, and where should we sell it?" get answered through the spontaneous order. Its power is seldom appreciated, but it is vital to providing the sustenance of life and to allowing people to adjust to change in pursuit of their interests.

To take another example, people move to San Jose to pursue their high-tech dreams, in part because the people with the necessary skill and experience (not just in design, but in related things like financing startups) are more likely to be found there. By taking advantage not just of what they know but what other people know in moving to places where high tech is well entrenched, people are able to acquire the necessary resources and information at lower cost. This phenomenon was unplanned and unpredictable, yet it happened, despite—or rather, because of—the spontaneous order. Over several decades

---

[9]Unilever's brands include Vaseline and Dove soap among many others.
[10]The story of Unilever in India is told in C.K. Prahalad, *The Fortune at the Bottom of the Pyramid: Eradicating Poverty Through Profits* (New York: Pearson Prentice Hall, 2008).

San Jose has metamorphosed from a sleepy town built on tourism and agriculture into the center of the high-technology capital of the world, Silicon Valley. And this is not just a phenomenon for wealthy countries. The traditional trading markets in developing countries are also full of people who have figured out how to buy products efficiently and where to sell them. Trading markets with many vendors selling many kinds of goods, like the traditional Arab *souk*, economize on the costs of searching for things to buy, just as Walmart or other superstores do in the U.S. Again, knowledge of how best to do things is harvested by reliance on self-interest, for the benefit of all.

The contrast can be seen by comparing two kinds of "ecosystems," not literal ones but metaphorical ones. One is used by people every day—it is the ecosystem of the smartphone, in which companies that design the phones and their operating systems (like the iPhone and Android interfaces) choose to rely on third-party app designers to decide what the phone will be able to do. App designers see what they think is an unmet desire and design software to satisfy it. It is not, in other words, Apple or Samsung that decides most of what the phone will be able to do. It is instead software writers who market their wares to consumers through the system set up by Samsung and Apple, some with great success,[11] others not so much.[12]

On the other hand, consider the "ecosystem" described and depicted in this essay[13] by the writer Howard Silverman. In it, the author confidently lists a series of jobs he views as clearly important for the economy of the future, including (for the area in which he lives, the Pacific Northwest) "feller buncher operators, specializing in individual tree harvest, and fisheries trust managers, enabling community driven marine stewardship in prosperous coastal areas."[14] (To get the full sense of how detailed Mr. Silverman's blueprint for our future is, look at the picture at the link.)

Are those likely to be the important jobs of the future? The only sensible answer is, "Who knows?" What will be required in the future is largely unknowable, because human possibilities are limitless, and it is almost impossible to acquire the necessary information now about what experiments will even be tried, let alone succeed, in the future. Thus, the trade-off among different human desires—what we must give up if resources are to be used this way—is also impossible to know. Rather, the future must be *discovered*. In the drawing for the article, it appears that there is a place for everything, or at least everything that passes Mr. Silverman's personal test of what is essential.

---

[11] http://www.businessinsider.com/here-are-the-most-popular-mobile-apps-of-2011-2011-12
[12] http://en.wikipedia.org/wiki/I_Am_Rich
[13] http://www.huffingtonpost.com/howard-silverman/jobs-of-the-future_b_1299922.html
[14] A *feller buncher* is a machine used in logging.

But its flaw lies precisely in the belief that the future is a thing certain, a target that we will inevitably reach.

Mr. Silverman's essay in some sense is harmless, because he does not assert that this is how the future *must* be, by the application of laws and taxes if necessary, but it betrays the planner's fallacy—the belief that the planner, in moving resources by the stroke of his pen, has enough knowledge to know the consequences of his decision. When government is fooled by its ignorance of its limits, things usually turn out differently from what was predicted, as when solar energy companies, flush with taxpayer subsidies because *everyone knows* solar is the energy of the future, are unable to sell their products and then go bankrupt, or when companies that received lavish governments subsidies are unable to profitably produce vehicle fuel made from coal, oil shale, and other unconventional sources. In the latter case, over $1 billion of taxpayer money was spent on the government Synthetic Fuels Corporation from 1980 until it was eliminated in 1985. Needless to say, most people who drive do so in gasoline-powered cars to this day.

▨ **Note**   Society is far too complex, and the future too unknowable, for anyone to make predictions that are more than mere wish lists or guesses about what may come about.

And government economic planning—the reliance on the force of law to *order* people to use resources in particular ways to achieve social goals instead of the decentralized competitive process of the spontaneous order—far more often than not generates these kinds of problems. When he was Vice President, Al Gore analogized government to a computer and made these observations in an interview with the magazine *Red Herring*:

> Just as you saw the progressive switch from central processing units to massively parallel supercomputing, our democratic system made it possible for the average citizen to participate in the decision-making of this nation by processing the decision-making directly relevant to him or her in an individual congressional district or state. Then, in the process of biennial or quadrennial elections, our process harvests the sum total of those decisions and uses it as a basis for guiding the nation.

Central processing refers to computers that operate independently, with one core processor doing all the calculations in sequence. In traditional computing architecture, the only way to get the computer to do more work is to make the processor more powerful. In parallel computing, roughly speaking, computing is instead speeded up by dividing a big calculation problem into smaller sub-problems and farming each one out to a separate processor. One computer, in other words, has multiple processors, and only at the end is the task completed at the highest processor (Wikipedia has a description of the technology.)[15]

So what the vice president is saying is that state governments and individual congressmen harvest information necessary for good decision making from individual constituents, who tell them about problems that need to be solved. This knowledge is then passed up the chain to Congress, which is able to use all the information collected to do what is best for the nation.[16] But information is not like that—it's not something harvested by a central authority, like a giant field of wheat being cut by agricultural machines. Information is possessed by individuals, and as it is passed up the political line from citizen to city councilman to state senator to Congressman to legislation, some of it is lost at every stop along the way. It is like electricity going through a substance that does not conduct electricity very well; much is lost along the way, so that by the time the state of California, for example, is deciding[17] how small houses should be and where they should be built, other unexpected problems arise. We saw how regulating land use ends up making home ownership for young families nearly impossible.

The same phenomenon was on display in the decision in the 1990s and 2000s by politicians of both parties to second-guess the decisions of real estate lenders as to who should and shouldn't get a home loan. The second-guessing was on the grounds that the percentage of people owning homes was actually not the best result, even though each lender and home buyer was interacting in the marketplace based on what he believed about the desirability of particular houses and the credit-worthiness of particular borrowers. Instead, home ownership was too low by some politician's arbitrary standard. (Should 60% of Americans own their own homes? 30%? 90%? Does anyone know?) Pressure was placed on lenders to relax their lending standards (with these standards sometimes criticized as racially discriminatory) to "allow" (as if there were some unnatural barrier having nothing to do with risk or opportunity cost) more Americans to buy homes.

Standards were relaxed, home lending went up, and home ownership for Americans reached a historic high in the middle part of the decade of the 2000s. Only later did those chickens come home to roost, when many of these borrowers proved—just as lenders had predicted when they had originally refused to make those loans—unable to make their payments, which contributed to the financial crash of 2007–8. The best evidence for the virtues of letting people make money off what they know is that the real estate market was functioning well prior to the second-guessing of its results by

---

[15]http://en.wikipedia.org/wiki/Parallel_computing
[16]The vice president expressed similar thoughts in an interview with the author Louis Menand. See Louis Menand, "After Elvis," *The New Yorker* (October 26, 1998).
[17]http://online.wsj.com/article/SB10001424052702303302504577323353434618474.html

bureaucrats, precisely because people lending their own money had incentives to try to make good loans and avoid bad ones. Only when lending below some arbitrary target set by bureaucrats became a potentially criminal matter were excessive risks taken.[18]

The bottom line is that information is simply too widely distributed for governments to have much wisdom about how to use scarce resources. Even events that are relatively easy to take precautions against in the abstract nonetheless happen, as anyone who has ever spilled his drink that he arrogantly set near his notes or laptop, secure in his "knowledge" that nothing can go wrong, can attest. Some of the difficulty in the idea of relying on central authorities to guide resource use can be had from a simple thought experiment, carried out by the author Virginia Postrel.[19] A single deck of cards has 52 elements. How many different card orderings are there? The answer is just less than 10^{68}, a number that is meaningless in the abstract.[20] But to get some sense of how big it is, note that it is far more than the estimated number of seconds since the Big Bang, more than the estimated number of molecules in the Milky Way galaxy. And yet that is the number of ways to combine a mere 52 objects. How many ways are there to combine all the available scarce resources with competing uses in an economy? In the answer to that question lies the essence of the planner's fallacy.

The Importance of Learning from Mistakes

But the alert reader may well object at this point that I have cherry-picked my examples. Rockefeller and smartphones and a historically well-functioning home-loan market are examples of *success* generated by relying on the spontaneous order to harvest and make use of socially valuable knowledge. Are there not many examples of failure as well? Indeed there are, but in failure too lies an important function of the spontaneous order.

---

[18]It should be noted that many place the blame for the housing disaster on progressively easier lending standards imposed by mortgage lenders at the time, including pressure on sales personnel to increase volume regardless of the risks. While certainly true as a proximate cause, this argument however raises more questions than it answers. Why did standards suddenly depart so much from historical norms? What were the likely consequences of engaging in riskier lending, and who would bear them—the people who made the decisions, the people who borrowed the money, taxpayers, or someone else? All we can say in terms of good rules for lending is that people who lend money should have the proper incentives to make good loans and avoid bad ones.

[19]Virginia Postrel, *The Future and Its Enemies: The Growing Conflict Over Creativity, Enterprise, and Progress* (New York: The Free Press, 1999).

[20]The calculation comes from noting that there are 52 possibilities for the first card. There are 51 cards left that can be laid on each of those 52 cards, and for each of those 52×51 combinations there are 50 possibilities for the third card, and so on. The total number of possibilities is $52 \times 51 \times 50 \ldots \times 2 \times 1$, which is about 8.07×10^{67}.

Businesses fail all the time. What then happens? The resources they were using are released to earn their opportunity cost in some other use. When a dry-cleaner closes, the storefront after the passage of some amount of time goes to a restaurant or an office-supply store, workers must find other work, the paper clips the dry cleaner would have used in his back office must be sold to someone else to use in some other back office, etc. If the business owner had known this was going to be the result, he would not have claimed the resources to begin with. Thus, even in the private sector, *knowledge is very far from perfect.* Business owners take risks, workers expect their careers to have a certain trajectory, and college students predict that their course of study will have certain results in the labor market. But life throws us curveballs—what we thought at a particular time turns out not to be what is so. Indeed, inherent in the word *risk* or *expect* is the idea that things can turn out differently than what we planned. This is just another way of saying that knowledge is costly and that the supply curve of knowledge is, like all others, positively sloping, so that at some point it becomes inefficient to try to acquire more before we act.

▓ **Note**   When a business fails, the resources it employed are then released and can be used more profitably elsewhere.

And this is the source of economic correction: businesses close at least as often as they open, companies introduce products that bomb in the market-place, people make investments in real estate or stocks and find that they go bad. Consider the case of a small business that fails quickly—a common occurrence. No one would purposely set out to engage in a failed economic activity, so it must be that the business expected something to happen that did not. In other words, it possessed information that was either insufficient or incorrect—it misjudged the number of people willing to buy that product, underestimated the cost of obtaining resources or its own time costs, or failed to anticipate changes in population, technology, local economic circumstances, or something else.

What, economically, does it mean that the business failed? It means that the revenue it earned from selling this particular mix of things to consumers was insufficient to allow it to retain all its resources (the owners of which must be paid compensation at least as high as the resources' opportunity costs). But this is what we *want* to happen—if resources used this way cannot earn their opportunity cost, society is better served by releasing them from this use. Failed economic experiments also yield knowledge—the knowledge of what not to do.

And it is not just businesses that fail shortly after their creation that can be damaged by faulty information. Companies that have long histories of success can fail to adapt to social change and pay the price. The Sony Corporation, mentioned at the beginning of the chapter, was once seen as the most innovative company in the world when it rode inventions like the Walkman, which made music portable for the first time by allowing people to take cassettes in little cases with them and listen to the music privately on headphones, to great commercial success. But it largely missed the boat when the preferred style of storing music switched from cassettes to digital files. At the same time, the television sets and computers that allowed Sony to reap huge profits in the 1980s and 1990s became standardized devices that many manufacturers could make, often in China, at less cost. As I write this, Sony, which sparked paranoid fears of a Japanese takeover of the American economy in 1989 when it bought Columbia Pictures Entertainment,[21] the producer of such legendary films as *Mr. Smith Goes to Washington* and *On the Waterfront*, has lost money for four years running. Sony has lost money both because it cannot make money on hardware anymore and because the movies it makes are less important as an entertainment option because of the rise of the Internet.

A company can even go from right to wrong to right again. The Apple Corporation was a star in the early years of the personal computer, but by the mid-1990s was losing money because of failed ventures such as its Newton personal digital assistant, as well as poor marketing and technology decisions regarding its desktop computers. And yet by 2012 it had—via its iPhone, iPad, and similar products, as well as an array of easy-to-use and powerful software—become perhaps the most successful and influential technology company in the world. The late Steve Jobs, Apple's long-time chief executive, was credited in particular (like John D. Rockefeller) with a gift for knowing what it was that consumers wanted out of technology, even if they did not know it themselves yet. And yet by early 2013 (after Jobs had died) it had had a series of disappointing product launches, its stock had fallen dramatically, and its ability to remain at the cutting edge was increasingly questioned.

Nothing, including the value of knowledge previously exploited, lasts forever. Apple was able to recover from its troubles in the early 1990s because of the ingenuity of those who ran it and worked for it, but there are no guarantees if it is unable to best predict which uses of the resources it controls create the most value for its customers. Even mighty Google, which rose to prominence and made its founders and many lower-level employees phenomenally wealthy by creating a better method of Internet search, now faces new competition[22] from people reimagining Internet search as built around one's Facebook friends or vocal requests asked of one's smartphone, rather than typing text into a search engine. And it is an interesting experiment to look

---

[21]A classic example of this paranoia was the novel by Michael Crichton called *Rising Sun*, which was later made into a movie.

[22]http://www.forbes.com/sites/beltway/2012/03/12/google-isnt-leveraging-its-dominance-its-fighting-to-avoid-obsolescence/

at changes in the Fortune 500, an annual ranking by *Fortune* magazine of the largest corporations in the U.S. (ranked by annual sales). Of the companies on the list in 1970, the *Economist* magazine reports, one-third were gone (through failure, merger, or acquisition) by 1983—only 13 years later. To take a particular case, Eastman Kodak, the maker of cameras and film, was number 43 in the first full list in 1955, rose as high as number 18 in 1980–1990, and went bankrupt in 2012.

■ **Note**   Google is flying high today, but if history is any guide, their dominance may not last long. Other companies will come along with cheaper and/or better substitutes for the wares and services they sell so profitably now.

Competition

Why do activities succeed or not in the marketplace? In each case, whether we are talking about a new business or long-standing one, competition is the playing field, and profits are the scoreboard, for economic success and failure. Competition between restaurants, between different ways of organizing a business, between using workers with and without college degrees to do particular kinds of work, between imported and domestic cars, between public schools, private schools, and homeschooling are all ways of discerning what does more for society at lower cost. Because knowledge is so decentralized, because predicting the future is so hard, the best way to achieve as much social progress as possible is to have as much competition as possible. Those competitive experiments that lose money will end, as they should, and those experiments that are able to make money will continue, as they should. Indeed, those experiments that make the most money are those where knowledge has proven most valuable. *Competition among products or companies is really competition among ideas, among different ways of deploying scarce resources to meet human needs.*

A humble example serves to illustrate what is going on. Imagine a random resident of town X who discovers that he can buy jam for $2.00 a jar while people 30 miles away in town Y, where people are insular and have high costs of living, pay $3.00 a jar for it.[23] (As a reminder, people who discover and capitalize on such price differences for the same good in different places are called *arbitrageurs*, and Hayek speaks of them in the quote earlier.) The $1.00 difference (minus whatever it costs him to get jam from stores in X to the hands of buyers in Y) represents the value to society of this knowledge.

---

[23]I owe this example to Walter Block, *Defending the Undefendable* (Auburn, Alabama: Ludwig von Mises Institute, 2008).

If people in Y were actually paying $5.00 a jar, it would be even more useful to society to save them money by seizing the opportunity to exploit this difference. Of course, the seller wants to charge as close to the price that prevails in Y as possible ($2.99 in the first case, $4.99 in the second). But that is the value of his knowledge, and so as the first to discover it he *should* benefit from it. The good news is that others will soon see him exploiting the opportunity and do the same—not just by charging a lower price, although that will be one method of competition, but also by offering a wider range of goods or more convenient purchasing options and locations. Eventually the benefits will spread widely among consumers as well, and indeed if more products are offered in better ways, the social gains will be even greater than envisioned by the first person who brought jam from X to Y.

But all competition is in some sense like this—discovering and exploiting opportunities to trade. Many American cities now have food trucks—large motor coaches out of which food is served, especially at lunchtime. There is nothing new about using vehicles to bring food to the diner instead of making the diner come to the food, of course; the American West had its chuck wagons, and armies their mobile canteens. In the 1980s and 1990s in Los Angeles, people discovered that they could make money parking these trucks near construction sites, which exploded in number during the real-estate boom of the 2000s. But in recent years truck owners have begun sending them to a wider variety of places, and some of these food trucks have developed cult followings, with owners using Twitter to announce where they will be. In each case, customers get something they didn't have before, and truck owners make money because they learned about this unfilled desire.

Food truck success in turn has inspired other types of information-based gambles. Companies have emerged spontaneously to lease trucks to chefs and handle the chores of ordering supplies, making it easier for would-be truck chefs to enter the business by lowering costs and allowing cooks to specialize in what they do best—cooking. More substantially, Rockefeller made millions of people he never met aware of the ways in which oil—when incorporated into gasoline, kerosene, and later jet fuel and plastics—could enable them to do new things (from throwing a Frisbee to being able to read at night, to flying around the world at much lower cost) that they could not do before. His compensation reflected the value of the possibilities that, by building his vast network to drill for, refine, and distribute oil, he informed society of.

▓ **Note** Companies that uncover latent demand—like the demand for food trucks—in turn spur the development of products and services to support them (like custom truck makers and food brokers who handle purchases).

But not everything pans out. Of course, some of those food trucks and truck-leasing companies fail, and they are those whose opportunities were revealed to be not sufficiently valuable relative to cost. The Segway scooter, which according to breathless media coverage at the time it came out was supposed to change the way we get around, has proven far too expensive for most uses, and therefore not revolutionary in the way (to go far back in history) the cart (still used today), the wheeled cycle, the vehicle powered by the internal combustion engine, or the airplane has been. The Apple Newton, the Nintendo Virtual Boy,[24] and the Ford Edsel were examples of new opportunities consumers elected to take a pass on, so society learned not to try mistakes like those again. Indeed, in the case of the Virtual Boy gaming platform, repeated price drops by Nintendo failed to find a point at which consumers thought this new opportunity worth it. Even Rockefeller would have been unknown to later generations had he not continuously innovated, creating new products such as paints and varnishes, investing heavily in speculative Ohio oil fields after oil in Pennsylvania—where the modern oil industry was born—became too costly to extract, creating new techniques to purify the high-sulfur oil found in Ohio, discovering new people to sell to in India and China, and on and on. Had he not done so, he would have suffered the same fate as our hypothetical jam seller would once the price of jam in Y had come down to just cents over $2.00. Instead, his *continuous stream of economically useful discoveries* changed the world. Competition is a merciless scorekeeper, but unlike every political process for allocating scarce resources ever conceived, it is completely objective: make enough money to cover your costs, and you get to keep playing. Those who succeed by its rules are those who discover and capitalize on the most useful information.

Profit as Markup

There is a commonly held contrary view of profit—not as the reward for discovering something valuable about how to use scarce resources, but as useless surplus piled up by overcharging for goods and then distributing them without rhyme or reason or "social justice" to people who don't need or deserve them. But the approach I'm describing suggests a different idea—of profit as the measure of the best use of scarce resources. Criticisms of profitable businesses are ubiquitous, and the larger and more profitable they are, the louder these criticisms often are. But consider a nonprofit institution—the university. For decades, college tuition in the U.S. has soared much faster than the rate of inflation, and this rise in the cost of procuring a college education is seen as a major social problem. But most colleges are nonprofit associations! They are legally bound to not seek to maximize the excess of revenues over costs, so the revenue that the university earns, much of it from students, need not be wasted as profit.

---

[24]http://www.time.com/time/specials/packages/article/0,28804,
1991915_1991909_1991900,00.html

Profit can be increased by two ways: revenues can go up (for example, via higher tuition without a correspondingly large drop in enrollment) or *costs can go down.* The absence of profit-seeking means there is little incentive to get costs down. Universities have many expenditures that might seem peculiar to someone trying to maximize profits. They are laden more and more by fully staffed administrators who are in charge of arguably extraneous (in the sense that what is invested in may not be justified by what is gained) activities such as "civic engagement," particular conceptions of "diversity, "athletics, and so on. (Note: the argument is not that such activities have *zero* benefits, just that their benefits may not justify their costs.) This—along with granting low teaching responsibilities to many professors, often those with the highest salaries, ironically—means that other teachers have to be hired to teach the courses these professors would otherwise teach.[25] These sorts of practices drive up costs.

These are not the only reasons for higher costs—extensive government subsidy of college education means that universities are incented to build more campuses and buy more frills. But the lack of the desire to pursue profit means no one has the incentive to discover what for students would be socially useful knowledge—how to provide more education at less cost. Partly due to the revolutionary technology of the Internet, for-profit alternatives are increasingly rising to challenge the old higher-education model. Some of them—offering "badges" for completing a curriculum or creating "massive open online courses"—offer tremendous potential. On the other hand, some for-profit colleges have revenue that comes mostly from students who take out student loans to afford the tuition. The money flows directly to the colleges (and especially to those who run them in the form of high salaries), while the students who acquire education that turns out to be of little value are, unlike most other debtors, currently unable to use bankruptcy law to discharge their debt burdens. What should happen is that competition should force such programs to offer more useful courses. But the model in which benefits accrue right now to firms while the costs are borne later *only* by borrowers (and taxpayers) may prove to be a deficient one, and if so we are likely to discover that only after a great deal of political finger-pointing, precisely because higher education is so extensively political.[26] The contrast with the hyper-efficient "supply chains" of for-profit corporations—which enable things like shipping produce in giant ships and planes around the world in a matter of days so that it arrives to stores fresh, and to distribute manufacturing

---

[25]It is instructive that some university professors refer to their "teaching load," suggesting that for them teaching is to some degree a distraction from other activities, for example research.

[26]The new communications technology is (I, with my very incomplete information, will speculate) likely to dramatically change the nature of higher education. In the course of this process, many mistakes will be made and many lessons will be learned. A theme of this chapter is that this process should be allowed to unfold as quickly as buyers and sellers want to make it unfold.

activities around the world at astonishingly low cost, *and* in which businesses are rewarded only for providing things that consumers want and are willing to pay their own money for—is conspicuous.

The Market as What We Know Together

Because competition is a way of rewarding useful knowledge and punishing false (*mistaken* is perhaps a better word) information, market competition is a way of amassing knowledge. There is an idea known as the *wisdom of crowds* which essentially means that many people acting independently to solve a problem will create a solution that is much better than the solution created by one person, even if that person is very intelligent or an "expert." *The Chronicle of Higher Education* published a fascinating account[27] on scientists trying to figure out how molecules of RNA in the body work by coming up with designs for molecules that will actually work in nature. Historically, one or a few highly trained scientists have developed programs that allow computers to try to build such models, with limited success. Now, scientists at Stanford farm this work out to thousands of gamers, each of whom comes up with his own design, with the players then collectively deciding which models among those they have created are best. The models produced considerably outperform those created by traditional methods.

Here we actually have a pretty good facsimile of the market process. There is decentralized knowledge (each player's idea), there is competition (to win the game), and there is a way of measuring the value of the result (whether it does or doesn't satisfy the scientists' goals). What is more, there is also continuous improvement as gamers learn from the results of previous rounds of the game how to make better designs, which is just like innovation that occurs in a market setting from watching both the successes and failures of others. The collective outperforms its most knowledgeable individual member (the scientist in charge). Note that the *reason* the process works is not because all participants are trying to solve a common problem per se, but because they are *competing* to solve it through a system that makes their private knowledge public and relies on incentives (the desire of gamers to win). This "market" has harvested all the knowledge available in this community at any moment in time about how to solve this problem.

It is perhaps not surprising that markets incorporate information on a massive scale. When the space shuttle *Challenger* exploded on January 29, 1986, the cause of the disaster was a complete mystery. An investigation that took months to play out eventually discovered that a part called an O-ring had failed,

---

[27]http://chronicle.com/blogs/wiredcampus/the-public-playing-a-molecule-building-game-outperforms-scientists/32835

causing fuel to leak into a place where it wasn't supposed to be, causing in turn a catastrophic ignition. But on the day of the explosion itself, this was completely unknown. There were four primary contractors on the space-shuttle program—Morton Thiokol, Lockheed, Martin Marietta, and Rockwell—and presumably the failure would be ultimately laid at the feet of just one of them. Yet on the day of the crash the stock of Morton Thiokol—the company that made the O-ring—fell more than 11.86%—a large one-day move—while none of the other three companies saw their stock fall more than 3.25%. The market collectively seemed to *know* that it was Morton Thiokol's fault. Even though presumably there was probably not a single trader who could explain in detail how the shuttle worked, traders made it their business to follow Morton Thiokol and other companies, to observe general and specific strengths and weaknesses of their quality control, management, and so on, and each trader who knew each little thing acted on it that day, with the *collective* result that the market partially anticipated the result of the federal investigative commission, with its exhaustive investigation, by months. The decentralized information used in each stock trade affected stock prices (each person who thought Morton Thiokol had many problems, for example, sold it and generated downward pressure on prices), and those prices assimilated all that information to produce the final result in the change in market value, on that day, of the company that ultimately proved to be at fault.

▨ **Note** The market seemed to know, before any official investigation, that Morton Thiokol had a major part in the *Challenger* disaster.

Of course, that could just be random chance; there were only four contractors, and prices would go on to fluctuate in the months before the commission made its judgment. But another striking example comes from World War II. In his book *Wealth, War and Wisdom* (Wiley, 2009), Barton Briggs investigates, among other things, the ups and downs of the stock market in the U.S. and Great Britain during World War II. Militarily, according to much contemporaneous press coverage, the most critical part of the European war was the Battle of Britain in the fall of 1940, when the Nazis, having defeated France and pushed British forces out of Western Europe, were bombing Britain continuously to gain control of the air and degrade British warmaking capacity in preparation for an invasion of the islands. Although Hitler would go on to conquer vast new territories in Eastern Europe, Greece, and the Soviet Union and obtain control over new military forces in Hungary, Romania, and Bulgaria in 1941, one could argue that the failure to invade Britain was the decisive moment for that country. However, press coverage continued to express uncertainty about whether Hitler could be defeated until the epic battle of Stalingrad, which ended with Axis defeat amid at least half a million casualties in February 1943. At that point the method, if not the timeline or ultimate cost, of victory could be seen by many.

But the financial markets did not see it that way. According to Biggs's analysis, the London stock exchange fell almost 40 percent between 1937 and early 1940, putting the lie to the hoary cliché that "war is good for business," but began to rise after the British saved many of their soldiers in France with their historic evacuation at Dunkirk. In the eyes of the public and British political leaders, the fall of France was the darkest hour yet, as well as a harbinger of darker times yet to come, in the form of an invasion of Britain. And yet in the eyes of investors, the saving of so many soldiers seems to have marked a turning point, meaning that the market collectively seems to have been a better gauge of the future than popular opinion. By the time of Hitler's defeat at Stalingrad, the market had more than doubled.

It was the same story, with slightly different details, in the U.S. After the attack on Pearl Harbor, Japan quickly expelled British, Australian, and Dutch forces from Malaysia, captured the mighty British military base at Singapore, then captured Burma and Indonesia, and by the spring of 1942 was conducting bombing raids on Australia and India. In the naval battle between the U.S. and Japan in the Coral Sea in early May 1942, Japan was able to inflict more damage on U.S. naval power than the inverse, but that marked the low-water mark of the market, which began a sustained rise through the end of the war, even before the Battle of Midway in early June 1942, which was decisively won by the U.S. Navy and was seen only in hindsight as the turning point in the Pacific war.

Financial markets—which are constantly incorporating the individual knowledge of each investor trying to trade on that knowledge for profit—are now increasingly used to try to predict events, and it is now widely accepted that the stock market begins to fall or recover before the broader economy does. The trouble is, of course, that at any time it is not clear whether the current fall is short or long term, which is why investing is so hard. That the market represents all of what is known doesn't mean it knows everything, and no single individual, as we have seen, is likely to know more than what everyone collectively knows.

Monopoly and Its Meaning, or Lack Thereof

People think they know things; sometimes what they think they know is right, and sometimes it is not. If competition rewards that which turns out to be true and punishes that which turns out to be false, then the first person to discover something of immense social value—the first person to inform others of a possibility in trade that didn't exist before—ought to make a lot of money. This is John D. Rockefeller's story. But not all new discoveries are the same. Some are easy to duplicate, whereas others depend on resources so rare that it is extremely difficult for other people to horn in on the extraordinarily high returns being earned.

It is critically important to understand this when thinking about competition and its absence. Most people are familiar with the word *monopoly*, which supposedly describes the opposite of *competition*. But *monopoly* is actually a word without any economic content, a word that does not map to any real economic phenomenon. The word comes from Greek, *mon* ("one") and *pōlein* ("seller"). But all producers of all goods face competition, because no demand curves are perfectly inelastic. Name any seller you like that you consider to be a monopoly, and it will turn out to face competition. Microsoft sells the Windows operating system, but ultimately this is just a way to manage information. People can use personal computers running on different operating systems such as Apple's Mac OS or Linux, they can use cell phones and tablets and forgo the need for a personal computer entirely, or they can use dictionaries, encyclopedias, and phonebooks. In each case they give up some things (convenience, perhaps) and get others (the use of the money saved in not buying a Windows machine), so that in each case we have an imperfect substitute for what Microsoft is selling.

John D. Rockefeller's Standard Oil? Rockefeller himself always noted that they always had competitors, always would, and indeed needed them. People had lived without heating oil before Rockefeller and somehow managed to live without petroleum jelly and varnish, and could easily do so again if Rockefeller's asking price were too high. The local modern electric utility? In some places, multiple companies offer electric power services, and even where they don't, one can still live off the grid by installing solar panels so as to minimize or eliminate one's use of the utility's electricity—or indeed live without electricity, as people did for most of human history. Of course, in some cases, the substitutes are not very good, but they are substitutes just the same.

From one point of view, no one is a monopolist, because all producers must deal with other producers who are selling goods that compete with what they sell. From the other point of view, everyone is a monopolist. Someone who owns a gasoline station that sells gasoline with the brand name BP may have to share that intersection with gas stations on two other corners, but his product is still distinct. It may allow people to accumulate points to be used by gas or junk food via a company-issued card, it may have a car wash whereas the other two do not, it may have a different mix of food in the market attached to it, and it may even require a right instead of a left turn, saving a tiny bit of driving time. These differences are not great, but they are differences, and in practical terms we have the opposite phenomenon from that in the previous paragraph—here substitutes are extremely close, but they are not perfect. So *all people*, because they sell unique products, are monopolists. What we learn from this is that the word monopoly is not helpful, and it depends on how we arbitrarily define the product. Either everyone is a monopolist, or no one is.

▓ **Note** Nobody really has a monopoly, because even if there are not direct competitors to your product or service, there are substitutes that might satisfy the same desires, so that people can always choose to go without *your particular product*. Alternatively, everybody has a monopoly, because each product is distinct.

From now on we will jettison the term monopoly. However, we have already learned, in Chapter 2, an idea to describe the degree of competition that is more concrete: elasticity of demand. We can speak of some producers—the makers of life-saving medicine subject to patent protection, the local electric utility—as having very inelastic demand. Products for which the substitutes are few and poor have inelastic demand. On the other hand, people selling other products—such as farmers growing corn that is essentially identical to the corn sold by thousands of other farmers—face extremely elastic demand. Generally, the more elastically one's product is demanded, the easier it is for one's profits to be dissipated by the *entry* of competing producers.

Consider first our jam vendor from earlier. He has discovered a socially valuable piece of knowledge—that residents of Y are paying a price for jars of jam that is one dollar higher than the price he can purchase them for in X. He begins buying them in X, selling them in Y at $2.99 a box, and thus earns a huge markup per jar sold. However, we must confess that although it took some work to discover this activity, and society is better off for our vendor having done so, the work is not excessively complicated. So what would probably happen is that other people would observe his cart on the streets of Y or observe him buying jam in large amounts in X, infer what is going on, and start trying to get some of that action themselves. They would do that by buying their own jam in X and selling them in Y at a lower price than $2.99. As more people are buying jam in X, they will drive up the price there. (The supply curve of jam in X is positively sloped after all, so higher demand for buying that jam against that supply curve will cause price to go up.) Combined, these two effects will eliminate the unusually high profits to this activity. The initial vendor had socially useful knowledge, but it was knowledge that required no unusually scarce resources to benefit from.

The Indifference Principle

Steven Landsburg has called the phenomenon just described the *indifference principle*. Ask yourself which is more desirable as a place to live: San Diego or Dayton? The answer at first seems to be San Diego, because of the weather, the nearby natural beauty from beach to desert to mountains, the ethnic diversity, the cuisine, etc. But note first that not everyone values these things. People who value ties to nearby family members, their perception of the nature of social interchange where they are ("people are friendlier here," people from everywhere seem to say), or the local habits they have acquired over a lifetime in Dayton have no wish to leave. But some will. And as they do, they will drive up the price of housing in San Diego. And with fixed freeway space, more people means more time spent in traffic. Eventually, as home prices go up and the freeways become more crowded, people more or less stop moving to San Diego. (In fact, California in general became a state with net out-migration of Americans in the last decade.)

What has happened is that the *excess return to living in San Diego has been competed away*. The new migrants drive up prices, and eventually the last person to move there basically could flip a coin as to whether to move or stay—in economic jargon, he is *indifferent* between staying and going. Our jam seller is in the same position—his excess profits should be competed away by people entering the business, who undersell him in Y and drive up the price in X. We can state this as a more general principle: *when an activity is easy to duplicate and entry is open, excessive returns should be competed away*. What makes the surplus to living in San Diego vanish is that anyone can move there, but housing and freeway space are scarce.[28] What makes our jam seller's high profits analogously vanish is that his activity, once he has learned of it and revealed it through his seizing profits by trading in the market, can be easily duplicated.

When the Indifference Principle Does Not Hold

But consider instead the phenomenon of the elite athlete. Albert Pujols[29] plays first base for the California Angels, and until 2011 played for the St. Louis Cardinals. Based on his salary between 2008–2010 for the Cardinals, he made over $20,000 per plate appearance during that time. The world is full of people who would be willing to do his job for free, and many others who would do it for substantially less than he is paid. But of course they wouldn't do it nearly as well as he does. Taking an average baseball fan off the street and writing his name in the St. Louis Cardinals lineup every night would mean an automatic out once every nine players instead of having Pujols's prodigious offensive production. The Cardinals, during the time Pujols played for them under contract, decided it wasn't even worthwhile to get rid of Pujols and replace him with another *major-league-caliber* baseball player who would have come cheaper, let alone someone who might've done it for $50 a night. Albert Pujols makes a phenomenally high salary because he has remarkably rare talent in an environment—Major League Baseball—where a large amount of money is divided up among a very small number of people. He is not nearly as subject to competition as our jam vendor.

---

[28]That the construction of housing in San Diego is artificially constrained by zoning and other government land-use planning makes it even more expensive there, but that is another problem.

[29]http://www.baseball-reference.com/players/p/pujolal01.shtml

As with Albert Pujols, so too with supermodels, musicians with very rare voices or instrumental gifts, and movie stars with unusually powerful public appeal, whether because of their looks or some other reason. All of these people possess a type of talent with very few decent substitutes and so are relatively invulnerable to competition, until such time as the public tires of them or their skills deteriorate with age. But this kind of skill need not be thought of as a mere gift of physical appearance or athletic talent. (It should be noted that most people who make it as supermodels, athletes, or entertainers have spent years in training or auditions developing their skills, so the word *gift* is only partly accurate.) What made John D. Rockefeller and Steve Jobs great was their very rare ability to see around the economic corner—to see what was coming or what needed to be done—before others did. Rockefeller, recall, had a whole series of innovations that meant that his money was not just made in his initial construction in Ohio of his oil-trading system, but in his discovery of and acting on one very valuable idea after another.

So, it is within the power of some to exploit the inherent and long-lasting scarcity of skills they possess. They as individuals are not subject to the indifference principle. Indeed individuals seldom are—the first expatriate Daytonian to buy a house in San Diego might have gotten it relatively cheap and later could have sold it for an immense amount of money. But the ordinary state of affairs is that high profits bring competition, and the only way to keep making money is to benefit from a resource in permanently short supply or to keep discovering *new*, also valuable, knowledge. Indeed, at the market level, the indifference principle is still in play. No one can compete away the immense returns of being Julia Roberts in particular, but for every Julia Roberts there are vast numbers of people who come hoping to be the next Julia Roberts but end up only doing local theater for low pay or waiting tables, thus in a sense losing more than is gained, if we count all the time spent waiting unsuccessfully to be a star. The same logic holds for would-be Major League Baseball players who spend years training but never get near the major leagues. On average, the *net income* (compensation minus opportunity cost) to all people who *try* to become major leaguers or Hollywood stars may well be zero.[30]

▨ **Note**   To make a lot of money, do something other people value a lot and be one of the few people who can do it.

---

[30]However, these activities are not without value, even to the person who fails to make it big, because he has fun playing and because sports teach teamwork, the value of pushing yourself, and other traits that are liable to be valuable. Becoming a better actor, even one destined to remain obscure, also has its nonmonetary rewards.

But many people make their fortunes large and small not by winning the race to be the next Hollywood movie star or NFL first-round draft pick, but by discovering valuable knowledge. The next section gives some thought to the process of trying to discover that knowledge.

Speculation

There is a way of thinking that economists probably overuse. When asked why businesses or industries or broad patterns of society are one way and not another, they say that if the other way were better that is what would be done. But this is flawed in that it assumes that the process of competition has always eliminated all better alternatives. Because there is a constant flow of new ideas and discoveries, and of people discovering unexploited opportunities, there is constant adjustment of resource use. And because not all ideas are created equal (competition will eliminate some and reward others), it is always *possible* that any individual's idea about how to rearrange the way resources are used will be a good one relative to the existing substitutes.

We actually have a word for the act of setting out on this journey to an unknown destination, although the word generally has a different, and indeed often negative, connotation in the public's mind. That word is *speculation*. Upon hearing it, many people think of people frantically buying and selling stocks or oil contracts in chaotic trading pits in New York or Chicago, or flipping houses.[31] These things are indeed speculation, although only a few of an infinite variety of *types* of speculation. Many people also view *speculators* as socially useless people or people whose rapid-fire buying and selling—of technology stocks during the late 1990s bubble in those assets, say, or of Florida condominiums during the real-estate bubble of the 2000s—needlessly inflate prices of these things beyond reason, causing social chaos when the bubbles pop. Many people even commit the fallacy of volition and assert that speculators purposely *cause* prices to go up so that they can make money. This charge comes up most frequently with regard to crude oil and gasoline prices, even among highly educated and accomplished people. Here[32] is Joseph Kennedy II, the founder of a nonprofit group that provides energy assistance to the poor and a former Congressman from Massachusetts:

> Because of speculation, today's oil prices of about $100 a barrel have become disconnected from the costs of extraction, which average $11 a barrel worldwide. Pure speculators account for as much as 40 percent of that high price, according to testimony that Rex Tillerson,

---

[31]http://en.wikipedia.org/wiki/Flipping
[32]http://www.nytimes.com/2012/04/11/opinion/ban-pure-speculators-of-oil-futures.html?_r=2&hp

the chief executive of ExxonMobil, gave to Congress last year. That estimate is bolstered by a recent report from the Federal Reserve Bank of St. Louis.

Many economists contend that speculation on oil futures is a good thing, because it increases liquidity and better distributes risk, allowing refiners, producers, wholesalers, and consumers (like airlines) to "hedge" their positions more efficiently, protecting themselves against unseen future shifts in the price of oil.

But it's one thing to have a trading system in which oil industry players place strategic bets on where prices will be months into the future; it's another thing to have a system in which hedge funds and bankers pump billions of purely speculative dollars into commodity exchanges, chasing a limited number of barrels and driving up the price.

There is nothing new under the sun here. Mr. Kennedy is not the first person to criticize "speculation." Vladimir Lenin, reacting to the chaos caused by his own policies after the Communist seizure of power, reacted with his typical terroristic excess, saying, "For as long as we fail to treat speculators the way they deserve—with a bullet in the head—we will not get anywhere at all." Closer to home, Abraham Lincoln also on several occasions expressed near-fanatical criticism of speculators. Of those who bought and sold gold during the Civil War, he asked in a meeting with the governor of Pennsylvania, "What do you think of those fellows in Wall Street, who are gambling in gold at such a time as this?" The governor replied, "They are a set of sharks" (a vicious carnivore, note), whereupon Lincoln replied, "For my part, I wish every one of them had his devilish head shot off."[33] After a major stock bubble popped in 1720, causing severe economic dislocation in Great Britain, the British government banned the issuing of any stocks by business, believing that the speculation in stock shares was useless.

Mr. Kennedy gives speculation some grudging praise, but this is a rare concession. People looking for simple explanations of complex financial trends often point their finger at "speculators" who make nothing real but through their "gambling" cause tremendous damage. So what can we make of this hostility? First, Mr. Kennedy's concessions are correct. The existence of oil-future contracts does allow people to manage risk. If Southwest Airlines is worried that fuel prices may be very high in two months at the holiday travel season, they can buy a contract that allows them to obtain delivery of the fuel during that time at a price locked in today. (This is what futures contracts are—contracts to buy or sell a certain amount of something at a given price on a certain date in the future.) Mr. Kennedy is right to raise that benefit of these contracts.

---

[33]David Herbert Donald, *Lincoln* (New York: Simon and Schuster, 1996): 502.

But in fact, the primary benefit of this market does not lie here but precisely in *the benefits speculation generates for the rest of society, not for the speculator.*

To see why, consider the problem in Figure 4-1, from a slightly different, and amateurishly drawn, perspective.[34]

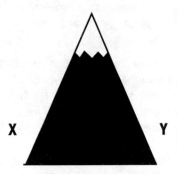

Figure 4-1. X and Y as places

X and Y are two villages separated by a mountain. They both produce their own grain, which they turn into bread. One year, Y has an unusually bad harvest. Someone in X hears information about it. He's not sure it's true, but he thinks it might be. He decides to buy a lot of grain in X for $4.00 a bushel and then at some expense transports it across the mountain to see if he can sell it at a much higher price in Y. It turns out he can. The harvest is so bad there that the price is $6.00 a bushel. The collective effect of all this buying grain in X forces up the price there, causing people in X to consume less. In ways that we have already discussed, the money he makes doing this reflects the value of his knowledge that right now grain is more valuable at the margin in Y—in other words, that on the whole, X and Y will be better off if people in X who have grain are persuaded by payment to give up some of it to be bought by people in Y. And some of the more risk-taking people in X who see him doing this may themselves decide to sell more grain themselves in Y instead of consuming it locally in X, forcing the price in X up further and inducing more restraint in X so that yet more grain is available for consumption in Y, which up to a point is what we want to happen. Naturally, we wouldn't want people in X to go without grain either, which will not happen because movement of grain from X to Y stops as soon as the rising grain price in X and the falling grain price in Y (because of more grain coming in from X) are even, once we include the cost of transporting grain from one place to the other. So, the price system is doing what it is supposed to do.

---

[34] I owe much of this analogy, although I do not implicate him in the artwork, to Don Boudreaux (www.baseball-reference.com/players/p/pujolal01.shtml).

So far we are on familiar ground. But what the enterprising individual in X has done, it should be noted, is to engage in act of speculation—he has guessed, based on some imperfect information that he has, that he can make money by transferring resources from one place to another. In this case, the only difference between the two forms of resource use is geographical—some grain is turned into bread in Y instead of in X.

But suppose we reconceive of what X and Y represent, as shown in Figure 4-2.

Right now **X**   →   The Future **Y**

Figure 4-2. X and Y as times instead of places

X and Y are now not geographic places but periods of time. Someone hears some information that the grain harvest for next year is likely to be much worse than usual. He's not sure it's true, but he thinks it might be. He buys a futures contract that will allow him to buy grain to be stored now and delivered at period Y, but when it is delivered he will pay today's price, allowing him to resell it at Y at the (higher, he hopes) market price prevailing then. But his doing so generates upward pressure in the market for grain to be delivered today. People who live in date X now and make it their business to pay attention to such things—call them speculators—notice this, and the more risk-taking people living in X now who see him doing this may themselves decide to sell more grain themselves in the future instead of consuming it "locally" in period X, forcing the price now (in period X) up further and thus inducing more restraint now so that grain is available for consumption in the future (in period Y), which up to a point is what we want to happen. There is no meaningful difference between transporting goods to different *places* on the basis of a belief that one can make money and transporting goods across *time* in the belief that one can make money.

The beauty of having contracts for delivering goods in the future is that when people expect the price of a good to go up in the future, they either buy it cheaply now (especially if it can be stored cheaply) or they buy futures contracts that allow them to buy the good at a now seemingly relatively low price in the future, which induces people to observe that the price of this good is likely to rise in the future. Either way, we learn ahead of time that a shortage appears to be in the offing, prices go up now, and we begin to economize on use now, leaving more grain available to be consumed in the future. So when people blame oil speculators for increasing the price of gasoline, what they are really blaming is a new belief that oil will be scarcer in the future for making it more expensive now, which speculators, having formed this belief through their research, are informing us of with their "gambling." If speculators could simply drive up prices at will, one would suppose that the price of oil would never go down, but of course it does. In addition, for everyone who buys an oil contract there is someone selling it to him, which indicates that people are disagreeing about the likely future circumstances of the oil market. It is only when sentiment about future prices tilts sufficiently toward the idea that they will rise a lot that those oil futures prices, and then shortly after the prices of oil now, rise significantly.

So all speculation is just making a guess about the future, and quite a bit of it has the salutary effect of bringing future developments to our attention now, alleviating the dislocation from those developments when they actually happen. Again, just as in the case of the financial markets we analyzed earlier, not every market prediction necessarily comes true. People lose money on futures contracts all the time, just as they choose college majors that don't lead to high-paying jobs or they open small businesses that do not succeed. But the collective knowledge that is reflected in the futures price is the best guess we have (remember the wisdom-of-crowds idea), and repressing speculation would take away people's incentive to try to learn about the future in order to make money off it. Venture capitalists speculate when they decide to invest money in company Y and not company X, although venture capitalists who disagree with the rosy assessments others are making about company Y, especially in light of the fact that it now costs more money to buy a share of investment in it, may choose instead to invest in X or seek out some new company Z. People who read that majoring in Y now leads to higher salaries than majoring in X may choose to major in Y in large numbers. The number of X majors shrinks, leading universities to hire more professors of Y and fewer professors of X, and indeed perhaps to open departments of Y for the first time.

Economically, all this activity is the same. Everybody buying, and everybody selling, is trying to pursue his self-interest as best he can while not possessing full information; maybe the future reveals him to be right, maybe it doesn't. Each person has information, but no one has certainty. And, for reasons we have seen throughout this chapter, allowing people to make money is a good way to motivate them to reveal their information by acting on it, and to do some research (that is, to harvest information) before acting. Censoring speculators would, in other words, leave us considerably more ignorant, and economic ignorance is not bliss.

▓ **Note**   In the end, speculators serve society by pointing out imminent shortages (or surpluses) and by helping balance supply and demand so there is enough for all.

Economics Out There

4.1. Read this *New York Times article*.[35] How is Mr. Rahr a speculator? What knowledge has he capitalized on to make money? Why are the drug manufacturers upset about his activity? According to the article, his activity causes "false signals" to be sent to manufacturers about demand for drugs in various places. Would you long expect Mr. Rahr to buy drugs that, because of lack of demand, he couldn't sell? What does your answer have to do with whether or not his actions cause these "false signals"?

4.2. This story[36] tells of how Hostess, the maker of Twinkies among other things, had to stop operations under the management of a "hedge fund." What economic information was generated by the failure of negotiations between the hedge fund and one of Hostess's labor unions?

4.3. Read this *Washington Post article*.[37] What information did Mr. Hettinga discover? Why was it valuable for him to discover it to begin with? One official with a dairy lobbying organization says the "market was damaged" by his activities. Can a "market" be damaged from competition from people like Mr. Hettinga, or just people in a market? If the latter, whose interests did he damage?

4.4. Read this 2006 New York Times article.[38] How should we judge whether Walmart's experiment in drug-selling created gains to consumers that justified the opportunity cost of the resources needed to make the experiment happen?

4.5. Based on what you read here,[39] describe some ways in which the spontaneous order took advantage of the invention of the car.

---

[35]http://www.nytimes.com/2005/01/26/business/26rahr.html?_r=1&
[36]http://www.cnbc.com/id/49853653/How_Hostess_Failed_Hedge_Funds_vs_Unions
[37]http://www.washingtonpost.com/wp-dyn/content/article/2006/12/09/AR2006120900925.html
[38]http://www.nytimes.com/2006/11/30/business/30pharmacy.html?pagewanted=all
[39]http://www.thelocal.de/society/20110128-32735.html#.UMjsx9chT4Q

4.6. These articles, one from *Forbes*[40] and one from the *New York Times*,[41] should be read together. What do the author in the first article and the President of the United States in the second believe they know about where things should be made? On the basis of whose knowledge has the decision to make Kindles and iPads in China actually been made? Whose knowledge do you suppose is better? Are there any benefits to Americans from making these things in China? (Hint: There are, and they are not just to consumers of *these* products. Think in terms of the opportunity cost of making these things here instead of in China.)

4.7. At the National Public Radio web site, there is a story[42] about a farmer making money off land purchases from real estate companies. What wrong information held by the developers was he able to capitalize on? What socially valuable knowledge did he reveal by his purchases, and what would he reveal if he later sold the land back to developers? Do you think it is strange that a farmer seems to be doing better in land buying and selling than a real estate developer?

4.8. Delta Airlines recently did something unusual and bought an oil refinery, according to this story.[43] What speculation Is Delta engaging in? How might other airlines make the decision about whether this is an economically efficient idea or not?

4.9. To what extent, if at all, do the stories here[44] and here[45] demonstrate the indifference principle?

4.10. This story[46] describes the Irish government refusing to pay for an anti-cancer drug, because of "cost-effectiveness" concerns. Is this a centralized or spontaneous-order decision? Is this—having health care services and pharmaceuticals in

---

[40]http://www.forbes.com/sites/stevedenning/2011/08/17/why-amazon-cant-make-a-kindle-in-the-usa/

[41]http://www.nytimes.com/2012/01/22/business/apple-america-and-a-squeezed-middle-class.html?pagewanted=all

[42]http://www.npr.org/2012/01/23/145627754/farmers-take-back-land-slated-for-housing

[43]http://travel.usatoday.com/flights/story/2012-04-30/Delta-buys-oil-refinery-in-a-bid-to-offset-rising-fuel-costs/54648888/1

[44]http://chronicle.com/blogs/wiredcampus/new-study-shows-e-textbooks-saved-many-students-only-1/34793

[45]http://www.marketplace.org/topics/world/energy-independence-us-its-pipe-dream

[46]http://www.irishexaminer.com/breakingnews/business/prostate-cancer-drug-zytiga-rejected-for-use-in-ireland-553060.html

particular paid for by taxpayers, with government officials approving or rejecting them—a good way to make such decisions? This is not a flippant question; the economics (health care is subject to decentralized information, opportunity costs, and other factors like any other activity) and ethics (unequal opportunity to consume health care services strikes many as unjust) of health care are not easy.

4.11. Consider this essay.[47] The author is very concerned about overstressed health-care workers, among other things. Does seeing patients at a faster rate have benefits for anyone? If so, do you think they exceed the costs? Does the author think he knows? What activities does the author think are truly valuable to people? How do you suppose he knows? How confident are you that doing the things he recommends—for example, mandating a 21-hour workweek—would have the effect on human contentment he predicts? What about the contentment of specific individuals, with specific goals and interests?

4.12. After the catastrophe of Hurricane Katrina, Walmart was able to do remarkable things to help victims, including selling them products they would be likely to want despite the difficulties of supplying them in a post-hurricane environment, if this account[48] is to be believed. What kinds of knowledge had Walmart harvested that enabled it to respond so effectively to consumer wants, even in an extreme situation like this? Why had it done so?

4.13. The Morning Star Company is a tomato-processing company based in California. Interestingly, it hires no managers—people whose job it is to supervise others and to whom others report. Instead it has its employees cooperatively work out what each of them should do. The company has been around for decades, is financially successful, and attributes much of its success to its lack of a rigid hierarchy. What are some of the advantages of such a structure for company profits? The disadvantages? Do you think this is a strategy that all companies should adopt?

---

[47]http://www.nytimes.com/2012/05/27/opinion/sunday/lets-be-less-productive.html

[48]http://money.cnn.com/magazines/fortune/fortune_archive/2005/10/03/8356743/

Public and Private Decision Making

Why Sugar Beet Farmers Get Government Subsidies but Apple Farmers Don't

Markets and governments are perhaps, along with religion, the oldest human institutions. According to some research,[1] stone axes may have been traded by humans hundreds of thousands of years ago. Adam Smith in *The Wealth of Nations* described the urge to "truck, barter and exchange" as a "general disposition" of men. As for government, the idea of a caste of humans with the power to forcibly extract resources (as with modern taxation) and use them for the ruler's purposes (sometimes for the broad benefit of the public, sometimes not) and to tell people what they are not allowed to do (or are required to do) has been around at least since humans made the transition from hunter-gatherer to agricultural society, the latter generating for the first time large amounts of produce that had to be stored and allocated.

---

[1]http://www.livescience.com/18751-hand-axe-tools-money.html

But the two institutions, because of the incentives they face, are different. To make this claim, the *people* who participate in each activity need not be different, one kind immoral and the other not, and I will assume throughout, in the usual economist's way, that they are all pursuing self-interest. But the self-interest of those in government often leads them to make different choices than occur when self-interested people interact in the market, and that is the focus of this chapter. Here we focus on situations in which government decision making is likely to lead to worse outcomes than when people trade what they own freely. The very real set of circumstances in which incentives mean that relying on markets to allocate resources with competing uses may be the inferior choice is deferred until Chapter 10.

▓ **Tip** Government is run by people, and the people in government have incentives, just like the people they govern do. When thinking about whether we are likely to get the results from government we want, it helps to think about the incentives of those in government, and not to automatically assume that this incentive, unique to those in government, is "to do what is best for the public."

Who Is the Government, and What Does It Want?

Actually, this question is not a sensible one. *Government* is not an organism with a brain and consciousness. It is rather a human institution, made up of individual human beings who are responding to the incentives they face. Individuals who work for the government want the same things as everybody else—money, prestige, authority over others, successful children, and an end to human suffering. They are no better, or no worse, than people who work for or own private businesses. But as we have seen, government is a distinctive social institution. It has power. What does power mean? To consider this I invoke Paul Heyne's idea of *coercion*. According to his view, to coerce someone *is to induce cooperation by threatening to reduce someone's options*,[2] or alternatively, to persuade someone to do something you want by offering a set of choices, all of which make him worse off.

Note that this is generally not what happens in a market setting—companies make offers to consumers or workers, and if they turn the offer down they are simply where they started, rather than worse off. But a robber who points a gun in one's face and says, "Your money or your life" *is* engaged in an act of coercion. So too is a boss who demands of a subordinate that she

---

[2]Paul Heyne, *The Economic Way of Thinking*, Ninth Edition (Upper Saddle River, NJ: Prentice Hall, 2000): 352.

sleep with him or lose her job. Power then is *the ability to coerce others*. As these examples suggest, it is not only government officials who possess power over others. But it is only government that is intrinsically *about* power. If the government wants you to do something, you either do it (and because you didn't voluntarily choose to do it, you are worse off) or you pay a fine or go to jail. Government is intrinsically coercive, and so its power should be rationed carefully.

Anytime the government exercises its lawmaking authority to take resources from some people and give them to others, or to prevent people from using resources they own in a way they would have chosen, it is leaving them worse off than they otherwise would be. This is not enough to argue that the coercion should not happen, but it should give us pause. Keep this in mind as we investigate the ways markets and governments decide the question of how to use scarce resources.

Problem 1: Government as Subject to Special-Interest Capture

The first problem descends from the analysis in Chapter 4 about competition and its value. Recall that competition is a way to enable people both to try out their knowledge (with the market rewarding socially valuable knowledge and punishing informational mistakes) and to drain away unusually high rates of return accruing to people who are the first ones to think of a new way to do something—in other words, to make the indifference principle play out. One circumstance that prevents competition from draining away these profits to the broader benefit of society is when a resource—whether it is Albert Pujols's talent for hitting a baseball a long way, Elvis Presley's voice and carefully crafted public image, or John D. Rockefeller's drive and knack for spotting things that ought to be done but haven't been—has so few substitutes that the owner of it can earn very high rates of return for an extended period of time.

The good news is that although individuals can (and should) earn immense amounts of money based on the value of their ideas over an extended period of time, history suggests that high profits for a company that is founded by one of those individuals can only persist for so long. We saw that Apple Computer itself was in a lot of trouble in the late 1980s and early 1990s, and is tremendously vulnerable to competition, as the once-mighty Nokia company was when the cell phones it made were swept aside by the smartphone revolution. Nokia may yet recover, and Apple may still prove to be a great innovator; all of this is left to the judgment of consumers. No company is invulnerable to competition—not the investment bank Bear Stearns (founded in 1923, died in the financial crash of 2008), not Bethlehem Steel (the twelfth largest company in the United States by revenue in 1955, vanished in 2003), not Chrysler (declared bankrupt in 1980, rebounded under bankruptcy organization, but bought and sold before declaring bankruptcy and being sold again in 2009), not Microsoft, not Google. Companies stay in business only with permission of their customers and of the owners of the resources they seek to use to make what they sell. Competition is an extremely vigorous force over the long term. In the long term, essentially, the demand for everything is elastic.

So every seller must constantly be on the lookout for entry from new competitors. But what if a seller could use the law to prevent such entry? Achieving that would be good for the seller but bad for the rest of society, and hence is a thing to be opposed, but it is distressingly common, often ironically in the name of protecting consumers.

For example, numerous states require those who cut hair and do makeovers to have cosmetology licenses. But in recent years, those who merely braid hair—a business that has grown both due to greater public demand and the arrival of many immigrants from Africa who want to enter the business—have also sometimes been required to go through the training that is required before the license is granted, which can amount to over 1,000 hours of course time, often in fields that have nothing to do with braiding. In Washington state, one must go through 1,700 hours of instruction[3] to get a license to be a barber or beautician, whereas one needs only 130 hours to become an emergency medical technician, which is a job where people's lives are actually at stake. The requirement, it should be noted, is not that one pass a test certifying the knowledge, but that one actually take the courses (for a fee of course), to the benefit of the schools offering the training.

State bar associations similarly require that to become a lawyer one cannot just pass the bar exam, but that one spend three years in an officially credentialed law school first, again at considerable expense in money and time. One story by National Public Radio has reported[4] that whereas several decades ago fewer than one in twenty occupations required a license, now about a third do.

Who benefits from these license requirements? In principle the requirements need not exist but could be replaced by customers deciding for themselves whether a seller of services—who might possess a non-mandatory certification offered by private agencies as a means to inform consumers that the certification's requirements have been met, a purely voluntary kind of certification that the spontaneous order could create—should be patronized or not. Consumers benefit, nominally, because they have assurance that the seller of services is safe or qualified. But obtaining certification is costly, and those costs will eventually have to be passed on, or else the number of sellers

---

[3]http://daily.sightline.org/2011/10/14/licensed-to-work/
[4]http://www.npr.org/blogs/money/2012/06/21/154826233/why-its-illegal-to-braid-hair-without-a-license

will have to decrease; either way, prices increase, partially canceling out or even outweighing greater confidence in the quality of the seller. Mandatory certification, of course, raises all sellers' costs. And mandatory or voluntary certification is not the only signal of quality; a long record of doing business with customers who come away from the experience very satisfied performs the same function, as do groups such as the Better Business Bureau (which monitors member businesses for complaints of fraud) and Consumers Union (publishers of *Consumer Reports*, which rates a wide variety of goods and services for safety, reliability, and cost).

But mandatory certification has one effect that is unambiguously bad: it makes it harder to enter a business and compete with people who already possess the certification. We would have more people willing to practice law, braid hair, and do contracting work if these things and others (such as auctioneering) did not require expensive credentialing. In states where braiders must get cosmetology licenses after training, the entire content of which is something extraneous to what they do, these requirements increase entry costs while doing little, arguably nothing, for consumers. And higher entry costs generate higher profits for existing sellers.

According to an account from *The New York Times* in 1997, at that time, when New York State's mandatory cosmetology curriculum requirement for braiders had been in place for a number of years, no one had successfully completed the curriculum, so that only those existing braiders who were demanding the license requirement and because of their political influence were exempted from having to take the courses could obtain a license. Those who are least able to afford the time and money required by the curriculum are those who would also be likely to charge the lowest prices and therefore would benefit consumers the most; but many of these competitors, alas, are immigrants with little political influence or knowledge of the American bureaucracy. Some people choose to enter the business anyway, without a license, but this makes them vulnerable to customers who refuse to pay, knowing that they can report the seller for operating without a license.[5] If the reader doubts that this credentialing—the requirement that licenses be acquired, often after the acquisition of expensive instruction—is usually about protecting existing competitors from competition from new entrants rather than about benefiting consumers, note that Louisiana requires florists to have a license, and Nevada requires one of interior designers.

---

[5]For more on how the people demanding the curriculum for braiding managed to get themselves exempted from it, see Lena Williams, "The Battle of the Braid Brigade," *The New York Times* (January 26, 1997). For information on the way the licensing requirement makes unlicensed braiders vulnerable to theft (that is, unable to benefit from the rule of law), see Monte Williams, "Bargain Braiders Battle for Heads: Hair Stylists From Africa Arrive, Driving Down Prices," *The New York Times* (May 19, 2001).

Note also that British Columbia ended the requirement that beauty workers, and people doing several other kinds of work besides, acquire a license, and there is no evidence the sky has fallen there. For many years, people in the United States got their hair done license-free without any outbreak of social chaos, as indeed they do in most countries around the world. Competition and reputation instead serve as their guides. (People who sell services that are performed unsafely are always very vulnerable to competition from those who sell them safely.) And note finally that civilization somehow managed to survive for many centuries without requiring workers to get permission from the government for entering a trade, with the uncredentialed lawyer Abraham Lincoln, who attended no law school and acquired no law license, being an instructive example.

Credentialing is an example of a much broader problem called an artificial *entry barrier*—a law or rule or specifically and arbitrarily applied government expenditure or tax that helps some sellers protect themselves from competition that would otherwise occur. Licenses are a common example, as are restrictions on imports (which protect domestic producers at the expense of consumers), and so are laws requiring that governments contract only with companies that have union contracts (preventing competition from companies and workers that wish to work outside a union framework). Other notorious examples include Jim Crow laws in the former Confederate states, and even more so the Black Codes that preceded them. The latter referred to regulations passed by white governments in the newly defeated Confederacy to limit the ability of freed slaves to compete with white workers. Here is an excerpt from the Mississippi Black Code, which was typical:

> Section 5. Every freedman, free negro and mulatto shall, on the second Monday of January, 1866, and annually thereafter, have a lawful home or employment, and shall have written evidence thereof as follows, to wit: if living in any incorporated city, town, or village, a license from that mayor thereof; and if living outside of an incorporated city, town, or village, from the member of the board of police of his beat, authorizing him or her to do irregular and job work; or a written contract, as provided in Section 6 in this act; which license may be revoked for cause at any time by the authority granting the same.

> Section 6. All contracts for labor made with freedmen, free negroes and mulattoes for a longer period than one month shall be in writing, and a duplicate, attested and read to said freedman, free negro or mulatto by a beat, city or county officer, or two disinterested white persons of the county in which the labor is to be performed, of which each party shall have one: and said contracts shall be taken and held as entire contracts, and if the laborer shall quit the service of the employer before the expiration of his term of service, without good cause, he shall forfeit his wages for that year up to the time of quitting.

Note that the law applied only to non-whites ("freedmen, free Negroes and mulattoes") and gave government officials (white, naturally) near-absolute authority to decide whether blacks could do work their customers wanted them to do. Needless to say, in the environment of post-Civil War Mississippi, it would be difficult for a newly freed slave to round up "two disinterested white persons of the county in which the labor is performed" to authorize his labor contract (which in this time would have been mostly for work or mechanical labor using skills that slaves had acquired either during or after their enslavement). Note finally the onerous conditions of contracting imposed on non-whites, who would have to return already-paid wages if they quit a job before their contract had expired. The arrival of Reconstruction forces meant the overturning of these Black Codes, but once the U.S. military left after the 1876 election, the codes substantially came back as the now notorious Jim Crow laws, which imposed mandated racial segregation on a wide variety of business activities. Like the Black Codes before them, Jim Crow laws, by preventing entry by non-white workers into many commercial activities, benefited existing white workers and damaged not just black workers but consumers too.

These entry barriers are common and also damaging, both to entrepreneurs who want to pursue a living and to consumers who must pay higher prices. A woman named Robin Smith, who had practiced as an independent paralegal for many years, once started a business doing routine legal work that did not require a lot of high-powered courtroom expertise (filing wills, for example) for much lower prices than lawyers were charging. She was successfully sued by the Oregon State Bar, a group that regulates and lobbies for lawyers in that state. The association also controls entry into the trade via the requirement that people who want to be lawyers pass American Bar Association-administered exams and go to ABA-credentialed law schools. The alleged offense was practicing law without a license, and the ABA's successful lawsuit resulted in her business being closed down. The Florida Bar did something similar to Rosemary Furman, a legal secretary who sold relatively uncomplicated legal forms and services to people of modest means, with the result that she was initially sentenced to actual jail time, although never served any.[6]

In the last 150 years, one of the most effective entry barriers in countries throughout the world has been the labor union. At its core, a labor union is simply an agreement by workers to negotiate their working conditions—salaries, promotion procedures (seniority versus productivity), procedures for arbitrating disputes between workers and management—collectively, instead of each worker negotiating for himself the deal that is best for him. The belief by

---

[6]If you are interested in looking up the relevant cases, their legal citations are *Oregon State Bar v. Smith*, 149 Or App 171; *Furman, DBA Northside Secretarial Service v. The Florida Bar*, 451 So. 2d 808.

supporters of unions, and it is not unreasonable, is that when workers cooperate by saying all of us will work at this salary or none of us will work at all, employers will pay more than when workers have to compete individually for jobs. When *companies* that sell *products* do this, they violate the law by committing an act called *price-fixing*, but unions—organizations of people that sell *labor*—are exempt from the laws governing price-fixing behavior in the United States and in many countries.

As we proceed through this section, it is good to recall the earlier argument that in terms of the entire society, a job is merely a means to an end, not the end itself. The aim of any business activity is to produce things that customers want to buy because these things create more value for customers than it costs to bring it to them. Increasing production costs by mere legal manipulation thus destroys value. Higher production costs make consumers worse off. It is true that lower wages make workers worse off, but it is precisely the function of the market to sort out these contending claims. If workers see that their interests are best served by negotiating collectively, then the principle of reliance on self-interest for the betterment of society suggests that they be allowed to do so.

However, the problem arises when the law requires that any time a sufficiently large percentage of the workforce—at present in much of the U.S., a bare majority is all that is required—approves representation by the union, they may impose the *legal obligation* on the employer to negotiate with it, whether the employer wants to or not, and impose on others who want to work for that employer the legal requirements to work under the union contract or not work for the employer at all. This prevents workers from competing on any grounds—more flexible scheduling, higher productivity requirements, less compensation initially or later, agreeing that the employer has the option of ignoring seniority in deciding which workers deserve promotion—not permitted by the union contract.

■ **Question 5.1** Why do you suppose labor unions so often demand in their negotiations that promotion and compensation be based on seniority rather than on merit or productivity?

But the world of course is full of workers—workers who are younger, who are ambitious to prove their worth for this or for a future employer, who can't work a standard 9–5 shift but who would be very productive if allowed to work weekends, the list is practically endless—who would love to compete on different terms. The union contract prevents that. And if the law requires the imposition of the union contract even though there are workers would like to work outside it, this is an entry barrier in the market for labor, just as surely as requiring 1,700 hours of cosmetology classes is an entry barrier in the market for hair braiding.

It is really no surprise that laborers who expect to benefit from limits on competition enthusiastically seek to be the exclusive negotiator for compensation and working conditions through the union-contract framework, and then to use this framework to deter other workers from filling the positions vacated by strikers. Such laborers cannot succeed in limiting employment terms to a collectively bargained contract unless all workers in a facility work through the union contract rather than work out their own terms., People trying to organize collective bargaining at a particular workplace, unsurprisingly, often want that support to be expressed through openly signing (or, critically, openly refusing to sign) a petition rather than secret ballots. Without a secret ballot, an individual's refusal to support collective bargaining is known by all.

During organizing or during a strike, such people will also have an incentive to use whatever tactics are legal, and sometimes some that are illegal, such as violence against the strikebreakers, to prevent competition from limiting their control of bargaining. And, as in the case of the Mississippi Black Codes, if their membership is of one ethnic group, they may seek to use ethnic-based rules to limit competition from members of different ethnic groups. This is undoubtedly why white labor groups were supporters of the 1879 Constitution of the State of California, which prevented the state government and any company chartered in the state from hiring Chinese workers.[7]

When a government agency starts out with a stated purpose of imposing rules to benefit a certain group in society—consumers, for example—but ends up enacting rules that benefit another group—like existing producers—we have a phenomenon known as *regulatory capture*. Often those who purport to speak for consumers demand that governments regulate prices that these advocates view as too high. Legal ranges for prices may be imposed, despite the deleterious effects of such controls noted in Chapter 3. Yet despite technological progress in the industry whose prices are being regulated, prices frequently do not come down. Instead, the companies being regulated work with the regulatory authorities to make sure these ranges, once seen as maximum prices, become minimum prices—below which no new entrant can compete legally.

For example, in 1938, at the tail end of Franklin Roosevelt's New Deal, the airline industry was in its infancy. Consistent with the tenor of the times, which owing to the Great Depression were marked by profound skepticism

---

[7]The California Workingmen's Party, founded in 1877 to stand up for a certain conception of worker's rights, had as one of its leaders a man named Dennis Kearney, an immigrant himself from Ireland, who had a habit of winding up speeches by saying, "The Chinese must go!" To him, the presence of the "Chinese coolie" in the United States served only to "degrade white labor." That Chinese workers and employers who hired them were both better off by having the right to contract and thus better serve their customers was of no concern to these white unions, as it is of no concern to anyone seeking to impose an entry barrier.

of business, legislation was passed in 1940 that resulted in the creation of the Civil Aeronautics Board. The Board was charged with (among other things) regulating airline fares and the routes the airlines were allowed to fly, with the goal of preventing exploitation of consumers through high fares. Here is how one author describes the change in the way airlines competed:

> In the 1930s nurse-stewardesses were a popular frill that not all young airlines could afford. By the late 1940s carefully chosen hostesses became more central to the maturing airline industry's marketing and service objectives because other avenues of competition had narrowed. After the federal government undertook economic regulation of the industry in 1938, airlines staked their reputation more closely on the quality of in-flight services and the charms of the stewardesses who delivered them. Deregulated airlines scrambled to win travelers' business with luxurious innovations in air transport and even more emphasis on fulfilling the promise of an attractive, attentive hostess.[8]

An entire television show (ABC's *Pan Am*) was once created on the mythology of the purported glamour of this era in flying, which stemmed from the fact that airlines were prevented from competing on the basis of lower prices. Most passengers would prefer more luxury (small white tablecloths for the tray tables, high-quality food) to less. (Those who want such things are still free to buy first-class tickets.) Some, perhaps many, male passengers would prefer very attractive flight attendants. But such things are subject to trade-offs, and what the results of freer competition have taught us is that many passengers do not care about them much and attach much more importance to getting where they're going quickly and cheaply. They are glad to give up these luxuries of a bygone era in exchange for lower fares, which were a major result of the airline deregulation of 1978, which ended government control over airfares.

Suddenly, how many flights there should be, from where to where, what should be charged for them, and the amenities that should be offered in-flight (flight attendants expected to flaunt their sex appeal, fine cuisine elegantly served) were no longer dictated directly or, through price floors, indirectly by bureaucrats, but instead came about through the spontaneous order, through the market negotiation process between buyers and sellers of airline flights. After competition played out without artificial government restraint, we learned something we did not know before—that frills are not important enough to justify the fares that supported them or the limitation on flexibility

---

[8]Kathleen Morgan Barry, *Femininity in Flight: A History of Flight Attendants* (Durham, NC: Duke University press, 2007): 39.

in introducing new routes. New airlines, a concept almost unknown during the years of airline regulation, began to rise and fall all the time after 1978. Society was clearly better off, but two groups that had fought hardest to keep the entry barriers of price regulation and a lengthy governmental approval process for new airlines struggled—the existing airlines and their unionized workers. Under regulation, they had been able to pass on higher wages to consumers in the form of higher prices. Many of the "great" airlines of the regulated era—Eastern Airlines, Pan Am, TWA—failed to survive the transition to deregulation. But air travel expanded far beyond the core market of wealthy leisure travelers and businessmen going far from home. It began to accommodate backpackers who wanted to see the world, full-time workers who wanted a quick weekend getaway, people who just wanted to fly home to spend time with old friends or see their children on the other side of the country,[9] and others whose willingness to pay to go from certain places to certain other places under certain conditions could never have been known to the Civil Aeronautics Board.

Yet it took 40 years to get rid of airline price and route regulation. What took so long? As noted, although airline regulation was bad for society as a whole, it was good for several groups in particular—the people who owned stock in the regulated airlines (which could charge higher prices and face less competition) and the people who worked for them.

The process by which political decisions get produced is not the simple democratic model taught in high school, that of "take a vote, and the majority rules." Instead, one has to invest resources to learn the knowledge about how regulatory agencies and legislatures make their rules. Indeed, bright law-school graduates and former congressmen with a lot of experience often specialize in helping people who want to get benefits from the government navigate congressional and bureaucratic procedures. We call these people *lobbyists*. Businesses will invest in the production of entry barriers by lobbying when they expect at the margin to make higher profits spending the money that way then they would by spending money competing in the market—especially competing against new entrants in possession of superior knowledge that would cause existing firms to lose business.

Ordinary people are busy, and paying attention to the lawmaking process for them is often difficult to justify. This is even truer when the costs of an entry barrier or other kinds of government regulation of the market are borne in small amounts by large numbers of people. For example, sugar-beet farmers in the United States benefit from the entry barrier of high *tariffs* (the formal

---

[9]The ability to move far away from home to pursue a career was also enabled by cheaper air travel, of course.

term for taxes on imported goods) and from dramatic numerical limitations imposed on imported sugar. There is no free lunch, so the cost of limiting entry into the sugar market in the U.S. is borne first by those who make goods that use sugar or who don't use it and instead substitute a higher-cost substitute such as high-fructose corn syrup. This in turn is passed on ultimately to workers and shareholders of these companies and to consumers who buy their products. But because the amount per candy bar or soda purchased is so small, it makes little sense for each consumer to spend a lot of time figuring out whether changes in the law could make those products cheaper.

But sugar-beet farmers who grow sugar in the United States each have a gigantic amount at stake if the tariffs and quotas are eliminated—very possibly hundreds of thousands of dollars per farmer. For the several thousand sugar-beet farmers in the U.S., it is indeed rational to pay very close attention. These farmers thus make campaign donations, scrutinize the laws governing the sugar trade, regularly communicate with their representatives in Washington, spend lots of money on lobbyists, and do the other things necessary to get things done in the manufacturing of laws. The lesson? Entry barriers involving arcane topics are likely to benefit small, well-organized groups who have a lot at stake, and their burdens are likely to be born in largely invisible ways by large groups. What Americans pay extra, because of limits on imports of sugar, for example, comes to about $150 per American per year.[10] Whether that is a small amount over the course of a year I leave to the reader's judgment, but if we add up all entry barriers in markets for all goods, the cost must be substantial.

Another informative example of regulatory capture is compensation for government employees. In many states, government-employee unions were long ago recognized as the sole legitimate bargaining agent through which workers could face off against taxpayers and their representatives. For public employees, the issues of their compensation and fringe benefits are critically important. For taxpayers, who have many other things, both in their private lives and with regard to politics, that they must pay attention to, time is extremely scarce. Naturally, there is a tendency for politicians to reward those who scream the loudest. A phrase of unknown provenance says that 90% of life is just showing up, and when lots of money and protection from competition are at stake, public employees, like many other relatively small groups before them, had the incentive to show up when the taxpayers did not. The result tends to give public employees compensation—especially taken as retirement benefits and job security—that is greater than that for private-sector workers who do similar work.

---

[10]http://drbseconomicblog.blogspot.com/2011/02/corn-and-sugar-subsidies.html

The Congressional Budget Office estimates,[11] for example, that the federal workforce earns 16% more in total wages and compensation than a private-sector work force with the same levels of education and experience would.[12] City bus drivers generally enjoy better wages and benefits than private-sector bus drivers do, and those who deliver mail for the U.S. Postal Service similarly are favorably situated relative to those who work for FedEx or UPS. In addition, the unions representing these employees can and do use their salaries, which come from taxpayers, to lobby against the privatization of the services they offer. Like any other pressure group, they lobby, make campaign donations, and buy televised political ads. If we assume a politician's primary interest is in electoral success, then he will have an incentive to inflate public-employee compensation and benefits now, secure in the knowledge that the bill will come due when someone else is in office.

Indeed, the short-term-nature of political decision making is rooted in the fact that future generations are not represented in any legislature, so there is a natural tilt toward spending now and paying later. This presumably is why so many U.S. states have run into budgetary crises[13] in part because of what has been promised in the past to public employees, relative to what is available now. The same problem is afflicting public pensions and health care systems in some European countries such as Spain and Greece, and may soon beset Social Security and Medicare in the United States. Promising benefits is in the short-term interest of politicians; paying the bill is not.

Overall, in the U.S. the value of the limitations on competition and special privileges[14] that Washington hands out can be gleaned from a *Forbes* magazine list[15] of the wealthiest counties in the U.S. Of the top ten, five are in Virginia or Maryland, adjacent to Washington, D.C. Some of this is due to federal employees who live there, but much of it is due to the presence of huge numbers of people engaged in regulatory and legislative warfare—the attempt to make sure Congress takes from those guys over there, who are perhaps not paying much attention, and gives to me. Whether people lobby to increase the amount taken from others and given to them or decrease the

---

[11] http://cbo.gov/publication/42921

[12] However, this gap is especially pronounced for workers whose highest degree is a bachelor's or a high-school diploma. The former earned 36% more in wages and benefits, the latter 15%. Those with professional degrees or doctorates received 18% less.

[13] http://www.pewstates.org/research/reports/the-trillion-dollar-gap-85899371867

[14] *Privilege* is a word with Latin roots, a marriage of *privus* ("private") and *legem* ("law"). That is exactly what favors handed out from Washington, D.C. (import barriers, extra highway projects funded nationally, farm subsidies, whatever) are: discriminatory assistance to specific groups in society at the expense of everyone else.

[15] http://www.forbes.com/2011/04/11/americas-richest-counties-business-washington.html

amount taken from them and given to others, they need high-priced legal talent and researchers writing advocacy reports to make it happen. That these lobbyists earn so much money is a reflection of what legislative privileges are worth. Indeed, the D.C. area fared better than almost any metropolitan region in the country after the financial crash in 2008 and subsequent depression, with home prices and income continuing to increase.[16] Note also that one county on the *Forbes* list, Los Alamos County in New Mexico, is nowhere near Washington but is dominated by a federal military-research laboratory, which means that it attracts many people who do business with the military, at high rates of pay.

▨ **Note**   Competing is hard. It is often attractive to people to get the government to limit their competition rather than doing the hard work of competing. The easier it is to do the former, the less competition we will have.

Problem 2: The Incentive to Accumulate Knowledge in the Private Sector and in the Government

In Chapter 4 I discuss the problem of decentralized knowledge. Here I discuss in more detail the incentives of the government to accumulate knowledge, and the consequences of this incentive system.

Knowledge is costly, and people invest in its acquisition as long as the marginal benefit to doing so is expected to exceed the marginal cost. But what is the marginal benefit of information acquisition for a politician or bureaucrat? In some cases, it's nothing more than the increase in his ability to acquire power or win elections. (In other cases, to be sure, it's the imposition of some set of laws that the politician or bureaucrat believes will improve society.) But given that the knowledge is down below, and the politician or bureaucrat is looking down from on high, he will never have the incentive to acquire all the knowledge he needs to make the decision in the most efficient way possible. This is why, recall, zoning and other land-use controls (for example, the declaration of some land as *wetlands*, which makes it illegal to use the land for any other purpose than the current one, which invariably means leaving it idle), create so many unexpected, negative consequences. The incentive to acquire

---

[16]Andrew Ferguson, "Bubble on the Potomac," *Time* (May 20, 2012). Available online at www.time.com/msgszine/article/0.9171,2115062,00.html.

knowledge is never as focused for a government decision maker—unless the knowledge is about how to be reelected or how to acquire the legal authority to accomplish some desired task—as it is for a private trader in the market. This is not a statement about who is good and who is evil, only about incentives. Market participants have a lot of their own resources at stake and tend to be much closer to the local knowledge that is needed to make a better decision. Politicians, in contrast, are distant and have different goals. It is no surprise that the rules they impose on who may be paid what, how land may and may not be used, which financial trades are and are not legal, and so forth generate so many surprising outcomes.

And thus we have Harold L. Ickes, longtime Secretary of the Interior and wartime "petroleum coordinator" for President Franklin D Roosevelt, pronouncing with complete confidence that the gasoline rationing imposed shortly before the U.S. entry into World War II could not possibly generate bootlegging (creation of a black market in gasoline): "Oil stations have to get their supplies from somewhere—you can't make gasoline in your bathtub, you know." In fact, wartime rationing generated black markets in a wide variety of goods, including gasoline. This frustrated the original goal of conserving fuel for the military and generated policing costs to try to get the various black markets under control. Why did Ickes make such an obvious mistake—obvious at least to someone with an appreciation for the depth of decentralized knowledge and for the ability of entrepreneurs to harvest it? I would guess that he was informed by his own recent experience of Prohibition, when people really did make bootleg alcohol in their bathtubs. But no other model of a black market for gasoline occurred to him, because he had no powerful incentive to go out and look for it.

In fact, gasoline bootleggers were cleverer than he imagined possible. Ickes thought about the problem in this way despite the experience of the 1930s, when equally extensive price controls were imposed under the authority of the National Recovery Agency. That agency was established in 1933 to try to end the Great Depression by micromanaging the price system—in particular by raising prices that in the judgment of the authorities were too low and lowering those that were thought to be too high. The result:

> The NRA was discovering it could not enforce its rules. Black markets grew up. Only the most violent police methods could procure enforcement. In Sidney Hillman's garment industry the code authority employed enforcement police. They roamed through the garment district like storm troopers. They could enter a man's factory, send him out, line up his employees, subject them to minute interrogation, take over his books on the instant. Night work was forbidden. Flying squadrons of these private coat-and-suit police went through the district at night, battering down doors with axes looking for men who were committing the crime of sewing together

a pair of pants at night. But without these harsh methods many code authorities said there could be no compliance because the public was not back of it.[17]

So, rules on which kinds of trades are not allowed beget unexpected consequences, and these consequences beget anger at those in the economy who are only pursuing their interest, often by working around the rules because it is better for both buyer and seller. That in turn begets more rules and more enforcement against these ne'er-do-wells. All of this ignores that costly information is a problem, and that giving people a reason to harvest it is the solution.

All the people who have been able to get a flight since 1978, who would not have been able to under the old airline price-control system, have deregulation of the airline industry to thank for it. It never occurred to any of the regulators that there was a social need for routes that were not authorized by law, and at fares that were lower but still economically feasible—provided only that people trying to make money were allowed the freedom to try to discover low-cost ways to run these flights. The airline industry itself, despite being subject to endemic bankruptcy and not being a particularly high-profit industry, estimates that the real price of air travel has fallen over 40 percent since deregulation, helping to turn air travel from a luxury into an ordinary, widely accessible form of transportation. This didn't happen immediately. It happened through trying out different types of competitive experiments until the airlines settled on funneling flights from many more cities through hubs like Chicago and Atlanta and, as noted earlier, trading off in-flight amenities for lower fares.

In contrast, consider this woeful tale[18] of an airport built in Castellon, Spain. The airport was extraordinarily expensive but ended up with a runway that was too narrow to handle most of the air traffic it was built to accommodate. It turns out also that the area where it was built was already served by several major airports, indicating that the marginal benefit of building a another one might be rather small. Imagine that building this airport were being pondered by a private developer. Is it likely that such fundamental mistakes as building an unnecessary airport or making the runway too narrow would have happened? It is not necessary to believe that the people who built the airport were acting with bad intentions—that they *wanted* to fleece the public. (Although some

---

[17]John Thomas Flynn, *The Roosevelt Myth* (Auburn, AL: The Ludwig von Mises Institute, 1956): 45.
[18]http://www.telegraph.co.uk/news/worldnews/europe/spain/9084202/
Castellon-airport-Spanish-ghost-airports-unused-runway-to-be-dug-up-
to-meet-regulations.html

of that was probably going on too, according to media reports[19] about this airport.) This example suggests that governments make a lot of bad decisions because, even if they are acting out of the highest motivations, compared to people with their own money at stake, there is very little incentive for decision makers to learn what needs to be learned to do the job well. Much sustained inefficiency that we observe around us, public or private, can be attributed to the lack of a compelling incentive to learn how to do things better.

Tip When there are great benefits to getting something right and great costs to getting them wrong, decisions are likely to be better. In the political system, sometimes those benefits and costs are not the same as they are in a non-political environment.

Problem 3: The Democracy Problem

Earlier I noted that small, focused groups often have an advantage in using the government to extract wealth at the expense of large, unfocused groups with little at stake per person. But when benefits are obvious, large numbers can be an advantage. American sugar farmers have an advantage over American consumers of sweets in lobbying the government because the latter seldom have the time to find out the details of the various government programs that take from them and give the farmers. (That these transfers of wealth are dispersed through many complicated laws and programs—subsidy of farmers, limitation on competition from imports, and so on—to begin with, rather than only one, is part of the informational problem for the consumer.) But sometimes having the public on your side allows you to use government to take from your neighbor.

In Chapter 3, during discussion of price controls, rent control is briefly mentioned. Legal ceilings on apartment rents are something that has a clear and obvious effect on large numbers of people, mostly tenants. Some tenants may know that allowing them to pay less rent than a landlord would charge in a free market constrains the landlord's possibilities, but may not care because they assume that as a landlord he has a lot of money to spare anyway. Others may well not know about the informational and incentive functions of prices, including apartment rents, which are set by the market. In any event, there are likely to be far more tenants than apartment-building owners in New York City. The City Council in New York reflects the will of constituents, and so it becomes nearly impossible in a democratic setting for rent controls, once done, to be undone. Tenants simply outvote landlords on an issue that is

---

[19]http://www.psmag.com/business-economics/spains-vacant-airport-typifies-european-woes-37884/

easy for tenants to understand and which clearly has major effects on their self-interest.[20] In most advanced countries, a majority of public expenditure is simply the redistribution of wealth from some to others, usually based on a system of taxation and distribution of benefits that results in taking more from those with a lot of money to give to those with less.

As evidence for this assertion, Table 5-1 presents data on the percentage of income and social security and government medical-care taxes paid by the richest 30 percent of the population in a variety of wealthy democracies, as well as payments received through retirement, medical, and other universal programs.

Table 5-1. Taxes Paid and Transfers Received by Richest 30%, in 2000

Country	Percentage of Total Taxes Paid	Percentage of Government Transfers Received
U.S.	65.3	23.0
Australia	65.1	6.5
Belgium	63.5	22.5
Canada	60.4	20.8
Denmark	65.3	23.0
Finland	56.8	18.3
France	67.9	25.1
Germany	53.6	30.7
Ireland	66.4	14.8
Italy	62.3	34.5
Netherlands	52.2	18.1
Norway	53.8	18.3
Sweden	53.3	25.8
United Kingdom	61.0	11.7

Source: Vito Tanzi, Government Versus Markets: The Changing Role of the State (Cambridge, UK: Cambridge University Press, 2011), Table 13.4.

---

[20]Potential future tenants, people who might move to New York City if only they could be confident of finding a place to live, do not get to vote for members of the New York City Council, of course.

In each case, the richest 30 percent pay substantially more than 30 percent of the taxes and receive less, often substantially less, than 30 percent of transfer spending. (Note also that, contrary to conventional wisdom, the United States is actually a country where the wealthy bear a relatively high proportion of the tax burden.) This may seem perfectly natural to many readers: *of course* the wealthy should pay more and get less; that is the nature of funding government. But a reaction of *of course* reveals how we have internalized the idea that redistribution from those with more to those with less is natural, and I would suggest that this policy and belief are normal outcomes in democratic societies.

Is this policy a bad outcome? Not necessarily; one could make all kinds of ethical arguments in favor of this purpose for government funding and expenditure. However, if such policies also have negative economic consequences (as they clearly do in the case of price controls, whether for New York City apartments or toilet paper and milk, currently hard to get in Venezuela, which is packed with price controls on such daily goods), then such consequences must be counted in the ledger of the effects of relying on government to preside over the decision of how scarce resources get used.

Problem 4: The Abuse-of-Power Problem

When government passes rules to change the way scarce resources are used, it is doing so because the result that has occurred when individuals have freely chosen to trade or not to trade is seen as undesirable. It thus must exercise power or coercion in the sense defined earlier. Unfortunately, because of Problem 2, the informational problem, government intervention frequently makes things worse. This naturally causes many politicians and bureaucratic rule makers to believe, as indicated earlier, not that their making the rules about how resources should be used is itself unwise because of what they don't know, but that they now *do* know these things and can make more rules to fix the problem caused by their first set of rules. And this argument assumes that the exercise of power is always employed with the goal of making society better in some way, as opposed to the goal of staying in power or rewarding political supporters and punishing political enemies. But for as long as men have had power over others, they have also had the potential to use that power to reward their friends and punish their enemies. And thus we have the final problem of excessive government control of the economy: the use of that power to abuse some economic actors.

In October 1929, the U.S. stock market fell dramatically, triggering several years of severe economic depression. In 1933, the new president, Franklin Roosevelt, and a new Congress had a mandate from the public to take dramatic measures to fix the economy. In the new government's judgment, one of the main reasons the American economy continued to struggle was that prices kept falling (a problem known as deflation), and the reason that they fell was because firms were competing excessively. Falling wages meant less willingness to buy goods and services, so the demand for all goods and services and hence their prices fell, and falling prices meant businesses and farm owners went bankrupt. In the new government's way of thinking, which many economic historians have disputed in recent years, this price-cutting increased unemployment and therefore caused wages to fall further, generating a vicious cycle. To break it, Congress empowered Roosevelt's administration to get workers and companies to cooperate in setting prices so as to eliminate what was seen as *harmful* competition.

Unsurprisingly, this generated tremendous economic problems, none of which was anticipated by the people drawing up the price regulations. This element of the story is familiar to us from the discussion of Problem 2. However, the reaction of government officials is what is of interest here. The federal government established policing authorities to inspect businesses to make sure that the pricing rules were being followed—the government, in other words, sent cops around to check whether the prices businesses were charging were the correct ones. At least one merchant, the tailor Jacob Magid of Jersey City, spent 3 days of a 30-day sentence in jail for offering to dry-clean a suit for $0.35 instead of the government-mandated minimum price of $0.40. (The regulations he violated, which also cost him a $100 fine for his $0.05 violation, were imposed by the State of New Jersey as reinforcement of the national price codes.) We do not know whether he emerged shaken or intimidated by the experience, but upon leaving jail after the remainder of his sentence was suspended, he pronounced the pricing rules "a good thing" and indicated he would comply with them.

The owners of one other business chose not to submit. The Schechter Poultry Corporation was a business owned by four Orthodox Jewish men, who ran a kosher butcher shop that among other things sold whole chickens. As part of the Roosevelt attempts to revive the economy, the Schechters had to operate their business consistent with something called the Code of Fair Competition for the Live Poultry Industry of the Metropolitan Area in and about the City of New York. Astonishingly, these rules prohibited customers from selecting their own chickens, which would strike most of us, I suspect, as a bad business practice for a butcher to follow, and which the brothers in particular felt violated their ethical duties to their customers. The right of customers to refuse specific birds was in fact part of the Jewish dietary laws, which the Schechters adhered to and which placed far more demanding obligations on them to satisfy their customers than any government rules.

Having to tell customers that they didn't have the right to select individual birds, often under the eye of government inspectors who frequently visited their store, naturally hurt their business. Despite their years of formal education, these government inspectors did not have the knowledge of particular circumstances and opportunities that a market economy harvests so effectively. One of the brothers, Joseph Schechter, once described one of the inspectors "by the name of Bob" as someone who "don't know from a chicken. And I started into teaching him what a chicken is, and my man and myself teach him what a chicken is, what a rooster is." Aaron Schechter described inspectors abusing his customers, saying of an inspector named Philip Alampi, "He told the customer that he is full of shit, and 'I am the Code Authority, and I got a right to do anything I want, and if you don't like it, get out.'" Later Aaron Schechter did manage to expel Alampi. He returned with a local policeman, and yet Aaron Schechter still refused to let the arbitrary bureaucrat, authorized by the faraway ruling class in Washington, D.C., enter.[21]

At the trial of the brothers (and remember, people were being put on criminal trial here for allowing customers to select the chickens they wanted to buy), the idea of government abuse arising from its ignorance about the economics of information was on display several times. The prosecutor asked Martin Schechter, "Your price is not very stable, is it?" (Remember, the goal of the government was to stop prices from falling.) Schechter replied, "The market isn't stable… We got our prices according to what the market might be." Prosecutors asked them who their "stockholders" were, a question that puzzled them, because there were only the brothers themselves operating without a formal contract among themselves or their suppliers. A businessman who bought and sold chickens (known as a middleman, whose role will be examined in Chapter 7) named Louis Spatz had the following exchange with the prosecutor Walter Rice:

> *Rice: You are an expert?*
>
> *Spatz: I am experienced but not an expert.*
>
> *Rice: You are not an expert on the effect of competitive conditions upon the prices of live poultry?*
>
> *Spatz: I am experienced—(he is cut off)*
>
> *Rice: Are you an expert?…*
>
> *Spatz: I am not an expert about anything.*
>
> …
>
> *Rice: You have not studied agricultural economics?*
>
> *Spatz: No, sir.*

---

[21] This history of the Schechter brothers and their trials is taken from Amity Shlaes, *The Forgotten Man: A New History of the Great Depression* (New York: Harper Perennial, 2008), Chapter 8.

Rice: Or any sort of economics?

Spatz: No, sir.

Rice: What is your education?

Spatz: None, very little. In my business, I am the best economist.

Rice: What is that?

Spatz: In my business I am the best economizer.

This is really a very striking exchange. Note the contrast between an *expert*, which to the prosecutor seems to mean someone with a lot of credentials and formal education that qualify him to say what the price of chicken ought to be, and the actual businessman Spatz's idea of *experience* actually buying and selling chickens, which is where he gets his knowledge about what the prices of chickens *in a particular set of circumstances* ought to be. According to Amity Shlaes' account of the trial cited in note 12, in order to make the poorly educated Schechter brothers look ignorant for the record, prosecutor Rice demanded to "have that word [economizer] spelled in the minutes, just as he stated it."

The jury ultimately convicted them, and the judge fined them $7,425—a huge amount for those people in those times. Joseph Schechter got three months in jail, Alex two, and the other two brothers one month each. But the brothers chose to fight, and what they were fighting for was a civil right. It was the right to peacefully pursue your goals in life through voluntary exchange with others in the market, and in doing so to be free from hindrance by a government at best motivated by unjustified confidence in its abilities, at worst by corruption or the desire to oppress. This right is every bit as important in allowing people to live with dignity as the other more well-known civil rights that we properly celebrate. They appealed the case all the way to the Supreme Court. The Court ruled in their favor, deciding that the law authorizing the massive web of price regulation, the National Industrial Recovery Act, was unconstitutional.

Such things have happened in the United States, where regulation of people buying and selling in the spontaneous order is by world standards relatively restrained. But in other places, the degree of oppression and humiliation that citizens suffer from regulation of the market is considerably worse. On December 16, 2010, a fruit vendor in Tunisia named Mohamed Bouazizi was once again harassed, as he was frequently, by police, who accused him of not having a required permit to sell goods. Every day throughout the world, people in such circumstances get out of this arrest by paying a bribe, but Bouazizi did not have the money. The police confiscated his scales and tossed his wares onto the ground. Bouazizi went to local authorities to complain and ask for his scale back, but could not get anyone who mattered to see him. Later that day, in desperation, he set himself afire on the street and died soon after. The result was angry protests that ultimately led to the ouster of Tunisia's longtime dictator, which itself sparked what is now known as the Arab Spring movement.

The reason the police could harass this man literally just trying to go about his business was that Tunisia, like many developing countries, has an endless list of rules that it is very easy to knowingly or unknowingly violate. The reason they wanted to confront him with this rules violation (and they had many rules to choose from) was that they could make money by taking a bribe to look the other way. In countries like Tunisia there is thus an awful dynamic that has been established: government officials establish rules just to have the opportunity to make money by writing them a certain way or, at the level of the local police officer or bureaucrat, ignoring the rule. (Think about campaign contributions to members of Congress in exchange for manufacture of entry barriers or for providing access to taxpayer money that their competitors who do not lobby or contribute so effectively will not get.) This makes careers in "public service"—the presiding over the creation and auctioning off of laws and their enforcement—the most lucrative in the country, ensuring that the country's best and brightest want to go into the bureaucracy and politics rather than start companies and create wealth.

The economist Gordon Tullock tells the story of the mystery of the popularity of customs-clerk jobs in a particular developing country. Customs clerks in some sense do very little that is of value—all they do is check to see whether imported goods are allowed or not under a country's (often very complicated) import restrictions and therefore decide whether people who desire those imported goods will be allowed to have them. And in the country Tullock mentions, these clerks have salaries that are extremely low. And yet they hold among the most desirable jobs in the country. To become a customs clerk one has to pass a very competitive examination, with perhaps only a few candidates out of every hundred passing every year. Many of those who fail simply wait until next year to try again, thus depriving the productive sector of the economy of their talents and effort during that time.

Precisely because these exams are so difficult, these people are among the best and brightest in the country, and so society pays the opportunity cost of them not actually creating wealth but merely presiding over its distribution. Why do such bright people try so hard to get jobs with such menial salaries? A big part of the answer is that the customs clerk owns a very powerful resource that is needed to obtain resources in this country—his permission. Like the owners of labor, skill, land, machines, and oil, economic theory predicts that the owner of this resource of permission will be likely to sell it to the highest bidder. In other words, he will only give it to those who pay the necessary bribes. Rules restricting exchange generate opportunities for politicians and bureaucrats to shake down citizen-supplicants who want either to get the rules written in their favor (in the case of politicians, for example, by outlawing competition for those supplicants) or to allow these citizens to violate the rules. This creates an incentive to write ever more of these rules. Thus it was that the Roman historian Tacitus, writing in the second century A.D. about the collapse of the Roman Republic and its displacement by the Empire, could write of the late Republic, "And now bills were passed, not only for national objects but for individual cases, and laws were most numerous when the Commonwealth was most corrupt." Laws were written, in other words, to reward and punish individuals who had or had not, respectively, paid the requisite bribe.[22]

Figure 5-1 provides some support for the idea that interference in the marketplace promotes abuse by government officials. Both axes measure data recorded by the World Bank. On the horizontal axis is an index of how many bureaucratic procedures are required overall to start a business, register a contract, and gain title to property. This is thus a measure of how many legal hoops citizens must jump through to do business with their fellow citizens. The vertical axis is the bank's corruption measure of how effectively a country controls corruption, which generally ranges from −2 to 3, with a lower number indicating more corruption. The figure suggests strongly that more government procedures are associated with more corruption. Indeed, many of the world's most corrupt countries are also among the world's poorest, which would suggest support for the model just developed, in which when governing is too intrusive, too much activity is diverted toward trying to become someone with the power to prevent someone else from trading, which means that less trading and more government predation happens. This forces the country into a quagmire of low productivity and an extensive amount of wasteful transfer of wealth presided over by highly educated and ambitious politicians and bureaucrats.

---

[22]The quote is from the *Annals* of Tacitus, Book 3, paragraph 27.

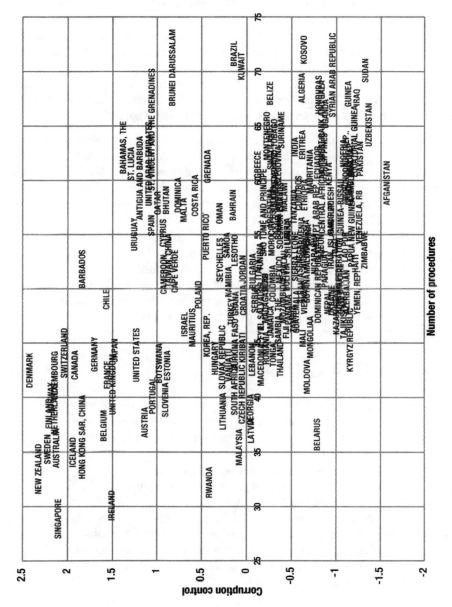

Figure 5-1. Corruption and government involvement in the economy

The final and, I would suggest, most important danger of extensive government intervention into the spontaneous order is that the rules developed to carry out the desired intervention empower government officials to abuse the citizenry and violate their most fundamental human rights. The power to regulate is the power to prevent people from using that which they own to make their way in the world, to achieve their goals in life, to provide for their families—the power to destroy, in other words. So, the road of rules and control is a dangerous one to start out on. As I note at the beginning of this chapter, government is as old as human society itself, and there are functions only it can perform. George Washington is supposed to have said that "a government is like fire, a handy servant, but a dangerous master."

I end this chapter with a quote from the writer Richard Fernandez, who describes how the rules of politicians and bureaucrats—sometimes done with conceptions of noble public interest and sometimes done for purely selfish reasons—come to create the kinds of societies that lead to results like Mohamed Bouazizi ending his life for desperate lack of any other choice:

> The common face of totalitarianism is not, as cinema often depicts, that of uber-Nazis marching in satanic rows, or of cultured madmen planning the extinction of millions with violin music softly seething in the background. Its quotidian face is one of petty, arbitrary, unappealable abuse. For the average man life under tyranny consists of being precisely zero in a society that can do anything — anything at all—to him.[23]

Answer to In-Text Question

5.1. Seniority-based promotion and pay prevents workers from competing against one another through lower salaries and working harder, making the lives of some of the workers (those wanting the most money for the least work) easier. Union advocates say that seniority-based promotion protects them from unfair behavior by management, which undoubtedly happens from time to time, despite its costs. But there are undeniable costs to promotion by seniority instead of productivity in terms of frustrating the ability to provide more of what consumers want and of allowing workers whose interests are different from that of union members to pursue them.

---

[23]Richard Fernandez, "An Event Foretold," April 20, 2011. Available online at http://pjmedia.com/richardfernandez/2011/04/20/an-event-foretold/.

Economics Out There

5.1. Read this blog entry.[24] Identify the entry barriers found therein. With regard to the author's claim that "the phenomenon of money in politics" is responsible for these barriers, which claim seems more reasonable to you—that the amount of government-manufactured entry barriers is more determined by the demands of campaign donors or by government officials' ability to use legal powers to supply these barriers in exchange for campaign donations?

5.2. This CNN story[25] is about a Thai student in the U.S. trying to make money by importing cheaper textbooks from Thailand and reselling them. The legal issues aside, explain how a victory for the textbook publishers suing him would increase their profits. Do you think this would give them an entry barrier or, as they claim, incent them to produce more textbooks (or both)?

5.3. The late author Michael Crichton, of *Jurassic Park* fame, once gave a talk at the Independent Institute.[26] In it, he describes how humans' efforts to shape the ecosystem of Yellowstone National Park in their preferred direction actually caused many unexpected side effects because an ecosystem is far too complex for humans to thoroughly understand. How is the economy a similar kind of complex system?

5.4. Read these four stories from various sources:

- Are Law Schools and Bar Exams Necessary?[27]

- You Think You Can Be a Hair Braider?[28]

- Uncertified Learning[29]

- Taxi Medallions Shackle Cabbies[30]

---

[24]http://blogs.hbr.org/cs/2012/12/how_corruption_is_strangling_us_innovation.html
[25]http://www.cnn.com/2012/10/26/justice/court-student-copyright/index.html
[26]http://www.independent.org/events/transcript.asp?id=111
[27]http://www.nytimes.com/2011/10/25/opinion/are-law-schools-and-bar-exams-necessary.html?_r=1&
[28]http://www.nytimes.com/2012/06/17/magazine/so-you-think-you-can-be-a-hair-braider.html?pagewanted=all&_r=0
[29]http://reason.com/archives/2001/12/13/uncertified-learning
[30]http://townhall.com/columnists/jeffjacoby/2012/03/11/taxi_medallions_shackle_cabbies/page/full/

These are all examples of entry barriers. What are the barriers? What costs do they produce? What benefits might they produce? In the end, do you think the barriers have benefits that justify the costs?

5.5. NPR has an article[31] about someone complaining about the power of the Internet merchant Amazon.com. Do Amazon's tactics benefit anyone? Whom do they damage? Who is more likely to be more able to effectively make their case to Congress and the bureaucracy responsible for regulating competition in the U.S.—the people damaged by Amazon's tactics or the people who benefit from them?

5.6. This blog entry[32] is a story about the government of Miami spending a large amount of money on Toyota Priuses that never got used. Do you think a private business would make a similar mistake? Why or why not? Which peril of public decision making does this represent? What incentives caused this to happen and indeed caused the government to purchase a car like the Prius in particular?

5.7. This article[33] is an occasionally comical story of the difficulties of starting a business in Greece. (Among other things, some would-be entrepreneurs must provide stool samples.) Who benefits from government rules making it more costly to start a business? How might the people who make the rules themselves benefit?

5.8. Reason magazine has a story[34] a about the licensing process for providers of in-home health care in Washington, D.C. In the article, the executive director of the D.C. Home Health Association is quoted as saying that the very low rate of approval for licenses is "like you saying to a certain extent that you have enough doctors in the District of Columbia so you won't license any more doctors…You can't do that really. No one ought to have the ability to do that. The marketplace will dictate that—if, in fact, doctors are not receiving enough clients. What will they do? They'll go where they can find the opportunity." To what extent is the "market" dictating the provision of home health care in D.C.? Given that doctors also must be licensed, to what extent is the "market" providing M.D.s (or not)?

---

[31]http://m.npr.org/news/front/145468105?textSize=small
[32]http://www.autoblog.com/2012/04/25/hundreds-of-5-year-old-municipal-vehicles-found-in-miami-that-we/
[33]http://www.ekathimerini.com/4dcgi/_w_articles_wsite2_1_21/02/2012_429208
[34]http://reason.com/archives/2013/02/14/dc-certificate-of-need

5.9. In the British paper *The Daily Telegraph*, we find a claim[35] that the government of Kenya now seems to exist primarily to provide money and goods to government officials, arguably so much so in fact that civil conflict over the election described was settled by expanding the number of government ministries. Relate this to the analysis here.

5.10. This account,[36] and this account,[37] show how important spite and envy are in human affairs. (The first link is to a relatively complicated scientific journal article.) Where are spite and envy, clearly costly human emotions, likely to be more important—in the market or in politics?

5.11. In an article at Bloomberg News called "The Disgusting Consequences of Plastic Bag Bans,"[38] Ramesh Ponnuru cites research and incidents indicating that banning plastic disposable garbage bags leads to outbreaks of bacterial illness, contracted from reusable bags not washed frequently enough.

    a. Is it reasonable to expect that such a side effect, if it proves to be real, should have been predicted when such bans were enacted? If you have heard of or experienced such bans, did you make such a prediction before reading this article?

    b. Do plastic bags have any other benefits (or costs) you can think of in terms of human goals and desires?

    c. Do you think the list of effects local governments considered when banning these bags were as extensive as yours in part (b)? Why do you suppose they emphasized the specific environmental benefits they did?

---

[35]http://www.telegraph.co.uk/news/worldnews/1895899/Kenyas-cabinet-soaks-up-80pc-of-the-budget.html

[36]http://www.plosone.org/article/info%3Adoi%2F10.1371%2Fjournal.pone.0041812

[37]http://reason.com/archives/2002/06/19/burn-the-rich

[38]http://www.bloomberg.com/news/2013-02-04/the-disgusting-consequences-of-liberal-plastic-bag-bans.html

Who Makes How Much, and Why

Why Finance Professors and Female Supermodels Make More Money

With, without

And who'll deny

It's what the fighting's all about?

—Pink Floyd, "Us and Them," 1973

In America, you look at the mansion on the hill and think, "One day that will be me." In Ireland, people say, "One day, I'm going to get that bastard."

—Bono, of U2 fame, *Sunday Mirror*, October 9, 2005

What did they want, those violent men, ragged, bellowing and wild-eyed, who with clubs and pikes poured through the ancient stress of distracted Paris? They wanted to put an end to oppression, tyranny, and the sword; they wanted work for all men, education for their children, security for their wives, liberty, equality, fraternity, food enough to go around, freedom of thought, the Edenization of the world.

—Victor Hugo, *Les Miserables*

The last chapter noted the costs of government rearrangement of resources and imposition of restrictions on people's freedom to trade with one another. And yet it must be admitted that such restrictions are common and are often imposed with some idea of improved justice in mind. Without question, one of the most frequent sources of belief in social injustice, and of social revolution itself, is the size of the gap in income and wealth between those who have more and those who have less. Widespread poverty has toppled many a dynasty in China and spawned revolutions with disastrously bloody consequences there, in Russia, and elsewhere in the 20th century. In modern democratic societies, this belief has led to a vast growth in government regulation of and displacement of private activity in spheres such as medical care and the provision of retirement income. In the U.S., violence over who should do work and how much they should get for doing it is far from unknown— it occurred in places like Chicago and the surrounding area,[1] Rock Springs, Wyoming,[2] and throughout the Northeast United States in the latter half of the 19th century and again in the 1930s. So it is worth exploring why people obtain the compensation they do in a market setting, so that we can better understand the consequences of using politics to do something about it.

The Market for Compensation

First, there are two terms that need to be distinguished: *income* and *wealth*. Wealth is simply a number, referring to the total amount of assets possessed— things that have value in market exchange. In common usage, wealth includes things such as cash, physical property (homes, cars), land, and financial assets such as stocks and bonds. Add the tradable value of all that up and you have how much wealth a person has. Before proceeding further, though, it should be noted that there is one asset that is typically not counted as wealth, but by this definition should be counted: a person's marketable skill. A person who possesses knowledge about how to design valuable pharmaceuticals but who is only 20 years old and hasn't started engaging in this task yet clearly possesses a resource of immense value, but this is not usually included when people say how "wealthy" this person is. (The reason for this is that this component of the person's wealth is not very *liquid*, a concept whose discussion is deferred until Chapter 10.) But no matter what you count and what you don't, wealth is measured merely as a number—that person is worth $4 million, for example.

Income is a little different. It refers to a one-time or periodic receipt of new wealth, which can be spent immediately on a nice meal (in which case it

---

[1]http://www.kansasheritage.org/pullman/index.html
[2]http://historymatters.gmu.edu/d/5043/

was not additional wealth for very long) or added to one's stock of wealth (by being put in a bank, used to buy stocks, etc.). It often has a time component to it—this person earns $40,000 a year, that person owns stocks that pay 3% dividends four times a year. But not always. If I receive $20,000 in cash from a deceased relative or win $10,000 in the lottery, many people would consider that income, although it is only received once, and legally it certainly qualifies as income, in the sense that you have to declare it on your taxes.

■ **Definition**   Wealth is what you have, and income is what you get, usually for performing some task and often measured per period of time.

But most income is not received as the result of chance events like these. Most income is received in compensation for providing value to someone else in exchange. The landowner who receives income from renting property to a resident or a store owner is providing that person with a place to live or do business, and the rent he receives, like all prices, is determined by supply and demand and hence, in part, by the value of that land to the tenant when he can use it for the purpose he wishes to use it for. So too with labor income, which is a sizable part if not the outright majority of compensation for most people for much of their life span, not just in the United States but around the world. And it is important to remember that the market for labor looks like any other market, as Figure 6-1 shows.

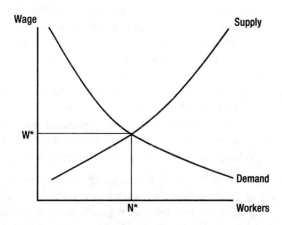

Figure 6-1. The market for a particular kind of labor

As before, the equilibrium price (in this case, the price for labor, W*, which I call the *wage*) and the equilibrium quantity (in this case of workers, denoted N*, with N sort of standing for *employment*) is found where the supply curve and the demand curve intersect. The supply curve tells us how the amount of labor that people are willing to supply varies with the wage, and the demand curve tells how much labor employers are willing to buy as the wage varies. The supply curve of labor is a function of how many alternatives workers have. People who have a spouse who is capable of earning quite a bit of money may demand a relatively high wage to induce them to come out of the home, and so their individual supply curve would be to the left. When there are very many workers capable of doing a particular job, the market supply curve for such workers is farther to the right, and the equilibrium wage is correspondingly lower.

The examples of labor-market violence from the United States cited earlier involved activities such as mining and manufacturing work, which in those days involved relatively little skill (in stark contrast to now, when operating advanced machinery often requires highly particular skills) and also occurred at a time of mass immigration. The result was that lots of workers were competing for the same amount of work. Thus, we are not surprised that the equilibrium wage would be lower. In general, immigrants with a particular skillset will compete against domestic workers with the same skillset and hence lower their wages and their job opportunities. We are thus also not surprised that domestic workers frequently oppose immigration of workers who might compete against them, whereas employers support more open immigration. In short, the more competition there is to do a particular kind of work, the more elastic and farther to the right the supply curve is, thus the lower the equilibrium wage is, other things being equal.

But the demand for labor is also critical in determining compensation. Fundamentally, the demand for labor is a function of how much revenue a worker can generate for his employer. Indeed, a sufficient condition for an employer to be willing to hire a worker is that the worker's wage be less than what economists call his *marginal revenue product,* which means "the amount that revenue for the business increases when that worker is hired." One more assembly-line worker hired increases the amount of output coming off the line, one more professor hired means more students are taught, one more lawyer hired means more billable hours charged, and one more software engineer hired increases the rate at which code is written and debugged. If hiring a worker brings more money in than the money required to pay all of his compensation (including benefits), hiring him makes profits go up.

As usual, what a worker is "worth" is not an absolute number but is context-dependent. A worker with a college degree in a particular field and a particular set of work experiences will be more productive in some circumstances than in others, and hence employees in some circumstances will be willing to pay more than employers in others. We have already seen how supermodels who possess spectacular good looks not available to most of us make quite a bit of money and are relatively invulnerable to competition. It also turns out that the top female supermodels make significantly more money than the top male ones, so that even within the rarefied circle of extremely good-looking people, compensation can vary quite a bit depending on the particular circumstances of the market.

At my university (and, I suspect, at most), professors in departments like accounting and engineering earn significantly more money than professors in departments like English and history. Indeed, it is not uncommon for a newly hired professor in a field like computer science to make more money than someone with 20 years of experience in a field such as philosophy. The person who comes off worse in such comparisons is likely to invoke the idea of "fairness," to say that he "deserves" more money, because he's been there longer, because he's older, etc. Of course, few of us can resist the temptation from time to time to believe that we deserve more than we are getting. But our supply/demand framework suggests that people do not get paid what *they* think they deserve—they get paid what *other people think they deserve, given the alternatives those other people have.*

▨ **Note**   You don't get paid based on what you think you deserve. Rather, you get paid what others think you deserve based on the alternatives they have (like working willing current workers harder, using a machine instead of hiring you, hiring someone else, outsourcing your skills, etc.).

And if true, this plays out two ways. First, on the labor supply side, people with many and good alternatives will have high opportunity costs of time, so that their supply curve will be farther to the left than those with fewer and poorer alternatives. This is, I suspect, a big reason why accounting and engineering professors make more than philosophy and history professors do. Philosophy and history professors have a lot of expertise, but for many of them it is not expertise that people will pay a lot for outside the university setting. But people in some departments have skills that are very lucrative outside the ivory tower, and so to get them to work for the university, the administration has to pay them enough to offset that.

The idea that you get paid what other people think you deserve plays out on the demand side as well. First, I'll introduce a new term: *human capital,* a perfectly good definition of which is *skill that other people think is valuable.* However, I will use the term *human capital* in addition to *skill* because *capital* suggests the idea of something that can grow and that one can invest in, not just something that one is born with. Some people are born smarter than others, but one can invest in marketable skills through formal education, on-the-job experience, building up a network of sales contacts, and so forth.

Personality traits are also part of one's stock of human capital—risk takers and people who have gifts of persuasion may earn more than others without these traits. And it is important to actually distinguish between skill and human capital in one critical way: skill is not the same thing as marketable skill. The ability to recite *Moby Dick* from memory while riding a unicycle is undoubtedly a rare skill (as of now, there may not be a single person in the world who possesses it), but it is not necessarily a skill that anyone is willing to pay for.

Instead of referring to a person's human capital as *more* or *less*, it is perhaps better to refer to it as *more valuable* or *less valuable*. (Even then, it would be more accurate to say *more or less valuable in a particular situation*.) People who have more valuable human capital in a particular relationship with any potential buyer of their labor will earn more than people who have less valuable human capital who are in that same relationship. So, some of the discussion about how to help people earn more money becomes more nuanced. Should we provide college education for more people to raise the average standard of living? It is true that on average, those with bachelor's degrees make more than those who only went to high school, but it is also true that not all bachelor's degrees are equally valuable in the marketplace. If a person emerges from college heavily in debt and with an education that makes him unattractive to those making decisions about filling jobs in which the recent graduate has interest, it will not help the graduate to complain that he "deserves" a better-paying job. Any employer who must earn profits to stay in business will hire employees based on what the employees can do for them—on how productive their human capital is when applied to the task the employer wants done.

Can we make any general statements about what kinds of human capital are "more valuable"? It is easy to be pessimistic. Why does one artist become popular while another languishes in obscurity? That seems to be a function only of vagaries in public taste. It is possible to copy the style of painters like Pablo Picasso or Claude Monet (and indeed popular artists often talk about who their "influences" are), but why the original source of influence becomes influential to begin with is largely a mystery. Yet many things qualify as *general human capital*, which means *widely applicable in a wide variety of tasks that employers will rate favorably*. Proper use of the English language, for example, is valued much more highly than improper use in a wide variety of jobs. Fluency in a foreign language might not be important in as many tasks, but is likely to be in more than a few. Other important elements of relatively general human capital include the habits of working hard, dedication to task, and showing up on time. A person who has these habits may well, in the expectation of the employer, have the potential to be a much more productive employee than someone with a particular university degree.

Specific human capital, in contrast, is *a highly particular ability that is only valuable in one or a few tasks*. When thinking about specific human capital, it is important to remember that many people pursue goals that have nothing to do with money. The starving artist is someone who is content to earn a little money doing something he loves, and I (and very many others) believe that it is much more important to have a job you love than a job you hate that pays a lot more money. People thus may acquire this specific human capital without expecting to make a great living. But with regard to monetary compensation, specific human capital—a degree in biology, work experience repairing computers (other than whatever value it signals in terms of doing work responsibly), knowledge of Java programming—will make much more difference in some tasks than others. Outside its appropriate environment, such capital is of little use.

Nowadays many people, lamentably, obtain PhDs in fields with little value attached to them by employers outside academia. Given that the number of jobs available in universities is much smaller than the number of people with those PhDs, the inevitable result is that those people compete the level of compensation down and become willing to take jobs as adjunct faculty (teaching one or two courses a term for minimal pay) in lieu of having the sort of full-time tenure-track job that they expected in graduate school. On the other hand, people with such unusual skills as knowing how to drive a Zamboni[3] have been able to parlay that into high-paying jobs as child-care workers. Elite programmers can write video-game software or create data-processing tools sold to millions of people. If this is a sufficiently rare skill, the people who do it will make a lot of money.

Ditch digging is not morally any less worthy than writing software, but it may be a skill possessed by larger numbers of people, and it is not a highly specialized skill—what one has to learn to do it well is modest. (This is not the same thing as being willing to exert the immense physical effort needed to do it well, which might be rarer.) Those who do it are subject to much more competition—the demand for their individual services, in other words, is much more elastic. Thus those who do it are easily replaceable, and over time competition should drive their wages down, in accordance with the indifference principle. This will change if machinery is created that allows many ditches to be dug by one person operating it, which in many ways has already happened because of mechanically powered construction equipment. That has raised the marginal product and hence the wages of ditch diggers. In that case, some ditch diggers will be replaced, but the ones who stay will make more, and more ditches will be dug thanks to the lower opportunity costs of digging one.

So, why do people make what they make? In short, because of supply of and demand for what they can do. Demand curves reflect the value of what we are being asked to purchase, and the demand for labor reflects the value of that labor not in some philosophical sense but to the person—an employer, typically—who might contract to buy it. (The value of human capital, in other words, is context dependent.) Supply curves reflect the ease with which more of a particular kind of human capital can be procured and the willingness of people to offer more labor in response to a higher wage. The market for labor, in other words, is like the market for anything else.

---

[3] http://www.npr.org/blogs/money/2012/03/29/149525587/the-200-000-a-year-nanny

Power in the Employer-Employee Relationship

Despite this, much regulation of the labor market comes from the belief that in the employer-employee relation, it is the employer who has most of the "power." In this view, employers can dictate wages to workers who are forced to accept them, and so workers need protection to ensure they make enough to live on. These protections include minimum-wage laws, the ability to require a company to negotiate all labor contracts through a union, guaranteed annual vacations, etc. This belief that employers have "power" and employees don't results in vastly different treatment of employers and employees under labor law. Under federal law, for example, in some contexts it is illegal to lay large numbers of workers off without providing six months' notice, whereas an employee need not provide six months' notice before quitting. Similarly, it is illegal for employers to discriminate against employees—by paying them less, refusing to hire them, or firing them—on grounds of race, sex, or age, yet employees are perfectly free to refuse to work for someone whose race, sex, or age they do not like.

Questioned about this distinction, people (or at least professors in other disciplines at my university with whom I have discussed this question) generally answer that the two parties are not the same. Employers are said to have the power in the bargaining relationship with their employees, and employees are said to be correspondingly vulnerable. By the definition of power used earlier, no one, when applying for a job, has power over anyone else. Both parties are free to negotiate over the terms of employment, and both parties are free to reject terms they find unacceptable, leaving them in the same situation as before. In fact, employees with relatively valuable human capital are able to use the alternative opportunities it generates to extract more compensation from employers all the time. The most obvious example is in professional sports, where players who are free to negotiate with other teams can use that freedom as leverage to extract higher contract offers from their current one. Of course, professional athletes are a very rare breed, and so a reader might reasonably object that this is not a fair example. But other people whose human capital is relatively inelastically demanded can also be said to possess most of the room for maneuver in a bargaining relationship. University professors, for example, frequently take job offers from other universities into the offices of their deans and tell them that they will take the job if they don't get a raise. (Legend has it that some professors actually go out and seek job offers precisely to use them to use them as bargaining leverage back home.) Software engineers in Silicon Valley routinely quit their jobs to look for something better. Research suggests that every month in the U.S. the percentage of Americans who change jobs within a field is about

3.2% and another 3.5% change fields at least to some degree.[4] Moving from one job to another frequently represents the exit from something worse to something better.

Of course, it is a different matter if you have been working at a car factory for 20 years and the factory closes. Workers in this situation have spent 20 years accumulating human capital highly specific to the job they have been doing—human capital that (for the same reason the factory closed) is not likely to be highly valued elsewhere, except perhaps in factories outside the country. If the workers are older, other potential employers will fear that they will not stay long in a new job and that their human capital (including physical strength, which is a component of human capital) is diminishing because of age. Many employers may be willing to offer such workers jobs, although such employers may be very rare locally, meaning that unless the employee is willing to move he will not be able to find such work. Even if he does, it is possible that compensation is much less than in his previous job. Without question, the mismatch between his specific human capital and what is currently most valued by the market leaves him much worse off. It is also possible that he and his coworkers may retain their jobs if they are willing to take substantial pay cuts.

This is not an exercise of power, but rather a reflection of changed market conditions. New ways have been found to bring valued goods to consumers at lower cost—for example, producing in foreign countries where workers have lower opportunity costs of time. The alternative is not preserving an obsolete ideal of "good jobs at good wages." As noted earlier, wages are purely a function of the alternatives workers have and the value to employers of the human capital possessed by particular workers. Indeed, some manufacturing jobs pay very high wages, precisely because workers have learned how to operate very productive machinery and/or possess high spatial-reasoning abilities that mean that workers themselves contribute a lot to the company's bottom line.[5] Workers in places like South Carolina or Ohio who are more than ten times as productive as workers in places like China and Mexico can earn ten times the wage and still have a job. And often this productivity depends on highly specific human capital.

Workers who possess such human capital often possess most of the bargaining leverage in their negotiations with their employers, whether they supervise complicated machines or design software concepts. (The actual writing of software code, as opposed to coming up with the idea for a game interface, for example, might be a fairly routine task that could be outsourced somewhere else.) In short, the key to earning a high salary lies in being indispensable (or nearly so, since nothing is perfectly inelastically demanded). The closer to indispensable you are, the more the leverage is yours and not your employer's.

[4]Giuseppe Moscarini and Kaj Thomasson, "Occupational and Job Mobility in the US," *Scandinavian Journal of Economics* 109 (4) (2007): 807–836.
[5]http://www.theatlantic.com/magazine/archive/2012/01/making-it-in-america/308844/

(Note, though, that in the long term, people who sell their labor are in the same competitive position as people who sell anything else—subject to a greater degree of competition than in the short run. But a person with a continual gift for creating new forms of near-indispensability will also be able to receive high rewards over a long period of time.)

In that sense, much of the history of labor-management (and labor-owner) relations in the U.S. is poorly taught and misunderstood. From the 1870s–1890s, and again in the 1930s, there was a great amount of often violent conflict between workers who abandoned their jobs over demands for higher pay (that is, went on strike) and the employers who had to answer to their customers by getting their product out on time at a good price. During those times, both because manufacturing was far more standardized and easier to learn than now and because of waves of new workers coming in from farms and foreign countries, workers were a dime a dozen, easily replaceable. The violence between workers and owners, which involved the police, the military/National Guard, private security agencies like the Pinkertons,[6] and unionized workers themselves almost invariably followed the same pattern: workers struck or wanted to strike, employers hired workers who were willing to work on better terms than strikers demanded, and violence was carried out or threatened against the strikebreakers, whom unionists dismissed as "scabs."

Contrary to the argument that labor-market violence was initiated by employers who wanted to "bust unions," research suggests that the overwhelming majority of court cases involving violence or threatened violence between workers and owners during this time exhibited this pattern: actual or threatened violence by laborers against those who wished to work, in an attempt to restrict competition.[7] Also contrary to the labor-is-powerless story, wages generally rose throughout most of this period of intense conflict (the Great Depression was an exception), the more so after the increase in labor supply slowed down with the decline in movement from the farms to cities and the imposition in 1924 of sharp limits on immigration. (These immigration limits may well have been unwise, despite their beneficial effects of restriction of labor supply for some Americans. Not only did they raise prices for consumers because of restricted competition for workers, they also deprived Americans of immigrants' entrepreneurship, ingenuity, and new ideas. But that is a separate question.)

■ **Tip** *Power* is not an appropriate word for thinking about employer-employee bargaining. What does apply is the degree of competition for the services one provides and its value to employers, and ultimately to consumers. To make a lot of money, be valuable and be very difficult to replace.

---

[6]http://en.wikipedia.org/wiki/Pinkerton_Government_Services%2c_Inc.
[7]Sylvester *Petro*, "Injunctions and Labor Disputes, 1880—1932," *Wake Forest Law Review* 14 (1978), 341—576.

The Distribution of Income

The title of this section is actually a horrible one, but I use it anyway because it is so common in public discourse. The phrase—especially when used in a context like *What can we do about the distribution of income?*—implies that "income" is a cake baked in an oven in City Hall, which politicians remove and take out onto the steps before cutting it up and "distributing" it to the grateful populace. But again, ignoring anomalous one-time circumstances such as slot-machine winnings or inheritances, income is generally provided as compensation for the provision of valuable services to others, with the degree of value context dependent as usual. It is thus unavoidably true that at any moment in time, income—whether it comes from current labor services provided or as interest payments on loans made in the past or as investment returns for having provided capital at a critical juncture in a company's growth—flow in larger amounts to some than to others, based on the value *to others* of what they have been able to provide in market transactions.

Thinking about "income distribution" this way means that data on it must be interpreted with some care. First, income ultimately accrues to individuals. Individuals, of course, earn compensation for the labor they supply, but even income that accrues to a business is ultimately distributed to individuals. These individuals can be the company's employees, from the CEO to the assembly-line worker, salesperson, middle manager, or custodial staff. Individuals can also include shareholders, who receive dividend payments on the stock shares they own (more on this in Chapter 7) or lenders who receive interest payments based on contracts they have signed with the business. But the U.S. federal government often publishes income data as "family income" or "household income."

The trouble with these statistics is that households and families vary by size. Three generations living in the same home are, from the point of view of government statistics, identical to a young single person who is living alone just one year after graduating from college and still working in his first job. We would not necessarily expect people of the same age or with different numbers of children and adults of working and non-working age to earn the same income, and as the proportion of households of different kinds in the population changes, "median household income" should change as well.

Indeed, if the salary of young people in their 20s rises enough to allow them to move out of their parents' home and live with roommates or alone, average household income may actually decline despite a higher standard of living, reflected in the ability of young singles to afford their own household. In addition, one must take into account the changing age structure of the population even at the individual level, because people's salaries (there are many exceptions, of course) tend to rise throughout their 20s, 30s, 40s, and into their 50s as they accumulate human capital through work experience.

Then, as retirement approaches, people begin to ease off accumulating human capital (because there is a shorter period of time to earn the revenue necessary to justify the cost of accumulating it) and suffer the negative salary effects of physical and cognitive depreciation. That is a fancy way of saying people in their late 50s and 60s generally find it more physically and mentally demanding to work hard than people in their mid-20s. (With seeming complete randomness, the government also counts some government transfer programs in calculating the distribution of income, but not others. Some in particular that are targeted to the poor are not counted.)

And people can be substantially mobile within the distribution of income across generations. From the 1970s through 2002, 63% of people without a college degree and 74% of people with a college degree earned more in real terms than their parents. For people in the bottom 20% of the income distribution, the figures were 81% and 96%. (Across all quintiles—20% slices—of the income distribution, for people with and without college degrees, only those in the top 20% who possessed no college degree did not out-earn their parents at the same age.)[8] Downward mobility, to be sure, is not unknown either. The researchers defined falling out of the middle class as growing up in a household where the adults' earnings were in the 30th to the 70th percentiles of the income distribution in the past, but were now below the 30th percentile. Among the most important factors that have been identified are: becoming divorced, widowed, or separated, or never marrying (especially men); failing to get education beyond high school; scoring poorly on tests of reading comprehension, math, and word knowledge; and serious drug use. Among ethnic and sexual categories, black men were also significantly more likely to drop out of the middle class, and white men were more likely to than white women.[9]

It has long been known that single-parent households are disproportionately represented in the poorest segment of the income distribution, and married families in the highest. Those in the poorest 20% are also less likely to work full-time, while those in the top 20% are far more likely to do so; a similar disparity exists for total hours worked. Americans at the 20th percentile of the distribution in 2006 (those who earn more income than only 20% of the population) had just over 12 years of education on average, whereas those at the 80th percentile (earning more than 80% of the population) had over 16 years of education.

---

[8]Ron Haskins, "Education and Economic Mobility," in Julia B. Isaacs, Isabelle D. Sawhill, and Ron Haskins, *Getting Ahead and Losing Ground: Economic Mobility in America* (Brookings Institution, 2008), Chapter 8.

[9]Gregory Acs, "Downward Mobility from the Middle Class: Waking up from the American Dream" (The Pew Charitable Trusts). Available online at www.economicmobility.org/reports_and_research/assets/pdfs/MiddleClassExecSUm.pdf.

I cite these statistics—which indicate the role of choice in outcome—not to assess blame, but merely to note that employers offer higher compensation to those who produce more for them. Some circumstances (for example, being in a single-parent household) substantially increase the difficulty of accumulating either education or on-the-job training, both of which improve productivity, as well as make it more difficult to work extended or irregular hours. Those who are married can benefit from two incomes and from specialization in what economists who study families call *household production* and *market work* (that is, one spouse concentrates more on household work, the other more on earning money). In other words, there are reasons why people earn what they earn that do not necessarily signal grand cosmic injustice.

Having said that, it would be foolish to claim that such factors entirely explain who earns what. Major economic changes can certainly catch significant percentages of the population unprepared. Under those circumstances, the people who are responsible for creating or who are well prepared for those changes do better, and the people whose work is made obsolete do worse. People who create web-based mapping apps gain immensely from their creativity, and the people who have worked for years producing the hardcover version of the *Rand McNally Road Atlas* lose out. This is unavoidable if we want to enable people to do more with less, to live better than those who came before us. However, those whose investments in specific human capital are now less valuable are undeniably hurt by this change, at least until they acquire human capital that is more valuable under the new circumstances. Insuring against the negative consequences of such adverse change (from the point of view of those workers, not the whole society) would probably require that a person invest thoroughly in more general human capital such as high-quality English, fluency in other languages, a solid record of achievement and reliability that can be documented for future potential employers, etc. This is the kind of human capital valuable in a wide variety of jobs. Having a lot of it makes it easier to find a new one.

In a dynamic, truly progressive society, change is constant, and so are fluctuations in income distribution. Insuring people against the consequences of progress while allowing that progress to play out primarily requires two ingredients: the widespread provision of very general human capital and the lack of legal or cultural barriers to entry in the new fields on the rise. Examples of the former include the provision of universal basic schooling; examples of the latter include ending the ability of competitors to get the government to kneecap their competition and legally limit certain jobs to certain arbitrarily chosen people. Historically, such practices have included the feudalistic practice of passing on trades from father to son. The origin of last names such as Smith, Carter, Baker and Dyer lies in the tasks once associated with these names, and the intimate tying of who your parents were to what you do was also the cornerstone of the Indian caste system, which still exists in residual form in rural India even today. But the modern-day equivalent of these restrictions exists in the entry barriers outlined in Chapter 5, which lower social mobility.

Despite the inevitability of income *non-uniformity* (a better word than *equality*, which suggests a morally desirable state of affairs), the state of income "distribution" is frequently seen as an indictment of a society, and governments across the world, as noted previously, take substantial steps to try to dampen it. Most notably, in the name of such distributive "justice," it is common for people to advocate that those who earn the most income pay a vastly disproportionate share of taxation. Yet as we saw in Table 5-1, it is not clear that such policies are effective. Among the countries listed in the table, only France and Ireland take a higher percentage of taxation from the top 30% of earners than the U.S., yet income distribution at any moment in time is likely to be far more non-uniform in the U.S. than in almost every country in that table (although it is perhaps hard to tell, given the transfer programs that are not counted in U.S. calculations). A great many things besides tax law affect the momentary distribution of income—age structure, immigration, and the rate of overall economic dynamism, just to name a few.

The Economics of Taste-Based Discrimination

Once upon a time, *discrimination* was a word with overwhelmingly positive connotations. People spoke approvingly of a person with discriminating tastes. That usage still exists, but if the only thing you hear today is that a person discriminates, your impression is not likely to be a good one. The original meaning has value in one of the two ways economists speak of discrimination, in that the person who discriminates is the one who makes an effort based on group traits to discard that which is less valuable in favor of choosing only that which is more valuable—for example, to avoid less productive workers and choose only more productive ones. This kind of choice is known as *statistical discrimination*.

But first we must take the uglier sense of the term. When people say that an employer discriminates on the basis of race, sex, sexual orientation, and so on, what is meant? (The same framework applies to landlords who refuse to rent or businesspeople who refuse to sell to members of certain groups, but I will speak of employers, because this is the kind of discrimination that most preoccupies the public.) Presumably what is meant is that the discriminator refuses to hire people from the disfavored group, or perhaps he hires them in limited numbers but pays them less (as was common in the post-Civil War U.S. for black Americans).

In yet more testimony to its usefulness, our supply/demand model can be used to think productively about this discrimination based on raw dislike, which is usually called *taste-based discrimination*. Consider the adjusted version of Figure 6-2.

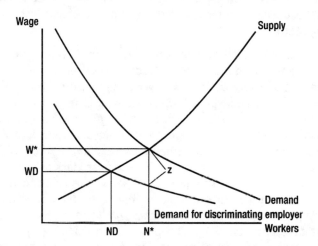

Figure 6-2. The market for a particular kind of labor, with taste-based discrimination by employer

The demand curve simply labeled Demand is the same as in Figure 6-1 but now reflects only employers who do not discriminate, and is for members of the disfavored group only. Discriminating employers, on the other hand, have a lower demand curve for members of this group. Their lower demand curve means that the discriminating employer is less willing to pay for any level of workers than the non-discriminating one. Why? Because his monetary gain—the productivity his workers generate—is partially offset because he dislikes them. Although at equilibrium, non-discriminating employers are willing to hire N* workers and pay them W*, to persuade non-discriminating employers to hire that amount they must be allowed to pay W* – z, with z representing the offsetting distaste discriminating employers have for their workers from the disfavored group. If there were only discriminating employers, they would pay a lower wage WD (the D standing for discriminating) and hire only the number ND of workers. If there are two separate labor markets, then workers caught in the discriminatory one will earn less and be hired less (or perhaps not at all, depending on the intensity of the employer's discriminatory tastes). Because this is more or less the common conception of taste-based employment discrimination, the model seems like a reasonable one.

But is this outcome likely to prevail over the long term? Discriminating employers are paying workers of equal productivity lower wages. Based on the indifference principle, we would expect those excess returns to employers to be competed away—for workers, in other words, to gradually be paid more until they are getting paid what their human capital makes them worth in this industry. The lesson? *Free competition is a powerful force against taste-based discrimination.* Is it guaranteed to eliminate all taste-based discrimination? Of course not. Compensation gaps having only to do with fundamental sex, race, and other differences[10] can exist, but there is an extensive history of competition eroding them.

During the brief interval between the end of the Black Codes, mentioned in Chapter 5, and the departure of Reconstruction soldiers, blacks in the former Confederacy saw their wages grow significantly faster than those of whites, despite facing widespread white racism. One of the most notorious legal cases in American history is *Plessy v. Ferguson*, which some Americans have heard of but whose details, lamentably, almost none know. The facts of the case were that railroads had begun, for efficiency reasons (lower costs, customer desires), to start running integrated first-class cars, but this practice was later banned by Louisiana's Jim Crow laws. The railroad then purposely had a man of mixed race but classified as "black" under Louisiana law defy the law demanding segregation of railroad cars by sitting in a whites-only cabin, to set up a test case. The case went all the way to the U.S. Supreme Court, which ruled that separate but equal public accommodations were constitutional. So, the facts of the case were that a business wanted to break down racial barriers, but the governments of the South, whose regulatory power had been captured by white racists, wouldn't allow it. It was 70 years before the federal government, through the civil-rights legislation of the 1960s, not only overturned Jim Crow laws but banned discrimination in public accommodation— laws that may well have turned out to be unnecessary had competition been allowed to follow its course.

In India, with a long history of harsh social and occupational segregation on the basis of their *jajmani* or caste system, economic reform in the 1980s and 1990s that loosened the government's limits on competition opened many opportunities to historically excluded castes.[11] And during Britain's colonial rule in what is now Malaysia and Singapore, people flocked to those places from China, despite a complete lack of voting or indeed any political rights, because local courts, operating under British law, effectively protected their rights to make contracts and buy and sell property—to compete, in other words. This was in stark contrast to the situation that prevailed among their ethnic compatriots back in China. People are black, white, brown, red, and yellow, but money (at least American money) is all green. Give people an alternative to

---

[10]As opposed, for example, to pay gaps arising from women having lower opportunity costs of time, or suffering human-capital depreciation while they are out of the workforce to raise children—an important factor in their continuing to trail men in salaries despite making up majorities of college undergraduates and law and medical students.

[11]http://news.bbc.co.uk/2/hi/business/4773425.stm

high-cost accommodation of discriminatory tastes, and people—entrepreneurs and customers—will grab it in the pursuit of money. Taste-based discrimination is extremely vulnerable to the power of the market.

■ **Note**   Taste-based discrimination is more difficult to practice with more intense competition (among businesses to hire workers, among landlords to rent to tenants, and so on).

Statistical Discrimination

I know from personal experience that when universities post an opening for a new young professor, they are very likely to receive over 100 applications. How to give them all the attention they deserve? It is very difficult, because of the deadline for decision making (applicants want to be informed in time to tie up their affairs where they currently live) and because the time taken by the professors making the decision has an opportunity cost—they must teach, do research, do dreary committee work, and so forth. The professors' task is to devote time until the marginal cost of another minute going over the pile of applications (a cost that is increasing, because time is being diverted from ever more valuable alternate uses) has caught up to the marginal benefit. The marginal benefit is likely to be falling, because one wants to hire the applicant likely to be the most productive by whatever criteria the department doing the hiring is using, but one is also becoming ever more familiar with the applicant pool as one spends more time on the task. At some point, in other words, more time spent reading files and discussing applicants is likely to be not worth it. Is this equilibrium amount of time likely to be one that leads to every publication of every applicant being read and every reference checked out? Not likely. Instead, shortcuts will be employed. Candidates who have already published research articles in excellent journals, who have solid evidence of excellent teaching, and who have degrees from first-rate universities are likely to get a lot of attention; others will get very little. And the hiring committee here is actually doing something that has a disreputable connotation—they are *stereotyping*. It is possible that the best candidate lies in the pile of discarded applications, among those candidates with degrees from second-tier schools and no evidence so far of excellence in teaching or research. But it is less likely, perhaps much less likely, and given scarcity of time, choices must be made about whom to interview.

Employers almost always engage in stereotyping. They look at previous work experience, quality of the university attended, testimonials by others, and other factors. Universities, too, stereotype when they try to pick the students who are likely to succeed there. They look at standardized test scores and read the students' essays and make their choices accordingly. (Which components of the applicant's package best predict his ultimate success, and the extent to which standardized test scores in particular do, is an active controversy.) Economists refer to this practice not as stereotyping, although it is that, but as *statistical discrimination—the use of categories an individual belongs to as sources of information about the individual.* The definition suggests a certain unfairness— why should a job applicant be judged by, say, his graduation from a particular university when he has his own individual productivity? But search time is not free, and at some point continuing to search becomes too burdensome. Employers use shortcuts to save costly time.

The kinds of information from which statistical discrimination is built have surprising range. A friend of mine who owns his own business, which at any time has several employees, has told me of receiving applications for job openings that list obscene-sounding e-mail addresses for correspondence, contain harshly critical remarks about former employers (and in one case, even an announcement in the application letter that the applicant was suing a former employer), and have cover letters riddled with grammatical and spelling errors. My friend is convinced, not without reason, that on average applicants with these characteristics are likely to be less productive than those without them.

But when people use group membership such as race or sex instead of college attended or GPA or grammatical quality of the candidate' materials to statistically discriminate, people object. This is probably because one is born into these former categories, whereas GPA and other non-innate characteristics can be affected by individual effort. But if racial groups and sexes differ by productivity, *these characteristics are informative, and it would be foolish to ignore them completely.* To be sure, they may not be very informative. But if the pile of applications is high enough, any information may have to enter the calculation.

It is important to say at this point that these group differences need not be genetic differences. A study by Duke University researchers generated an astonishing amount of controversy by showing that black students, as well as admits of all races who were children of Duke alumni, had a much higher chance of switching out of demanding majors in the sciences and economics. The authors found that the entire gap was explained by differences in academic preparation, and was in the case of black students unrelated to racial category per se. On the other hand, there is a vast scientific literature, for example, generally but not unanimously supporting the idea that men take more risks than women. (Think of the different driving habits of women and men.) Men are also more prone to violence. Why do these differences exist? The profit-maximizing business owner does not care. He is not doing social science and cares only that they exist, not why. It is possible that ethnic group membership or sex will carry weight in the decision to offer a job, just as graduating from Harvard or having a high GPA does.

Negative stereotypes of groups exist all over the world, toward ethnic Malays in Malaysia and Singapore, who on average are less economically successful than

Chinese in those countries, and in India, where stereotyping against members of lower castes exists. But stereotypes need not be negative: Thomas Sowell cites the examples of Mohawk Indians in New York, who have a reputation for skill in the construction trade in New York City. Gardeners in Los Angeles once included many Japanese and now are dominated by Latinos. Insurance companies make money off statistical discrimination by giving female and older drivers more favorable auto insurance rates than the young and male (especially young men), and not without reason: males 16–25 in the U.S. are by far the likeliest to have an accident or get a ticket. (Insurance companies, which only pay out in the event of an accident, of course use a history of getting ticketed, even without causing an accident, as yet another layer of statistical discrimination.) Women also pay lower life insurance rates because they are less likely than men to die young.[12] There are of course many men who will not have accidents, and many women who will have one or more, but (in conjunction with other information such as type of car owned, neighborhood of residence, etc.) insurance companies have discovered that the sex of the insured is informative with regard to the expected costs to the company of taking on the policyholder. For women, this statistical edge results in a positive stereotype. According to the Scandinavian insurance company Tryg, Danish people on average are much worse skiers than Norwegians,[13] which generates interesting questions discussed further in Problem 6.4 later in this chapter. So is it really a surprise that groups differ in ways that affect the human capital they bring to market on average, even if no individual in the group necessarily has those traits, positive or negative?

In sum, statistical discrimination is unlike taste-based discrimination in that it is something done not in opposition to but in the service of making money. Unfortunately, it is for that reason harder to displace than taste-based discrimination. Unless the group-based differences vanish, the only way to escape taste-based discrimination is for the stereotypers to come up with ways to more closely tie productivity information to the individual. The more an employer (or landlord, or insurance-policy underwriter) knows about a particular individual, the less information is imparted at the margin by group membership. In a perfect world, every employer would know every applicant's productivity with certainty. But "perfect world" here means "costless information," and that is a world that can never be. Banning statistical discrimination in the face of costly information will lead to worse decision making—employees on average will be less productive, admitted freshmen will perform on average worse in school, etc. But because group membership, whether the group is

---

[12]http://www.guardian.co.uk/money/2004/sep/19/europeanunion.genderissues
[13]http://www.thelocal.no/page/view/norwegian-skiers-100-times-less-clumsy-than-danes

"black females" or "Harvard graduates," is imperfectly informative, there are always incentives to develop new individual-specific measures of productivity, especially productivity and skills tests.[14]

▨ **Note**   Statistical discrimination is harder to reduce through competition than taste-based discrimination, precisely because it is done to try to increase profits.

There is now more good news (at least from the employer's point of view): many job applicants have left footprints all over the Internet, which employers can readily access to find out information about these applicants that is informative regarding their likely productivity. The bad news is that at least some of this information is damaging. My business-owner friend I mentioned earlier reports seeing online pictures of applicants passed out from excessive alcohol consumption or with captions like "**** yeah, it's 4/20" (a date that apparently has grand significance in the marijuana subculture). One need not rely on stereotypes about young men or graduating from a "party school" after finding individual-specific information of that sort. Note that individuals too can try to disentangle themselves from stereotypical judgments—or, more accurately, associate themselves with more favorable ones—by dressing for job interviews or, in a broader context, adopting the public norms of majority culture. Many economists view "assimilation" by immigrants and members of minority groups as a way of persuading evaluators that they do not share the negative features that these evaluators statistically associate with their group.

▨ **Tip**   The more precise an employer's information is about a particular job applicant's expected productivity, the less he needs to rely on statistical discrimination. In the Internet era, very specific information about most individuals is available, and not all of it is flattering. So think twice before uploading that picture; it may be there forever.

Who Makes What, by Ethnicity and Sex

As just noted, there are indeed ethnicity- and sex-based differences in income, not just in the contemporary U.S. but in every society in history. According to some estimates,[15] adjusted for cost of living, the group of people who live

---

[14]Google has developed famously eccentric questions (http://online.wsj.com/article/SB10001424052970204552304577113003705089744.html) for applicants, whose answers, they presumably think, give some information about productivity in doing what Google wants done.

[15]http://www.newgeography.com/content/002019-regional-exchange-rates-the-cost-living-us-metropolitan-areas

in the Western states have the lowest standard of living in the U.S., and those who live in the Northeast have the highest. The group of people in the sixth decade of their lives (that is, in their 50s) earn more than the group in the third decade. But of course the group membership that draws the most attention are differences by race, ethnicity, and sex. Two kinds of comparisons are particularly popular: what members of non-Hispanic white (NHW) males make compared to males from other groups, and what women make compared to men. Figures 6-3 through 6-5, based on data from the Current Population Survey of the U.S. Bureau of Labor Statistics, show annual earnings for various groups relative to NHW males and NHW females, and male/female earnings for the racial groups officially designated by the U.S. government (B = black, A = Asian, H = Hispanic, M = male, F = female).

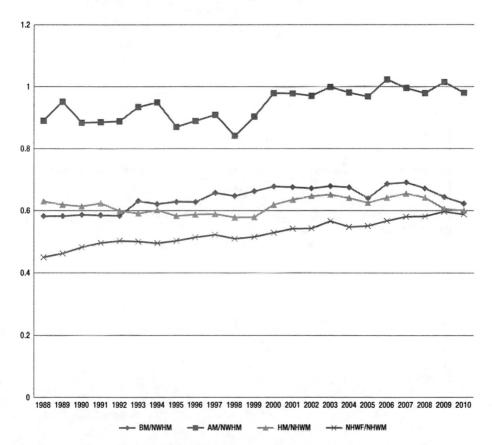

Figure 6-3. Annual income relative to non-Hispanic white males (NHWM).
Source: U.S. Bureau of Labor Statistics

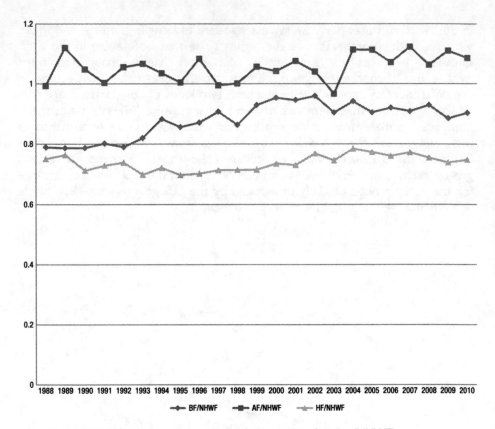

Figure 6-4. Annual income relative to non-Hispanic white females (NHWF).
Source: U.S. Bureau of Labor Statistics

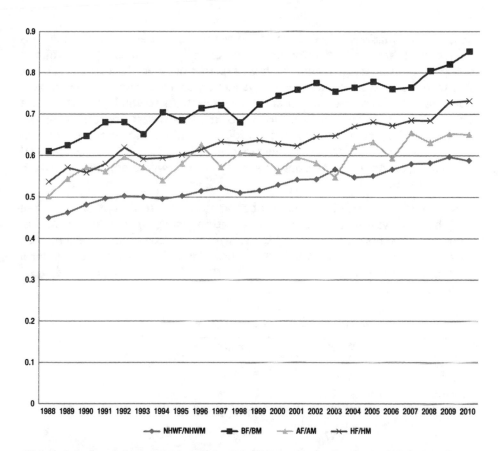

Figure 6-5. Female/male income within each ethnic group, by sex. *Source: U.S. Bureau of Labor Statistics*

The definition of *earnings* in the government statistics used here includes wage compensation, which is most of compensation for most people, as well as investment income. The figures collectively tell three stories. First, Asian males and females have approximately the same earnings as, respectively, NHW males and females. (Asian females actually slightly out-earn NHW females.) Second, women make less than men, although the ratios of female to male compensation within each racial/ethnic group have been rising. Third, black females have seen their earnings rise to very close to those of NHW females, although progress stopped in the early 2000s. Fourth, Hispanic males and females have seen their wages rise very little relative to those of NHW males and females.

So why do average earnings differ when we divide the population into groups by race/ethnicity or sex? Because statistical discrimination is really a reflection of underlying group average human-capital differences, there are really two possible explanations for groups to have average incomes that differ substantially: taste-based discrimination or human-capital differences.[16] Which of our two prime candidates provides the best explanation? Recall first the argument that taste-based discrimination is always vulnerable to elimination by competition, and then the counter-argument that vulnerability to elimination is not the same thing as actual elimination. Note also that Asians earn approximately the same as NHWs, so either any taste-based discrimination somehow exempts them, or Asians have far more human capital than NHWs but taste-based discrimination nonetheless brings their earnings down to approximately the level of that of NHWs.

However, taste-based discrimination becomes harder to accept once we see that there are vast differences in compensation *among different kinds of Asians*. Table 6-1 presents data from the U.S. Bureau of the Census on annual median earnings for different subgroups in the broader group that the U.S. federal government categorizes as Asian.[17] (The data do not distinguish between immigrants and native-born.)

Table 6-1. Median Earnings for Different Asian Subgroups

	Males	Females
Indians	$51,904	$35,173
Japanese	$50,876	$35,998
Chinese	$44,831	$34,869
Pakistani	$40,277	$28,315
Korean	$38,776	$28,403
Filipino	$35,560	$31,450
Thai	$32,879	$25,403
Vietnamese	$31,258	$24,028
Cambodian	$28,706	$21,911
Laotian	$26,664	$21,857
Hmong	$25,187	$20,237
All Asians	$40,650	$31,049
All workers	$37,057	$27,194

---

[16]This assumes that the differences do not result from other factors best classified as random, for example the tendency of a group to specialize for historical or cultural reasons in occupations that pay less. This may actually be a large contributing factor.

[17]Source: Terrance J Reeves and Claudette E. Pennett, *We the People: Asians in the United States* (Washington, D.C.: Bureau of the Census, December 2004), Figure 15.

Some of these Asian subgroups earn more than the median U.S. worker, and some earn less. The fact that median compensation varies so widely among different types of Asians is hard to square with a theory of pure taste-based discrimination if that means malicious prejudice against people who are racially or ethnically different from you. Why would the amount of taste-based discrimination be much greater against Laotians and Hmong than against Indians and Japanese? Such taste-based discrimination exists, in the contemporary U.S. as in every other society in history, but as noted earlier, competition is a potential remedy—those who discriminate in employment lose high-quality workers to those who don't.

Does human capital then explain earnings differences? Groups certainly do differ in the average amount of various human-capital components. Table 6-2 uses data from the federal National Center on Education Statistics to break down college graduating classes for different years in the U.S. from the 1970s to the 2000s by sex and race/ethnicity. In each case, a comparison is made between the percentage consisting of each group and that group's overall representation in the college-age population. If the figure is in bold, this indicates that that group's percentage of the college graduate pool in that year is meaningfully higher than its percentage of the overall population. If the figure is italicized, the group's percentage of college graduates is significantly less than its percentage of the overall population. If the number is neither in bold or italics it means that the percentage that group represents in the graduating class is not significantly different from its share of the population.[18] For example, in the class of 1977, NWH males were 47.7% of college graduates, which was significantly greater than their percentage of the population.

Table 6-2. Race/Ethnicity and Sex Groups as a Share of College Graduates

	NHWM	BM	HM	AM	NHWF	BF	HF	AF
1976–7	**0.477**	*0.027*	*0.011*	0.010	0.403	*0.036*	*0.009*	0.007
1988–9	0.460	*0.022*	*0.012*	0.019	**0.445**	*0.035*	*0.016*	0.018
1996–7	*0.344*	0.029	0.022	**0.028**	**0.424**	0.052	*0.031*	**0.031**
2003–4	*0.318*	0.031	0.037	**0.030**	**0.415**	0.062	*0.041*	**0.036**

Source: National Center on Education Statistics

In 1977, NHW males were the only group overrepresented among college graduates, whereas Asian males, Asian females, and NHW females had roughly equivalent shares of both the graduating class and the overall population. Black males and females and Hispanic males and females were both underrepresented.

---

[18]Here *significant* refers to statistical significance, at the 10% standard.

By 2003–4, Asian males and females and NHW females were overrepresented in this crude sense, whereas NHW, black and Hispanic males, and Hispanic females were underrepresented. As noted earlier, years of formalistic education are not the same thing as human-capital acquisition, not by a long shot. But it is striking that Asians have a higher propensity to go to college, while the wages for both Asian males and females have caught up to those for NHW males and females for the data depicted in Figures 6-3 through 6-5. Groups also differ significantly in their propensity to have children outside of marriage and to go on to graduate degrees. And the average woman works significantly fewer hours per week in the market than the average man. So it would not be a surprise at all if human capital told most if not all of the story of these group-based earnings differences, which would mean it is silly to speak of "overrepresentation" or "underrepresentation," unless groups are by design deprived of the opportunity to invest in human capital.

▓ **Note**   Compensation differences on average among groups do not by themselves indicate discrimination against members of those groups.

Economics Out There

6.1.   This headline writer[19] observes a seeming paradox: "Home Health Aides: In Demand, Yet Paid Little." Can you resolve this paradox?

6.2.   In this *Guardian* article,[20] we learn that the European Union wants insurance companies to charge men and women the same premiums for auto-accident insurance. What kind of discrimination were the companies engaging in? Is it any different, from the social point of view, from charging very young and very old drivers higher premiums than those in the middle age range, which insurance companies also often do?

6.3.   *The Weekly Standard* presents evidence[21] that Asian-Americans are harshly damaged by admissions policies at elite universities in the U.S. The ethics of such policies aside, if the charge is true, what kind of discrimination do you suppose it is?

---

[19]http://www.npr.org/2012/10/16/162808677/home-health-aides-in-demand-yet-paid-little
[20]http://www.guardian.co.uk/money/2004/sep/19/europeanunion.genderissues
[21]http://m.weeklystandard.com/Content/Public/Articles/000/000/015/463ufyzo.asp

6.4. An article[22] indicates that Norwegians on average are *much* better skiers than Danes and hence less likely to be injured. If Norwegian ski resorts were responsible for the costs of ski accidents on their property, would they be justified in charging higher ticket prices to people with Danish citizenship?

6.5. New York City manicurists charge women more than men,[23] despite that being illegal there. Why might they do this? (Hint: it may involve the analysis in Chapter 2.)

6.6. The *Wall Street Journal* has another article telling of classical musicians upset at their pay.[24] Playing classical music at a world-class level is a rarefied skill. Yet why might people who can do it make so little money compared with other world-class professionals? How valuable does the market consider this human capital to be, and why? Go to this *Reason* article[25] for some additional insight.

6.7. The British paper *The Daily Mail* reports in "Hair-raising ruling: Denmark says that both men and women's haircuts must cost the SAME PRICE"[26] that charging different prices by sex for hairstyle services will be banned.

   a. If it takes more time on average to style a woman's hair than a man's, do you think that is a good reason to have a price difference?

   b. What if women are willing on average to pay more than men for good-looking hair?

   c. What do you think will happen to the price men pay for hair styling because of this new rule? To the price women pay? To the number of hair salons and barber shops in Denmark?

---

[22]http://www.thelocal.no/page/view/norwegian-skiers-100-times-less-clumsy-than-danes#.UMoJt9chT4Q
[23]http://online.wsj.com/article/SB10001424052702304019404577420651136722954.html
[24]http://online.wsj.com/article/SB10001424127887323639604578369150649193988.html
[25]http://reason.com/archives/2012/10/05/classical-musicians-take-to-the-barricad
[26]http://www.dailymail.co.uk/news/article-2265959/Denmark-rules-men-womens-haircuts-cost-SAME-PRICE.html

The Middleman and the Entrepreneur

The Economy's Matchmakers and Little Revolutionaries

Up until now we have paid attention largely to abstract things—markets, information, competition, and so on. This chapter investigates the role of two particular actors in the economic drama who play starring roles in it: the middleman specifically, and the entrepreneur more generally.

The Middleman

What do Apple's iTunes, Walmart, and a literary or theatrical agent have in common? None of them directly produces things that consumers buy. Although two of them directly sell to consumers, one doesn't even do that, but as an agent merely negotiates with music or publishing companies that will eventually sell the work produced by writers or actors to the public.

To think about what these people do, imagine what would have to be done if they *weren't* there. If Walmart (and, just to make the argument more persuasive, all other retail stores) disappeared, consumers would still like to buy microwave ovens, hammers, and patio furniture. There would still be companies that wanted to stake claims to scarce resources to make these things in response to this demand. But now it would be up to the companies and the consumers themselves to find each other. A consumer interested in buying a microwave would have to seek out manufacturers and then either go to one of its retail stores or use its mail-order service to get the microwave he wanted. Could such a thing be done? Almost certainly. Could it be done at lower cost than the current system centered around Walmart and other retail stores? Almost certainly not.

Suppose you are new to Hollywood, and no one has ever heard your name. You certainly want studios or theater groups to hear of it. You may not know where to audition for the roles you are interested in or who the right people to contact are for someone with your specific thespian human capital. At the same time, the studios and theater groups simply do not have time to meet and audition everyone in Los Angeles who wants to be a star. If studio personnel spent all day long meeting and sifting through these people, many more people would have to be hired to hire the actors who actually perform in the movies. The result? The spontaneous order's creation of a different kind of work for the modern era of mass entertainment: the agent. The agent seeks out potential actors, decides to represent them (or not), and brings them to the attention of the people who need actors in their productions. The studios and directors then find it easier to cast their films, and would-be stars brand new to Hollywood find it easier to concentrate on acting rather than learning the mechanics of the movie business.

iTunes performs a similar function. Musicians record their own music, and iTunes merely sells it. The iTunes search system makes it easy for fans to find the music they want and even suggests music they might like based on what they have ordered in the past. (Other music-subscription services have similar systems, as does Amazon.com for books.) To be sure, unless the musicians directly retail their music to iTunes, then in this case there is more than one layer of activity between those who make the good (recorded music) and those who consume it (listeners/fans). In particular, many record labels (as they are still called, in deference to the vinyl records on which music used to be released) look for and sign music acts, record their music digitally, and then sell those wares to consumers—and also to aggregators such as iTunes, Spotify, or Rhapsody. The employees of these record labels—whether their job is going to clubs every night looking for the next big thing, deciding which acts to sign, or organizing promotional concert tours—do not themselves make music. And the musicians who do make it ordinarily do not sell directly to consumers.

▨ **Question 7.1**   Under what circumstances do you think musicians might choose to sell directly to consumers, and how you think they would go about making themselves known to fans?

Walmart, iTunes, and agents are all examples of *middlemen*, which we can define as someone who does not himself make the product that consumers buy, but buys it from others and sells it to the consumer. Sometimes, as in the case of a record company, the middleman adds value to the product, by organizing songs on CDs for example. But often, as in the other cases, the middleman simply offers the product unchanged to its final buyer.

The middleman has a very specific economic function: namely, to lower the costs of manufacturers and sellers finding one another. For buyers to find sellers and buy directly from them, and for sellers to find buyers and sell directly to them, is too costly because each side lacks knowledge about the other. Absent iTunes and record companies, consumers must find recording artists on their own—through word of mouth, going to clubs, or other relatively costly methods. Finding good music (in a context-dependent sense, that is, good to the particular fan) is not impossible this way, but it is costlier than allowing Apple and the labels to organize the available music in a format that is easy to access. The literary agent tells book companies which authors have which types of books available. (And then the bookstore or Amazon organizes the book companies' products for consumers.) The real estate agent makes it easy for house buyers to know what's for sale and lets sellers know who the buyers are and what they're willing to pay.

Many people react negatively to middlemen (sometimes to extreme degrees, as we will see later). They believe their role is unnecessary, that they only drive up costs. But middlemen are a huge part of any economy. Poor countries have traders who specialize in buying products in larger quantities in big stores in the countries' bigger cities and then reselling them in small villages or in those same cities from small carts. These people are usually known as peddlers. On their carts can be found fruits, sundries, textiles for sewing, shoes, and all manner of other goods bought in bigger quantities and resold in smaller ones. The retail establishments or wholesale stores where they buy their goods to begin with are like retail establishments in developed economies (whether physical, as in the case of Walmart, or virtual, as in the case of Amazon.com), and they are also middlemen. Indeed, as already hinted at, it is common for several layers of middlemen to lie between the maker of a product and its final purchaser, as in the case of a musician who is paid by the record company, which then pays money to iTunes, which then resells the digital music to the consumer.

In highly developed societies, there can be many middlemen for any particular good. Why do consumers buy this way instead of "cutting out the middleman"? Because it is a more effective way of buying, presumably—it lowers cost (in money or time), increases buying and selling options, or both. We have the seemingly paradoxical result that increasing the number of stages in getting a good from producer to consumer causes the costs of getting it to go down. But it is no paradox at all, once we remember that information is costly.

If a maker of a product sells directly to consumers, he must spend time seeking out customers, and the opportunity cost of this time is time not spent not devoting attention to increasing production and product quality. Customers in turn must spend time seeking out manufacturers, leaving them fewer resources to actually buy the product. Middlemen specialize in knowledge about where buyers and sellers are, and their compensation reflects this. (Recall the jam reseller earlier.)

Note The middleman exists so that sellers can specialize in production and buyers can save on search costs. The middleman, in turn, specializes in learning about buyers and sellers.

An article from 1920 headlined "Farmers to Fight Grain Middlemen: American Bureau Federation Discusses Plans for Cooperative Marketing" describes the federation's efforts to increase farmers' income by eliminating the middleman. The group's official name was actually the American Farm Bureau Federation, and in those days it was an organization of farmers that sought to act collectively to increase the price they could get for their produce and provide information about farming techniques to its members. (It now also specializes in lobbying the government for special privileges in the manner discussed in Chapter 5.[1]) In particular, a leader of the group, J. R. Howard, was quoted as saying: "We plan to organize local grain interests in every State, so that the producers will have control of the grain until it reaches the manufacturer. This is a fight against the broker and the middleman." (The "brokers" actually were middlemen too.) The article goes on to indicate that such middlemen charged farmers $50 million a year for their services. As the quote suggests, the Bureau also sought to eliminate the speculator, but as we learned in Chapter 4, the speculator is only the deliverer of news, not the maker of it.

It is now the second decade of the 21st century, and despite the Farm Bureau's best efforts, grain middlemen are still with us. And this is not surprising, because they perform all manner of valuable functions that make food cheaper. First, many farmers produce in volume. With such wide geographic dispersion, going to the farmers to buy would be very costly for sellers of food such as bakeries, restaurants, and grocery stores (who manufacture nothing except the opportunity to buy conveniently and are thus middlemen themselves) to slog through as they searched for the products they wanted either to sell directly (groceries) or make into food (bakeries, restaurants). So the makers of grain store their grain in grain elevators, which keep track of every farmer's deposits of grain during harvest season and upon receiving

---

[1]The web site of the American Farm Bureau now describes it as the "unified national voice of agriculture." Most groups that lobby the government often claim to be the sole representative of some large and important group in society.

authorization to sell that farmer's grain package it with the grain of other farmers and sell it in larger quantities. Those who buy the grain may in turn sell it to other middlemen who deal in even larger quantities. Eventually it ends up in the hands of those with the transportation equipment to ship it in very large quantities across the nation or around the world, where it ends up on the grocery shelves or in a bakery backroom or restaurant kitchen.[2] The result? Measured as a percentage of our income, the amount we spend on food is less than it has ever been.

And yet at the same time, the percentage of the food dollar that goes to the farmer has declined, from $0.41 in 1952 to $0.21 in 2001. Where did the rest of it go? Some of it goes to advertising (which serves in part to inform consumers of what choices are available) and a very small amount of it goes to packaging—but most of it goes to people who stand between the farmer and the consumer, from the grain elevator all the way to the grocery store. This is not surprising, because in food systems all over the world, middlemen are part of the distribution system. In Africa, parts of which are among the poorest regions in the world and where farms are often very small, there may be three or four middleman between farmer and consumer.[3] As mud crabs produced in Bangladesh have become more popular in other parts of Asia, the fishermen sell (live) crabs to collectors, the collectors sell to fatteners, who mass the crabs and fatten them for 10–21 days, and the fatteners sell them to agents who gather them in even larger amounts and send them to the capital of Bangladesh, Dhaka, in preparation for export, whereupon exporters buy them in presumably even larger quantities and send them to retailers overseas.[4] (These overseas retailers too are middlemen.) Even in a poor country like Bangladesh, people are immensely clever in creating new chains of specialization to get things from where they are originally made to where they are wanted. The freeing up of farmers in China in the early 1980s to sell their crops privately instead of to the government led almost immediately to the spontaneous generation of middleman activity in the production of strawberries, and I would guess in all other crops else as well.[5]

---

[2] The dramatic improvements in the technology of container ships since the end of World War II has allowed farm-production activity to be disbursed across much greater distances. For example, it is possible to get summer fruit from New Zealand and Chile in American supermarkets in the winter.

[3] A.A. Enete, "Middleman and Smallholder Farmers in Cassava Marketing in Africa," *Tropicultura* 27 (2009): 40–44, 42.

[4] Zannatul Ferdoushi, Zhang Xiang-Guo, and Mohammed Rajib Husan, "Mud Crab (*Scylla* sp.) Marketing System in Bangladesh," *Asian Journal of Food and Agro-Industry* 3 (2) (2010): 248–265.

[5] For evidence on strawberries, see Wan Guowei, Abe Jun, Mohammed Munsur Rahman, and Zhao Hong, "An Analysis on Formation and Function of Farmer Middleman in Strawberry Production: A Case Study in XT Village of Hangzhou City, China," *Journal of International Farm Management* 4 (1) (June 2007): 1–17.

Despite the caution expressed in Chapter 4 on inferring the permanent inevitability of something from the fact that it exists right now, the fact that middlemen are found in the production of food throughout time and space suggests they are doing something valuable for society. The farmers in 1920 who wanted to avoid them were thus tilting at windmills. Middlemen exist in the getting of food from farmers to consumers precisely because it is efficient for people who make things to specialize in that and not so much in marketing and in searching for final consumers, and for consumers to be able to find large amounts of goods in one physical or virtual place. On the highways in Kansas, one sees many signs that say "One Kansas farmer feeds several hundred people, including you." True enough, in the sense that absent farmers, the only way people could eat would be to grow their own food. But *absent everybody else in the food-distribution system who stands between the farmer and the people who eat,* his food would be much more expensive, consumers would thus consume less of it, and farmers would live much worse.

As usual, there is a hidden logic in the spontaneous order. Middlemen are people who make money by searching for (actually, by finding) more efficient ways to get stuff from those who make it to those who want it. Middlemen can discover ways to package foodstuffs in amounts that are cheaper to transport per unit. They specialize in having backup sources of supply (either other farmers or other middlemen somewhere in the middle of the distribution chain) if there are problems growing in one particular region due to weather, war, or some other reason. And they can use the price system to tell them where demand is suddenly higher and suddenly lower, enabling the shifting of resources from lower- to higher-valued uses. All this happens because they make money doing so, and indeed it is the opportunity to make that money that causes middlemen to sprout up to begin with.

Note   Consider the overlap between what these middlemen do and what speculators do; middlemen must frequently speculate about where things are likely to be found and where they are likely to be desired. Our intrepid traders who took wheat from X to Y both geographically and across time were middlemen too.

Financial Middlemen

One of the most important classes of middlemen in any economy of any level of sophistication—be it ancient Rome, medieval Venice, or modern America—is that of the middlemen for funds, otherwise known as the *finance industry*. Imagine you are someone with a great idea. To bring your ideas to market will take a great deal of cash right now. Research on production technology, on consumer preferences, and on locations for production has to be conducted, factories have to be built, employees will have to be hired. But as great as you are convinced your idea is (and as Chapter 4 shows, competition will be the judge of that), money is the one thing you lack. That is all right; there are plenty of people with lots of money sitting around doing nothing. But where are they? You could go out and try to find them, perhaps by knocking on every door in the city and asking people if they have any money to spare and if so are willing to invest it with you. But it would be much easier to go to a bank, or even a venture-capital fund (which pools money the way food distributors pool foodstuffs) and ask them instead.

There are two reasons for this. First, it's easy. Banks, venture-capital firms, and other financial middlemen spend money to make themselves known to people who have promising ideas. This saves you what we call *search costs*. Second, they know what they are doing compared to some random guy whose door you just knocked on. They have specialists who guide them on which ideas are better and worse, which would-be recipients have well-thought-out business plans, and so forth. There are no sure things of course; venture-capital firms make bum investments all the time. (Banks are immunized against this risk to some degree by the fact that they insist on collateral, which they can seize if the loan payments are not made.)

What we have here is a classic middleman. It is the function of banks, venture-capital firms, and every other element of the financial industry to match people with ideas and no money to people with money and no ideas. For each side of that transaction, it would be very difficult to find the other. Thanks to the existence of financial middlemen, they don't have to. Even the ordinary bank customer who simply wants to borrow money to buy a car or home benefits from this institution. By investigating how likely you are to pay the money back after looking at your credit report (in other words, by engaging in statistical discrimination), the bank will offer an interest rate that reflects the expected cost of providing you with funds that otherwise would go to some-one else. And the standard middleman benefits are still there. The would-be homebuyer need not wander around cup in hand, looking for someone who happens to have the money he needs. The bank collects funds from many depositors, pays them an interest rate to persuade them to forgo the use of their money for a period of time, and lends that money at a somewhat higher rate to people who want to use it to consume (buy cars or homes) or invest (in their own business ideas). Each depositor has no idea what happens to the funds he deposited, and each borrower has no idea whom the funds bor-rowed came from. Indeed, given the electronic nature of modern banking, the idea of borrowed money belonging to some particular depositor doesn't even make sense.

The bank collects money from some people and lends it to others and in so doing lowers the cost of borrowing, therefore creating opportunities that would otherwise not exist. It is a classic middleman, from the giant global banking company Citibank on down. Indeed, a revolutionary development of recent years has been the opposite of Citibank: microlending,[6] which was originally developed by a man named Mohammed Yunus[7] to lend money to the poor of Bangladesh who did not have access to credit. Most of his borrowers were women, and just as he thought they would, many were able to succeed without the collateral and connections that traditional borrowers there use in dealing with traditional lenders. Similar activities have spread to the U.S., with companies like Kiva and Kickstarter providing a way to match people looking for funds and people who have them, but on a much smaller scale than in the typical bank. This is a powerful response of the spontaneous order to the emergence of the Internet, and an indication too of the importance of financial middlemen.

This in turn is strongly suggestive of what is given up once such middlemen begin to be regulated in the same way many emergent social institutions are. Such regulations may or may not achieve their avowed goal, but they will surely raise the cost of doing business—of matching up those with dreams and those with the resources to make them happen. Note finally that we can match up the middleman role of finance with its important role in speculation by noting that much investment in embryonic businesses is highly uncertain. People who want to perform this financial middlemen function must have an incentive to seek out information on which investments are likely to be the most profitable, and it follows that they should avoid having artificial incentives to make loans that are likely to go bad.

▨ **Note**   Financiers—investment banks like Goldman Sachs, commercial banks like Citibank, venture-capital firms, hedge funds, and so on—are largely middlemen. They marry people with ideas or goals—but not many resources—to people with lots of resources but without many promising options for what to do with them.

The Middleman in Society

Given the essential function that middlemen perform, the way they have often been seen in the public eye is unfortunate. In fiction by such distinguished writers as Shakespeare, Dickens, Balzac, and Dumas, the banker or financier is depicted as obsessed with borrowers' collateral, unimaginative, greedy, unfeeling, and even incompetent in any matters (love in particular) that do not involve money.[8]

---

[6]http://en.wikipedia.org/wiki/Microcredit
[7]http://en.wikipedia.org/wiki/Muhammad_Yunus
[8]For a survey of how many authors of fiction depict bankers, see Johnson Brigham, *The Banker in Literature* (Charleston, SC: BiblioBazaar, 2009).

A compelling example of the middleman is provided by the experience of R. A. Radford, who was a trained economist by the time he joined the military during World War II. He was taken prisoner and held in a German POW camp. After returning, he wrote a scholarly article about his experience. One aspect of life in the camp that caught his attention derived from the fact that all prisoners were eligible for weekly packages from home and the Red Cross. The Red Cross packages contained uniform amounts of canned milk, jam, butter, biscuits, sweets, and cigarettes. Some prisoners also got clothing, toiletries, and cigarettes from home. Almost immediately, a trade, particularly in cigarettes for food, developed. This is not surprising; demand for any good is context dependent, and not everybody smokes or is a fan of canned milk. If everyone starts out with the same goods, but doesn't have the same tastes, opportunities arise for people to become better off through trade (a small model of the entire economy).

But which people like which goods? That information is costly. Quickly traders developed who made it their business to find out the best place to get surplus amounts of things from people who didn't want them so much in exchange for things they wanted more, which the traders had acquired from other people. Seen from the point of view of the middleman developed in this chapter, these people were clearly doing the prisoners a favor. But were they admired for their hard work and ingenuity, as a high-tech entrepreneur might be? Hardly. In Radford's account:

> Taken as a whole, opinion was hostile to the middleman. His function, and his hard work in bringing buyer and seller together, were ignored; profits were not regarded as a reward for labor, but as the result of sharp [i.e., devious] practices. Despite the fact that his very existence was proof to the contrary, the middleman was held to be redundant.[9]

And it is often like this. People with no practical experience in buying and selling are convinced that the middleman markup is pure social waste, gouging simply because one has the opportunity to. The Soviet Union's first dictator Vladimir Lenin viewed middlemen as parasitical and exploitive, even though they reappeared almost immediately when, because of economic collapse brought on by his policies, Lenin was forced to loosen control over exchange of goods and services among people in 1921. A key belief of the populist movement at the tail end of the 19th century in the U.S. was that middlemen connived to force farmers to accept lower prices for their output, and that farmers could do better by cutting them out. (This belief was very similar to

---

[9]R.A. Radford, "The Economic Organisation of a P.O.W. Camp," *Economica* 12 (48) (November 1945): 189–201.

the hostility noted earlier of the American Farm Bureau to "middlemen" and "brokers".)

In feudalistic Japan, there were four social classes. Samurai warriors were at the top, farmers and fishermen second, artisans who made consumption goods (clothing, eating utensils, tools, and so on) were in the third tier, and mere merchants were at the bottom. There, as in so many times and so many places, merchants were thought of as parasites who added nothing and merely lived off the work of others. They were not allowed to interact with members of the other classes except for clear business reasons, and for many centuries were segregated in their own parts of town. (The great Chinese scholar Confucius, from whose work Japan probably got the idea, also relegated merchants to the bottom of four classes.)

Occasionally, this condemnation reaches alarming levels. Violent and nonviolent targeting of stores owned by members of ethnicities vastly overrepresented (in the statistical sense) in merchant activities—a phenomenon that economists call the *middleman minority*—has frequently occurred. The world is full of such minorities, who have chosen to specialize in middlemen merchant activity. They don't produce tangible goods but sell the produce of others, the availability of which they have discovered by looking for it. These minorities often encounter intense hostility from those who do not understand their indispensability. South Asians in East Africa (expelled previously by law in at least two countries in that part of the world), Korean merchants in New York City (the victims of boycotts),[10] and Chinese in Southeast Asia have been among the victims since the end of World War II.[11] Jews were relegated to finance in medieval Europe by laws that prohibited them from engaging in other activities and by contemporaneous Christian theological doctrines against charging interest. They often drew resentment because they were perceived as charging unjustifiably high interest rates. Especially in such ethnic contexts, middleman minorities are often seen as parasites, and indeed that word, along with *bloodsuckers* and other terms suggesting vermin in need of elimination, is applied to these groups all too often.

Such ignorance about the function of the middleman is both widespread and tragic. Even economists, before the revolutionary development of the theory of costly information, were inclined to believe that only actual "productive"

---

[10]http://www.city-journal.org/2011/21_1_nyc-koreans.html

[11]It is said that the Chinese in Indonesia, who are relatively prosperous and dominate merchant activity there despite their small share of the population, always have a packed suitcase—in case hostility suddenly breaks out against them and they need to evacuate their families in a hurry. Such an event did happen in 1998 after a financial crisis had broken out the previous year. Many Chinese-owned businesses were looted or burned, Chinese women were raped, and hundreds of people were killed, both Chinese and non-Chinese.

activity was valuable. A school of economists in France in the 18th century called the physiocrats[12] believed that all wealth was based on farming, fishing, and hunting, all of which depended on soil, the ultimate resource. Anything else—manufacturing or, especially, the mere reselling of goods produced by others—therefore did not add value. Even today, some modern economists, along with many in the broader public, distinguish between "useful" work such as manufacturing and the empty casino gambling that they perceive finance to be. But because the middleman's role is so essential, he always appears or reappears despite the risks of public disapproval. (The economist Walter Block has argued the one reason prices are higher in poor neighborhoods in the U.S. is that middleman merchants, especially those of different ethnicity from local residents, must be compensated for enduring local hostility.[13])

Whether it is people engaged in microfinance and crowdsourcing (discussed earlier), ancient traders from Phoenicia and Middle Age merchants from Italy who moved spices, cloths and metals at great risk across vast ocean distances, or George Bailey, the banker in the classic film *It's a Wonderful Life*, middlemen exist precisely because there is a demand for their services. In their absence society would be much poorer with regard to the decentralized knowledge they were not around to harvest, and therefore much poorer in general.

▒ **Note**   Middlemen are often seen as doing nothing more than marking up something produced by someone else, who did all the real work. The lack of understanding of their critical role in producing information has frequently fed a sometimes-dangerous hostility.

The Entrepreneur More Generally

The middleman is someone who performs the function of getting goods from where they are made to where they are used. By the time a middleman reaches the stage of Walmart or Bank of America, it may be hard to see where the original middleman opportunity was spied and seized. As it happens, the Bank of America was founded as the Bank of Italy by an Italian immigrant named Amadeo Giannini in San Francisco in 1904. It specialized in serving Italian immigrants who were turned down by other banks. (Note the example of competition addressing taste-based discrimination.) Giannini took the name Bank of America from one of the banks he bought during his rise. Walmart was founded by Sam Walton, who had accumulated human capital specific to the retail business as a worker at a J.C. Penney store and as a franchisee for two other stores. He learned how that business worked, combined it with

---

[12]http://en.wikipedia.org/wiki/Physiocracy
[13]Walter Block, *Defending the Undefendable* (Auburn, AL: Ludwig von Mises Institute, 2008).

his own unique insights about how it could work better, and his innovative approach led to a global corporation that saves consumers 25% on their food expenses and more on the purchases of some other items. (Note that lower prices raise one's standard of living just as surely as higher income does, a fact often forgotten in criticism of Walmart.) As we have seen, the economic term best applied to these giant ventures is *middlemen*. But they are mere examples of another broader type of economic actor, which we call the *entrepreneur*, a word that comes to English directly from French. It has the same etymological roots as *enterprise*, which *The Oxford English Dictionary* indicates combines the words for "between" (*entre*) and "to take" (the French verb for which is *prendre*, with a past participle of *pris*). So the original meaning of *enterprise* is to take something in hand, with the implication of controlling and directing it. That, it turns out, is also the economic function of the entrepreneur, whose role I now explore.

The Entrepreneur as Residual Claimant

Imagine that someone wants to open a small stationery store, where he will sell greeting cards, office supplies, and so on. He does some calculation and expects to incur the following expenses:

Workers: 3 @ $20,000/year = $60,000

Annual rent for storefront: $100,000

Annual expenses for merchandise: $50,000

Annual miscellaneous expenses (utilities, office supplies such as paper clips for his own use, and so on): $10,000

Total = $220,000

What is his goal? Economists often model business owners as having the goal of maximizing profit.[14] *Profit* is defined as revenues minus costs. I have purposely omitted revenues—the money the business brings in—from the figures just given for the stationery store. I will instead assume, properly, that when this person opens his business, its success is not a sure thing. I model this by assuming in particular that he doesn't know what his revenue will be. We do know the sum of his monetary costs: $220,000. How much profit he makes in monetary terms depends on what his revenue is. Let us assume that it turns out to be $270,000 per year. If we subtract monetary costs from this then he seems to be earning a profit of $50,000 ($270,000–$222,000) annually.

---

[14]Many people also reap the satisfaction of being their own boss, although no business owner can dictate the prices of the resources he needs, or dictate that consumers buy things at the prices he prefers. So in some sense even a business owner answers to others.

But we are neglecting at least one cost that is very important in terms of predicting his decision making but which does not show up in the figures yet: the opportunity cost of devoting himself to his new business. He had some other activity, probably a salaried job, that he must sacrifice to become his own boss. Let us suppose that he was an engineer, and his annual salary was $100,000. When we include this figure (as we should), his $50,000 in seeming profit turns into a $50,000 loss (ignoring any intrinsic value he attaches to running his own business.) At this point we must distinguish between *accounting profits* and *economic profits*. Accounting profits are defined as *revenues minus explicit monetary costs,* in other words *money in minus money out.* But the profits that are relevant for decision making, economic profits, are defined as *revenues minus all costs, including non-explicit, non-monetary costs.* In this example, the only non-explicit cost is the cost of the work the owner gives up, but it is a substantial one, enough to make him change his decision from "continue operation of this business" to "shut this business down."

▓ **Note**   Economic profits drive decision making, and these profits are defined relative to what the entrepreneur would earn elsewhere if he did not engage in his venture. But a company (a farm, for example) can earn profits in an accounting sense even as farming as a whole may not generate any economic profits, and hence not induce other people to enter the farming business.

What level of revenue would be enough to persuade him to continue operating the business? Any level that fully covers all costs. If we add the $100,000 opportunity cost of the owner's engineering work to the explicit monetary costs, we get a figure of $320,000 for economic costs. (Economic costs are all costs, explicit and non-explicit, that go into the calculation of economic profits.) Revenue of $320,000 would leave him indifferent between keeping the store open or not, and anything above that would cause him to keep operating the business.

But while revenue is uncertain, it is decisive in determining his compensation. If he was wildly pessimistic and actual revenue turns out to be $1,000,000, his economic profit equals $1,000,000—$320,000 = $680,000. If it turns out he was not wildly but merely mildly pessimistic, and actual revenue is $400,000, he earns $400,000–$320,000 = $80,000. And if it turns out that he was actually optimistic, and revenue is only $200,000, he generates an economic loss of $120,000, and the business shuts down (as it does for any amount of revenue less than $320,000).[15]

---

[15]Note that because of the way economists define losses, any losses mandate shutdown. In practice, the owner may be willing to stick it out, but this willingness is encoded into the idea of his opportunity cost of time—economic losses mean that this is not the best use of these resources, including his time. Accounting losses can be withstood for a time, but not economic ones.

So, the owner's compensation varies widely, depending on how the prior uncertainty that existed before the establishment of the business plays out. This is in stark contrast to his employees. Assuming the business doesn't fail (which of course it might), their compensation is the same rain or shine: $20,000 a year.[16] If the business does fail, the owner of course loses as well. He and his workers will both have to earn their opportunity cost by engaging in their next-best labor-market action. If the owner has made long-term commitments to secure the resources he needs to operate his store (in particular if he signed a long-term lease), he's still on the hook for these payments regardless of whether his business closes.

In general, the owner is facing much more uncertainty and risk than his workers. Indeed, uncertainty is what generates profit opportunities in the first place. He thought he saw an opportunity—and grabbed it. But if his seizing of this opportunity is easily duplicated by others, such as our jam vendor from before, temporary profits are eliminated by the movement of resources from where they are earning less to where they are earning more. Nonetheless, he saw something others didn't, and it is only a continual tide of these new (uncertain) opportunities that prevents the indifference principle from being in operation all the time, everywhere. As discussed in Chapter 4, those who possess information about unexploited opportunity that turns out to be correct make money, and those whose information turns out to be incorrect lose money. Our stationery-store owner is the very example of this. He thinks he can make money by using resources in a different way from how they were used before, but he doesn't *know* that he can. And the risks that he is wrong are not small. There are lots of claims in cyberspace about the failure rate of small businesses, and solid information is hard to find. But one estimate based on rigorous research[17] suggests that 36% of businesses founded in 1992 were gone by the end of 1994, and 71% of them were gone by the end of 2002—within 10 years.

Profit—which comes from the exploitation of opportunity—is often fleeting. The only reason there is any profit at all is because there is a constant tide of new ideas and improvements and seizing of these previously unseen opportunities. From the point of view of an individual entrepreneur, only a continuous flow of innovations insures that he continues to earn money, as with a Rockefeller or Jobs. If your innovation is easily duplicated, in contrast, profits are competed away.

---

[16]Actual compensation can be more complicated than this. Many business owners, to give their employees a very direct interest in the success of the business, will adjust their compensation according to that success, either through raises in good times or giving them a share of profits as part of their pay.

[17]http://smallbiztrends.com/2008/04/startup-failure-rates.html

Economists refer to this relatively risky nature of the owner's compensation by calling the entrepreneur (the person who takes a perceived opportunity in his hands and acquires command over resources to try to exploit it) a *residual claimant. Residual* just means "what's left over." In this case, it means what's left over after all other resource owners have obtained the compensation necessary to persuade them to allow the resources they own—their land, time, etc.—to be used for the purpose the entrepreneur wants to use them for. $100,000, for example, is what is necessary to persuade the owner of the storefront to rent it to the entrepreneur so that it is used for selling stationery instead of selling fast food. $20,000 is the amount necessary to persuade each worker to participate in the selling of stationery rather than doing whatever he would be doing otherwise. So, after the owners of these resources have received compensation necessary to secure their cooperation in the entrepreneur's idea, the entrepreneur is only left with the residual—big, small, or negative.

Being exposed to this greater uncertainty, it seems reasonable to suppose that the owner would insist on some measure of control over how decisions regarding the business are made. And indeed he does. It is he who makes the rules (but only after knowing that the owners of the other resources he needs, especially his employees, will consent) about opening and closing hours. It is he who makes the rules (but only after paying a price that the vendors from whom he buys his wares are willing to accept) about what merchandise will be sold. It is he who makes the decision about the terms under which he will or will not offer refunds to customers. And so on. The nature of business is that *owners are exposed to uncertainty in their compensation in exchange for greater control over how the business is operated.* This is the essence of the bargain in the idea of the entrepreneur as residual claimant.

Our stationery store, in which one owner really does make these decisions himself, is an obvious example of this bargain at work. But many companies are not small storefronts with single owners. They are large, perhaps multinational corporations that have leaders (known as presidents or chief executive officers). Individuals do not own these businesses in the same way that our hypothetical stationery-store owner does. Rather, they are owned by many stockholders.

Here it is worth briefly discussing what exactly *stock* is. One can think of it as a piece of paper (although most stock now merely exists as ones and zeros in a computer) that is issued by a company and bought by individuals who think it is worth buying. Traditionally, this piece of paper entitles them to a share of the company's profits, paid four times a year as a *dividend.* In exchange, they literally own a portion of the firm and can contribute to decisions on every detail about how it is run. To be sure, for many large companies there are millions of shares of stock outstanding, and so most holders of that stock exercise no meaningful control over its decision making. Indeed, even large stockholders may have little role to play in day-to-day decision making. Instead, the stockholders delegate this decision-making power to the officers of the firm—the chief executive officer, chief financial officer, assorted vice presidents, and the other elements of the company's management. But even here the ultimate word is that of the stockholders. If the existing management team is seen to have run the business in such a way that profits are not as high as they could be, stockholders can and frequently do band together—perhaps under the leadership of someone with a lot of money who can buy a lot of shares of stock in an attempt to make his voice heard—to try to change the way the business is run. They may demand ending unprofitable product lines, closing surplus factories, acquiring businesses that should be acquired, whatever.

■ **Note**   Stock shares are shares of ownership in the company that issued the stock. Usually the reason for owning stock is hope that its price will increase, which will happen if the company is run profitably. Ultimately, through the ability to band together, stockholders can direct these companies, although they do not usually exercise day-to-day control.

Although often disparaged as "corporate raiders," it is the function of such large shareholders to put their money behind their belief in the information they have harvested that the corporation is underperforming. They thus perform a critical function in allowing shareholders to assert meaningful control over the company. So, even though there is a degree of separation between ownership and decision making in a large corporation that is not there in our stationery store, it is still fundamentally true that the owners exercise ultimate control.

The Entrepreneur as Social Reorganizer

Let us take a broader, society-wide perspective on what our stationery-store owner has done in opening his business. Previously, all the resources he has now claimed were being used for some other purpose (perhaps low-value). His workers were working elsewhere (or unemployed), the storefront was being used for some other business (or was idle), and the office supplies and merchandise that would otherwise end up in his store ended up someplace else. What this means is that society's fixed (at any moment in time) stock of resources has been moved from some other uses to a new one. Because the entrepreneur has presided over this reallocation of resources, we can also refer to him as a *social reorganizer—somebody who moves resources from some uses that he judges to be less valuable to society to uses that he believes to be more valuable to society.* Society is a little bit different after he opens this business than it was before, as indeed it will be again if the business fails, or if it expands (perhaps he opens several stores and even eventually develops a regional, national, or global franchise) and claims even more resources. In short, our stationery-store owner is a mini-revolutionary, and his revolution is carried out without firing a shot, purely through securing voluntary cooperation (through perceived potential mutual gain) of other resource owners.

Because of incomplete, costly information, there are always ways to do things better than they are being done now. The entrepreneur is the agent of attempted change, and if his venture succeeds he leaves society better than he found it. This is true whether at the obvious, large-scale level—for example Henry Ford revolutionizing freedom of movement by lowering the costs of getting from point A to point B with his Model T—or at a more modest level, such as our stationery-store owner giving his customers a place to buy his wares that is more useful for them than the alternatives they had before. Successful entrepreneurship, on a small or large scale, rearranges resources and improves society. Once those improvements accumulate, the total amount of change can be astonishing, as we will see in Chapter 9.

Answers to In-Text Questions

7.1. If it becomes possible for musicians on their own to discover places where large numbers of people who will buy their music are likely to "be," either physically or virtually, they will tend to do their marketing themselves. I have attended free concerts where CDs are sold, and music can presumably be marketed either by the song or by the whole CD in particular places on the Internet. It is easy for musicians to announce at their concerts that they can be visited on Facebook or Twitter, and their music can again be sold there. At least temporarily, the Internet has allowed sellers of this particular product to go around the traditional middleman, which is something that cuts against the general trend over the centuries of more and more middleman and specialization.

Economics Out There

7.1. A screenwriter gave up the Hollywood life to move to Nebraska and sell, of all things, gongs.[18] What resources did he rearrange? How did he want to use them? What was his goal?

---

[18]http://www.npr.org/2012/03/04/147791832/a-hollywood-writers-second-act-gongs

7.2. Read this *Businessweek*[19] article. What is the entrepreneurial innovation, the rearrangement of resources, going on in this experiment? Critics assert that the spread of "concierge medicine" may lead to unequal access to health care resources based on income. Keeping in mind that it is generally true that greater wealth allows people to have more choices, is this criticism an important one to keep in mind in thinking about the ethics of this economic experiment?

7.3. Here's an interesting article on banking.[20] Again, identify the entrepreneurial innovation going on. Do you think Walmart and Amazon are making your local bank obsolete? In the end, how will we know?

---

[19]http://www.businessweek.com/articles/2012-11-29/is-concierge-medicine-the-future-of-health-care
[20]http://www.forbes.com/sites/johntamny/2012/10/14/amazon-com-exposes-the-fraudulent-nature-of-the-2008-bank-bailouts/

Time and Risk

Some Economics of Now and Later

No matter what it is that people want, it sometimes seems that there is inevitably a market for it. Got an old cell phone you want to unload but don't want to haggle? Done.[1] Interested in a paternity test but don't want to go to a doctor to get one? Get it from the paternity testing truck.[2] Got a rambunctious cat but are too frail or otherwise unwilling to corral it yourself? There is someone in New York[3] who will, for a fee of course, do it for you. So perhaps we should not be surprised that there are extensive markets that allow people to engage in trade across time. Such markets, which are among the oldest in continuous existence, sprout up because people with different goals in certain circumstances find it worthwhile to forgo using their resources now or to acquire the use of resources now that they don't currently possess. To understand how some of these markets function, this chapter discusses the ideas of investment, trading across time, attitudes of individuals toward risk, and the markets that these opportunities and attitudes generate.

Investment

Investment is, along with *capital*, one of the most widely used yet inconsistently defined terms in economics. But many different things that we think of as "investment" really boil down to the same thing, which is *the sacrifice of an*

---

[1] http://marginalrevolution.com/marginalrevolution/2012/12/vending-machine-auction-markets-in-everything.html
[2] http://newyork.cbslocal.com/2012/08/15/whos-your-daddy-truck-offers-answers-with-dna-tests/
[3] http://www.nytimes.com/2012/02/18/nyregion/jordana-serebreniks-unusual-vocation-cat-catcher.html?_r=2&

opportunity now for what one believes to be a better opportunity in the future. This simple category of action encompasses a phenomenally large range of things. A company that earns revenue now may choose to distribute it to various groups of people now. It may choose to pay higher wages to its workers in hopes that it can keep them. Or, an individual owner may choose to take it as profit, which he may then spend on his own consumption. In the case of a publicly owned corporation, the management of the firm may correspondingly choose to distribute higher dividends to the firm's stockholders. But on the other hand, the owner or managers of the firm may believe that the better action to take is not to use those revenues now in the ways just described, but to spend them on increasing the productive capacity of the firm so that it will earn even more revenues in the future.

The obtaining of another degree at the margin—high school, bachelor's, graduate, or professional—also involves giving up opportunities now, because that degree must be paid for and because to get a college degree, one generally chooses for now not to work full-time. This acquisition of human capital results (it is hoped) in future income that is sufficiently higher to justify the sacrifice made now. Individuals may choose to take some of their pay and use it not for consumption now but to buy various financial instruments, such as stocks and bonds, or do something more prosaic like putting the money in the bank. For some reason, when an individual does the latter we call it *saving*, whereas when he does the former we generally call it *investing*. But from the point of view of the economy as a whole, the actions are really the same: resources that could have been spent now on consumption are instead put aside so that more consumption is available later. This is the general framework of what investment is.

▓ **Note** Investment is any sacrifice of opportunities now in the hope of using the resources saved to generate more opportunities later. This is true for individuals investing in higher education, companies investing in research and development, or governments building infrastructure that will last a long time.

Interest Rates

But if one puts part of one's salary in the bank or in the stock market, as already noted an opportunity cost must be paid—the action of using that salary to consume now. If a business forgoes the distribution of revenue now, the people who would have received that revenue must be willing to accept that they will not in fact get it now. So, to persuade people to take these actions, there must be found an amount of potential wealth in the future sufficiently large to convince people to forgo the sure opportunity now.

How would this work? Think about a simple loan. I lend you $1,000, and you pay me back $1,100 a year from now. This loan thus has an annual interest rate of 10%. We have also clearly engaged in exchange, just as people do in the job market or the market for paper clips. But what have we traded? You are getting $1,000 right now, and I am getting $1,100, but not until a year from now. In other words, the lender gives up the opportunity to buy $1,000 worth of things now in exchange for the opportunity to buy $1,100 worth of things in a year. The interest rate we agree on is thus an indicator of a price—in this case, the price of wealth right now in terms of wealth in the future. In general, if the interest rate is i% (for example, 10%), this means that to get $1 today requires giving up $$(1 + i)$ a year from now (that is, $1.10). If the rate is 20% instead of 10%, getting your hands on $1 today requires you give up $1.20 a year from now. Present wealth, in other words, is now more expensive in terms of future wealth. The economics jargon of what an interest rate reflects is that it is an *intertemporal price—the price at which wealth across different periods of time trades.* (*Intertemporal* just means "across time.") Note that this means that a phrase one sometimes hears—that the interest rate is the price of "money"—is simply wrong. The price of a dollar is just a dollar; why would anyone give up dollar and get back less than that? Rather, in a sense, the interest rate is the price of money (or of any form of wealth, technically—many ancient societies defined interest rates in terms of grain) *now*.

There is a market for loans, and this market functions like any other. As the price of getting a loan—the interest rate—goes up, the amount that potential lenders are willing to supply goes up. (The supply curve for loans, in other words, is positively sloped.) The law of demand is also in effect in the market for loans, so that the higher the interest rate, the less potential borrowers are willing to borrow. The interest rate is just another equilibrium price—in this case, the price that coordinates the willingness of borrowers to borrow and the willingness of lenders to lend. The market must—and will—find a rate that is sufficient to persuade people with wealth now, but no perceived high-value uses for it currently, to offer it, and to persuade people with potentially high-value uses for it, but no wealth now, to offer wealth later (principle plus interest) that they expect to earn from that wealth they borrow now. Interest, in other words, is the price that allows people with resources but no ideas for future productivity (lenders) and people with wonderful ideas but no resources (borrowers) to engage in what they expect to be mutually beneficial exchange. (Recall that this phrasing was also used in the description of the finance industry.)

▨ **Note** An interest rate is the price, in terms of wealth to be repaid later, of obtaining wealth now. (Or from the lender's point of view, the price in terms of wealth received later, of giving up control over wealth now.)

Like any price, the price at which wealth in different periods of time trades differs for a variety of reasons, because of where both the supply curve and demand curve are located. Note also that the market for loans is really many different markets, depending on the term of the loan. One can borrow over a very short term—three months, say—or a very long term—30 years, the longest term over which the U.S. government borrows, and also a very common term for home loans. (During World War I, the British government took out loans to be paid back in 100 years.) In general, if you're willing to lend to someone and give him longer to pay it back, the chances that he will default go up. In addition, your money, which has alternative uses, is locked up for a longer period of time. As a general rule, therefore, longer-term interest rates tend to be higher than shorter-term rates. In addition, poor credit risks have a higher probability of default, and the interest they are charged must cover this probability. This is true whether they are companies with iffy prospects (who must pay high interest rates when they borrow from financial institutions or issue bonds) or individuals with bad credit ratings, who end up at payday lenders instead of borrowing at lower rates from conventional banks.

People attempting to get their very small company started may be charged high rates, for example, if the company is seen as highly speculative, but they may be willing to pay those rates if they are convinced of the value of their idea. In addition, the more easily risk can be spread around and insured against, the more willing people are to supply loans, and the lower interest rates will be. People who can put up collateral, or who live in societies with highly developed credit markets, get credit supplied more readily, that is, they pay lower interest rates. Indeed, much of human progress is partly creditable to the creation of social institutions in general, and financial institutions and instruments in particular—from metal coins to banking to futures contracts to modern "credit default swaps"—that have allowed people to lend with more confidence. It is not surprising that interest rates on the highest-quality loans were often 33% in antiquity, yet rates on such loans in the most stable countries have fallen relentlessly over time, from 10–15% percent in medieval times to a good deal less than 5% now. This democratizing of the access to credit in turn has increased the number of people who can engage in entre-preneurial experimentation and therefore has increased the amount of such experimentation and social progress.

It is also worth noting that a lender expects that the interest rate he gets on his loan will cover *inflation*, which is the decrease in buying power of his money over the course of the loan. If inflation is 5% a year, and he charges 4% on a $1,000 loan to be repaid in 1 year, the $1,040 he gets back actually buys less than the thousand dollars he lent out. If he expects inflation to be 5% and he charges 5%, then what he gets back buys exactly the same amount of stuff as it did before—stuff that costs $1,000 when he lent out the money costs $1050 when he is repaid. But this means that he gets no advantage from giving up wealth now in exchange for wealth in the future. What we say in this case is that the *real interest rate*—the rate he gets over and above the rate of inflation expected to occur over the course of the loan—is *zero percent*. Because having wealth to lend right now is valuable, we would expect him to get more than just an inflation adjustment for giving up that wealth now. And so the actual interest rate that one pays is really implicitly divided into two parts. One part is this real rate, which is compensation for advancing wealth to somebody else right now. Like provision of anything valuable, provision of wealth now has value that ought to be compensated—in this case, by the provision of more wealth later. The proportion of the interest rate that compensates the lender for the depreciation in the value of his money over the course of the loan is the *expected inflation* component. The formula for the interest rate actually paid (called the nominal interest rate) is thus:

Nominal interest rate = Real interest rate + expected inflation rate

Thus, in high-inflation societies, interest rates tend to be very high, just to cover the fact that money is losing value very rapidly. These high interest rates are part of the reason high inflation destroys lending markets, which I discuss in more detail in Chapter 11.

▓ **Note**   The actual interest rate paid on a loan will be higher than what the lender expects the inflation rate to be over the course of the loan. Only after the lender is compensated for this expected depreciation in the buying power of money can he earn a real interest rate, which, possessing wealth now desired by the borrower, he will. (How high the real interest rate is is a function of the supply of and demand for loans.)

Risk and Risk Trading

As has been emphasized repeatedly, one of the most important, if not the most important, economic phenomena is that of costly, dispersed information. Looked at another way, this simply means that the future is difficult to predict. Just as people have different attitudes toward certain kinds of food or toward what (if anything) they want to watch on television, they have different attitudes toward risk. Risk means exposure to multiple possible outcomes, some better and some worse. Some people are willing to pay a lot to avoid it, some are not much bothered by it, and a few even go out of their way to seek it. This difference in attitude is known as *risk preference*.

To think about different attitudes toward risk, including your own, conduct the following thought experiment. Suppose I offer you the following bet: flip a coin, and if it comes up heads, I pay you $100. If it comes up tails, you pay me $100. If you are not willing to take that bet, you have some degree of what is known as *risk aversion*, which means that you are unwilling to take a "fair bet." What is a fair bet? It is one for which the expected value is zero. In this case, you have a 50/50 chance of winning $100 and a 50/50 chance of losing $100. In the language of probability, the expected value of this bet is zero.[4] Some people will take a bet in which losing requires that they pay $100 to the professor while winning means the professor pays them $120. Others will not even take that bet, but will take one in which winning means receiving $200, and losing still means only paying $100. The more you have to receive in the event of winning to be willing to tolerate the chances of losing $100, the more risk-averse you are. If you are willing to take a bet in which losing means you pay the professor $100 and winning means you will get $99 (or less), you are said to be *risk-loving* or *risk-preferring*. In the case that you are willing to take a fair bet but are not risk-loving, in other words you will not take a bet with negative expected value, you are said to be risk-neutral.

People have all sorts of different attitudes toward risk, and these differences (as with all differences among humans) generate opportunities for mutually beneficial trade. In this case, the phenomenon we are talking about is called *risk-trading*. Risk-trading happens when a person who is less willing to be exposed to risk pays someone who is more willing to be exposed to it to bear the risk for him. This is an extremely common phenomenon. There are two factors that make it possible. The first is that people have different risk preferences. If one person is very risk-averse, and another is less risk-averse or even risk-loving, the second person may be willing to bear the risk of some event in exchange for payment. (Often, as we will see, this payment only happens if the event generating the risk turns out well.)

The second way risk-trading can be enabled is if the party that chooses to bear the risk is able to capitalize on something called the law of large numbers. The law of large numbers basically means that the more events with the same risk an individual is exposed to, the more reliably he can predict his eventual gains or losses. If one flips a coin one time, there is a 50/50 chance one will get no heads at all. If one flips it twice, there is still a one in four chance of no heads, and one in eight if it's flipped three times. But if one flips it 1,000 times, the chances of having no heads are essentially zero, as are the chances of only getting heads 25% or less of the time. In fact, with 1,000 flips, one can be quite confident that the percentage of heads will be close to 50%.[5]

---

[4]In general, if an event has two possible outcomes with monetary outcomes A and B, the expected value of the event is $p_A A + p_B B$. In the example here, A is +100 and B is −100, whereas $p_A = p_B = 1/2$. A one-third chance of winning $200 and a two-thirds chance of losing $100 would also be a fair bet.

[5]Ironically, as the number of flips goes up the chances of getting exactly 50% heads goes down. The chance of getting exactly 50% with only one flip is one in two, whereas the chance of getting exactly 500 heads in 1,000 flips is very small. However, the chance of getting less than 25% heads or less than 25% tails with 500 flips is also very small, and the chances of getting somewhere between 480 and 520 heads is fairly high.

If one or both of these conditions exist, we expect to observe entrepreneurs creating ways to trade risk. One of the most obvious examples of how this is done is insurance. Assume that all houses are the same—that they are all worth $100,000 to the owners and that each house has a 0.1% (1 in 1,000) chance of being destroyed in a fire every year. Most people only own one house, and if it does burn down it is a catastrophe. If they are risk-averse, they are willing to pay more than the expected loss from a fire each year (0.1% × $100,000 + 99.9% × 0 = $100) to insure against this potential disaster. The more risk-averse they are, the more they are willing to pay in insurance premiums. The insurance company, in contrast, has many customers. In any given year, they may have more customers' homes than expected burned down, and in other years, fewer. But the more customers they have, and the longer the period of time we are considering, the more predictable their payouts become. So, if they charge a premium of $110 or $120, it is almost a license to print a small amount of money. The insurance business is simply an exercise in risk-trading between risk-averse customers and less risk-averse (because of the law of large numbers) businesses.

Question 8.1 Under what circumstances could the insurance companies charge $120 instead of $110?

Another example is the tort lawyer. You may have seen, either on late-night television or on the back of the phone book, lawyers who (often very aggressively) promise to represent clients in a way such that if the client wins nothing, the lawyer gets paid nothing. This system is called a *contingency fee*, and it means that the attorney takes a fixed fraction (often one-third) of whatever amount the attorney is able to recover, whether via an out-of-court settlement or at trial. If the client receives nothing, since one-third of zero is zero, the client pays nothing. The more he does receive, the more in dollar terms the attorney's fee is.

The client is in a similar position to the homeowner in the last example. He has only one case, and is thus exposed to a relatively large amount of risk. The attorney, in contrast, has many cases, and so his expected income over all of them may be relatively easy to predict. If the client paid his attorney by the hour, he would be exposed to the possibility that his legal fees would exceed the amount recovered, leaving him worse off than when he started. The outcome would be the worst if he went all the way to a trial verdict (so that the hours billed are likely to be the highest) and then recovered nothing. Such share payments in lieu of payment for hours worked are actually quite common. It is how real estate and entertainment agents are paid. In many developing countries (including Europe and the United States in earlier periods), farmers work land as sharecroppers—an arrangement in which the rent they pay is not a fixed amount but instead a share of the crops they are able to reap.

Other examples of risk-trading abound in any market economy. But for purposes of our discussion, the most significant example of risk-trading is the organization of the firm itself. Recall from the previous chapter that one of the models of the entrepreneur is as residual claimant. His pay depends entirely on the performance of the firm overall—a relatively risky scheme of compensation, especially for a new company at its most uncertain stage. The employees, in contrast, are exposed to risk primarily to the extent that the firm may fail. Even then, if they have alternative employment available to them, the consequences of being exposed to this risk may be less for them than for the owner, who may have a huge fraction of his wealth tied up in the business.[6]

So, the trade discussed earlier—the owner taking on more risk in exchange for control and for the potential to earn very high rewards—is also a form of risk-trading. This suggests that people who start and run businesses tend to have more tolerance for risk than people who work for salaries. Because the number of such people in any society may be a rather small percentage of the entire population, it may be rather important (via allowing those entrepreneurs who successfully discover and take advantage of valuable opportunities) to give that small slice of the population a reason to take those risks. If not, as we are about to see in Chapter 9, the future may not be what it could be.

▓ **Note**   Risk-trading is a key part of any economy. It is also the cornerstone of business creation, with the entrepreneur as residual claimant staking claim to the residual in compensation for bearing much of the risk of business failure.

Answers to In-Text Questions

8.1. The most obvious answer is that people who are willing to pay $120 to avoid an expected loss of $100 are more risk-averse than those who are only willing to pay $110 to avoid the same expected loss.

---

[6]Not always of course; many entrepreneurs already possess wealth from prior business ventures, and many employees, for reasons of highly specific human capital or generally depressed economic conditions, may actually have very poor alternatives to their current job.

Economics Out There

8.1. Sometimes the real boundaries between economic categories are fuzzier than depicted in the textbooks. A 1997 issue of *Businessweek* tells the story of a person in Silicon Valley who quit her job and took one as a receptionist with many responsibilities at a small technology company. She got a salary much smaller than in her previous job, but also a lot of company stock and options to buy more later at a guaranteed price. What kind of attitude toward risk do you think she had relative to someone who insists on being paid only in salary? Was she a residual claimant?

8.2. In his essay "On Usury," the writer Hilaire Belloc argued that we should distinguish between productive and unproductive loans, with only the former being a justified reason to charge interest. He provided an example of each type:

> Supposing a man comes to you and says: "There is a field next to mine which is a very good building site; if I put up a good little house on it I shall be able to let that house at a net profit—all rates, taxes and repairs paid—of £100 a year. But I have no capital with which to build this house. The field will cost £50 and the house £950. Will you lend me £1,000, so that I can buy the field, put up the house, and enjoy this nice little income?" You would presumably answer, "Where do I come in? You get your £100 a year all right; but you only get it by my aid, and therefore I ought to share in the profits. Let us go fifty-fifty. You take £50 every year as your share for your knowledge of the opportunity and for your trouble, and hand me over the other £50. That will be five percent on my money, and I shall be content."

> This answer, granted that property is a moral right, is a perfectly moral proposition. The borrower accepting that proposition certainly has no grievance. For a long time [theoretically, forever] you could go on drawing five percent on the money you lent, with a conscience at ease.

Now let us suppose that man comes to you and says: "I know the case of a man in middle age who has been suddenly stricken with a terrible ailment. Medical aid costing £1,000 will save his life, but he will never be able to do any more work. He has an annuity of £100 a year to keep him alive after the operation and subsequent treatment. Will you lend the £1,000? It will be paid back to you on his death, for his life has been insured in a lump payment for the amount of £1,000." You answer: "I will lend £1,000 to save his life, but I shall require of him half his annuity, that is £50 a year, for every year he may live henceforward; and he must scrape along as best he can on the remaining £50 of his annuity." That answer would make you feel a cad if you have any susceptibilities left, and if you have not—having already become a cad through the action of what the poet has called "the soul's long dues of hardening and decay"— it would be a caddish action all the same, though you might not be disturbed by it.

It seems therefore that there are conditions under which you may legitimately and morally lend £1,000 at five percent in perfect security of conscience, and others in which you cannot.

Is the latter loan merely an exchange of something valuable for something else also valuable, or is there more to it than that?

8.3. On his blog[7] at *The New York Times* web site, the economist Paul Krugman displays a chart showing the long-term trend in U.S. tariffs—they go up and down over time, but the general trend has been down. What does freer international trade do in terms of the reliability of supply of various resources? What does it do to the competitive risk faced by any individual businesses that compete with foreign firms and that get resources from them? Do you think freer trade over the centuries is one of those innovations alluded to in this chapter that has served to lower interest rates over the long term?

---

[7]http://krugman.blogs.nytimes.com/2009/11/07/us-tariff-history/

The Entrepreneur and Some Economics of the Future

Our Ever-Brighter Days, and How They Happen

Q: Is the future going to be better than the past?

A: It always has been.

It has probably never occurred to you to think about it, but the man who invented the snowblower is responsible for saving at least hundreds of lives. Shoveling snow is vigorous exercise, especially when done under the burden of several layers of winter clothing. It is quite an exertion for someone who is middle-aged or older and thus prone to heart disease. It used to be common in winter to read about people who suffered heart attacks while shoveling snow and died shortly thereafter if not immediately. But the invention of the snowblower changed all that. It allows people to do a necessary but histori- cally unpleasant chore with much less work. It is almost certainly true that the inventor of the snowblower, whom Wikipedia credits[1] as being Arthur Sicard of Quebec, did not create it or the successful company to market it with the goal of saving lives. Rather, he thought it would sell because people were looking for a tool to save them time and discomfort. So, in a sense the lives saved are a free benefit of his entrepreneurial experiment. It turns out more generally that entrepreneurs like Mr. Sicard are a prime if not the prime mover of human achievement and progress, and so it is worth considering the magnitude of what they have done.

Pessimism Amidst Miracles

In the course of my work I meet professors from many disciplines, and I try to read ideas from people with a wide variety of points of view. A sentiment that I sometimes run into that always disappoints me is the reluctance of people to have children. It must be admitted that there are good reasons for deciding not to have children, in particular if one is confident that one will make a terrible parent, or if one has life plans that do not leave room for them. But the belief I want to investigate here is that it is a bad idea to have children because the world into which one would bring them is terrible and getting worse. I often run into this sentiment, particularly from people who have strong beliefs with regard to the environment. Strongly religious people also often worry about the collapsing state of morals, but these religious people often also believe that they are religiously obligated to have many children, so this type of pessimism does not so much affect their decision to bring children into the world or not.

Throughout the world, especially but not exclusively in wealthy countries, birth rates have fallen spectacularly in the last several decades. Some of this is easy to understand economically. Wealthy societies mean that people can easily earn enough during their working years not just to fund their own retirement, but actually to leave large amounts of wealth behind for their children. They therefore do not have large numbers of children to care for them in their old age. And in some ways the opportunity cost of the action of raising children is much higher than before, because of the intense time commitment required to do it properly, and in the U.S. in particular, owing to the high cost of purchasing their higher education. But many kinds of pessimism are completely misplaced.

Such pessimism is easy to understand. Popular entertainment and news companies often emphasize it. But this is because broadcasters know that if you want people to watch, emphasize stories involving violence, the more hideous the better. And so local news follows the "if it bleeds, it leads" principle; it is

---

[1]http://en.wikipedia.org/wiki/Snow_blower

replete with video of robberies, the aftermaths of shootings, spectacular car accidents, and so on. At the level of national and international news, we hear of wars, famines, and environmental devastation. Both people of the political left and right have their own favorite catastrophes. People of the left worry about environmental calamities, worsening standards of living, and "income inequality," while those on the right worry about the breakdown of long-standing moral codes, the spread of ignorance about the glorious past of their society, and also about falling standards of living.

If you want more evidence of the omnipresence of pessimism, consider pop culture. Most readers are familiar with the term *utopia*, which is taken from a 1516 novel by Thomas More describing a perfect society of the future. There is a corresponding antonym, called *dystopia*, and there are plenty of books and movies representing the idea that things are getting relentlessly worse, or indeed that they have already collapsed. In the 1993 movie *Falling Down*, the main character played by Michael Douglas is caught one day in a traffic jam on his way to work when he decides to just get out, abandon his vehicle, and start walking. His day winds up with him killing himself on Venice Beach, but not before strolling through a Los Angeles beset with white supremacists, selfishness, and greed, vast income inequality, and senseless street crime and outbursts of violence. The *Terminator* movies depict a world in which the few remaining humans fight the killing machines that they themselves inadvertently created.

And these examples barely scratch the surface. What is striking about dystopian fiction, besides its frequency, is the nature of the things imagined to do humanity in. Frequently, mysterious, powerful corporations have either engineered human disaster or are actually using it to their benefit. In the 1975 movie *Rollerball*, corporations actually run the world, and one part of the corporate ruling class, called the Energy Corporation, runs a sport characterized by extreme violence whose goal is to make sure no player can succeed for too long (to make people unwilling to believe in the power of the individual to succeed). In *Blade Runner* (1982), the Tyrell Corporation plays a large role in operating the world—and a lovely world it is, characterized by pollution so severe that the sun is almost never seen and most natural life has been wiped out and by seemingly inescapable police surveillance. In the *Terminator* series, it is the Cyberdyne Corporation that (unwittingly) sets down the path that leads to humanity's near-destruction. Skepticism of business and its role in society, without all of the dystopian overtones, is also far from rare. The movie *Alien* has a sinister "company," never explicitly identified but which might (based on letters on various items in the film) be the Weyland-Yutani Corporation. In the immensely popular movie *Avatar*, a private corporation seeks to seize control of a faraway planet's resources even if it means destroying the society of the planet and enslaving everyone on it if necessary. At the level of the individual's relation to business, such movies as *Wall Street* (both the 1987 original and 2010 sequel) depict financiers not as middlemen linking ideas and money but as greedy destroyers of all that is decent and noble. In Arthur Miller's *Death of a Salesman*, considered among the greatest of all American plays, the title character is a seemingly helpless near-slave of his ruthless corporate employer, which resolutely refuses to ease his emotional burdens by letting him work closer to home and fires him when he reacts angrily to its refusal to do so.

Seen from the opposite point of view, utopian visions often rest on the abolition of commerce. Plato's *Republic*, the ancient Greek philosopher's guide to the ideal society, abolishes private property. In the *Star Trek* television series and films, the various intelligent beings who inhabit the galaxy produce amazing technological and material advances, but have no desire for material things and generally use no money, human nature apparently having been adjusted somehow to move beyond self-interest. How people were motivated to create all the marvelous technology is not specified.

Another common theme of dystopian art is environmental catastrophe. Films like *Silent Running* (1972) and *Blade Runner* depict human-caused mass species extinction. *Logan's Run* (a 1967 novel made into a movie in 1972) and *Soylent Green* (1973) both hinge on overpopulation. *Logan's Run* depicts a future U.S. in which everyone is executed at 30 to avoid overcrowding. *Soylent Green* is set in a world in the later stages of being destroyed simultaneously by overpopulation, global warming, and mass extinction, depicting a society in which people passively and unknowingly consume a product made from the flesh of the dead in order to stay alive. *Waterworld* (1995) is about a lawless world after the polar ice caps have melted, the *Mad Max* series of movies is about the collapse of civilization after the near-exhaustion of the world's oil, and *The Day after Tomorrow* (2004) depicts the catastrophic effects of humans dumping greenhouse gases into the atmosphere. Even children are not protected from the genre; the generally very charming movie *Wall-E* (2008) is about humans living a life of utter but empty leisure in space because their ancestors made the earth uninhabitable by treating it as a mere bottomless trashcan.

It is striking how far these works of art part from what actually happened in the depicted year that in reality has now already passed or is about to. *Blade Runner* takes place in 2019, and the decision to prevent anyone from reaching old age that is the basis for *Logan's Run* takes place in 2000—because of rapid growth in the numbers of young people. As it turned out, as noted above, economic growth has caused population growth rates to plummet, and predictions made several decades ago about the number of people and what they're going to do to the planet now look wildly pessimistic if not paranoid.[2]

---

[2]George Orwell's *1984* is another example of disproven dystopia. Although there the nightmare there is political, the predictions were in most respects equally misplaced.

In contrast, there are very few movies made about a future that is brighter in every respect than the present, where people get along more or less (amazingly well by historical standards, in fact), where racial conflict and war are much less severe than they once were, where many health problems that used to be scourges are now largely solved.[3] And yet that is pretty much how the future always turns out to be.

The Way Things Used to Be

One of the unfortunate negative effects of modern technology is that people tend to think more in terms of the here and now, because they don't depend on the recounting of ancient myths and struggles for knowledge or entertainment. One reason Homer's *Iliad* and *Odyssey* became classics is that they were orally recounted by traveling professionals before eager crowds for centuries before they were finally committed to paper. But in our age of instant information, that is a poor way to spend an evening, and in general our electronic age has probably made what's happening now seem very important, and what happened before, so to speak, yesterday's news. People have always had a natural tendency to suppose that everything that matters in human affairs started within the span of their own lives, despite the thousands of years of human civilization that preceded them. (When I ask students to identify the most important innovations in history, invariably many offer up the computer or the Internet. Important as these seem to be—admittedly at a time when they are still in their infancy—they do not yet compare to the wheel, writing, mechanical power, or even eyeglasses or the mechanical screw.)

In fact, most of human history was frankly awful. In 476 A.D., the last Western Roman emperor (the 8-year-old boy Romulus Augustulus) was forced by the barbarian invaders to leave the throne, and Western civilization entered what we call, not without reason, the Dark Ages. During this long span of history, not only was life miserable, it was unchangingly so for centuries. Uncountable millions of numbers of people were born with no chance to travel more than five miles from where they were born. Life expectancy was perhaps 30 years, and the rate at which young children died was staggering. Many people didn't make it to adulthood, and those who did died not from cancer and heart disease, diseases of advanced age that are the preoccupations of the modern

---

[3] *Star Trek*, by depicting a brighter future achieved in part by overcoming grubby commerce, is the exception that proves the rule.

world, but in horrible ways: from smallpox, plague, and yellow fever.[4] Now all of these diseases are preventable by vaccine and other public-health improvements. On and on it went like this, generation after generation. Not only did you live the same life your great-great-great great grandparents did, you had every reason to expect that your great-great-great-grandchildren would live that life too.

But from about 1780 on, everything changed. Consider Figure 9-1.

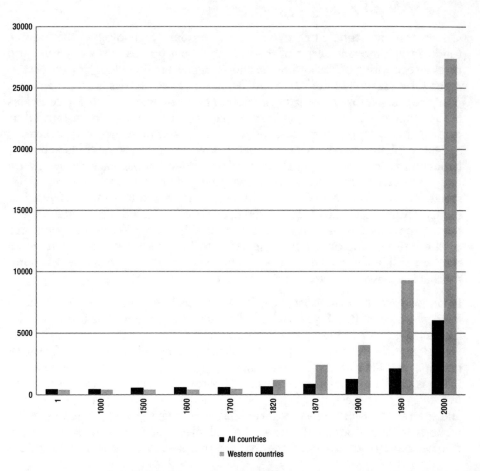

Figure 9-1. Per capita GDP over the very long run (1990 $US)

---

[4]Indeed, as late as 1821, thousands of people died in Barcelona, Spain, from yellow fever, whose lethal effect lies partly in its victims bleeding profusely from every orifice until they die. Similarly, in the pre-antibiotic era, President Calvin Coolidge's teenage son died from an infected blister after playing tennis at the White House.

Figure 9-1 shows per capita gross domestic (GDP) product over a very long period of time. Per capita GDP, the total amount produced in a society divided by population, is a good index of material standard of living. (I discuss GDP in more detail in Chapter 11.) Looking at the chart, one sees the pattern is nothing much to write home about until 1820. Indeed, the stagnation of the Dark Ages is plainly visible in the figures for Western countries. But sometime before 1820 (1780 is probably the best guess) something dramatic changed—standards of living, especially in Western countries, began to increase substantially and without relent. Many people in 1870 had standards of living that were unimaginable in 1700, and we live now in ways that were inconceivable to even the wealthiest people in 1870. In fact, in the United States, since 1820, every generation (if a generation is defined as 30 years) can expect to live 40–50% better than its parents did. Here are some other things we know about life in the United States:

- Since 1965, the average American man has 6–9 more leisure hours per week, the average woman 4–8. This is equivalent to an extra 5 weeks of vacation. Less-educated adults have seen the biggest increase in leisure time.

- Since 1900, the average workweek has declined from 60 hours to 40.

- In 1900, almost 75% of males aged 16–19 were in the labor force. Now, only about one in four teenagers works, and many work as much for spending money as to provide their families with essential income.

- In 1900, only about 25% of the population could retire at 65. Now, about 84% do, and most who don't retire keep working because they simply want to.

- In the 19th century, the average woman spent about 70 hours a week on household chores. In 2011, men and woman combined spent fewer than five.

- Life expectancy since 1900 has gone up from 48 to 78 years.[5]

And this hardly begins to state the ways in which life is different. It used to be common for Americans to live with their parents until and even after they got married. Now for many it is expected that they leave home at a young age. (Indeed there is a stigma to being a "boomerang baby" who returns home

---

[5]For leisure time per week, see Mark Aguiar and Erik Hurst, "Measuring Trends in Leisure: The Allocation of Time Over Five Decades," *Quarterly Journal of Economics* 122 (3) (August 2007): 969–1008. For teenage labor-force participation in 1900 see Sobek, Matthew, "Male labor force participation rate, by age: 1850–1990." Table Ba391–403 in *Historical Statistics of the United States, Earliest Times to the Present: Millennial Edition,* edited by Susan B. Carter, Scott Sigmund Gartner, Michael R. Haines, Alan L. Olmstead, Richard Sutch, and Gavin Wright. New York: Cambridge University Press, 2006. http://dx.doi.org/10.1017/ISBN-9780511132971.Ba340-651. For teenage participation now see Allison Linn, "A Teen With a Job Becomes a Rarity in US Economy," http://lifeinc.today.com/_news/2012/05/03/11489527-a-teen-with-a-job-becomes-a-rarity-in-us-economy?lite. For workweek length, see Stephen Moore and Julian Lincoln Simon, *It Is Getting Better All the Time* (Washington, D.C.: Cato Institute, 2000): 98. For retirement at 65 in 1900, see Marilyn Gardner, "A World Without Clocks," *The Christian Science Monitor,* (September 22, 1981). For retirement at 65 in 2011, see Haya el Nasser, "More Americans Delay Retirement, Keep Working," *USA Today* (January 24, 2013), which indicates that although 16.1% of Americans worked past retirement in 2010 compared to 12.1% in 1990, only 13% kept working because they were worried about finances, along with another 6% who kept working to make up for recent declines in the stock market. For time on chores in the 19th century, see Moore and Simon, p. 11. For time on chores in 2011, see Bureau of Labor Statistics, American Time Use Survey, 2011 results news release, available online at www.bls.gov/news.release/atus.nr0.htm. For life expectancy, see Table 21 in Elizabeth Arias, "United States Life Tables 2008," National Vital Statistics Report 61 (3) (September 24, 2012), available online at www.cdc.gov/nchs/data/nvsr/nvsr61/nvsr61_03.pdf. The statistic on labor force participation by 15-year-olds is a guess on my part. We do know that in 1900 the median number of years of school completed was fewer than 8 for males of 21 years of age, and high-school graduates made up fewer than 25% of that group. From that it can be presumed that most 15-year-old males were working. Fifteen-year olds are now strictly limited in the work they may do because of the Fair Labor Standards Act of 1938, but even before this time, high-school graduation rates began to surge. These data on education are from Claude S. Fischer and Michael Hout, with John Stiles, *Century of Difference: How the Country Changed in the Last One Hundred Years* (New York: Russell Sage Foundation, 2006).

after graduating from college.[6]) If one wishes to read more vivid testimony about how good we have it, consider the following from the writer Steven Pinker on what life was like in Europe in the 17th century:

> *Our ancestors...were infested with lice and parasites and lived above cellars heaped with their own feces. Food was bland, monotonous, and intermittent. Health care consisted of the doctor's saw and the dentist's pliers. Both sexes labored from sunrise to sundown, whereupon they were plunged into darkness. Winter meant months of hunger, boredom, and gnawing loneliness in snowbound farmhouses.[7]*

Truth be told, this doesn't sound much different from life in Rome in the second century B.C.:

> *Ordure as well as water flowed through her streets. If the noblest and most enduring virtues of the Republic found their expression in the murmuring of a public fountain, then its horrors were exemplified by filth. Citizens who dropped out of the obstacle race that was every Roman's life risked having shit—literally—dumped on their heads. Plebs sordida, they were called—"the great unwashed." Periodically, waste from the insulae would be wheeled out in barrows to fertilize gardens beyond the city walls, but there was always too much of it, urine sloshing over the rims of fullers' jars, mounds of excrement submerging the streets. In death, the poor themselves would be subsumed into waste. Not for them the dignity of a tomb beside the Appian Way. Instead their carcasses would be tossed with all the other refuse into giant pits beyond the easternmost city gate, the Esquiline. Travelers approaching Rome by this route would see bones littering the sides of the road. It was a cursed and dreadful spot, the haunt of witches, who were said to strip flesh from the corpses and summon the naked specters of the dead from their mass graves.[8]*

In terms of filth on the streets, although not in terms of the disposal of dead bodies, such scenes still exist in many cities in many poor countries. But in the cities of wealthy countries—a club that has expanded considerably in recent

---

[6]Even in the miserable economic climate in December 2011, only 24% of Americans 18-34 said they had moved in with their parents at any point recently for economic reasons. Kim Parker, *The Boomerang Generation: Feeling OK About Living With Mom and Dad* (Washington, DC: Pew Research Center, 2012), http://www.pewsocialtrends.org/files/2012/03/PewSocialTrends-2012-BoomerangGeneration.pdf. (See responses to question 29.)
[7]Steven Pinker, *The Better Angels of Our Nature: Why Human Violence has Declined* (New York: Viking, 2011): 693.
[8]Tom Holland, *Rubicon: The Last Years of the Roman Republic* (New York: Anchor Books, 2005): 16.

years by moving beyond Western Europe, the U.S., Canada, Australia, and New Zealand to include Japan, Taiwan, South Korea, Singapore, Chile, and several other nations—they are inconceivable. Go back less than 20 generations (or far fewer than that in the newly wealthy countries), and the ancestors of 99.9 percent of the people reading this lived on less than a dollar a day, if they weren't outright slaves or serfs.

As with our material standard of living, so too with the tendency of humans to do violence to one another. Random, senseless violence is another preoccupation of modern pop culture—think of the appeal of slasher movies, for example. In fact, violence both in war and as homicide has declined spectacularly over the centuries in the industrial world. Despite the ghastly death toll of the two world wars, both the frequency of and death rate in war declined throughout the 20th century. Europe itself is now, along with parts of East Asia, the most peaceful region of the world, where people have long lives, and, compared to earlier generations, crime is by historical standards a non-factor (although fear of crime, driven in part by the media, is not). Homicide rates in Europe are less than 10% of what they were in the Middle Ages, when they were already considerably lower than what they were, according to many estimates, in the pre-agricultural hunter-gatherer societies often wrongly romanticized by writers. According to Pinker, whose research provides the information used in this paragraph, there are several causes for this decline in violence.

But one that is worth our attention is the gradual spread throughout the world of the market process—the widening and deepening of ties through the market that connect us in ways that give us opportunities for mutually beneficial bargains. Politics, as we have seen, is very often zero-sum (meaning the only way one person or group wins is for another to lose), whereas market exchange is by definition positive-sum (that is, win-win). I don't do business with you unless I expect to be better off, and the same is true for you. But politics is all too often about whether the government gives me something and you pay for it, or vice versa. The more we rely on markets to decide who gets what, the greater the possibilities for us to decide that the way to get what we want is to peacefully trade with other people rather than forcibly take things from them. The decline in human violence, partly driven by the spread of the market as the way of deciding who gets what, has been one of the great triumphs of human history, even if it doesn't make for a good movie.[9]

---

[9]In addition to the spread of market exchange to a greater and greater percentage of the population in a larger number of countries, Pinker also credits the spectacular decline in violence to the ability of governments to establish enough authority to provide law and order, and to the spread of abstract thinking, which allows people to see others as having interests and moral rights equal to their own.

Statistics about the bounty of modern life are everywhere; we worry now about the homeless in our major cities, but as late as the mid-19th century European cities, notably London, had a vast population of "vagrants," "paupers," and "street Arabs" (homeless children).[10] Between 1990 and 2010, vaccines are estimated to have saved 20 million lives. Since 1960, the average daily caloric intake in developing countries has risen from 1,900 to 2,700, the latter about what a person needs daily to live a physically active lifestyle in good health. And we live longer, have more free time, have opportunities to travel that would be unimaginable to previous generations, and have exposure to more of the world's diversity than ever before. (Think about how easy it is not just to go to China or Brazil but to learn Chinese and Portuguese, thanks to the glut of teachers and software, compared to even 50 years ago.) We are actually smarter too. A person who scores 100 on an IQ test now, which is by design the average score, would have scored 118 as recently as 1950, and 130 (putting him in the 90th percentile) in 1910.[11] Literacy is essentially universal in many societies, which is all too easy to take for granted. At the time of the French Revolution, literacy in France was probably very far below 50%, but illiteracy essentially doesn't exist there now.

In addition to dystopia, another common theme of culture is nostalgia. In America, for example, many television shows and movies have been devoted to the golden age of the 1950s and even the 19th century, when people cared more about each other, and the complications of modern life—the violence, the dehumanizing nature of modern industrial society, the decay of family life—didn't yet exist. But for people who think things used to be better, there is good news. It is possible to live a 1950s life, with 1950s choices. Indeed, occasionally people conduct such experiments and report the results, not all of which are bad. (Two examples, both by women, are here[12] and here.[13]) But to live this nostalgic life, not only will you have to give up all communications technology beyond the rotary phone and over-the-air television channels. Your house will also be smaller, although it will cost less. Air travel will be unaffordable. Many modern medicines that we take for granted will be unavailable. If you are disabled, your ability to manage in modern society will be profoundly limited, and you will almost certainly not work. So even the recent nostalgized past is not necessarily all it is cracked up to be. And the

---

[10] The fictional detective Sherlock Holmes relied on such children as his "Baker Street irregulars," who helped him in some of his investigations.

[11] The vaccine figure is from UNICEF, available online at www.unicef.org/immunization/index_coverage.html. The calorie figure is from Thomas R. DeGregori, *Origins of the Organic Agriculture Debate* (Ames, IA: Iowa State Press, 2004): 128. The IQ data are from Pinker, Chapter 9.

[12] http://www.lfpress.com/life/2010/01/08/12397666.html

[13] http://www.jenbutneverjenn.com/2010/05/welcome-to-50s-housewife-experiment.html

future? There is a long tradition of saying it is going to be awful, not just in popular culture but among people who think for a living, as among those who govern us.

■ **Summary** Doomsdayism sells books and movie tickets, but any way you slice them the numbers say things are getting better all the time.

How Intellectuals and Politicians Have Seen the Future in the Past—a Brief History

The discussion so far strongly suggests that the main story of the human condition is now progress—by technological, medical, intellectual, material, or any other criteria. And yet the public conversation frequently acts as if this progress doesn't exist. And that is substantially because the people who set the parameters of this discussion—intellectuals and politicians—either can't or won't see it. Here we look at the long history of such unjustified pessimism.

Malthusianism

It has been said that there is a difference between knowledge and wisdom. Nowhere is this more obvious than in the tendency of highly educated, highly credentialed people to think that everything is getting worse. In my research on this topic, I have been unable to nail down the first appearance of this belief. But a good place to start is probably with the English demographer and (unfortunately) economist Thomas Robert Malthus, who had a view of population dynamics that still bears the name "Malthusian." For Malthus, the primary good that people cared about was food (not an unreasonable view in the late 1700s and early 1800s, when he wrote his most famous works), and food was produced through two resources: land and people. When times were good, people tended to have a lot of children, and given that land was fixed and its productivity could not be enhanced, this meant that eventually population overtaxed the land's productive capacity. This led to famine, which killed off so many people that the ratio of persons to land fell dramatically, which meant that the amount of food per person, and hence general prosperity, could go up again. Mankind was forever trapped in this boom-and-bust cycle.

Ironically, even as Malthus was writing, the great long boom that had begun in the late 18th century was beginning to make a real difference, but he couldn't see it. Rising productivity was allowing people to grow more food on less land, because it turned out that the resources that went to produce food went far beyond land and labor and included various productivity enhancements such as more advanced mechanical tools, ever-cleverer techniques to rotate crops and to grow the right crops in the right places, and eventually chemical enhancements to productivity such as pesticides and fertilizers.

Luddism

Shortly after Malthusian doomsdayism, the Luddite version emerged. The Luddites were supposedly named after Ned Ludd, a weaver from England who destroyed knitting machines in a fit of anger whose source history does not reliably record. In 1811, upset by automated looms that were replacing unskilled textile workers, those workers began adapting Ludd's tactics to save their jobs by destroying machinery and continued to do so (along with threatening factory owners and local officials) until the movement was crushed in 1813. Their belief was that if machines destroyed jobs, those whose jobs were destroyed would forever be unemployed. Society would be divided into a small class of those with work, and a large underclass without. Needless to say, this future failed to play out. For the next 200 years, unemployment in industrialized countries usually ranged between 3% and 10%. The reason the mass-unemployment scenario didn't occur is that released workers are an idle scarce resource, and their underuse (or non-use) provides an opportunity for new economic activities to take place—either new enterprises in existing activities or the creation of new activities entirely. Out of destruction comes renewal, rather than permanent stagnation. Despite this logic, and 200 years of mass unemployment in the industrial and post-industrial era consistently failing to appear for an extended period, the idea that work permanently disappears, in a way that deprives people of income rather than providing them leisure because of machines replacing men, can still be found—by the author Jeremy Rifkin[14] for example.

Marxism

Despite the fact that most societies once governed by people who called themselves Marxist have changed their systems (and two still nominally Marxist societies, China and Vietnam, rely more and more on property rights and free exchange to decide who gets what, with the beneficial results that one would expect), the most famous kind of doomsdayism is probably the Marxist variety. Here we must note that in the Marxist vision, doomsday is only a way-station on the road to Utopia. What was supposed to happen was that the people who owned the factories would constantly have power over workers and could keep a "reserve army of the unemployed" to bolster this

---

[14]http://www.foet.org/books/end-work.html

leverage. They would pay workers only a subsistence wage, just large enough to enable them to buy the food and shelter they needed to be able to keep working, but pocket for themselves all the profits thereby generated. If workers tried to improve their lot, they could be cast aside and replaced by the unemployed.

In the context of the mid-1800s—with vast movements of labor from countryside to city, and from Europe to North America, which represented constant rightward shifts in the supply curve for people doing factory work—this had a certain surface plausibility. But wages in fact rose throughout this period as they did before and after, and the predicted revolution of the working class never actually arrived in an industrial country, only in agricultural ones like 1917 Russia and 1949 China. In the meantime, living standards rose relentlessly in the so-called "capitalist" societies, and communism became (in addition to one of humanity's great crimes) a dinosaur ideology.

Permanent Economic Stagnation

Sad to say, economists are not invulnerable to the doomsday mentality. A certain kind of economist is especially likely to invoke the idea of the "end of progress," or of "permanent stagnation." To be fair, this way of thinking is not as common as it used to be; it was especially popular during the Great Depression, unsurprisingly. The writer Deirdre McCloskey summarizes this point of view:

> During the 1930s and early 1940s the prospect of diminishing returns deeply alarmed economists such as the British economist John Maynard Keynes and the American follower of Keynes at Minnesota and Harvard, Alvin Hansen. They believed that the technology of electricity and the automobile were exhausted, and that sharply diminishing returns to capital were at hand, especially in view of declining birthrates. People would save more than could be profitably invested, the "stagnationists" believed, and the advanced economies would fall into chronic unemployment. In line with the usual if doubtful claim that spending on the war had temporarily saved the nonbombed part of the world's economy, they believed that 1946 would see a renewal of the Great Depression.
>
> But it didn't. Stagnationism proved false. Instead, world income per head grew faster from 1950 to 1974 than any time in history, and the liberal [i.e., pro-market] countries boomed. That is, innovation prevented the return to capital from declining.[15]

---

[15]Dierdre McCloskey, *Bourgeois Dignity: Why Economics Can't Explain the Modern World* (Chicago, IL: University of Chicago Press, 2010): 134. In economics writing, *liberal* generally means *pro-free market*.

This idea that we have run out of progress to make is also not new. A Roman named Julius Frontinus is said to have said that "[i]nventions reached their limit long ago when I see no hope for further development."[16] It is known that the Scottish physicist William Thomson, in a letter written to Major B.F.S. Baden Powell on December 8, 1896 (just a few years before the flight of the Wright Brothers at Kitty Hawk), announced his refusal to join Britain's Aeronautical Society, because "I have not the slightest molecule of faith in aerial navigation other than ballooning or of expectation of good results from any of the trials we hear of." So, the belief that we have hit the wall economically and technologically has been around awhile. Make a note of that remark about inventions; we will return to it. In the meantime, note that all of these doomsday visions have proven spectacularly false.

Overpopulation/Sustainability

And yet doomsdayism is still with us. Its most prominent modern form is environmental doomsdayism, which itself takes two forms, both based on the idea that there are too many people in the world: sustainability and overpopulation.

As near as I can tell, the modern fear of overpopulation dates to work by the Stanford biologist Paul Ehrlich in the 1960s.[17] In a 1968 book of the same name written with his wife Anne Ehrlich, he coined the phrase "the population bomb." A copy of it dutifully sat on my parents' bookshelf, and it warned readers (not, thankfully, including my parents, who never urged their children to go out and not give them grandchildren) that there were simply too many of us humans. We couldn't possibly manage to grow enough food to feed them all. (Recall how this theme shows up in the 1970s in *Soylent Green* and elsewhere, which reflects the broad cultural influence of Erlich's work.) Unlike a lot of doomsdayists, and to his credit, Professor Ehrlich did actually make predictions. Thankfully, they did not come true. He predicted in particular

---

[16]Sometimes rendered as "I also lay aside all ideas of any new works or engines of war, the invention of which long ago reached its limits, and in which I see no hope for further improvement."

[17]The broader eugenics movement, which sought to improve the quality of the human race by making sure the "good" types of people reproduced and the "bad" types—the poor and the dark-skinned—did not, was also worried about overpopulation, especially of darker people, as documented extensively in Robert Zubrin, *Merchants of Despair: Radical Environmentalists, Criminal Pseudo-Scientists, and the Fatal Cult of Antihumanism* (New York: Encounter Books, 2012). The Erlichs describe being appalled by the tide of desperate people they saw on a visit to India. Since they appear to be concerned more with the problem of too many people generally rather than too many of the "wrong" type of people, it is not fair to call them eugenicists. But historically many others who advocated population control have clearly been in this camp.

that hundreds of millions of people would die in famines in the 1970s. The annual global death rate would "substantial[ly] increase." But malnutrition as a percentage of the population has in fact declined by about half since the book was published, and calories consumed by the average person worldwide have increased substantially.

In a speech on the original Earth Day in 1970, Ehrlich pronounced that "In ten years all important animal life in the sea will be extinct. Large areas of coastline will have to be evacuated because of the stench of dead fish." And Great Britain? Not so great anymore. "By the year 2000 the United Kingdom will be simply a small group of impoverished islands, inhabited by some 70 million hungry people... If I were a gambler, I would take even money that England will not exist in the year 2000."

And here is another prediction, from Sandra Postel of the Worldwatch Institute, an organization that has long been concerned about "sustainability":

> As a result of our population size, consumption patterns, and technology choices, we have surpassed the planet's carrying capacity. This is plainly evident by the extent to which we are depleting natural capital. The earth's environmental assets are now insufficient to sustain both our present patterns of economic activity and the life-support systems we depend on. If current trends in resource use continue and if world population grows as projected, by 2010 per capita availability of rangeland will drop by 22 percent and the fish catch by ten percent. Together, these provide much of the world's animal protein. The per capita area of irrigated land, which now yields about a third of the global food harvest, will drop by 12 percent. And cropland area and forestland per person will shrink by 21 percent and 30 percent, respectively.[18]

This prediction was made in 1994, and the doom prophesied in it was supposed to have happened by now. And yet much of 1994–2010 was a global boom, when people became better nourished and more prosperous, untroubled by such things as "per capita availability of rangeland" and "the fish catch." (I investigate overfishing and why it happens in Chapter 10.) But having certain amounts of these things are not goals per se, because they are resources—means to an end, not the end itself. The end is, and always should be, human welfare. If people are eating better (and they are), it is generally because we can get more food with fewer resources than before, as has happened around the world for decades. The planet per se has no "carrying capacity"; this can only be defined relative to our ability to convert

---

[18]Sandra Postel, "Carrying Capacity: Earth's Bottom Line," *Challenge* (March/April, 1994) (4-12): 4–5.

its resources into human purposes, something that constantly improves over time because supply curves shift right thanks to technological improvement. Pay attention to outputs—human welfare, manifested as nutrition and health, opportunity, peaceful coexistence, and so on—and not to inputs.

■ **Note** Pay attention to outputs like improved health and economic opportunity throughout the world and not to inputs like carbon-based fuels, cropland available, and so forth. You'll put your mind at ease.

The older sustainability concerns, in which humanity outruns the means to feed itself, date back to Malthus and have been given a gloss for our media age by people like the Ehrlichs. But now, after several decades in which the things that population doomsdayists were most concerned about failed to happen, a new set of concerns about sustainability has been expressed. Some of these involve human pollution of the environment, especially carbon dioxide, which influences climate. In earlier decades, most concern about pollution involved substances that are directly toxic to human health—poisons in the air and water. But a huge body of research shows that as countries industrialize, while their pollution may initially increase, it eventually declines sharply as its people become wealthy enough to be in a position to trade off some economic growth for cleaner air and water. In every major city in the United States, for example, the air is much cleaner now than it was in the early 1970s, when laws requiring strenuous efforts to prevent pollution first began to bite.

In addition to other concerns about running out of rain forest and cropland, the latter seemingly hard to reconcile with the declining proportion of the world's population that is malnourished, the primary concern of the new sustainability movement is climate. Fairly representative is the following, which is from the promotional materials for the 2006 film *An Inconvenient Truth*:

> *Humanity is sitting on a time bomb. If the vast majority of the world's scientists are right, we have just ten years to avert a major catastrophe that could send our entire planet's climate system into a tail-spin of epic destruction involving extreme weather, floods, droughts, epidemics and killer heat waves beyond anything we have ever experienced— a catastrophe of our own making.*

This prediction, it should be noted, was made in 2006, so as I write this the time limit for preventing these catastrophes is already over half over. Whether humans influence the climate, and if so by how much, is a question of chemistry, and I am not in the least qualified to answer it. If chemists say that human emissions of carbon dioxide interact with solar radiation and the surface of the earth in ways that should cause atmospheric trapping of heat to increase, it is basic chemistry and that is that. Predictions about what will happen to the climate in the future are also a scientific matter, although one considerably harder to resolve (at least so far) using the scientific method. Climatologists typically fit their models to the data they have available from the past. This is an acceptable scientific method, and economists use it all the time. But the acid test of a climate model, or an economic one, is its ability to predict the future. As far as I know, climatologists have not been able to consistently accurately predict in several decades of climate modeling what global temperature would do in light of human carbon-dioxide emissions.

Here's what we do know. Predictions of climate doomsday fit comfortably within a long tradition of doomsday philosophizing, none of which has been borne out. We also know that it does not follow that just because human activity influences the environment—even the climate—a massive, centralized government program to limit the human activities that generate these effects is called for. Such dramatic intervention in the trading networks people have built over time is frequently called for by people most concerned about carbon-dioxide emissions, and indeed given the role carbon-based energy plays in modern life, intervention from on high could hardly help but be sweeping, even compared to prior anti-pollution measures. But carbon dioxide is not emitted by people out of malice. Emissions are instead a byproduct of useful human activity—ambulances taking people to the hospital to save their lives, young people getting on airplanes exploring the world, people in buildings all over the world taking night classes in rooms lit by electricity to improve themselves, people reading books for pleasure and edification, factories churning out medicines and electricity-generating and transportation machines, people being liberated by central heating and air conditioning from freezing in the winter and suffering heat stroke in the summer, and so on. The benefits of those activities must of course be considered in addition to the costs.

Even the benefits of climate change itself must enter our deliberations. It may well make many areas of the world more agriculturally productive (although it will surely make some areas less productive as well). The problems of government limitations on human exchange that were discussed in Chapter 5—the problems, in other words, that government regulation creates in limiting the ability to use scarce resources to meet human goals—must also enter our calculations. In discussions of environmental problems, people will often raise the "precautionary principle,"[19] which says that when humans engage in activities that *might* damage the environment, we must err on the side of caution—we must allow no action that might cause such damage to occur, even though we don't yet have scientific certainty that it will. But the precautionary principle cuts both ways. It is true that allowing the activity to go ahead might lead to the environment being changed by human activity in this particular way

---

[19]http://www.sehn.org/ppfaqs.html

(although humans have always changed the environment, as do all living things, since they first emerged), so that the current state of the environment, itself a product of hundreds of millions of years of interaction among living things, is something that must be given up to allow humans to take the actions they are contemplating.

But if you prohibit people from changing the environment, that also has costs—businesses don't get started or expanded, people don't have access to food and medicine at lower cost (a substantial cost in poor countries), dreams don't get pursued (and surely human satisfaction must be taken account of in our deliberations about the impact of greenhouse-gas emissions), they don't get to drive a car but instead have to take public transportation, which deprives them of a significant amount of mobility. Most substantially, the expansion of government control over what we may not do—you may not drive certain kinds of cars (or perhaps someday any kind of car), you may only employ certain technologies to control the climate in your home (in other words, you will have to forgo some amount of climate control), your consumption of electricity and all you get out of it will have to fall—also carries costs.

And it also carries risks, because we know from Chapter 5 that governments tend to choose relatively poorly because of lack of information, that their tools of control tend to be hijacked by special interests, and that they tend to use the power that they possess to punish their enemies and suit their own interests. Expansion of government control over how people can recombine scarce resources, in other words, also ought to be subject to a precautionary principle. There is no way to take environmentalists' precautionary principle seriously without accepting uncritically the idea that the social cost of changing the environment as it currently is exceeds the social cost of preventing *any* environmental change. This is madness.

It is also unwise to view nature as a temple that cannot be profaned, as something that humans spoil whenever they interact with it in any way. Human alteration of the environment is not an act of sacrilege, but something done in the pursuit of human happiness and achievement. Sometimes, if the damage to other humans, either now or in the future, from human interaction with the environment is great enough, then the actions may have to be limited (a topic explored in detail in Chapter 10.) But humans, like all species, are constantly changing the environment in the course of surviving and advancing, and what they do is worthwhile in making other humans better off. The Grand Canyon is indeed extremely beautiful, and it would be a tragedy if future generations were not allowed to see it in all its beauty because humans had altered it. But this kind of beauty is not all there is. Humans create their own kind of beauty. The Golden Gate Bridge is beautiful, as is the Sistine Chapel, as is the Manhattan skyline, as is a chrome-laden Harley Davidson motorcycle. So too is a well-crafted cell-phone interface. Indeed, the network that has been built to allow us to link with one another over the Internet and cell-phone networks is profoundly beautiful in a certain way, as are the commercial networks that people build to trade with one another and pursue their goals.[20]

The risks to human dignity, achievements, and welfare from the expansion of the state to keep the climate exactly as it is right now (itself a dubious proposition given the other factors, notably the cycles of the sun, that also affect it) may well exceed the costs that result from changes in the climate. This is especially true because the spontaneous order reacting locally can deal with the latter—if the climate changes, flood-control systems can be built, people can move, new technologies can be produced, different crops can be invented and then grown in various places. The number of possible human reactions to changed circumstances, climate or otherwise, is limitless. For many decades, coastal cities in the United States have had to deal with the problem of subsidence, the threatened surrendering of coastal land to the ocean because of some combination of rising sea levels and the pumping out of groundwater and oil and gas. Local authorities have managed these problems through combinations of letting the water reclaim some areas and building various kinds of infrastructure to divert the water. The end result is that life, and human achievement, go on.

So what do the facts say in terms of threats to humans from climate change? In the grand scheme of things, weather-related events are an infinitesimal contributor to human mortality. In 2002, 57 million people died worldwide from all causes. Accidents killed 5.2 million, including 1.2 million who died in auto accidents. War killed 200,000, and other violence 600,000. Deaths from "weather-related extreme events," in contrast, summed to 19,900, and have been declining throughout the last 90 years.[21] And the vast majority of these deaths occur in countries that are very poor—countries, in other words, *whose economies have not yet grown enough to allow them to buy protection against the climate.*

What *does* kill the most people? Disease, both communicable (parasites, tuberculosis, AIDS, and malaria, for example) and non-communicable (heart disease, cancer). And disease is something that can be controlled with prosperity; there is no malaria or yellow fever in New Orleans or Florida anymore, although they were once endemic. If control of greenhouse gases were to come at the expense of economic growth for the poor, thus, it would do much more harm than good. There is a cost of not doing anything about climate

---

[20]I have written that human commerce should be seen philosophically as a kind of beauty in an article published at http://www.independent.org/publications/tir/article.asp?a=690, a work also referenced in this footnote.

[21]The data in this paragraph are from Civil Society Coalition on Climate Change, *Civil Society Report on Climate Change* (London: International Policy Press, 2007), available online at www.csccc.info/reports/report_20.pdf.

change, but there is also a cost of "doing something" about it, too, a cost that can vary with the means we choose to address this problem. The notion of opportunity costs of actions taken—for example, electricity that doesn't get generated and pesticides that don't get applied because of environmental desires of people in wealthy countries, where the tradeoffs are different—can help us think more comprehensively and sensibly about sustainability.

▓ **Note** Climate change, and environmental problems generally, are costs resulting from the benefits of the valuable use of modern technology. Unavoidably, controlling these costs requires giving up some of these benefits, and sometimes the tradeoff will be worth it, sometimes not. The costs will often hurt the poor the worst, and will increase as the solutions become more centralized and hence inflexible. Excessive government control of the exchange process is also something to take "precautions" against.

The final environmental fear is a different kind of "unsustainability": resource exhaustion—the idea that we are running out of oil, coal, aluminum, rare-earths metals, trees, etc. Usually such thinking operates by making some calculation of per-person use of, say, oil, and then predicting population and economic growth, estimating the amount of oil in the ground, doing some simple arithmetic, and finally pronouncing authoritatively that the oil will all be gone in year X. But this way of thinking about resource sustainability ignores two related phenomena. The first is the mediating role of prices. Oil is valuable because it does useful things for people. If it becomes more costly to extract, its price will go up, inducing consumers to use less and entrepreneurs to invent new technologies to find more, or to find substitutes they can sell profitably. Indeed, as noted earlier, oil itself from the point of view of human purposes was once seen merely as a wasteful by-product of salt mining; sperm-whale oil (and before that, wood) was used to heat buildings. It was only with the discovery of new technology allowing oil to do what we take for granted now that it became useful, replacing the older sources of heat, concerns over whose "exhaustibility" were also expressed once upon a time. (Indeed, John D. Rockefeller, by making oil and, indirectly, natural gas a cheap source of heating, may have done more to save whales than anyone who has ever lived, although he is seldom credited with it.)

As it once was with fears of England running out of wood and the oceans running out of whale oil, so too it is now with oil. And yet these predictions are not new, as the science writer Ronald Bailey notes:

> *Predictions of imminent catastrophic depletion are almost as old as the oil industry. An 1855 advertisement for Kier's Rock Oil, a patent medicine whose key ingredient was petroleum bubbling up from salt wells near*

> *Pittsburgh, urged customers to buy soon before "this wonderful product is depleted from Nature's laboratory." The ad appeared four years before Pennsylvania's first oil well was drilled. In 1919 David White of the U.S. Geological Survey (USGS) predicted that world oil production would peak in nine years. And in 1943 the Standard Oil geologist Wallace Pratt calculated that the world would ultimately produce 600 billion barrels of oil. (In fact, more than 1 trillion barrels of oil had been pumped by 2006.)*
>
> *During the 1970s, the Club of Rome report The Limits to Growth projected that, assuming consumption remained flat, all known oil reserves would be entirely consumed in just 31 years. With exponential growth in consumption, it added, all the known oil reserves would be consumed in 20 years.*[22]

The chief geologist of the state of Pennsylvania, then the most important oil-drilling region in the U.S., argued that "[t]he U.S. has enough petroleum to keep its kerosene pumps burning for only four years." He said this, alas, in 1874. To restate: what resource doomsdayists always ignore is both the ability of prices to let us know about scarcity long before a resource is physically gone, and the ability of the profit motive to come up with other ways to do things.

Modern environmentalism can be dated, perhaps, to the publication of Rachel Carson's book *Silent Spring*, which warned of pesticide overuse and generated a consciousness that led to the first marking of Earth Day in 1970. To the extent that it is a movement that makes us more aware of costs of our actions that we did not know about, it is a useful idea. To the extent that it views all habitats without humans as sacred, and human activity as a poisonously disruptive force, it has become a religion, a belief system rather than anything anchored in science. Humans impact the world around them, as they, like all life forms, always have. There are some aspects of the natural world that we ought to preserve for future generations to see because of their inordinate beauty—it is easy to justify (on grounds laid out in Chapter 10) creating a national-park system, for example. But to suppose that the environment as it is today, the set of species found in particular numbers in a particular place, is untouchable is to make a completely arbitrary choice, to impose your beliefs about how land should be used on other people with different goals from you.

Thus it is, for example, that in California a solar-energy project that promises to produce electricity with less pollution (greenhouse and otherwise) is now

---

[22]http://reason.com/archives/2006/05/05/peak-oil-panic

threatened with fatal legal obstacles because of its effect[23] on a proportion (not even the entire population) of a species of desert tortoise. This is the arbitrary privileging of one interest—the desire of some people that a certain number of a certain kind of turtle be found in a certain place—over all other conflicting interests. It is the kind of conflict that politics is bound to produce. Environmental fetishism fundamentally neglects the limits the restrictions it advocates impose on human possibilities and achievement.

■ **Note**   Environmental rules in particular should be judged in a comprehensive cost/benefit framework.

Why We Think Things Keep Getting Worse

So, people can and do complain about the results of the market process all the time. They lament that there is too much poverty (even though the poor in modern societies today have opportunities unimaginable to an 1870s tycoon or a 1770s king), the environment is falling apart, etc. But complaining exclusively or excessively about these dissatisfactions suggests a certain ignorance about the past. The data demonstrate clearly that across a wide variety of dimensions—health, opportunity, exposure to culture, violence—things are better, and have been getting better for a long time. Why is the contrary so often suggested? To oversimplify a little bit, there are three kinds of people who actually have an interest in promoting the view that things are getting worse. As noted above, one of them is people in the media and entertainment businesses. It is a natural human drive to want to be shocked and alarmed, perhaps because our evolutionary drive makes us very sensitive to threats. So profit-maximizing media and movie companies, have powerful incentives to churn out blood and gore and fear in the news, in movies, in books. And this output in turn may reinforce our fear and dystopian inclinations. We are hard-wired to be scared, to be alarmed, to perceive risk. So it is unsurprising that the media and entertainment industries trying to maximize profits emphasize danger.

The second sort of person who has both an interest in propagating fear of this or that and the platform from which to do so is the intellectual. For purposes of this discussion I will define an intellectual as someone who traffics in ideas and wants to persuade other people (other intellectuals and the general public alike) that his ideas merit our attention. This class includes university

---

[23]http://latimesblogs.latimes.com/unleashed/2010/01/clash-of-environmental-ideals-in-the-mojave-desert-solarenergy-project-vs-endangered-desert-tortoise.html

professors, authors, journalists, and others. In the postwar world, with the spread of higher education and democratic politics, the intellectual has become a distinct participant in a vast market, the market for ideas.[24] Just as someone who makes pens is naturally inclined to think that his company's pens are the best product at the best price, intellectuals tend to believe that the ideas that they are selling are not just good but the best ones. But if one sells the idea that everything is getting better, the natural response is to do nothing.

On the other hand, if as an intellectual you are selling the idea that there is some terrible problem that must be solved, then the natural response is to listen to the intellectual for ideas about what to do. Such intellectuals, I think, have a natural incentive to see big problems, because they believe their highly specific knowledge is the key to solving these problems. They generalize their knowledge, and suppose it is all that matters in terms of thinking about human problems—to make society better, they often think, *you must listen to me.* (I leave it to the reader to decide whether I am committing the same error in this book.) There is not necessarily anything dishonest about this, although the unwillingness to look beyond your own tiny sphere of knowledge bespeaks a parallel unwillingness to think critically.

To predict the future, it is not enough to know the chemistry of pesticides, or of atmospheric carbon dioxide, or of the biology of biodiversity. One must also know history, politics, economics. The implication of the tendency of many intellectuals to overemphasize the importance of the specific things they know is that they naturally tend to paint things in the worst possible light, and equally naturally tend to think that they must be relied on for solutions. If they are believed, this will provide them with both the satisfaction of public approval, material advantages from people buying their books, and even the rush of having the political system adopt their views about how to regiment society. They are also naïve about government and how it really operates.

Finally, there is the political class. When people see problems, they want to be protected. Intellectuals offer this possibility of protection, but not nearly as much politicians do. If we become convinced that we are on the edge of environmental crisis, a family-structure crisis, a race-relations crisis, or whatever crisis will get the job done, naturally we want someone to save us. And politicians are all too eager both to persuade us to listen to them describe how terrible things are and to run into their embrace to save us from that which they have so strenuously warned us about. On this I leave you with the words of the noted wisecracking Baltimore writer H.L. Mencken, who said on one occasion that "[t]he whole aim of practical politics is to keep the populace alarmed (and hence clamorous to be led to safety) by menacing it

---

[24]This is not to suggest that intellectuals are merely a postwar phenomenon, just that the market for ideas has grown dramatically in recent decades.

with an endless series of hobgoblins, all of them imaginary," and then went on to add that "[t]he urge to save humanity is almost always only a false-face for the urge to rule it."

How Things Got Better

Why have so many wonderful things happened, and so many horrible things failed to happen? As noted earlier, a key part of the story is the creation of positive-sum situations. But this only describes the environment, not the precise driver of the changes. And I will contend that the person responsible for the most human progress—the people who do the heavy lifting that has made life so much better over time—is the entrepreneur in his role as social reorganizer.

In the American South, one can still occasionally hear people refer to refrigerators as *iceboxes*. The reason for that is that once upon a time, before the invention of mechanical refrigeration, food was placed in a box that was cooled by ice, and the term stuck around after the technology changed. But it has probably never occurred to you to ask how it is that one could ship ice to a place like Dallas, Texas, and sell it every day in the summer, given that the temperature there could easily be over 100 degrees for days on end. In fact, the story of how ice came to be shipped across great distances is an amazing story of entrepreneurial triumph. In September 1833, the U.S. ship *Tuscany* arrived in the blisteringly hot city of Calcutta, India with a shipload of … ice. How such a thing became possible had to do with a Bostonian named Frederic Tudor, who after visiting the Caribbean had decided that there was money to be made shipping ice from the U.S. Northeast, where it was all too plentiful in the winter, to a place where it was desperately wanted during the seemingly endless summer. Because this had never been done before, it was up to him figure out how to do it. After trial and error, he finally found information that earned reward from the market—in particular, that storing the ice in a ventilated chamber with sawdust insulation allowed ice to be profitably taken from the Northeast to the Caribbean. While in the Caribbean, he realized he could make more money taking fruit in both directions—apples from New England to Cuba, oranges the other way. So ice was harvested in the American Northeast and upper Midwest, allowing for the chilling of fruit and flowers.[25] By 1833, Tudor could use what he was calling his "ice plantations" to ship ice to Calcutta, where in September more than 100 out of 150 tons made

---

[25]One of the places Tudor's workers got their ice was near Walden Pond, which local resident Henry David Thoreau in his journal took a dim view of because of the disturbance, although he expressed amazement that his "pure" water would end up in India, mixed with the "sacred" water of the Ganges.

it from Boston after a four-month journey. Later, other entrepreneurs working through the spontaneous order began to ship American beef to London, where Queen Victoria pronounced her first taste of the U.S. product "very good."[26]

In the context of the 19th century, this is an amazing achievement. But in fact entrepreneurs are constantly doing things that others think are impossible. That is what it means to reorganize society—to do something that others have, out of ignorance of the idea itself or of knowledge about how to make it work, left undone. Although there are of course a number of great individuals who have done great things through social activism, leading military campaigns, or politics, the prime mover of history—of changes in how we live—has been the entrepreneur. He has been the lone genius like Thomas Edison, who believed that by tinkering in his lab, things thought to be undoable actually weren't. He has been the eccentric dreamer, like the Wright brothers, who thought that William Thomson[27] and the uncountable thousands who thought the way he did were simply wrong, and that it was possible to make a heavier-than-air flying machine, which has gone on to provide boundless opportunity for people to see new places, to do business with people in faraway lands, and to generally shrink the world. They have been the graduate students at Stanford who had the vision to see[28] that there is a better way to rank web pages, by how popular they are with everybody else rather than by the keywords the web page designers select themselves. They then used this insight to create Google, which in addition to organizing the information on the Internet much more effectively, has given us new maps, new tools for translators, new ways of sharing our lives, and perhaps soon new ways to drive cars.[29]

These are the people who make history. With a small number of exceptions—Edison, Ford, the "robber barons"—history books do not concentrate on entrepreneurs and the role they have played in reorganizing society for the better, and when they mention them, they often emphasize their negative aspects. But it is they at least as much and perhaps in some ways more than

---

[26] The data and details of Tudor's story, who like many entrepreneurs had failure mixed in with success, was recounted in "The Ice Trade Between America and India," *Mechanics' Magazine, Museum, Register, Journal and Gazette*, April 9, 1836 (http://todayinsci.com/T/Tudor_Frederic/IceTradeAmericaToIndia.htm) and Henry G. Pearson, "Frederic Tutor, Ice King," *Proceedings of the Massachusetts Historical Society* 65 (Oct. 1932-May 1936), pp. 169-215, available at http://www.iceharvestingusa.com/Frederic%20Tudor%20Ice%20King.html.

[27] http://en.wikipedia.org/wiki/William_Thomson,_1st_Baron_Kelvin#Pronouncements_later_proven_to_be_false

[28] http://infolab.stanford.edu/~backrub/google.html

[29] http://www.wired.com/magazine/2012/01/ff_autonomouscars/all/1

presidents, kings, popes, and generals, who have allowed us to escape the life "infested with lice and parasites," and the city with ordure flowing through the streets. It is true that many improvements in our lives have been built by science and by governments—the discoveries of vaccines, the construction of public-health infrastructure, etc. But to be a scientist is not to be a seller— a person who actually figures out ways to make scientific breakthroughs practically useful and distributes them via the construction (in the pursuit of self-interest) of trading networks to those who can benefit from them. To invent a marvelous medicine is not the same thing as figuring out how to get it into the hands of as many people as possible, and to make it at lower resource cost. And such contributions as government has made to prosperity have been built mostly on the wealth generated by people buying and selling in the market, whether they are grand visionaries like Ford or small-scale dreamers like our stationery-shop owner.

How is it that entrepreneurs' dreams become life-changing reality? A while back I mentioned the year 1780, and while one could quarrel about the exact year that the modern miracle began, it is clear that around that time in England something changed that led to the creation of modern industry, whose benefits have since spread around the world. England was a country that protected property rights better than most, and following their two revolutions in the 1600s those rights were sufficiently well entrenched to set the table for the Industrial Revolution. A key lesson of all economic history is that for entrepreneurs to work their magic, they must have the freedom to try, which means also the freedom to fail. From both successes and failures, society learns how to do things better. The fruits of economic freedom are plain to see not just in the achievements already of those countries that have relied on it the longest, but in the new success in places like China and India, where the degree of control the state has over private individuals in the economic arena has loosened dramatically in recent decades. Entrepreneurs make progress, and economic freedom makes entrepreneurs.

This freedom to experiment is necessary because the future is almost impossibly hard to predict. It is not hard, in addition to the earlier predictors of doom, to find more mundane predictions about what the future would be like that failed to hold true. Artists gave it a shot, predicting (without much accuracy in the end) at the beginning of the 20th century what life would be like in Paris at the end of it.[30] Science-fiction writers have also tried, imagining robots that would resemble humans physically, while cognitively remaining very fast computers. Such is the nature of the droids in *Star Wars* and, comically, the robot character in the over-the-top campy 1960s TV series *Lost in*

---

[30]http://publicdomainreview.org/2012/06/30/france-in-the-year-2000-1899-1910/

Space. (Look up a picture of this character if you want to see an example of what robots turn out not to look like.) Instead, they are industrial robots, like the one here.[31]

The movie *2001:A Space Odyssey* had, by 2001, an elegant space station that among other things gave people a place to rest on their way to the permanent base on the moon. We have had space stations, of course, but they are considerably more spartan. That movie also featured the human-like computer HAL, which malfunctioned when it was asked to lie like humans, forcing a human crew member to destroy it. In fact, computers became the incredibly useful things they are not just by becoming more powerful but by being linked together, first in local area networks and later across the planet through the Internet.

When the artificial language Esperanto was created in the second half of the 19th century by Ludwig Zamenhof, it was assumed by many that it would become the language of the world, shoving aside widely spoken but parochial languages like English and French. In fact, perhaps precisely because it was a centrally planned language with a set of rules imposed by its designer, Esperanto had no chance against the spontaneously ordered, constantly evolving languages that people actually speak. Indeed, if there is anything close to a world language now it is English, itself a spontaneously ordered combination of Germanic and Latin-descended languages that absorbs foreign words (*pajamas, ennui*) happily and is constantly in motion. Language is constantly evolving and wonderfully effective despite (because of?) the lack of central design. In that, it is like all economic change.

Much of humanity's progress does not come from mere small extensions of the status quo, but consists of dramatic advances that come from unexpected places. They became important precisely because a free society already existed to create them, play with them, and see how best to use them. An example is the antibiotic penicillin, which was the result of an unexpected contamination of a laboratory experiment, which gave Alexander Fleming and other scientists a moment to seize in order to transform the way we treat bacterial diseases. (Antibiotics, like vaccines, have probably saved tens of millions of lives since their invention.) Tim Berners-Lee, the person credited with inventing HTML code (the primary language for building webpages), probably had no idea that his invention would lead to people engaging in microlending to fight poverty and fund businesses, solving previously unsolvable scientific problems through crowd-sourcing, and doing things as mundane as watching cats making music or a robust defense of Britney Spears on YouTube. Charles Townes, one of the men credited with helping invent the laser—a device now widely used to fix detached retinas and address retinal

---

[31]http://en.wikipedia.org/wiki/File:FANUC_6-axis_welding_robots.jpg

damage caused by years of high blood sugar in older diabetics—was asked by *The Economist* in 2005 to talk of this use, and he replied by saying he had never heard of a detached retina. So it goes in a society willing to rely on the freedom to constantly experiment, in part on the basis of other experiments before yours.

The seductiveness of big centrally directed plans—the siren song of the politician who tells us that such-and-such are the jobs of the future or that the preservation of our way of life requires keeping this or that bankrupt company afloat with taxpayers' money—probably comes from the way they seem to reflect our instinct as individuals. We are constantly, and properly, urged to prepare for the future by saving for retirement and our children's education, to buy insurance against unexpected calamities, and so on. Many feel a little dismissive at the person who is unprepared, and this is a belief that cuts across cultures. Aesop had his fable of the ant and the grasshopper; the great ancient Indian sage Kautilya wrote in his work *Arthashastra*, which was advice for the leader who wanted to be wise, that "Tomorrow's deed should be done today. What is to be done in the afternoon should be done in the forenoon." Or, more straightforwardly, "Money should be saved for difficult days." But this is advice for the *individual*, given precisely because the individual cannot predict what may come, and savings are a way to be ready for anything. The problem in the economy, in contrast, is that because we cannot from our satellite predict what people will invent or see down on the ground, what the details of trade-offs in the economy are, we must *avoid* committing to a specific path. The future is not a thing to be reached, it is a thing to be discovered or, better still, created.

The song "The Internationale," originally written in France in 1871 as an anthem for the then-rising socialist movement, suggests in its American version that a better future only comes from organized agitation, even violent revolution— that, to quote its words directly, through socialism "a better world's in birth" and that "[t]he earth shall rise on new foundations." Alas, it didn't work out that way, as socialism failed in Russia, China, and pretty much everywhere it was tried for reasons outlined earlier in this book. It turns out that building a brighter future does not involve a lot of marching and violence against one's oppressors. It is actually rather boring, not the stuff of movies or novels. It is nerds working late into the evening at Microsoft, it is stationery-store owners hoping their little economic experiment succeeds, it is hard-working immigrants in Los Angeles putting in 60-hour weeks so they and their children can move up to something better. It is competition and exchange and experiments successful and unsuccessful. It is not sexy, but it is how the future happens. There is only one dystopia, and it is the planner's. Economic planning almost never works—regulating monopolies only strengthens them through regulatory capture, minimum wages for women unemploy them, helping "the working class" by strengthening unions keeps many workers from finding work, rent control limits lodging for the poor, zoning rules make housing impossibly expensive, 116 agencies (the number of entities in the federal government controlling financial trading) worth of stock regulations don't eliminate financial turmoil but do raise the cost of issuing and trading stock, and a $750 billion economic stimulus doesn't lower the unemployment rate.[32]

On and on it goes, but still we never learn. Any society with decentralized, costly information—which is to say any society at all—must endure periods of instability and even painful retrenchment if it is to progress. It is entrepreneurs who carry out this process, who do the hard work of discovering a brighter future. Granting entrepreneurs the freedom to do their thing, including the freedom to fail, is the best solution for making a better world if that world is full of imperfect people making imperfect decisions. With any luck, with the passage of time, the role of the entrepreneur in building our better future will be more appreciated.

■ **Note**   Progress is substantially the entrepreneur's doing, regardless of the scale of his entrepreneurial experiments.

Economics Out There

For good summaries and criticism of doomsdayism, read these two articles, one from the *New York Times*,[33] and the other from *Wired* magazine.[34]

9.1. Take a look at this video.[35] Do you think the market price of a washing machine accurately reflects its value, overstates it, or understates it? What other unappreciated modern miracles can you think of?

9.2. This article[36] and another from the *San Francisco Chronicle*[37] discuss the environmental costs of each human life. Should we conclude from this that the world has too many people?

---

[32]I owe this way of thinking about the contrast, if not all the items in the list, to Dierdre McCloskey, *The Bourgeois Virtues: Ethics for an Age of Commerce* (Chicago: University of Chicago Press, 2006).

[33]http://www.nytimes.com/1996/09/29/magazine/the-optimists-are-right.html?pagewanted=all&src=pm

[34]http://www.wired.com/wiredscience/2012/08/ff_apocalypsenot/

[35]http://www.youtube.com/watch?v=BZoKfap4g4w

[36]https://www.mja.com.au/journal/2007/187/3/personal-carbon-trading-potential-stealth-intervention-obesity-reduction

[37]http://www.sfgate.com/homeandgarden/article/GREEN-Maybe-None-Is-having-a-child-even-one-3236285.php

9.3. What should we really be worried about? Here is one person's estimate.[38] Why do you suppose we tend to exaggerate some risks so much, while being so ignorant of others?

9.4. The writer Virginia Postrel has written often on progress, and one of her essays on this topic is "No Flying Cars, but the Future Is Bright."[39]

    a. She mentions FedEx, Facebook, and Starbucks as examples of progress. Are they really? Why or why not? What about cheap air travel, which was made possible substantially by airline deregulation?

    b. Why do you suppose people think of progress in terms of space flight and flying cars? Is the absence of such things a sign of lack of progress?

    c. Is the modern era in fact largely devoid of "disruptive technologies"?

9.5. Crisis or not?[40] Why or why not?

---

[38]http://www.ecolo.org/documents/documents_in_english/Bernard.Cohen.rankRisks.htm

[39]http://www.bloomberg.com/news/2012-12-16/no-flying-cars-but-the-future-is-bright.html

[40]http://www.bbc.com/future/story/20120308-touch-and-go-screens

The Things Only Government Can Do

The Economics of "Market Failure"

Much of this book to this point has been a caution against—some might say a tirade against—excessive reliance on government to make sound decisions when resources are scarce, people pursue their self-interest, and information is costly. But as noted previously, government is among the oldest human institutions, and human institutions do not persevere so long—since the dawn of settled agriculture, perhaps 7,000 years ago—unless they bring some benefits. And although much of what government can do, as we have seen, is inimical to human achievement precisely because prices ordinarily provide incentives for people to use scarce resources to greatest social benefit, it turns out that sometimes market prices provide poor incentives. Government, by using its power to take command of resources or limit how they are used, can in fact use them more efficiently under these circumstances. The conditions required for this to be true, which also have relevance even outside the question of government versus private responses to resource-use decisions, must be carefully delineated, and this chapter does that.

Setting the Table for the Entrepreneur and the Market

The analysis so far has indicated first that markets, operating via the signals given by prices, cause resources to move toward where they can create the most value. In addition, it has argued that giving entrepreneurs (and everyone) the incentive to harvest costly decentralized knowledge ensures that as much of that knowledge as can be used will be used. But this *requires* that the government set up the institutions that allow people to trade, institutions that are easy to take for granted. Thus, it is important to understand that from the economic point of view the first task of government is to *facilitate trade*.

Foremost in the effort to facilitate trade is giving people confidence that their property is secure from seizure, both by private thieves and by agents of the government itself committing thievery under the color of authority. Recall our stationery store owner from Chapter 7. In recounting his little revolutionary act, we have actually assumed quite a bit. We have assumed first that it was a straightforward matter for him to come to an agreement with the owner of his storefront, to sign a contract that would allow him to use the space for a specified period of time in exchange for a specified payment. But who will make sure this agreement is held to? To some extent, it is self-enforcing. A store owner renting the store space who suddenly refused to pay the rent (perhaps by physically threatening the shopping-center owner) would acquire a reputation of being a deadbeat, and an owner of a shopping center who suddenly expelled his tenant halfway through the lease, perhaps by relying on his own private muscle, would have to cope with the reputation of being unreliable. So, people can uphold their agreements without the law.

Hasidic diamond traders, who operate in New York, Antwerp (Belgium), Israel, and India, among other places, are famous for doing business with one another without contracts, a common practice among middleman minorities. But sometimes people have honest disagreements about what a contract means—whether the store owner or shopping-center owner really can get out of the lease agreement—so the government's courts provide a means for resolving these conflicts. The ability to enforce contracts makes people willing to commit to trade with each other, especially with people they don't know well, which increases the amount of trade that occurs. In addition, if the person who owns the shopping center wants to sell it, the government can guarantee that the rights to decide how the property should be used can be reliably transferred from the old owner to the new. If someone vandalizes his property, lowering its value by making people more reluctant to do business there and increasing his costs, the state can after due process of law inflict the necessary punishment, thus deterring (imperfectly) that damage.

In general, in addition to enforcing contracts, another key function of government then is *to protect the property rights of people from being violated.* Government punishes those who steal cars or rob others at gunpoint, who commit acts of violence, who write contracts they never intend to fulfill (by selling fraudulent medicines, for example), and do other things that result in the destruction of value. *Enabling exchange by enforcing property and contract rights is the first economic task of the state.* A society without meaningful enforcement of property rights is one in which people have to waste inordinate amounts of resources defending themselves from others—by driving around in very costly armored vehicles, living in fortresses, and hiring private security guards, for example—all of which claim resources that could have been used to create wealth. And everyone's potential gains from trade are lowered when people are unwilling to shop in or do business in certain neighborhoods because of the sense of danger. A society without contract enforcement is one in which people lack the confidence to do business with people whose reputations they do not know or trust (in other words, people for whom information on reliability or creditworthiness is too costly to obtain). If the would-be stationery-store owner is sufficiently worried that the contractual agreements he enters into will not be enforced, or that his profits will be taken (by robbers on the way home from work or by the government in the form of an unanticipated tax on his profits), he will not take the risk of opening the store to being with.[1]

■ **Note** To talk meaningfully about exchange and property rights, we must assume an entity that can enforce property and contract rights. In every successful society, the government performs these tasks.

Note that, contrary to the claims of some, protecting property and contract rights is not something that benefits primarily the rich but actually the poor. The rich find it much easier to buy their way out of dangerous neighborhoods and can buy security protection that the poor cannot afford. The rich can leave their region or country if things get too bad, and they can rely on their reputations and their collateral to get access to capital. It is the poor—lacking assets to pledge as collateral or to use to protect themselves and their property

---

[1] The owner runs the risk of too much government as well as too little. If there are 1,000 regulations that his store might violate, he runs the risk nearly every day of police officers coming in demanding bribes to look the other way rather than cite him for the 40 or 50 obscure rules he is currently breaking. He might also have to worry, if the government itself can violate his property rights with impunity, that some official could take his store and give it to a crony just at the moment as it is starting to succeed. These things routinely happen every day in countries around the world.

(whether in rich countries like the U.S. or poor ones like Brazil or India, poor neighborhoods are the most dangerous ones)—who benefit most from the establishment of the rule of law. The law, uniformly and reliably enforced for rich and poor alike, is the key to providing the poor the capacity to work their way into something better. It is also the poor, people like Mohammed Bouazizi, who are most vulnerable to the power of the state to change the rules and to use its power to abuse and rob the citizenry. It is the poor who suffer most from high crime, abusive police, bureaucrats' shakedowns, and the inability to get justice from the courts. The poor do not have access to these things until their rights are respected before the law. (If you do not believe that it is the poor who benefit the most from establishment of law and order, think about who is victimized most by crime and violence in contemporary America.)

▨ **Note**   Property rights benefit the poor the most.

When Prices Are Wrong

But there are times when simply allowing people to establish ownership of and use property in particular ways (whether it is actual land, other physical property such as vehicles, or abstract but nonetheless valuable property like human capital or time) actually leads to inferior results for society as a whole. To see how this happens, I will repeat a point I made in Chapter 3: prices are a way of making people take account of the consequences for everyone else of their choices. If they are not allowed to freely move up or down, bad things happen because people do not have to face all of these consequences.

Recall that the reason this happens is that supply and demand reflect, respectively, social cost and social value. The supply curve tells us the price producers need in order to be willing to produce various quantities of goods, and this reflects the alternate uses the resources needed to produce this good have—in other words, the opportunity cost society must pay to use resources to produce any amount of this good. Demand tells us how much people will buy at any price, which is a sign of what each quantity is worth to them. Excessively high (low) prices lead to an adjustment downward (upward) in price and a corresponding adjustment in quantity, so that the price system reconciles the conflicting uses we have for scarce resources. In the (very simple) example from Chapter 7, those resources were a store location in a shopping center, the time of five workers, the supplies needed to run the stationery store, and the time of the entrepreneur/owner.

But now consider another kind of market—the market for steel. Manufacturing steel, like selling stationery, is an action that requires the imposition of costs on society in order to produce something that other members of society value. To oversimplify dramatically (to make the problem easy to explain), assume that to manufacture steel requires the entrepreneurs who own the company to stake claims to the following resources: the time of their workers, land to put their factory on, iron ore, and miscellaneous supplies. Just as in the case of the stationery store, the steel company will purchase these resources and combine them in whatever way maximizes profits and will only stay in business if the price they get for the steel they produce exceeds the combined opportunity cost of these resources. So far, the problem is just like that of the stationery-store owner. We may rely entirely on the market process to decide whether this steel company should continue to exist or not, and if so how much steel it should produce.

But in fact, the action of manufacturing steel imposes a major social cost that is not generated in any significant way by the action of selling stationery. In particular, the manufacture of steel also generates substantial air pollution. Is this a social cost? Certainly. It damages the health of others, and air pollution has also been shown to damage personal property of others—car windshield wipers and tires wear out faster because of damage from all the gunk in the air in places like Los Angeles and Houston, for example. Next to human health, this is a secondary effect, but we still want to count it. The difference between this cost and other costs is that the entrepreneurs making decisions about the steel factory need not take account of this cost when they decide whether to pollute, and if so how much.

The pollution is thus an example of an *external cost* or *negative externality—a cost of an action taken that is imposed on others but that does not have to be taken account of by the person taking the action.* This is distinct from the cost imposed by the decision of the entrepreneurs to hire workers, buy land, and acquire all the other resources they need to make steel. Taking the action of luring them away from other uses also imposes costs on society, because those resources are not being used for some other purpose. But the entrepreneurs must take account of this cost because they must pay the owners of those resources a price that persuades the owners to allow them to be used for the purpose the entrepreneurs want to use them for. (This was a point made in Chapter 7.) We call these kinds of costs *private costs—costs that must be taken account of by the person taking the action,* or in the jargon of the economics trade, costs that must be *internalized* by the decision maker.

The same negative-externality effect is actually at work in traffic jams. When someone decides to take a trip in a car, he must take account of the private costs he imposes on himself. Among others, there is the marginal cost of the gasoline his car uses on the trip, wear and tear on the car, and the time costs he has to spend driving. He will not take a trip unless the benefits he expects to receive from it exceed these costs. But in fact he also imposes costs on others, because the fact that he is on the road means that other drivers have to slow down. He thus imposes external time costs on them. This effect may seem very small, but one need only look at a freeway in Los Angeles or Atlanta at rush hour to understand how small costs imposed by any individual can add up to dramatic costs in the aggregate. There is thus again a clear distinction between private costs and external costs. In a delicious irony, drivers who complain about the traffic problem *are* the problem, by their very presence on the road.

The trouble with external costs is that they are not included in the prices that guide decision making, but should be. Thus, the statement I made earlier about prices giving people reasons to take account of the consequences of their actions for others is no longer operative. Another way to think about it is in terms of our supply/demand model from Chapters 2–3. It can take account of the external-cost problem by altering it, as shown in Figure 10-1.

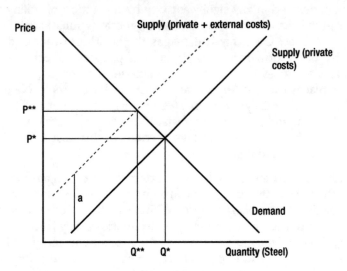

Figure 10-1. Supply and demand with a negative externality

The solid black curve labeled "Supply (private costs)" is the supply curve based on the cost of a steel maker obtaining control over land, workers' time, iron ore, and supplies. In essence, it is the supply curve we have been using up until now. But this curve neglects the external pollution costs. The dashed curve labeled "Supply (private + external costs)" incorporates these costs. It is assumed, for the sake of convenience, that each unit of steel produced imposes costs in the amount *a* on society, so that the two supply curves are parallel. This may not be true, but it makes explanation easier. The demand curve is just the demand curve, and reflects the value of various quantities of steel to society, measured as usual by what buyers—other businesses using steel in making the things they make; no one buys steel to keep around the house—are willing to pay. The graph simply depicts the idea outlined earlier, that the total cost to society of producing steel is higher than the costs that the steelmakers take into account when deciding how much steel to produce.

This means that the market equilibrium is not the best one, in the sense used in Chapter 3. Recall that that equilibrium occurs where the supply curve crosses the demand curve, at price P* and quantity Q*. But we want steel producers to take account of all of their costs, not just the private ones. If they had to take those into account, their decision making would be different. I denote this equilibrium with two asterisks instead of one, because it is a better equilibrium for society overall, if it can actually be achieved. If we incorporate the pollution costs into our decision making, as we should, then the price of steel will go up to P**, and quantity will go down to Q**. The failure of the steelmakers to take account of the external costs in their decision to make steel in whatever quantity means that *steel is underpriced*, that is, that the price does not reflect the full social cost of the action of making steel. Precisely because steel is too cheap, it is over-consumed. If we can figure out some way to lower steel production, preferably in a way that directly requires steel consumers to take account of the external costs their decision to buy steel imposes on society, in addition to the private (and therefore already internalized) ones, society will be better served.[2]

The traffic problem is the same in its nature, although not necessarily in its solution. Every traveler should be required to take account of the crowding costs imposed on other drivers if we are to achieve the efficient amount of (that is, reduce the number of) car trips. However, there is a way to make this happen. If the road is privately owned, the owner of the road will charge a price that takes account of the negative impact of each paying driver on his other paying drivers. This reveals a powerful insight about what negative externalities really are. They are simply *a property right that is missing* or, more accurately, *a right that is too costly to enforce*. Road space is typically (although not always) available free of explicit monetary charge. If it were not, the owners of the road would set the price in the same way that the owner of the stationery store does for the things he sells. Frequently, costs that are external at the local level are not external at the level of the person making the decision.

For example, in restaurants if smokers and non-smokers are at adjacent tables there will be local externalities. If you like to smoke with dinner, and I hate having my meal surrounded by cigarette smoke, then your act of lighting up makes my meal worse and thus imposes a negative externality on me. Critically, note that if you are not allowed to smoke with dinner, that makes the value of your meal worth less to you as well. In a sense, no matter how we best allocate the right—either I get the right to tell you not to smoke or you get the right to blow smoke over my table—someone will lose out. However, the restaurant owner wants to maximize profits. He will therefore have an incentive to trade

---

[2]Note that even if steel producers are initially made to bear these costs—for example, by installing pollution-control equipment or paying a pollution tax on every ton of steel they produce—these costs will be passed on to consumers, as they should be.

off what smokers are willing to pay to smoke with their meals and what non-smokers are willing to pay to eat without the irritation of others' smoke. At the level of the restaurant owner, in other words, there are no external costs. The system of property rights is sufficient to enable him to make the decision that balances the conflicting interests properly.

Note finally that the possible solutions to this conflict over the air are not limited to *allow smoking everywhere* or *allow smoking nowhere*. The restaurant owner also has it within his power to set up smoking and non-smoking sections, and to do so in ways that really do allow non-smokers to eat in the way they prefer. Thus, laws to prohibit smoking in all bars and restaurants, which of course exist in many locations, are actually inefficient, because they ignore the interests of smokers. (Although it makes no difference to whether the argument is a good one or not, I say this as someone who does not smoke and does not like the people at the table next to me to do so.) That restaurant owners in areas without laws that prohibit smoking do come up with a wide variety of smoking policies for their restaurants is testimony to the power of the spontaneous order in promoting social experimentation and the accommodation of disagreement about how scarce resources (restaurant seating in this case) should be used.

■ **Note**   Externalities only matter if there is no market decision maker who can internalize them.

But whereas smoking in restaurants and taking up space on a road are locally external costs that can be internalized higher up by decision makers who own, respectively, the entire restaurant or the entire road, sometimes negative externalities are really not amenable to this kind of solution. The pollution problem in particular cannot be solved by relying on property rights. The problem of pollution, in essence, is that there is no way to enforce a right to air (or water, in the case of water pollution). There is no way to meaningfully enforce the idea that this air is mine and that air is yours, so that you are not allowed to pollute "my" air without my consent. In economic terms, a property right to air—dividing the air into mine and yours—is too costly to enforce, so there is no point in trying. In such circumstances, we have to try something else. One could require that certain kinds of pollution-control machinery be installed on all cars and in all factories. The problem with this approach is that the decisions about which controls to require will be made by self-interested politicians and bureaucrats, who will be ignorant about all possible pollution-control options and may have an incentive to favor those who are closest to them or give them the most cash, as suggested in Chapter 5. A better solution is simply to limit the amount of pollution a factory is allowed to emit and leave it to factory owners to decide the lowest cost way to get pollution down to this level. This solution allows us to take advantage of the spontaneous order to solve the pollution problem in the lowest-cost way possible by allowing the company to innovate in its pollution-control techniques.

Note that I say *limit* and not *eliminate* pollution. The reason is because of what pollution is. In economic thinking, pollution is not a sin, it is simply a bad (and unpriced) side effect of doing something good. The manufacture of steel, as with most actions that generate pollution, is an activity that also generates many social benefits. Steel enables modern transportation, allows the creation of taller, stronger buildings (both commercial and residential), and is generally nearly indispensable to modern life. As of now, there is no way to manufacture it without generating external pollution costs. So, bringing pollution from the steel industry down to zero would mean having no steel, which be a different kind of—and much more substantial—cost. The trick is to balance the two good things—less pollution and modern life—at the right place.

It is sometimes proposed that rights to pollute be created, in the form of permits that can be acquired which entitle the holder to generate the amount of pollution specified in the permit. These permits would be tradable like any other kind of property, allowing those companies that have no way of reducing their emissions except at very high cost to buy the permits from companies that can reduce emissions at very low cost. Such programs exist for air pollution in the Southern California region and for carbon emissions in the nations of the European Union. Unfortunately, because of such problems as uncertainty about how the market rules might change, it is not clear that these programs achieve substantial cost savings. It is also possible simply to tax the output of the item whose manufacture generates the pollution. In the situation in Figure 10-1, this is an easy solution. Every steel company should simply be required to pay tax in the amount of a on every unit of steel they produce. This approach makes the pollution generated into a private cost, eliminating the externality problem. Because a is the amount of social cost that the manufacturers were not taking account of because it was external and not private, the market now properly harmonizes the cost of manufacturing steel with the value to society of making it.

As a practical matter, though, pollution externalities may not be constant over all ranges of production, and so this approach too may have limits. Sometimes, outright bans might be the lowest-cost way to solve externalities. If your loud parties are keeping me awake in the apartment upstairs, that is a negative externality imposed by your guests on me, and the typical approach to that is simply to have the police threaten legal sanction for those who do not get the noise down. That is almost certainly the most straightforward way to solve that problem, rather than having people buy and sell "permits" to make noise. So, all we can say about the negative externality is the following: *if a reliable property right can be created or already exists at some higher level of decision making, the externality problem can be resolved easily. If not, we just have to do the best we can in figuring out the lowest-cost way to solve it, by the application of some kind of government rules if necessary.*

Positive Externalities

In principle, there is no reason why the value to society of an action taken cannot *exceed* the value to the person taking the action. Thomas Sowell cites the example of mudflaps. With the exception of the value that some people take from having what we can charitably call mudflap artwork on the backs of their vehicles, almost all the social value of installing a mudflap actually accrues to other drivers. One's own vehicle does not ordinarily throw rocks that damage one's own windshield. Instead, the crack happens because of a rock that somebody else's car threw up. Again, as with the case of an outright ban on loud parties, the most straightforward solution is probably just to require that owners of sufficiently large vehicles (certainly semi trucks, perhaps large pickup trucks as well) install them. People who keep their homes well maintained do so at some cost to themselves, but some of the benefits flow to the neighbors in the form of less irritation from looking at dilapidated property and from higher property values. The social benefit to a well-maintained home, in other words, is greater than the private benefit to the homeowner. Of course, this is often an externality that is local at the level of the individual owner but which real estate developers properly internalize by including rules on home upkeep in their housing-association rules.[3]

What to Do

The externality problem is a complicated one. It is easy to invoke whenever we don't like the choices someone else has made. Almost any action can be held to cause emotional externalities to people who get sufficiently upset because the action was performed, and many actions that are more concrete externalities are trivial in scale. Paul Heyne has noted that "the beginning of all wisdom on this topic is a clear recognition that negative externalities cannot be completely eliminated."[4] Good manners (knocking on your neighbor's door and asking him to turn the music down, keeping your property well maintained) eliminate many negative externalities, and self-sorting through the market process eliminates others.

Near where I live, which is in the countryside a bit but where many larger homes are currently being constructed, there is a farmer who has erected a sign by the road that tells others that agricultural activities from time to

---

[3]Note that these are not the same thing as zoning rules, because there is no criminal penalty for failing to observe them and because it is much easier to choose whether or not to live in a particular housing development on the basis of its rules rather than, for example, to choose whether or not to live in California, which has extensive land-use controls imposed on the entire state.

[4]Paul Heyne, *The Economic Way of Thinking*, Ninth Edition (Prentice Hall, 2009): 322.

time generate noise and stench, that he was there first, and to keep that in mind when deciding whether to move here and complain about it. People sufficiently bothered by such things will be inclined not to live there rather than move there and demand that the externality—the result of farming as it is most efficiently done, externality aside—be eliminated by legal action. In cities, one often observes families with children, or singles who want to live near active night life, tending to self-sort into neighborhoods full of others like them, meaning that not every problem that crosses a property line calls out for a law. But we must confess that there are times when the externality is so pronounced that we must consider legally mitigating it in the interest of the greater social good.

The "Market Failure" of Nonexcludability and Nonrivalry

Several times a year, public television and radio stations have fundraisers. In these events, the stations engage in various activities to persuade people to give money to support something that they can get for free. As an aside, as best I can tell, the ways in which public TV stations do this has changed over time. When I was young, they had the pledge drive, in which staff members of the stations standing in front of a phone bank beseeched the public to give money. Later this was replaced by an auction, in which local merchants would donate goods to be sold to the highest bidder, with the station getting funds. Now, it seems that they run previously aired concerts and other beloved programs designed to appeal to public TV viewers to give money, usually accompanied by a prerecorded announcement by the station and a continuous subtitle with the number to call. This shows that even nonprofit institutions like public TV stations still respond to some degree to incentives, and to some degree are entrepreneurs constantly in search of new ways to do things.

The audience for public broadcasting values it as a good. But public broadcasting is unlike many goods in that one can consume it whether one pays a monetary price or not. (One must still pay a time price, although increasingly new entertainment technology allows people to watch shows when they want to rather than when the TV network wants them to, allowing the viewer to select the block of time with the lowest opportunity cost.) Standard economic theory would predict that people would tend not to pay money for things that they can get, in monetary terms, for free. And indeed the vast majority of people who consume public broadcasting do not contribute to the stations they watch and listen to. There would be a simple way to solve this problem, which is the way private, for-profit broadcasters solve it, that is, by charging businesses for the rights to broadcast commercials on these stations. But public broadcasters are unwilling to use these methods, and so they choose the method of begging instead. This means their budget is lower, but it also means they are less constrained in their broadcast choices, by not having to worry about whether advertisers are willing to be associated with certain programs. (Or maybe they face *different* constraints, since they *do* have to worry about what their donors want to watch.)

I'll Eat, You Pay: Nonexcludability

The core problem of the public broadcaster is actually relatively common. It is called *nonexcludability*, which means *the inability to prevent people who do not pay for a service from consuming it.* In a sense, this too is the problem of a property right that is too costly to enforce. If technology were available that allowed only people who paid for public broadcasting to receive it, in the same way there is technology (and there are laws and social norms) that prevents people from walking in to Walmart and walking out with a computer without paying for it, the public radio station would simply make its signal available only to those who had paid. Indeed there are such technologies, such as cable, satellite radio, and satellite TV. In these technologies, nonpayers are clearly excludable. Thus, these companies need not go periodically to their audiences pleading for money. And even over-the-air broadcasters possess one excludable resource: their programming time. Only those who pay for ad space actually get to run them on a commercial radio or television station, and so, as with all normal market processes, the amount of commercial time, and the specific commercials that fill it, are entrepreneurial decisions made in the context of the known trade-offs, so as to maximize profit.

But nonexcludability presents a significant economic problem. If people do not have to pay, no matter how valuable an action taken by an entrepreneur is to them, entrepreneurs get inadequate signals as to how valuable the action is, and under-produce it. In general the things will, depending on the circumstances, be overused or under-produced. In the public radio example, the fact that many consume without paying probably means that there is less public radio then there should be, evaluated by the usual economic criterion of whether a marginal increase in the production of it would create more marginal value than marginal cost. The reliance on the volunteer model means that public radio stations have fewer reporters, less variety of music, fewer features on their web sites, and so on than listeners would be willing to pay for—if only some way could be found to get them to do so.

What to do about such underpayment? As with externalities, if it is possible to make the good excludable, that is the ideal solution. For example, there is constant warfare between for-profit makers of digital content (software, books, songs, etc.) and some of the users of such content. When a book means a physical good that one buys at a bookstore and holds while reading, the value lost to nonpayers consuming the product is relatively small. One person who buys it can share it with a friend, or a person can at great expense (probably much greater than the cost of simply buying the book) copy it. He can also borrow it from a library, but libraries typically wait until prices have come down before ordering books, so libraries are a poor substitute for the customers who want the book the most and are most willing to pay the most for it. So, there is a nonexcludability problem for physical books, but it is small.

But the turning of more and more human knowledge, including books and music, into digital form has generated new problems for creators of such content. In principle, one can write a book or record a song, have one person pay for it as digital content, and then watch helplessly as that person transmits it freely around the world. One response to this nonexcludability problem is the law-first response, to impose legal penalties on people who access such content without paying for it, in violation of what are known as copyright laws. In addition, in an effort to prevent so-called "piracy" of content, many sellers of DVDs, digital music, etc. include coding that makes it difficult for the content to be copied.[5] When one downloads music from iTunes, for example, one cannot just e-mail the music at will to all of one's friends. Naturally, people who want to access this content without paying for it, and to allow others to do the same, try to break these digital barriers through their own computer coding. This practice is generally illegal under the 1998 Digital Millennium Copyright Act and other laws in the U.S. and elsewhere. Given the large number of people engaging in efforts to break through the copying barriers imposed by content producers and access the content, the battle against piracy is probably a losing proposition, although the entertainment industry is nonetheless committed to fighting it.

---

[5]Some of these barriers are implemented as much to enable what is known as *price discrimination*—charging different prices to different people for the same products—as to prevent copying. When one buys a videogame or DVD in East Asia, regional coding will sometimes mean that one cannot use it on a machine purchased in North America. This means that consumers cannot buy the content where it is cheaper than in their local market and then have it shipped, nor can they buy it where it is cheaper and resell it where it is more expensive. The fact that price is set differently in different markets is an act of price discrimination by the sellers of the content—trying to match prices to willingness to pay. If people in Asia aren't willing to pay as much for video games as people in North America, then it is profitable to charge people in North America more, and regional coding helps achieve this. Other examples of price discrimination include giving veterans and some students discounts for movie tickets (their average willingness to pay is lower), charging higher prices to airline customers to buy their tickets a few days before the flight leaves (done mostly by business travelers or others with higher willingness to pay), and college financial aid, which operates by extracting from every applicant detailed financial information, which also suggests his personal willingness to pay. What do you suppose would happen if a seller were required by law to charge the same price to all customers? (Go to http://www.insidehighered.com/news/2012/04/17/supreme-court-will-hear-case-major-implications-textbook-prices to read a legal case that involves price discrimination in the college-textbook market, although it is not the central issue in the case.)

The author Stephen King in 2000 tried a different approach, releasing a book called *The Plant* one chapter at a time online, and "charging" a dollar for each chapter, but without restricting people's access rights if they didn't pay. This model is very similar to the public broadcasting one and it had similar results. Some people did contribute, but King said he would not continue to put out chapters unless 75% of those who downloaded chapters paid the fee. In the end, he decided not to finish releasing the book, because too few people were paying. It remains unfinished, an example of a valuable product that is under-produced because those who are willing to pay are not *made* to pay as a condition of acquiring it—an example, in other words, of nonexcludability, although a nonexcludability that King consented to.

Nonexcludability can also result in over-consumption as well as under-production. The classic example was provided by the writer Garrett Hardin, an ecologist very concerned about over-consumption of the world's natural resources. He asked us to think about a pasture that is used for grazing by a group of people, each of whom owns his own cattle. The pasture is not fenced in, and anyone is free to use it. Each cattle owner is assumed to be interested only in maximizing the income from his own cattle. Each time a cow grazes, the owner of the cow receives the entire benefit, but there is less grass available for all the other owners. Thus, benefits are private but costs are collective. This, he claims, is a recipe for overuse of the resource. In deciding how many cattle to own and how frequently to graze them, each owner will consider only his own private benefit. This will mean that there are too many cattle, and that the pasture is over-grazed.

Hardin's example itself turns out not to be such a problem, precisely because individuals, left their own devices, have come up with ways to manage this problem by allocating *rights* to use the "common" pasture—in other words, by making it not so common after all. Closely knit communities seem to be able, according to the research of another economist named Elinor Ostrom, to limit overuse. In a far different time and a far different place, Governor William Bradford of Plymouth Plantation in 1623 fretted over the fact that his colonists chronically ran short of grain and produce. He eventually decided, in consultation with the colonists, to change the method of ownership from a common field worked by all to a series of private plots of land, each entrusted to one family. The result? According to Bradford's own testimony:

> This had very good success, for it made all hands very industrious, so as much more corn was planted than otherwise would have been by any means the Governor or any other could use, and saved him a great deal of trouble, and gave far better content. The women now went willingly into the field, and took their little ones with

them to set corn; which before would allege weakness and inability; whom to have compelled would have been thought great tyranny and oppression.

The experience that was had in this common course and condition, tried sundry years and that amongst godly and sober men, may well evince the vanity of that conceit of Plato's and other ancients applauded by some of later times; that the taking away of property and bringing in community into a commonwealth would make them happy and flourishing; as if they were wiser than God. For this community (so far as it was) was found to breed much confusion and discontent and retard much employment that would have been to their benefit and comfort. For the young men, that were most able and fit for labour and service, did repine that they should spend their time and strength to work for other men's wives and children without any recompense. The strong, or man of parts, had no more in division of victuals and clothes than he that was weak and not able to do a quarter the other could; this was thought injustice. The aged and graver men to be ranked and equalized in labours and victuals, clothes, etc., with the meaner and younger sort, thought it some indignity and disrespect unto them. And for men's wives to be commanded to do service for other men, as dressing their meat, washing their clothes, etc., they deemed it a kind of slavery, neither could many husbands well brook it. Upon the point all being to have alike, and all to do alike, they thought themselves in the like condition, and one as good as another; and so, if it did not cut off those relations that God hath set amongst men, yet it did at least much diminish and take off the mutual respects that should be preserved amongst them.[6]

The making of a nonexcludable resource into an excludable one, in other words, not only increased production but increased people's respect for one another, perhaps because it made them more conscious of the costs they imposed on others in their decisions. Markets and property rights once again became a way to peacefully and productively resolve conflicts over scarce resource use.

But in other circumstances, this over-consumption, which is called *the tragedy of the commons* (a term Hardin invented), is a severe problem. In recent years the European Union has expressed great concern about overfishing by its fishermen in the waters of the Mediterranean, in the North Sea, and off the coast of Northwest Africa. This problem has arisen because in recent decades

---

[6]http://press-pubs.uchicago.edu/founders/documents/v1ch16s1.html

there have been dramatic technological improvements in the ability of fishermen to harvest more fish with fewer resources, particularly through the use of large drift nets, which stretch miles across the ocean and trap huge numbers of fish, which the fisherman then sell. Unfortunately, those fish are necessary to produce the next generation of fish, and so to take them now imposes negative externalities on future generations of fishermen. But since that cost will not be borne by any individual fishermen, he neglects it.

This is the overuse version of the nonexcludability problem in a nutshell: benefits are privatized, costs are externalized. As a result, fish stocks in these regions (and elsewhere) seem to have declined substantially in recent years. Indeed, if each farmer is aware of the tragedy of the commons problem, he has an incentive to take as many fish as possible as quickly as possible, before some other fisherman does, in the manner of two people both given straws to drink out of the same glass—each one feels compelled to drink faster to make sure he gets it and the other guy doesn't.

Other examples abound. Apparently, people who run marathons are growing increasingly irritated at people who run in the races without paying the necessary entry fees.[7] Operating a marathon requires acquiring control over scarce resources, in particular the time of staff members, the food and water that runners use during and after the race, T-shirts and medals, and the police who must be hired to shut down roads and patrol them while the race is going on. Apparently the nonexcludability problem is partially combated by race organizers hiring people to try to look out for counterfeit bibs that that these so-called "bandits" print themselves using the latest technology, but this is largely futile. There was also a time when American coffee shops used to charge people for access to Wi-Fi on their premises, because they had the problem of people buying one coffee and staying for hours and using the Internet, preventing the tables from being used by other paying customers. (In some other countries this charge is still the practice in places like Starbucks. Why the practice is different in different places is an interesting topic for speculation.) During the Occupy Wall Street protests in 2011–2012, a group of activists, secure in their knowledge of the wickedness of private property, took over[8] a foreclosed home in New York City and announced that it would be made available to the homeless. By the time journalists got around to visiting the house two months later, the original occupants were gone, and there were new squatters occupying the property. Meanwhile, the property had been destroyed and valuable equipment stolen—over-consumed, in other words.

---

[7]"Fleet of Foot and Blissfully Bold, Freeloaders at the Marathon Wear Fake Bibs—but Win No Prizes," *The Wall Street Journal* (November 5, 2011), available online at http://online. wsj.com/article/SB10001424052970203716204577015830896749236.html.
[8]http://pjmedia.com/richardfernandez/2012/02/20/702-rue-vermont/

But once again, the problem is not greed or sin or insufficient lack of green consciousness; the problem is simply an inability to establish property rights. Private fish farms exist all over the world, and they never run out of fish. The reason for that is that when the farm's owner sells a fish to some middleman who wants to sell it to a restaurant or a supermarket, the fisherman must think about the consequences for his own future fish stocks. In addition, private fish farms can erect fences that prevent those unauthorized by the owners from harvesting the fish there. In short, a nonexcludable resource in the ocean is an excludable one in a fish farm. If nonexcludable resources can be made excludable, the tragedy of the commons is solved.

Southern Africa has long had a problem with poaching of large mammals, elephants in particular. But in the 1980s and 1990s, several southern African governments stopped using environmental ministries to create national parks to try to manage elephant populations and prevent poaching, and replaced this approach with one in which local authorities were given the rights to manage their own elephant populations in their own self-interest. Whereas for the poacher the primary task is to get elephants as quickly as possible so that their ivory may be sold to make goods (primarily medicines sold in the Far East)—meaning that the best choice is to look for elephants and shoot them—giving local people an ownership right to the elephants gave them both better incentives than the government had to fight poaching and an incentive to manage the populations intelligently. As a result, sharp population declines were reversed[9] in countries like Zimbabwe, partly by obtaining the ivory by simply culling it from tusks without killing the elephant.

Even without guidance from a very distant administration in Washington, new landowners in the American West in the latter half of the 19th century developed cattle branding as a way to distinguish the cattle of different owners, and later entrepreneurs developed barbed wire to make cattle excludable. As a result, in sharp contrast to relatively rare animals which some humans value but which lack property-rights protection (also known as endangered species), no one ever worries about running out of cattle. (The unowned buffalo of the Plains, in contrast, were nearly hunted to extinction, partly but not entirely as a tactic of war against the Plains Indians.) Again, the spontaneous order is very creative in coming up with ways to solve "market failure" problems.

Sometimes, whether a situation reflects over-consumption or under-production really depends on the perspective from which one looks at the problem. In February 2006, in the town of Monett, Missouri, the local fire brigade—which is funded entirely by dues collected from people who choose to pay them—went to the scene of a house fire but refused to put the fire out because the home was owned by someone who was not a member of the association.

---

[9]http://econjwatch.org/articles/an-ivory-tower-take-on-the-ivory-trade

His unwillingness to pay annual dues meant that the association had less money to spend on equipment purchases and maintenance, and so to provide service to all comers—in other words to make the resource nonexcludable—would have resulted in, depending on how one looks at it, over-consumption by the residents given the amount of equipment bought, or inadequate equipment bought given the number of people to be protected.[10] But no matter how one looks at it, nonexcludability is a social problem. The inability to make users pay fees commensurate with the value they attach to particular goods means that resources are used inefficiently. When nonexcludable resources can be made excludable, just as when external costs can be made internal, the problem ceases to exist.

But once again, the creation of private property rights is not always possible. The problem of air pollution mentioned earlier can also be thought of as a tragedy of the commons problem. Clean air and water are common, unowned resources. People "over-consume" them by dumping pollutants into them in the course of their private activities. Eventually, the air and water become dangerously poisonous. Here, as suggested previously, there are no alternatives to using government to limit these costly decisions. In such cases as overfishing on the open sea (it is very difficult to divide up the ocean into mine and yours in a meaningfully enforceable way) or air pollution, government intervention to limit this over-consumption has the potential to force resources to be used more efficiently.

A similar problem occurs nearly every day in the campus restaurant where I get my afternoon snack. Every morning the floor is clean, but people choose to "consume" this clean space by leaving food all over it. By the time I get there, the place is routinely filthy. Ideally, the cost of that dirtying should be borne by the people causing it. The expense necessary to police each diner's behavior (and the negative effect it would have on demand to attend or work at my university if people, both those who clean up after themselves and those who don't, felt like they were constantly being monitored) means that those who consume the clean space cannot be excluded. In principle, social norms, as Elinor Ostrom suggested, are sufficient to keep the nonexcludable, rivalrous resource from being over-consumed. (Indeed, some public spaces are not trashed in this manner, although many are; I am hard-pressed to think of an explanation other than differences in the probability of being caught or differences in moral codes that will explain this.) Most problems of dirtying the environment have this tragedy-of-the-commons feel to them.

But note also that the definition of "dirtying" is context-dependent. Every major-league baseball game is attended by thousands of individuals, many of

---

[10]A similar event happened in Tennessee, as recounted here: http://www.dailymail.
co.uk/news/article-2070834/Firefighters-watch-couples-home-burn-
ground-hadnt-paid-75-subscription-fee.htmls.

whom throw all kinds of trash on the stadium floor over the course of the game. And yet the next night when the first fans enter the ballpark, all of that trash is gone. Obviously, the owners have seen to it that this trash is hauled away expeditiously; because their consumers have made it clear to them that they attach value to the seating being litter-free when they get there, even as they apparently also value the ability to throw peanut shells at will on the ground. The contrast to many public highways, where litter is common, is striking.

Nonrivalrous Consumption—of Public Goods

The Coca-Cola Corporation is famous for protecting its "secret formula," the ingredients and instructions for making its famous signature drink. Indeed, the secrecy of the recipe (although versions of it can be found all over the Web) is marketed by the company as part of the product's appeal. There is now a World of Coca-Cola in Atlanta, a sort of theme park/museum for the sugary, caffeinated drink, and the formula is actually said to be in a large vault there, with the vault (although of course not the formula itself) on display in the building. Taking for granted the company's assertion that the formula really is a secret, it is clear why they would want it to remain so. The formula is a form of knowledge, and the thing about knowledge is that your having it doesn't prevent my having it also. Unlike many goods—for example, a sandwich, where my consumption of it leaves less available for you—if you and I both copy the formula down, the fact that I know it doesn't mean you can't also know it. Our brains can both "consume" the knowledge at the same time. But we cannot both consume the same sandwich—it must only go to one of us. In most contexts, including some of the ones mentioned in Chapter 4, making knowledge publicly available is actually a good thing. It is better if more people know how to read and do math than if fewer do, and it is good that a new scientific breakthrough is immediately propagated to the scientific community. Einstein's theory of general relativity, the formulas in Newtonian mechanics that it partly replaced, the Darwinian theory of evolution, the economic distinction between marginal and sunk cost, and every other form of scientific knowledge can be held simultaneously by many people. Indeed, it can be acquired at near-zero *marginal* cost by a large number of people. Think about a number of people sitting in a large lecture hall, listening to a physics professor talk about Newton's three laws of motion. The student in the middle of the front row sits, listens, and learns, but the student sitting right behind him does much the same thing, with no extra effort required on the part of the professor. He speaks simultaneously to the entire classroom.

This characteristic of some goods, whereby consumption by one person does not come at the expense of consumption by others, is called *nonrivalry*. Its opposite then is called *rivalry*, which means that when I consume it there is indeed less available for you. Most of the goods discussed in previous chapters have been rivalrous. If I buy a computer, the only way you can buy one is for one more to be made. If six cupcakes have been baked, my eating one means one less for everybody else. And in some of this chapter's examples too, the good in question is rivalrous. An elephant slain and its tusks' ivory turned into medicine means that there are fewer elephants available for others. The examples in the prior paragraph, in contrast, are nonrivalrous. At first, nonrivalry seems to contradict the idea of scarcity—if I can consume without lowering the amount available for you, what exactly is scarce? But remember that the *production* of the goods still requires acquisition of resources that *are* scarce.

Nonrivalry introduces a complication into market decision making. The increase in production of a good resulting from one person's decision to pay for it actually becomes available to many other people at the same time, so that the total social value of the decision to pay for the good is actually much greater than the value to the individual who makes the payment.[11] In some sense, in fact, the action of making a nonrivalrous good available is really just generating a large-scale positive externality, that is, a positive externality that affects many other people.

What kinds of goods might have these characteristics? Think about flood control. Suppose we survey each individual who might be potentially protected by a levee constructed next to a river to lower the probability of it flooding and ask him how much he would be willing to pay to construct it. When answering this question (assuming he answers it honestly and is only considering his self-interest), he will think about the benefits of having the levee protect his own house. If it exists, it will provide some protection for his house against the risk of flooding. But the levee will protect all homes in the neighborhood simultaneously. And the higher the levee, the higher the flood has to be before the levee is breached. So in terms of benefits to residents, higher is better. But each individual is only thinking about his own private benefits, even though social benefits for every extra row of bricks in the levee are much higher than the benefits to any individual homeowner. The result of the fact that any individual's financial contribution has far greater social benefits than private ones to that individual is that each individual, under voluntary provision of resources to build the levee, contributes too little. Each individual *free-rides*, in other words, just as in the public-radio example.

Our flood-control system has another problem, namely that there is no way to build the dam in such a way that only those who have paid for it are protected by it. This of course is the excludability problem already discussed. When a good is both nonrivalrous and nonexcludable, it is called a *public good*. (Note that this definition is very specific and is not the same thing as *a good*

---

[11]Technically, the marginal social value of one individual's purchase of a nonrivalrous good is actually equal to the sum of the marginal values of all the individuals who can consume it. This is a mathematical detail that is not particularly important for the discussion that follows.

used by the public.) What to do about this problem? One way to overcome it is to have the government simply forcibly extract the amount of resources necessary to build the levee to a height at which the marginal value of the last dollar spent—a little more protection for a slightly more serious flood times the damage *to all homes* if this flood happens—equals the marginal cost to the citizens of the last dollar taken from them. Such direct provision, or at least construction, of a good (management can be contracted out to a private company, although owing to the power of government workers in government decision making, outlined in Chapter 4, this may not happen) is nearly universal for some kinds of goods. Almost every country on earth takes money from its citizens to pay for its military, which provides a non-excludable product—how can the military defend everybody but me?—that is probably also nonrivalrous (adding 10,000 more soldiers simultaneously makes everybody safer from invasion from Canada or Mexico). So too is the navigational information provided by GPS. So too is mosquito control in hot, Gulf Coast cities. In each case, if individuals contributed voluntarily, they would do so by treating their own private benefit from increased contributions as the full social benefit, when in fact, their contribution is benefiting many others as well.

Infrastructure also has this quality to some degree. A broadband network can, up to a point, be used by many people simultaneously, as can a road grid or electricity system. If a private company sought to build such a system, an individual's willingness to pay would reflect only the value of the grid to him, even though the broadband cables, roads, and power lines can simultaneously be used by many. Thus, relying on such private fees paid voluntarily would lead to a system with too little capacity. Therefore, infrastructure is often built under public authority.[12] Again, once the infrastructure has been constructed, each individual can pay for his own use, so there is no reason that governments must *manage* infrastructure that has already been built. But it is plausible that government construction of it by reliance on forcibly confiscated tax revenues yields an outcome that is better than the free-market solution. It is up to the government perhaps (at least for now) to launch satellites that make GPS navigation possible, but the software enabling one to use it can be designed in an excludable way. And thus…

Excludability Is the Key Issue

Another example of a nonrivalrous good has already been mentioned: broadcast signals. If I am watching ESPN in my apartment, there is not less ESPN signal available for you. This is a classic example of a nonrivalrous good, as

---

[12]Note, though, that access to broadband cable is excludable, requiring a device that can access the information of the company that offers the service. The ease of laying these cables down has made broadband excludable from the beginning.

is any radio or television broadcast. But the signals are excludable, and so there is no reason to suppose that relying on private entrepreneurs to decide how many television programs to broadcast will fail to capture the full social value of these programs. If a lot of people like the television show on a cable channel, advertisers will pay higher fees to advertise on that show, which makes that channel more willing to carry it. The advertising space itself is both excludable and rivalrous, so no issue of "market failure" presents itself. Over-the-air broadcasts can be accessed without paying a fee, but the commercial spaces are also excludable and rivalrous. What these examples suggest is that nonrivalry per se is not a bar to private production—what matters is whether nonpayers can be excluded. The very fact that advertising rates for radio and television shows are based on ratings is evidence that buyers and sellers of advertising take account of the nonrivalry effect when deciding what programs to broadcast on. If universities offer courses over the Web (a nonrivalrous medium), all that is required to elicit the right amount of such courses is the ability to limit participants to those who pay whatever price is charged.

Indeed, the modern telecommunications/Internet revolution has demonstrated that as long as nonpayers can be excluded, there is sufficient incentive even to construct infrastructure for nonrivalrous goods. Cell-phone towers now dot the landscape, with several companies often building their networks of them from sea to shining sea.[13] Much broadband infrastructure has been publicly constructed, especially overseas, but much of it has also been laid down at private expense, as some railroads were, contrary to conventional wisdom, in the 19th century.[14]

The reluctance, for electoral reasons, to means-test many government-benefit programs—in other words, to only make them available to people whose income falls below a certain level—is a practice that enables another tragedy of the commons. People can consume government spending, which is provided by others, and only think about the costs to themselves, in the form of higher taxes they personally will have to pay. There is a natural tendency to

---

[13]One of the most frequent obstacles encountered is not any public-goods problem but special-interest opposition by those who find the towers aesthetically displeasing or, despite much evidence to the contrary, to be emitters of dangerous radiation. This opposition is willing to get the government to forcibly deprive others of the opportunity to communicate so that their tastes may be indulged (http://ridgewood.patch.com/articles/poll-is-cell-tower-opposition-nimby). This is an illustration of the ability of small, motivated groups to disproportionately affect the political process, as noted in Chapter 5.

[14]For an interesting account of how one private entrepreneur, James J. Hill, was able to build a private railroad and make money from it, while other railroads looted the taxpayers and purposely built the railroads inefficiently to extract more government subsidies, see the account of Mr. Hill's life given in Chapter 3 of Burton Fulsom's *The Myth of the Robber Barons* (Hemdon, VA: Young America's Foundation, 1987).

want to displace the expenses of, for example, medical care and retirement onto other people. Government spending thus becomes a sort of commons, which the citizenry over-consumes. Even means-tested programs (programs that can only be used by people whose income is below a certain level, like food stamps or Medicaid) are subject to this problem, if people who will pass the means test are allowed to vote on whether to enact the benefit. This is undoubtedly part of the reason why government spending has expanded to incorporate so many activities that individuals were expected to fund on their own in previous generations, with retirement and health care being the two biggest examples. Government spending thus becomes a kind of unfenced pasture, which the citizenry over-grazes.

The Creation of Scientific Knowledge

As noted earlier, the discovery of new knowledge—such as the creation of new radioactive elements, the conducting of experiments that reveal unknown truths about atomic structure or the cataloging of plants and animals in the rain forest—creates a good that is nonrivalrous. Again, the fact that one person knows a thing doesn't leave any less of the knowledge available for anyone else (although each person has to spend resources individually to acquire the knowledge). But in some contexts, companies may want to keep information they discover about how to create better products secret— and *better* here, as always, means *of more value to consumers, as revealed by their willingness to pay*. The Coca-Cola formula is one obvious example. But companies often hold their employees to agreements not to reveal *trade secrets*—information that, if it falls into the hands of a competitor, will lower the company's profits by increasing the substitutability of competitors' products. This is information that is costly to create (how many unsuccessful experiments were there before the Coca-Cola secret formula was perfected?), but which can be possessed by many people simultaneously. If most of the social benefits flow to others, the incentive for the company to invest in producing knowledge is insufficient. But if the knowledge can be made excludable by keeping it a secret, then the company keeps all the benefits itself. It is thus adequately incented to create a better-tasting soda, a better tablet computer, a better piece of word-processing software, etc.

But if all knowledge is nonrivalrous in this way, there is nonetheless some knowledge that we do not want kept secret. If individuals produce it and try to keep it secret, society will suffer. Scientific knowledge is generally of this character. The discovery of a new scientific principle may have implications for increasing productivity in many industries and thereby dramatically improving the way we live. But those applications are very far down the road and involve commercial skills that the scientist probably does not possess. Therefore, the market is not effective in getting those who benefit from the knowledge the scientist creates to pay him for its social value. The fact that scientific knowledge generates so many nonrivalrous benefits and that those benefits are often created in unpredictable ways many years after the discovery is made (and often after being modified by other scientists) is often used to argue that governments—that is to say, taxpayers—should fund basic scientific research.

Crowding

Note finally, with regard to public goods, that they may not be nonrivalrous over all levels of consumption. To listen to a lecture inside a classroom is to consume a good that is nonrivalrous up to a point. It doesn't matter whether there are 2 students in the classroom or 50—the lecture is available in identical quantity to all of them. But as more and more students enter the classroom, crowding starts to set in. All the seats are used up, requiring students first to sit on the floor and then to crowd closer and closer together. The discomfort makes it harder to assimilate the knowledge from the lecture. Even if the lecture is held outdoors, as people get farther and farther away from the microphone, the value of the lecture is lower and lower. This *crowding*—the turning of a nonrivalrous good into a gradually more rivalrous one once the number of consumers reaches a certain level—means that the good can no longer be treated as purely public. Shortly beyond the primary entrance to the Grand Canyon on the southern side there is a viewing area, and everybody standing on it gets the same spectacular view of the canyon below. But the more crowded the viewing space gets, the more unpleasant it becomes, and if it were crowded enough that a new person could enter only after someone else exited, the space would be completely rivalrous.

Many of the infrastructure examples mentioned earlier, especially roads, fall into this category. If an interstate highway has sufficiently few cars that no one car meaningfully slows down the others, then it is close to a nonrivalrous good. Once the road has been constructed, therefore, the primary reason to charge for use is merely to keep the road maintained. But once enough cars are on the road, each additional one meaningfully slows down every other car on the road. (This is of course the situation prevailing on many freeways in many cities around the world.) The proper price to charge then must include the negative externality of these crowding effects, and if the road were privately owned, the owner would of course have every incentive to charge that price. It used to be true that broadband cable and many web sites with unexpectedly large numbers of visitors were subject to crowding, but as technology improves, this effect is diminishing. As always, the key task is excludability. And many goods are nonrivalrous at small levels of consumption, but become rivalrous at higher levels. If the good is excludable—the ability to enter Yosemite National Park, or to use a swimming pool—then controlling quantity will be one thing that the owner of the site will want to do.

The Taxonomy of "Market Failure" and its Absence

Table 10-1 summarizes the pure categories of goods, with examples in each category.

Table 10-1. Taxonomy of Market Failure

	Rivalrous	Nonrivalrous
Excludable	Private good Sandwich, car, PC, fish raised on fish farms, plants and animals raised on private land	Club good Cable TV, movie theater (up to seating capacity), a lecture you have to pay to get into (up to seating capacity)
Nonexcludable	Tragedy of the commons Clean air/water, non-fenced pasture land, fish taken from the ocean, plants and animals taken from the wild.	Public goods National defense, the construction (although not necessarily the operation) of infrastructure, the creation of basic scientific knowledge.

As the chapter has suggested to this point, it is in the second row—the nonexcludability row—where potential "market failure" arises.

Conclusion

The reader may have noticed by now that the language in this chapter has been rather equivocal. Whether or not any particular potential "market failure" justifies government action to address it is, I confess, not an easy question to answer. As noted earlier, government has been around since humans first began settled cultivation. It was created from the desire of some people to be in control of the distribution of the new surplus that was created from the productivity advantage cultivation has over hunting and gathering (that is, to have power over who eats and who doesn't) and from the need to enable people to work more effectively together (that is, to correct "market failure"). If one is trying to resolve this difficult question of when to rely on government and when to rely on free people interacting on their own terms to solve social problems generated by scarcity, we might start with a general rule of thumb: *if people can solve this problem better on their own, let them; if not, rely on the state, but do not have unrealistic hopes about what it can achieve.*

In practical terms, there is one essential task that history suggests only government can achieve. None of the virtues of the market process can be achieved without it. That task is the establishment and preservation of law and order. If people can freely prey on one another, it does not make any sense to talk about "property rights." Punishing those who steal and commit violence, and who deceive in the course of their interactions with other people, is acknowledged by social thinkers of all stripes as an essential task of the state.

The second arena of state action, which is fuzzier, is the correction of "market failures." Without question, individual interaction through the market sometimes leads to worse outcomes than when those actions are limited by the state. But the state is not perfect; it uses its immense power to punish its enemies and reward its friends, often by taking wealth from the former and giving it to the latter. It is often captured by special interests. Its decisions are often flawed because of its inability, relative to individuals acting in their own interest, to harvest costly decentralized information. But sometimes it is the only game in town.

When there are externalities or problems of nonexcludability—in other words, when property rights that we wish were there are too costly to enforce—the state may make things better, although it may also make things worse. A good rule of thumb is that the more important the effect per person, and the greater the number of people affected by it, the more likely it is that government restriction of individual freedom will do good. Environmental pollution, because of the ways it damages human health and because of the complete inability of individuals who have no direct contact with one another to resolve their conflict over property use, is likely to be a prime candidate for government activity. (But only up to a point; if people with extreme views on how much pollution, pesticide residues, etc., should be allowed capture the regulatory process, much will have to be sacrificed in the course of the government producing the regulations it enacts under their influence.) National defense is easy to abuse—a people convinced of their military superiority may wish to seize things by war instead of obtaining them peacefully)—but the fact that almost every country in history has resorted to government seizure of resources, including conscription, to defend the country suggests that defense has major public-goods aspects.

Over the centuries, more and more human activity has taken place in the market, and this is a good thing. Even when governments do things, they don't do them with the same severity and cruelty as was once true. If the government had announced it was going to build the Golden Gate Bridge or the Empire State Building by conscripting slave labor, people would have properly been outraged. But many ancient monuments throughout the world were built this way, so it is a sign of progress that the state nowadays gets the resources it needs by demanding money (taxes) rather than labor. Over the long course of time people have come to understand the dangers of ceding too much power to government.

Throughout this chapter when I have used the term "market failure" I have put it in quotation marks. That is because this "failure" is defined only relative to an ideal in which market prices incorporate all aspects of every action. However, governments fail too, for reasons covered in Chapter 5. The solutions about how to solve any market failure—for example, imposing a tax of just the right amount on just the right people, or setting up a trading market for rights to pollute the air that will function just like the existing market for wheat—work perfectly on the blackboard, but the government we have is not the government of the blackboard. (To consider an absurd yet revealing example of the difference between what the law ought to be and what lawmakers want it to be, one need only consider this example[15] of a proposal to tax all men because of the social cost imposed by violence against women committed by some—perhaps a very small percentage—of them.) Ultimately, the question of whether a particular market has the shortcomings defined by the term "market failure" can be objectively answered. It must be characterized either by externalities or nonexcludability. The question of whether that failure is substantial enough to justify government action is not so easy to answer; every citizen has to decide for himself.

Economics Out There

10.1. All of the following qualify as potential "market failures," because they have the characteristics of the situations discussed in this chapter. Which characteristics are they? Can the market solve them on its own, or do they necessitate some kind of government intervention?

- Private Property May Become Preserved[16]

- Wi-Fi a "Basic Human Right"?[17]

- Plan Would Expand Ocean Fish Farming.[18]
  (In addition, why are the oceans often overfished, while fish farms never are?)

- Some Cafe Owners Pull the Plug on Lingering Wi-Fi Users[19]

- Tax men for abuse of women?[20]

---

[15]http://archive.mises.org/2568/a-man-tax/
[16]http://www.foxnews.com/story/0,2933,124358,00.html
[17]http://www.theregister.co.uk/2005/10/04/sf_wifi/
[18]http://www.nytimes.com/2005/06/06/national/06fish.html?pagewanted=all&_r=1&
[19]http://www.nytimes.com/2005/06/13/technology/13wifi.html
[20]http://www.iol.co.za/news/world/swedish-mps-want-men-taxed-for-women-abuse-1.223297#

Macroeconomics

The Big, Often Blurry Picture

I suspect that when many people pick up a book about "economics," they expect to be reading about such things as unemployment, inflation, and economic growth. And yet it is not until here, in the final chapters, that I address these questions. The reason for that is related to something I hinted at in the introduction: an *economy* is merely a description of the ways in which people with different interests in the presence of scarcity reconcile those differences. It does not make any sense to describe the functioning of an entire economy unless we understand this fact and use it to think about the terms under which people relate to one another and about how much they can expect to gain at any moment from participating in "the economy." So-called "macroeconomics"—the study of aggregate-level phenomena such as unemployment, inflation, and economic growth, usually at the level of the nation-state—depends critically on so-called "microeconomics"—the ways in which *individuals* respond to the incentives they face.

■ **Note** Macroeconomics (overall economic growth, the rate of inflation, and so on) is utterly dependent on microeconomics—the daily decisions we make based on the incentives that either motivate us to act, or don't.

To talk of "the economy" is to make crude generalizations about a vast conglomeration of individuals, some of whom at any moment might be doing well, some not so well. So it is with all aggregate descriptions of complicated phenomena. One may say at any moment that one's body (or more likely, "health") is bad, because one has a cold. But one's brain still functions normally, one's heart still vigorously pumps blood, one's arms and legs still do exactly what is expected of them. It is only the runny nose, the coughing, and the fatigue that mark departures from the norm. People might describe "the earth" as "in crisis," but life in all its marvelous complexity still reproduces, and many kinds of pollution, including natural pollution such as dangerous diseases, decline. (Remember the stories of the conquest of public filth and infectious diseases in the discussion of the environmental benefits of economic growth in Chapter 9).

Another reason I resisted speaking of "the economy" as a whole until the end is that to speak this way encourages a fallacy of control, a mistaken belief in the omniscience and omnipotence of politicians in the face of constant economic change. People who are concerned about their prospects or poverty, or the prospects or poverty of their neighbors, will be eager to listen to any politician who promises to fix things, and politicians either out of deception or delusions of grandeur will be all too happy to oblige these wishes. But what if we entertain a terrifying thought? That thought is that any set of politicians may be powerless to do anything about the short-term fluctuations of "the economy." If the economy is really 310 million people (in the case of the U.S.—7 billion if we think globally) interacting in the presence of costly, decentralized information, the president—let alone any particular senator or representative—may in other words get far too much credit when "the economy" is looking up and far too much blame when it is, by conventional ways of looking at things, struggling. Economists over the years have been very willing to deceive themselves about the amount of control they can provide politicians with, especially in the short run. (The long run, as we will see, has more possibilities.) If I were to put this discussion of "the economy" at the beginning of the book, readers might well wonder, after reading about the difficulty of achieving many macroeconomic goals, whether economics has any use at all, when in fact, in terms of analyzing the trade-offs of individuals, it is profoundly useful. So keep these themes in mind: (1) The economy is a complicated, evolved structure, so any modeling of it taken as a whole must be of limited use; (2) the power of any political system to influence it over the short run may be very constrained. With that in mind, let us proceed to the first task, which is to define some terms.

■ **Note** Because at any moment people's opportunities and available resources differ, the idea of talking about how "the economy" is doing is unavoidably imprecise. In addition, it may generate an unjustified confidence that any problems in "the economy" can be easily fixed.

The Concept of Gross Domestic Product

Gross domestic product (GDP) is the *estimated monetary value, measured at prices at which things are actually sold, of everything produced and sold within a jurisdiction (a country, multinational organization, county, state, and so on) in a given period of time*. The jurisdiction is usually a country, and the period of time is usually a year.[1]

To build a very simple model of how GDP is calculated, imagine that people consume only two goods: food and clothing. Table 11-1 represents the quantity and price of food and clothing consumed (and produced—assume there is no foreign trade) in 2010.

Table 11-1. A Simple GDP Model

2010	Quantity	Price	Value = P × Q
Food	10,000	$10	$100,000
Clothing	4,000	$50	$200,000
GDP			$300,000

Here it is worth saying a few words about economic modeling. The model in Table 11-1 assumes, as if we live in some dystopian science-fiction future, that there is only one kind of food. The market-equilibrium price is $10. Clothing, too, is uniform (so to speak), and every year 4,000 units are produced and sold at $50 each. Reality is naturally much more complicated. There are many kinds of food—high-end, low-end, meat, vegetables, grains, junk food, and so on. So too with clothing. And real people consume far more than two goods. They buy cell-phone services, paper clips, medical consultation and treatment, child-care services, on and on. But to express this more complicated reality would simply require adding more rows to the table, generating little marginal insight while generating high marginal costs because of extra computational complexity. So in this simple but illustrative example, the GDP is the sum of the value of all food sold in 2010 ($100,000) plus the value of all clothing sold in 2010 ($200,000), or $300,000.

But when one reads about GDP, one usually sees it expressed as *real GDP*. To think about what this means, imagine that for some reason (and we'll get a better feel for what that reason might be later in the chapter), next year the amount of food and clothing we consume is unchanged, but the price of each has increased, so that the new figures are as shown in Table 11-2.

---

[1] There is also a term called *gross national product* (GNP) that is defined differently, but for many countries, including the U.S., these differences do not matter significantly, and so I will speak of GDP rather than GNP from now on. If you read a report the news about one or the other in the U.S., you can treat them as essentially the same.

Table 11-2. The Same Economy, Next Year

2011	Quantity	Price	Value = PQ
Food	10,000	$12	$120,000
Clothing	4,000	$75	$300,000
GDP			$420,000

So what we call *nominal GDP*—current quantities times current prices for each good, the latter of which are $12 and $75 respectively—has gone up by 40% ($120,000/$300,000), and yet we aren't materially any better off. For this reason, economists like to talk in terms of real GDP, which means *GDP based on this year's quantities, but some previous base year's prices*. If we use 2010 prices and multiply them by 2011 quantities (unchanged from 2010, by assumption), we find that real GDP in 2011 is the same as that for 2010: $300,000. The economy did not grow at all, in other words.

Let us do one more year (see Table 11-3).

Table 11-3. Two Years On

2012 (nominal)	Quantity	Price	Value = PQ
Food	11,000	$13	$143,000
Clothing	4,400	$75	$330,000
GDP			$473,000

In 2012, clothing prices are stable, food prices are higher again (again, don't worry about why yet), and quantities of both goods are higher. So, nominal GDP grew by 12.62% (($473,000 − $420,000) / $420,000) over last year's $420,000, whereas real GDP, using 2011 prices as the base, requires that we multiply this year's quantities times 2011 prices (see Table 11-4).

Table 11-4. Two years On, in Real Terms

2012 (real, 2011 as base year)	Quantity	Price	Value = PQ
Food	11,000	$12	$132,000
Clothing	4,400	$75	$330,000
GDP			$462,000

So, growth in real GDP in 2012 was ($462,000 − $420,000) / $420,000 = 10.5%. Why make this distinction? Ultimately, what we are interested in is how much better (at least materially) people are living, and this is measured in this simple model by how well fed and well clothed they are. To get quantity changes, we have to net out price changes from growth in nominal GDP. Calculating real GDP allows us to measure how much the quantity of each good, weighted by its share of the economy, has gone up or down. From this point forward, when I speak of changes in GDP it will mean changes in real GDP. As a reminder, the actual calculation of GDP (done by the U.S. Bureau of Economic Analysis) has, in effect, a table with very many rows for the very many goods and services produced in a modern economy. It is also subject to constant revision as new goods and industries are born and old ones fade away.

Note   GDP is, approximately, the value, as determined by buyers and sellers interacting in the market, of what was produced and sold in a particular place in a particular year.

The Broader Significance of GDP

Economists do emphasize GDP growth a lot and often equate it with growth in the *standard of living*, implying that growth in GDP is synonymous with improvement in the quality of life. Indeed, I engaged in this exercise myself when I showed the figure on growth in GDP around the world and the West in particular in Chapter 9. But many criticize this focus on GDP, arguing that it neglects things in life that really matter. It is certainly true that GDP is limited as a measure of quality of life because it can only measure things that are explicitly traded in a market. Some services that are provided out of love rather than for money—for example, parents leaving their jobs early to watch their children play Little League baseball—are important parts of human happiness and achievement, of the life well lived, but do not show up in GDP. In addition, precisely because it ordinarily cannot be mediated through the price mechanism, environmental damage such as that generated through pollution damage is not incorporated into GDP, and indeed remedying it may *lower* GDP growth. On the one hand, companies that make goods that control pollution see demand increase after anti-pollution regulations are imposed, but on the other hand, installation of pollution-control equipment raises costs for the products made in the factories that must install it, lowering GDP. On the other hand, reducing pollution lowers health damage, which on the one hand lowers demand for health-care services, which lowers GDP, but on the other hand allows workers to be more productive, which raises it. By now, we have to keep track of so many hands that it is clear that one can't make any unambiguous statements about the relation between pollution control and GDP. We can generally rely on the intuition that pollution is a market failure, and people would be willing to pay to get rid of some of it if only property rights to clean air and water existed. So, in this dimension, GDP is clearly an incomplete measure of human welfare. Other things that GDP does not directly measure, such as crime, also reflect this phenomenon. Crime is damaging to human happiness, but controlling it adds to measured GDP in the short run, even as in the long run it might make it harder for people to cooperate in producing things, because they're afraid to go out, because certain neighborhoods must be avoided, and so on.

But I contend that GDP is still a very good measure of quality of life. I will muster two arguments in this regard. First, global migration (apart from refugees fleeing to neighboring countries due to civil war) is overwhelmingly from low-GDP to high-GDP countries. (Some of my research suggests that this is true even when we take account of the fact that high-GDP countries tend to be politically freer than low-GDP ones.) This suggests that the material benefits available in high-GDP countries are things that people value. Secondly, we can spare a few moments' reflection to think about what it is exactly that GDP buys. In the anti-consumerist stereotype that is fairly common nowadays, high GDP allows people to buy bigger houses, bigger plasma TVs, a third car, and trips to Disney World, but nothing of profound value.

This view I totally reject. It is growth in GDP that has allowed us to buy public health (for example, clean water and vaccinations that have vanquished many communicable plagues in wealthy countries), safer accommodations (solid roofs and floors instead of thatched-leaf and dirt ones, climate-control technology, and so on), opportunities for personal enrichment and travel, exposure to new ideas, and a host of other things that the critics of focus on GDP growth claim to value. (In general, countries with high per-capita GDP also have less crime and invest more in pollution control than countries with lower per-capita GDP.) So I will take it as given that although production of some goods generates negative externalities—so that more production of them, other things being equal, makes some people worse off—trying to achieve a growing economy is a perfectly valid goal, maybe the primary goal, of economic policy.

▓ **Note**   Per capita GDP is not a perfect measure of the quality of human life, but it is probably the best one we have.

Unemployment

As noted in Chapter 9 in the discussion of Luddite doomsdayism, the unemployment rate in the economy has fluctuated between 3–10% for most of the time it has been measured in the U.S. However, it should be noted that the definition of *unemployment* does not exactly correspond to that used by most people, which would probably be: *want a job, don't have one.* Instead, the

Bureau of Labor Statistics counts as officially unemployed only those who did no work for pay in the last week, but who have actively looked for work in the last four weeks. (For some reason, people who have been on layoff within the last week but expect to be recalled within the next six months, a situation that historically has affected manufacturing workers most, are also counted as unemployed.) If one has not looked for work in the last four weeks, one is not in what is called the labor force (although the BLS keeps track of such people in other categories). And the unemployment rate is simply those who are officially unemployed divided by the sum of those who are officially unemployed plus those who did at least some work in the last week, with this sum being the *labor force*. Unemployment, in other words, is given by this formula:

$$\text{Unemployment rate} = \frac{\#\ of\ unemployed}{labor\ force} = \frac{\#\ of\ unemployed}{unemployed + employed}$$

As written, the definition looks perfectly sensible, but those who have not looked for work in the last four weeks are not counted as being in the labor force. Some of these are people who have chosen to stay home and care for children, or who are full-time students or retired or otherwise not particularly interested in work at this time; excluding them from the calculations is perfectly reasonable. But some are people who have simply given up on looking for work because they cannot find jobs they are willing to accept, even when they are willing to accept relatively low wages. Most people would accept that many of these people qualify as "unemployed" in the common-sense definition of the term, but they are not so counted. Figure 11-1 shows the combined percentage of the population that is in the labor force—that is, either working or officially unemployed. It too wanders within a relatively narrow range, ranging between approximately 58% and just over 67% between 1948–2011. Much of the surge in the 1960s was probably due to the larger percentage of Americans who were of traditional working age, owing to the entry of baby boomers into the workforce, as well as the surge of American women into careers.

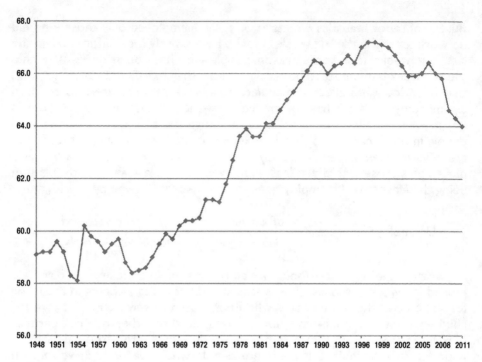

Figure 11-1. Labor force participation 1948–2011

Figure 11-1 indicates that this rate peaked in the mid-1990s and has fallen more or less steadily since then, including sharply during the so-called Great Recession, which started in late 2007. This drop is probably due to some combination of an increase in people who have stopped looking for work out of frustration, baby-boom retirements (the first baby boomer reached 65 in 2010), and a rise in claims for disability,[2] some of the latter reflecting people choosing to receive government checks instead of paychecks. As we will see, the economy is prone to natural fluctuations, and the unemployment rate with it. But that does not stop unemployment, when it is at the high end of its historical range, from being a very potent political issue.

Money

Next we turn to money. We have a natural tendency to think of *money* primarily in terms of the pieces of paper with images of important national figures or architectural landmarks on them—*currency*, in other words. But in fact the definition of money is a little trickier than that. First note that money is

---

[2]http://www.bloomberg.com/news/2012-05-03/disabled-americans-shrink-size-of-u-s-labor-force.html

simply a way of holding a person's wealth. Again, wealth is slightly different from income, in that wealth is generally a number (usually translated into currency units) and income is more likely to be considered as a number per period of time. So we say someone's total wealth is $200,000, while his income from his job is $4,000 a month.

How did we come up with this figure of $200,000 for "wealth"? Probably this person holds his wealth in several forms. He may own part of the equity in a house. (In other words, he has borrowed to buy the house, and only paid part of the money back. Were he to sell the house before the loan had been paid off, he would be responsible for paying the loan back, and would be able to keep the remainder of the cash.) He may have some money invested in the stock market, either directly or through a retirement plan at work. He may have an account at the local bank that is credited currently with a certain amount of "dollars." Add it all together, along with the value of his miscellaneous personal property (cars, entertainment, and information technology, and so on), and this will probably constitute what he thinks of as his wealth.

Strictly speaking, *wealth* is everything that a person owns that could be used in trade with others. Although all those things certainly qualify, recall that he also owns another form of wealth—another asset, in other words—that we have not counted. This asset is his skill, or his human capital (to use a term from Chapter 6). If a person has received extensive training in video-game design or carpentry, those are certainly valuable assets. If he wants to, the person can with some difficulty convert this asset into something he wants to consume. He can do this in two ways. The most straightforward way is simply to find someone who has use for that training and is willing to pay him for its use—a company that sells video games to consumers, or a company that builds houses. Alternatively, he could directly exchange his services for something someone else has that he values. Unfortunately, this process, known as *bartering*, is very cumbersome. It requires that what I have coincide with what you want, and vice versa. Unless you, the pediatrician, need your house remodeled, and I, the contractor, need my child's broken arm set, we have no opportunity for such barter Having some kind of asset that everybody will take in any exchange means we need not have this coincidence of desires. So, sometimes money is known as a *medium of exchange*, which we can define as *the asset that all sellers will accept in exchange for that which they sell.* Note that U.S. paper currency says on it that *This Note Is Legal Tender for All Debts, Public and Private*, which is suggestive of this idea of the medium of exchange.

Unfortunately, not all the assets that this person holds are as useful as others in market exchange, which is to say they will not be accepted as legal tender for all debts. For a person to trade on, for example, his skills requires at a minimum going to work and waiting until he is paid in the asset known as cash, or perhaps waiting longer (until he finds someone to barter with) if he chooses to rely on barter. In addition, in some sense he "owns" part of his house, but if he wants to go to the store and buy dinner, he can't carve a couple of bricks off and take that in as payment. Nor will the grocery store accept any of his personal property, which in any event he probably gets use out of and doesn't want to give up. The one asset that he does possess that any seller of any product will take is his physical currency, with wealth credited to a bank account and accessible via an ATM card a close second in terms of acceptability (limited only by the ever-smaller number of businesses, for example some vendors in farmers' markets, that do not take debit cards). This is how we should think about money—not as a specific asset, for example the green pieces of paper with deceased prominent citizens on them, but as all kinds of assets that satisfy a certain minimum level of universal acceptance in trade with others. This trait—the ability to use an asset to obtain in trade that which one wants from others—is called *liquidity*. Money, then, is simply all the assets that have at least a certain minimum level of this liquidity. By any definition we can come up with, paper currency will certainly qualify, and we should probably also always count money stored in accounts accessible by an ATM.

Given that money, however we define it, is the easiest asset to use in exchange, why would one ever store one's wealth in any other kind of asset? For wealth such as skill, storage (in one's brain) is essentially free, and converting this wealth into exchange power is relatively hard. Other kinds of assets, for example a house, also provide consumption services—namely, you get to live there—in addition to being a store of wealth. But some assets—stocks, bonds (more on what these are below), real estate where one does not live—do not have this quality. Although they are worth something, they are not easy to use to obtain other things. But one quality they do have is that they either pay out income periodically (if one owns an apartment building, one earns rent monthly from the tenants, and if one owns various stocks, one often earns dividend payments from the companies that issue the stock), or they have a chance of going up in value over time. Money, unless one puts it in a bank, earns no returns, and if there is inflation (about which more below), simply holding one's wealth as cash in the house exposes one to this inflation tax. (Holding one's wealth as cash also exposes one to the risk of theft of one's wealth by others, in the form of robbery or burglary. Banks can also fail, although in the U.S. bank deposits are partially insured by the federal government.) So there's a trade-off. On the one hand, the types of assets that we call "money" have the benefit of being very easy to use in market exchange. On the other hand, other kinds of less-liquid assets tend to grow in value and be less exposed to some kinds of risk, whereas cash tends to lose value over time and be more exposed to these kinds of risk. So most people ordinarily choose to hold some fraction of their wealth (often a very small fraction for older people with a greater amount of wealth accumulated over their lifetimes, which they have invested in less liquid kinds of assets) in very liquid forms, and the rest of it in forms that they cannot access immediately but which will grow in value over time. Those most liquid forms we will call money.

In the modern era, we have generally thought of paper currency as the most widely, indeed near universally accepted, medium of exchange. There are some times and places when this is not true, especially when the government implicitly breaks the deal by which currency is not promiscuously supplied (which causes inflationary problems, to be discussed soon). But currency, or something like it, is almost as old as civilization itself; some have suggested that the Incas of what is now Peru, a not very advanced civilization even by the standards of the time, were the most advanced civilization not to have some form of money. Thus, the productivity-enhancing effects of having a medium of exchange seem to be substantial. Some ancient settlements in what is now China used cowry shells as the medium of exchange, and to this day many Chinese characters involving money use the symbol meaning sea-shell (贝, *bei*). Other areas of Australia, Africa, and the South Pacific have also operated with seashell currency. The items people would use as a medium of exchange depends on the confidence that they have that those items will retain their value, primarily by not being over-supplied. Some years ago in the West African country of Cameroon, beer-bottle caps with prizes on the inside were for a time accepted as currency by many,[3] which suggests that they were more desired than the Cameroonian currency, the CFA franc. One supposes that this was because the supply of these caps was relatively predictable, and owning one gave the right to some other specific kind of wealth. Interestingly, even though the caps themselves only entitled the holder to one specific prize, the prizes themselves were sufficiently widely useful and sufficiently valuable that many, especially taxi drivers, were willing to accept them in lieu of cash.

So to repeat, by this way of thinking there is not a definite class of assets known as "money," but money rather is simply the set of assets that are the most liquid. The U.S. federal government does have official measurements of money. The most widely used and monitored (by the government, for reasons of policy discussed below) measure is known as M1, and its primary components are paper currency held by the private sector but outside bank vaults plus demand deposits. *Demand deposits* are official terminology for a set of different kinds of bank accounts, dominated by checking accounts. As noted previously, in any society where the currency is intelligently managed, that paper currency will be the most liquid asset, as close to a universally acceptable medium of exchange as it is possible to have. Demand deposits are not quite that liquid; there are some transactions (often off-the-books ones) where using an ATM card or writing a check would be undesirable, and there are even some registered businesses that will not take checks or debit cards. But the number of the latter has declined with the rise of debit cards, which settle immediately (although at the cost of a fee charged to the merchant), as opposed to the

---

[3]http://www.upi.com/Odd_News/2005/08/17/Beer-caps-replacing-cash-in-Cameroon/UPI-48211124301944/

old paper checks, which take longer to clear.[4] The "clearing" process is suggestive of how banking works. When I use a debit card or write a check at your business, my bank electronically deducts the amount of payment from my numbered account and transfers it to yours, whether at the same bank or not. With a check, the process is the same, but historically paper checks had to be transferred from where they were written to the bank where the deposit existed, which then transferred the money out of the writer's account and into the receiver's. A lot of money is purely notional in this way, rather than an actual piece of paper with a numerical amount on it.

There are slightly broader federal measures of money as well. M2 includes everything that is in M1, as well as savings deposits and what are known as *time deposits*. A time deposit, also known frequently as a *certificate of deposit*, is an account in which you give a bank cash or transfer funds out of your demand deposit, and the bank sets up an account and promises to pay you a slightly higher interest rate than you would get from a checking or saving account, in exchange for your not touching the account for some fixed period of time. Obviously, acceding to a requirement that one's account stay untouched for a period of time makes that account less liquid than one from which one can withdraw money at will, and so these time accounts properly belong in a category of money defined by lower standards of liquidity. (Whether savings accounts in the modern age of debit cards are less liquid than demand deposits is an interesting question, but in any event they are included in M2 and not M1.)

The final thing to note about money is that, fundamentally, banks create most of it. Once this used to be literally true in the case of paper currency; banks would issue their own currency notes, which were as good as they were acceptable to other people. In Hong Kong, the government issues paper currency, but so too do three private banks. But nowadays currency issuance is monopolized in most countries by the national government. And so banks cannot create at will the single most liquid kind of asset. But if I go to my bank and borrow $5,000 to start a business, then that bank will create an account for me and credit it in the amount of $5,000. *By the definition of how M1 is calculated*, its quantity has just gone up by $5,000. Of course, I immediately withdraw that money to spend on my business plan; for the sake of argument, say I immediately withdraw all of it. (The fact that the merchants are willing to take my debit card suggests that the money contained within the account it represents really is a nearly universally excepted medium of exchange.) It would seem at first that the money supply has just gone down by $5,000, exactly canceling the bank's loan. But in fact M1 is still ahead $5,000, because

---

[4]Currency by itself that is in circulation in the economy rather than in bank vaults is known as M0, but since demand deposits are almost as liquid and their value vastly exceeds that of current U.S. currency, the value of this circulating currency by itself is not so interesting.

the businesses where I spend that money will in turn deposit it in their banks. So a bank loan actually increases the money supply. Indeed, since any deposits into a banking system can be lent against, and the businesses where I spend my loan deposit those funds into their banks, those banks will then all lend against much of that (minus what they keep as reserves), increasing the money supply further. This process goes on until the amounts in question are too small to lend out.

The process by which newly created loans ricochet through the banking system is known as the *money multiplier*. On the other hand, when I pay the loan back, say in the amount $5,200 (which includes interest), the bank transfers money from my account (which has been swelled to at least $5,200 because of the success of my business) and into its own coffers, and thus the money supply has gone down by $5,200. Thus, the quantity of money—in other words, the quantity of the most liquid forms of wealth—goes up only when banks are making loans at a faster rate than loans are being paid back, and goes down when the opposite circumstances prevail.

So if money can be created in this fashion at will, why don't banks create more of it? The reason is that they don't want to make a loan unless they are confident that the loan will be paid back. Furthermore, deposits credited in the account of one bank will not be accepted as payment by businesses unless people are confident that that the transfer of virtual, liquid wealth from that bank's computers to the computers of the bank of the business owner will really increase the business owner's wealth. If business conditions are generally bad, and/or banks are failing left and right (as they did, for example, in the early years of the Great Depression), banks become unwilling to lend except to the safest borrowers. So the creation of loans is limited by the particular economic circumstances, whether deriving from an individual's creditworthiness or the overall state of the economy, that determine whether loans are wise or not. Loans have opportunity costs; anything that is lent to you is not being used to buy something that in the judgment of the bank might be safer—the transferring of electronic deposits to very reliable Swiss banks, the purchase of gold, even the buying of U.S. government debt, the creation of which is explained in more detail in the next chapter. So, in fact, money cannot be created at will, because its creation, even though it is a private act of a bank, has an opportunity cost. Influencing this opportunity cost, and therefore influencing the rate of bank lending, it turns out, is a key task when government attempts to manage the economy in general.[5]

---

[5]This explanation of money and how it works is very similar to that in Chapter 14 of Paul Heyne, Peter Boettke, and David Prychitko, *The Economic Way of Thinking*, 12th Edition (Upper Saddle River, NJ: Prentice Hall, 2010).

▩ **Note** Because *money* simply means *the most liquid ways of holding wealth*, the dividing line between what is money and what is not is arbitrary. But banks have it within their power to create what the government defines as "money" simply by lending money to someone and therefore crediting his account with a higher balance.

Inflation

Very closely related to the official notions of "money," and the rate at which these measures of "money" grow, is the idea of inflation. Note first that inflation refers not to high prices, but to prices increasing over some significant period of time. The city of Tokyo is one of the world's most expensive, but the rate at which prices have increased in the last 10 years, for example, is not particularly high. So, Tokyo is not a high-inflation city, merely a high-cost one.

Note also that our ability to measure or estimate inflation falls short of some actual overall theoretical idea of rises in all prices, for the same reason that measured GDP is not the same thing as all valuable activity. There is simply no way to keep track of the fluctuations in the rate at which the money price of every good in the economy changes. In addition, different people can consume different combinations of consumer goods. Younger people like smartphones, more people in middle and old age than you might think[6] like tablet computers, some people like to eat at restaurants, some people like to eat simply at home, and so on. Products also change their features all the time, and their prices change accordingly. A 2013 model car is a very different thing from a 1990 model car, and so simply saying that the 2013 version is more expensive does not imply that the price for the same amount of consumption has gone up. So these kinds of quality changes must also be accounted for. Measuring inflation, in short, is a tricky thing.

Nonetheless, despite this problem of costly, decentralized knowledge, the government does try. The most widely used measure (and one adequate for all the analysis that we will do here) is called the Consumer Price Index. Data on it are published once a month, and one will often read in news articles reporting on this month's data how much higher (they are almost never lower) prices are than a year ago. The CPI is almost always used to make this claim about overall "inflation." How is it calculated? Economists working for the Bureau of Labor Statistics select a basket of goods that they decide some hypothetical ordinary American is likely to consume frequently. They then survey what the prices are for these goods every month and attempt to adjust for changes in

---

[6]http://money.usnews.com/money/blogs/the-best-life/2011/04/25/why-the-ipad-appeals-to-older-users

the quality of the products. Every month, they are published in an index, which is measured against some base year, the choice of which is arbitrary (similarly to the GDP base year). The year-to-year change in the price of this basket of goods is the best measure we have of the "inflation rate." Figure 11-2 shows the CPI from 1870–2011, with the base year (when the index takes a value of 100) being the average of the period 1982–1984.

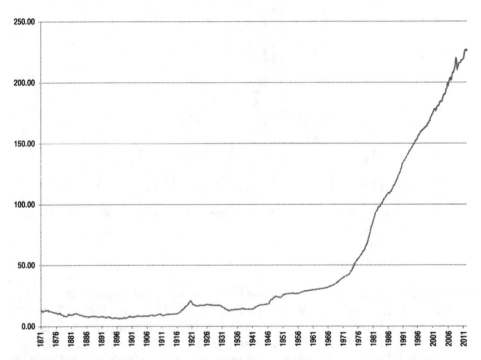

Figure 11-2. U.S. Consumer Price Index, 1871–2012 (1982–1984 = 100). *Source: U.S. Bureau of Labor Statistics*

Inflation can also be shown as the annual rate of change, as in Figure 11-3 (which is shown, because of data limitations, for a shorter period of time: 1960–2011).

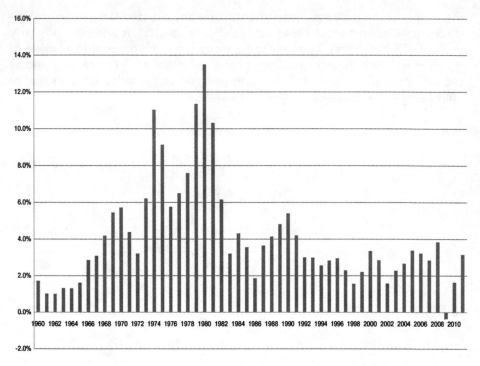

Figure 11-3. U.S. annual inflation rate, 1960–2011 *Source: U.S. Bureau of Labor Statistics*

So, when the inflation rate is higher in Figure 11-3, the slope of the rate of increase of the Consumer Price Index in Figure 11-2 is also higher. Both diagrams tell the same story, which is that inflation was highest (that is, consumer prices grew at the fastest rate as measured by the CPI) from approximately 1968–1981. Figure 11-2 suggests that there was no tendency toward inflation and even some deflation from 1871 to about 1920, there was modest inflation from 1920 until the early 1970s, and then temporarily the rate of inflation grew in the late 1970s and early 1980s, before falling back to a level that was not as high as during that time but is nonetheless higher than what prevailed before 1920. So, in general, to the surprise of few readers, I suspect, a lot of things are much more expensive now in money terms than they were several decades ago. The analysis of aggregate demand management in Chapter 12 tries to explain these patterns.

No one will be surprised to read that inflation is an economic problem, but perhaps the reasons will not be what the reader expects. When asked why he should worry about inflation, the typical person might answer, "Because everything is getting more expensive." But in theory, this is no problem at all. If all prices adjust immediately and in the same proportion, this kind of inflation has no effect on economic activity—on the ability of people to trade productively with one another. Why? Because one of the prices that will adjust automatically is the price of all kinds of human capital and other sources of income that people use to buy the goods whose prices are going up. To take a simple example, if the prices of all consumption goods went up by 10%, all your income came from your salary, and your salary also went up by 10%, there would be no problem, apart from the minor inconvenience of having to carry around paper currency that was worth 10% less. Even very large price increases, say 10,000% a year, would be no problem as long as they were consistent (in other words, the prices of everything, including the price of one's skill and labor, also went up by 10,000%). All this simply requires is that we periodically add zeros to the currency. Some countries from time to time have in fact removed zeroes from their currency to try to restore faith in and stability of the currency, precisely because the inflation they are trying to control is far from benign. But inflation, in fact, generates all manner of economic difficulties, and so it must be that the way I stated the nature of inflation—all prices change by the same amount, along with compensation—is mistaken.

In fact, prices do not change in this uniform, mechanistic way, and this is why inflation becomes a problem. The primary problem arising from non-mechanistic inflation derives from what prices are supposed to do in a market economy—give people guidance on the consequences of their decisions and hence induce them to make better decisions from the point of view of the entire society. The robotic model of automatic adjustment of all prices in uniform proportions that I just described is not what real inflation looks like. For a variety of reasons, prices for different goods adjust at different rates. Tenants might sign contracts one year at a time, so that apartment rents adjust rather slowly. But the cost of acquiring, for example, heating oil may change on a day-to-day or even an hour-to-hour basis. In a high-inflation environment, people who own buildings may be reluctant to be exposed to this risk of putting apartments on the market (their heating costs may rise dramatically, but their rents are frozen until the end of the year), and so perhaps apartments will be converted to other uses. Someone who is committed to a two-year contract to build a factory or skyscraper for a fixed price may find at the end of the contract that the money he is being paid back will buy less than he expected it to, because of inflation that has occurred in the meantime. Indeed, in general, inflation exacts its biggest toll on exchanges carried out over a long period of time. Assets that hold their value best in a time of high inflation—land, for example—may see a purely artificial and unnecessary increase in demand, which comes at the expense of, for example, investing in new entrepreneurial experiments.

Note Inflation is a problem precisely because prices—and wages—do not rise in lockstep fashion. Rather, prices for different goods and services rise at different rates, meaning some people in the economy can get hurt more than others by a run of high inflation, and the usefulness of prices as a guide to action declines.

When I was young, I used to listen to AM radio late at night, and it would sometimes be possible to pick up signals from stations in different cities. The value of that activity depended on how much of what I heard was actual language that I could make out and how much of it was just static. If there was a lot of static, listening to the station was just about useless. Prices are information in a market economy, and inflation decreases what engineers might call the "signal-to-noise ratio" that people get from the prices they see. The more chaotic the overall inflation situation, the less informative specific prices become about which activities are useful and which are not, because prices are not changing at uniform rates. The whole ability of the price system to reconcile conflicting uses for scarce resources unravels. In some ways, the effect that inflation has on the ability of prices to give guidance to economic actors about what they should do is like the pernicious effect of well-documented grade inflation[7] at U.S. universities on the informational value of a transcript. Just as someone reading a transcript now has little idea if someone who got an A in 2012 is as capable as someone who got one in 1970, someone who sees the price of gasoline going up by 8% when general inflation is 10% may not be able to tell whether gasoline is "really" cheaper relative to other goods, which is the only way that matters.

The second problem with inflation is that it represents a tax on long-term thinking. When there is high inflation, paper currency loses value in market exchange almost right before one's eyes, and so there is no reason to put it away in the bank. Instead, one wishes to spend it as soon as one gets one's hands on it. But of course the entire financial system, which partly funds the process of entrepreneurial experimentation, is a series of middlemen who take money from people with no particularly good uses for it and lend it to people with potentially very good uses for it but no money on hand. If people become unwilling to save, the whole entrepreneurial process grinds to a halt. Indeed, a closely related problem to the unwillingness to save is the unwillingness to lend. If the inflation rate is zero percent, and one lends money for five years, even if one is wrong about the inflation rate that prevails over the next five years, one won't be wrong by much. Inflation might be 2%, or it might be −1% (in which case it would be deflation). Either way, one can be pretty confident what the money one gets repaid in five years will buy. If inflation is very high, this is not true. If inflation is 100% this year, it might be 500% next year and in 2000% in five years. Or it might be 300% next year and 500% in five years. Thus, the opportunity for error is much greater. The fact that lending money to entrepreneurs is already a very risky endeavor means that people are very unwilling to court the extra risk of high inflation, which would devastate the value of the money they are paid back in the future. In short, in addition to taxing saving, inflation makes lenders unwilling to lend for any period of time.

---

[7]http://www.gradeinflation.com/

▓ Note Long-term credit markets basically disappear in high-inflation countries because no one wants to save and no one wants lend over an extended period, and thus so too does entrepreneurial risk taking.

In addition, precisely because inflation may damage the prospects of some people (namely, people whose costs may go up faster than their compensation), people work very hard to try to avoid this punishment. They will in other words try to rearrange how they hold their wealth—get out of money, get into real estate or gold or other assets that are likely to preserve their value. But none of this is free. Some people don't know, at least initially, how to manage their wealth in a high-inflation environment, and so they are penalized by foolishly holding large balances of, say, cash. Eventually they find their way to offices that more knowledgeable people found out about long ago, the offices of financial advisors who, for a perhaps substantial fee, will help people manage their assets in a way that protects them against the inflationary tax. But all of the time and effort spent defending oneself against this inflation, plus the resources paid to the professionals who manage wealth for people unable to protect themselves, are a sort of deadweight cost, an unnecessary cost made necessary only because of the presence of inflation.

In high-inflation societies, even the act of businesspeople having to constantly change prices is another sort of deadweight cost. In some cases of very high inflation, known as hyperinflation, food markets have been known to raise the prices of the goods they sell several times a day. This is also deadweight cost from the point of view of society as a whole, because those workers could be spending their time trying to find out more valuable products for their customers to buy, trying to figure out how more efficiently to organize the shelf space, and so on. Expressed this way, the cost seems rather small, but in hyperinflationary societies it is not, and in fact is part of the much larger problem of the *opportunity costs of managing inflation*.

Finally, the fact that inflation playing out in a non-mechanistic way makes many people substantially worse off means that people demand the government "do something" about the problem. But most of the things that the government ends up doing, whether the people directly demand them or not, will make things worse.[8] Governments impose price controls, for example, forbidding sellers from raising prices above some certain percentage every year. This simply prevents these sellers from passing on their higher monetary costs to their customers, and unavoidably causes them to decrease their willingness

---

[8]An exception is government action designed to bring inflation dramatically down, as occurred in the early 1980s in the U.S., for example.

to take risks and to supply goods. Groups with more political influence in society (be they unionized workers, government workers, retirees, or others) will demand that the government act in a discriminatory way protect them (and only them) from inflation—for example, by requiring that their contracts include automatic adjustments to take account of the average calculated inflation rate. (In post-World War I Germany, as inflation rose, the government relied on ration cards to allocate increasingly scarce foodstuffs.)

Citizens without so much political influence, on the other hand, will not get these benefits, and so will lose out to those with more political influence in the ability to acquire goods and services. And ultimately all of this serves to increase the amount of government control over the economy, of the ability of government to dictate who gets more and who gets less, who gets rewarded and who gets punished. Given the pernicious effects of government control over the economy outlined in Chapter 5, this cannot be good. A striking account of how inflation affected the ability of the economy to function properly was given by Anna Eisenmenger, a resident of Vienna, as inflation began to surge in immediate post-World War I Austria, whose hyperinflation, which peaked in 1922 at 1,426%, is not quite as well known is that of postbellum Germany:

> In the large banking hall a great deal of business was being done… All around me animated discussions were in progress concerning the stamping of currency, the issue of new notes, the purchase of foreign money and so on. There were always some who knew exactly what was now the best thing to do! I went to see the bank official who always advised me. "Well, wasn't I right?" he said. "If you had bought Swiss francs when I suggested, you would not now have lost three-fourths of your fortune". "Lost!" I exclaimed in horror. "Why, don't you think the krone will recover again?" "Recover!" he said with a laugh…

> Heightened class-consciousness is daily being instilled into the manual workers by the Socialist government, and, in heads bewildered by catchwords, leads to an enormously exaggerated estimate of the value of manual labor. Only in this way could it come about that the wages of manual workers are now far higher than the salaries of intellectual workers. Even our otherwise honest old house-porter is demanding such extravagant sums for performing little jobs that I prefer to do the heavier and more unpleasant household work myself…

> I survey my remaining 1,000-kronen notes mistrustfully, lying by the side of the pack of unredeemed food cards in the writing table drawer. Will they not perhaps share the fate of the food cards if the State fails to keep the promise made on the inscription on every note? The State still accepts its own money for the scanty provisions it offers us. The private tradesman already refuses to sell

his precious wares for money and demands something of real value in exchange. The wife of a doctor whom I know recently exchanged her beautiful piano for a sack of wheat flour.[9]

In this extract, we see much of what was discussed earlier. There are the arbitrary goods whose value is preserved in the marketplace, that is, some prices inflating at higher rates than others. (In addition to the piano mentioned, Eisenmenger's husband's collection of cigars was also useful in barter, but note that it was wheat whose value relative to that of a piano soared.) There are people running to politically ambitious people, in the form of socialist politicians, for protection. There was Eisenmenger herself, ignorant about how to protect herself from inflation and thus vulnerable to its ravages. The diary itself does not mention the disappearance of long-term lending, but one must suppose based on historical experience that this too occurred.

Austria is far from the only example of hyperinflation in the last hundred years. The worst cases during this time are listed in Table 11-5, according to Steve Hanke's and Nicholas H. Krus's calculation.[10]

Table 11-5. Hyperinflations

Country	Highest monthly inflation rate	Time required for prices to double
Hungary	1.30×10^{16}% (July 1946)	15.6 hours
Zimbabwe	79,600,000,000% (Nov. 2008)	24.7 hours
Yugoslavia	313,000,000% (Jan. 1994)	1.4 days
Germany	29,500% (Oct. 1923)	3.7 days
Greece	11,300% (Nov. 1944)	4.5 days
China	4,120% (May 1949)	5.6 days

These are of course extreme cases, and the chaos that such inflations introduce is also extreme. But relatively "moderate" inflation has also been far from rare in the last hundred years. Many Latin American countries and Israel, among others, have suffered inflation in the hundreds of percent per year. Even in the U.S., where inflation peaked at just under 14% during the period of worst inflation, the period of wringing it out of the economy was associated with very low rates of GDP growth.

---

[9]As reported in Adam Ferguson, *When Money Dies: the Nightmare of the Weimar Collapse* (New York: PublicAffairs, 2010), pp. 21-22.
[10]http://www.cato.org/sites/cato.org/files/pubs/pdf/WorkingPaper-8.pdf

So inflation is clearly a costly phenomenon. Why does it happen? There are two reasons. The first is, according to some, a side effect of policies designed to stimulate an economy that is growing too slowly for public tastes, which is again a topic for the next chapter. However, the other reason is related to the direct, socially toxic incentives of politicians. They seek to benefit from something called *money illusion*, the short-term response by people to the creation of "money" by banks in response to changed incentives given to them by the government, which pumps up economic growth, but only for a brief period.

To see how money illusion works, imagine the following: you wake up one morning, go to your ATM to withdraw money, and you find that the amount of cash in your checking account has mysteriously doubled. Being an honest sort, you immediately report this error to your bank, but they assure you that there is no mistake, that everything is as it is supposed to be, so you needn't worry about it. Undoubtedly you treat this as an unexpected gift, and you go out and spend some of the money on purchasing goods. However, suppose that in fact *everyone's* bank account doubled overnight, and everyone goes out and spends some of the money in about the same portion you do. The underlying productivity of the economy has not changed. The amount of the various scarce resources needed to produce things that people value is the same as it was yesterday, there has been no technological improvement that allows us to produce more with less, and so there is no reason to think that this should result in any long-term increase in economic activity. In fact, the money price of goods and services is just an artificial unit of measure. Thinking in terms of the previous idea in which all prices and earnings increase in the same proportion, whether we say that the amount of "money" needed to purchase a new car is $10, $10,000, or $10 million, is completely arbitrary, as long as one's income is adjusted accordingly. It is like expressing height in the larger quantity of centimeters instead of the smaller quantity of inches; the actual height of the person is the same either way. And so the extra money in the economy should eventually play out simply as higher money prices of goods, which, as we have seen, once we move away from the mechanistic inflation model, becomes a serious social problem.

But it may take people a short time to figure out that their increase in money—which after it plays out is *not*, note, an increase in wealth—is not just confined to them. And so when the government increases the amount of "money" in the economy and distributes it through the banking system, whether by printing it or through other means outlined in the next chapter, people may for a short time engage in more economic activity because the increased liquidity of the economy is confused with increased wealth. Why would the government do such a thing? It may be in the government's short-term interest to cause people to think the economy is performing better, because then they may return the government to power. This effect is known as the *political business cycle*. It is unclear how important it is, but to the extent that it exists it suggests that governments will be prone to manipulating the economy's liquidity in their own political interest. If one accepts the common definition of inflation as "too much money chasing too few goods," this will result over the long term in increasing inflation, which may eventually have to be wrung out of the economy at significant cost.

▨ **Note** The government sometimes adds liquidity to the economy in a way that makes it seem as if we are all wealthier, at least in the short term. It is quite possible for this political business cycle to result in inflation.

Sometimes the highest levels of inflation result from an even more direct incentive—the government must create money simply to pay its bills. When governments spend more than they take in in taxes, they are sometimes able to simply borrow money, by issuing what are known as bonds. Once upon a time, bonds were mostly in the form of paper—you may have seen old-fashioned savings bonds that are still sometimes given to children by relatives when the children are born—and now they are electronic credits. A bond is a promise to pay a person who has lent the government money. He has done this by buying a bond in a certain amount of money, in exchange for which the government pays him interest periodically over a certain period of time, before he gets the money he originally spent purchasing the bond back. A person may, for example, spend $9,800 on a U.S. government bond, which means that the government now has that additional amount of dollars available to spend on things it wants to purchase. Depending on the kind of bond, you may receive regular interest payments, or you may simply receive a higher amount when the bond expires—say, 13 weeks later at $10,000. Either way, you are in essence lending money to the government. (Large corporations also issue bonds.) The bonds issued by the U.S. federal government in particular are known as Treasury bonds, after the Department of the Treasury that issues them.

For many governments this is a routine matter. But if the cumulative government debt becomes too much, people may begin to doubt that the bonds issued by this government will be paid back. They will thus stop buying the bonds, and the government will become unable to borrow money, in the same way a person who had defaulted on numerous loans would be unable to borrow money from a bank. Then, if government spending continues to exceed taxes, the only way for the government to pay its bills is simply to print new money and to give that as payment to those selling it goods. But all of this printing money, again for the same reason as above, does not create any additional productive capacity. Instead, it simply adjusts upwards the monetary prices of more or less everything (although not at the same rate, as already indicated.

As prices of things get higher, the government must print even more money to pay its excess expenditures, and indeed as inflation damages economic activity, its tax intake will fall even further, worsening the problem. The country thus enters into a hyperinflationary spiral, which are the sorts of situations seen back in Table 11-5. Hyperinflation, in other words, is always and everywhere a political phenomenon. It would thus be nice to insulate the portions of the government responsible for managing the amount of "money" in the economy from daily political pressure, because absent such insulation, that pressure tends to lead both to creating "money" every time an election comes up and to printing more money to fund more government spending, which if it exceeds taxes by enough for long enough, leads to hyperinflation. Thus, there is a phenomenon in many advanced countries called independent central banking, which we turn to in the next chapter.

Macroeconomics

Stabilizing the Economy, or Not

As noted in the previous chapter, "the economy" is really, in the case of the U.S., just a description of the trading relations among our 310 million people at any given moment. As one might imagine, when there is a constant tide of private-sector economic experimentation, and information about prospects and outcomes of those experiments is costly and dispersed, this description is unavoidably vague. At any moment, some people may be doing better and some not so well, and the economy is constantly in flux. What is more, there is some reason to doubt how effectively people in Washington, D.C., can push the buttons they have in front of them to make "the economy" better when it seems to be going badly on balance at any moment.[1] But people understandably dislike circumstances in which unemployment is high, and economic growth (growth in real per-capita GDP) low. In the modern era, in which it is assumed that government is primarily a vehicle to solve social problems (as opposed to, say, an organization designed to enable people to solve their own problems by setting up and enforcing contract and property rights and addressing market failures), when "the economy" is bad, many people, especially those suffering the most, will demand that government "do something." Economists in the 20th century created a vast apparatus of theoretical tools to tell government officials what to do when it is time to "do something." Because "the economy" is so complex, encompassing many different individuals with their own specific circumstances, I personally am somewhat skeptical of the ability of these tools to achieve their goals. However, many people much smarter than I developed these tools and believe in their use. This chapter therefore describes how

---

[1] Why do I say "on balance"? Because in a big society like the U.S., there will always be some activities that are becoming more valuable and hence expanding, no matter the overall average state of "the economy."

much of the modern macroeconomic policy—that designed to stabilize the economy in particular—is said to work, and evaluates it.

The Goals of Economic Policy

To understand the goals of what is generally seen as good economic policy (as opposed to the goals of any particular politician at any moment, which is a different thing entirely), it is helpful to look at a diagram showing growth in U.S. real GDP per capita from 1870–2010 (Figure 12-1).

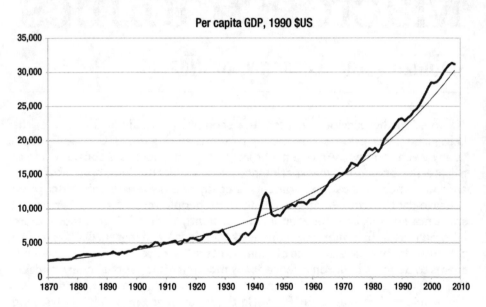

Figure 12-1. Growth in real per-capita U.S. GDP, 1870–2010

Recall first from Chapter 11 that real per-capita (that is, per-person) GDP refers to analysis of changes in quantities, while holding prices fixed at some base-year standard. In the chart shown in Figure 12-1, the base year is 1990. In addition, the thick line represents actual GDP. The thin curve represents the best fit of what is known as an *exponential function* to these data. In other words, this is the smooth exponential function that most closely approximates the actual data on U.S. GDP growth.[2] The details of this function are not important, but the estimation of it indicates that over this time real per capita GDP in the U.S has grown at an average annual rate of 1.97%.

---

[2]If U.S. economic growth were exactly characterized by an exponential function it would indicate that the U.S. economy grows at some fixed rate every year, without fluctuations around that trend.

This means that the material standard of living has doubled about every 35 years, consistent with the discussion throughout Chapter 9 about things constantly getting better. This pattern of growth is the first key thing to notice about Figure 12-1. We should not be surprised that, over time, income per person tends to grow. There is a constant flow of new entrepreneurs with new ideas, people figuring out new ways to meet human needs by using scarce resources differently, and the best ideas are the ones that best survive the competitive process. New ideas allow us to find useful resources where none were known to exist before. The former waste product of oil, the scientific plaything that was the laser, and the one-time laboratory curiosity of the semi-conductor that went on to power the computer are vivid examples. History is a constant tide of technological improvement.

In most countries, long-term growth of real per-capita GDP is an important objective of government policy. This is as it should be. There are some people who object, as noted in Chapter 11, that GDP is not a very good measure of quality of life. Accordingly, some people have developed alternative measures of what they view as the important components of quality of life—the Human Development Index[3] or the Genuine Progress Indicator,[4] to name two. Indeed, a former king of the South Asian country of Bhutan once said that his goal was to maximize something he called "gross national happiness."[5] But I would argue that maximization of real per-capita GDP growth is in fact what we should be aiming for. GDP is not a perfect measure of human welfare, but it is an objective index. The prices used to calculate it, to the extent that the calculations are correct, reflect the value people actually attach to various goods themselves, as revealed through the market process, as opposed to the value an arbitrary but powerful individual might assign to, say, a mandatory minimum wage, a piece of land being preserved as wetlands instead of being used for a parking lot, or a Beethoven symphony.

Because the market process is a way to reconcile conflicting human desires as efficiently as possible, a growing economy reflects the fact that human desires *as humans themselves define them* are being better satisfied than before. Thus, the more rapidly an economy grows, the more comprehensively human desires are being met, even when particular desires of particular people conflict (as they usually do). These other measures, in contrast, depend on the subjective interpretations of the people who construct them (the King of Bhutan, for instance) to determine what is important. When the economy is growing, people are living together more productively and helping each other to achieve their goals more effectively. Hence, economic growth is a worthy goal of economic policy, perhaps the single worthiest one.

---

[3]http://en.wikipedia.org/wiki/Human_Development_Index
[4]http://en.wikipedia.org/wiki/Genuine_progress_indicator
[5]http://en.wikipedia.org/wiki/Gross_national_happiness

But there's another thing to note about Figure 12-1. Although the general pattern over the long run is a positive one, in the short run there can be significant instability. Per-capita income may grow on average at 1.97% per year, but in any given year it may grow more than that, less than that, or even fall. Inspection of Figure 12-1 suggests that these periods are not rare. The two worst episodes in absolute terms were the 1930s (the Great Depression) and the demobilization after World War II. It turns out that when looking at the percentage by which real GDP per capita—instead of its absolute level—fell, we see that there were also serious economic reversals from 1873–1878 and 1893–1895.

These fluctuations are normal. Figure 12-2 shows a slice of U.S. macroeconomic history—namely, growth in real per-capita GDP over a portion of the earlier data set, from 1890–1921.

Figure 12-2. Growth in real per-capita U.S. GDP, 1890–1921

So, even in the short run, there are substantial economic fluctuations, even from one year to the next, and GDP itself is merely an average of all growth across all goods whose market trade is measured by the government. This seemingly constant instability generates a significant problem—not economic, but *political*. When GDP is falling (or even, in an economy with rapid growth like China, not growing as fast as it was before), this means that more people than usual have planned for a future that is not going to happen, at least not yet. Companies have, more than usual, staffed their factories and offices in the belief that demand for their products will increase by a large amount, but it turns out that this does not happen, and demand for what they sell may even decrease. Given that businesses cannot hold onto their resources unless they can pay them compensation at least as high as their opportunity cost, and given that this requires that they make economic profit, this declining demand, which may occur in many places simultaneously, requires that costs come down. One way this brutal yet inescapable economic arithmetic plays out is that workers are let go.

▒ **Question 12.1**   If there is a layoff, and the factory is subject to a collective-bargaining contract, according to what rules and procedures might these layoffs be carried out?

And make no mistake about it—an increase in unemployment is a problem that the citizenry wants politicians to address. People who lose their own jobs naturally want "the economy" to recover so that they may find good jobs again. And people who are merely worried about losing their jobs may also want the government to "do something." This is unsurprising. Losing one's job is a major setback. Many people depend on income from employment as their primary source of resources to fund their consumption, their retirement savings, and so on. If they cease drawing this compensation, their horizons diminish considerably. So *if* we can lower economic instability—make it so that hiring is not far above trend sometimes and far below it at other times, and losing one's job is not a constant fear, and we can do this *without* sacrificing economic growth (in other words, without sacrificing the ability of people to reconcile their conflicting needs, and ensuring that our children live better than we do, as we live better than our parents did)—this would seem to be a worthy goal. (If stabilizing the economy comes at the expense of slower growth on average, the trade-off is not so clear.)

▒ **Note**   In the long run, a well-managed economy will grow because of new ideas. In the short run, anything can happen because of unpredictable change that is often brought about by such ideas. If the short-run changes are bad ones for more people than usual, this becomes a political problem.

Precisely in the belief that this is the case, that government can and should stabilize the economy, for much of the 20th century the government in most advanced nations, including the United States, has under the guidance of many smart economists engaged in such stabilization policies, which are often known as *aggregate demand management*. (I will use this term and *economic stabilization*.)

Its goal is to iron out economic fluctuations—to prevent severe downturns, which put people out of work in large numbers, from happening and to prevent excessive booms too, on the assumption that it is their unsustainability that leads to severe economic contractions in the first place.

The "Business Cycle"

The term *aggregate demand management* is revealing. It suggests that there is something called *aggregate demand*. To this point, we have thought about demand as something that occurs in individual markets—there is a demand for shoes, for accounting services, for paperclips. And this demand depends on the quantity and quality of available substitutes. But *aggregate demand* means we're aggregating everything—it refers to the general demand for *all* goods. Already, this seems a little peculiar, because goods do not really have a single price. Rather, each good has a price, and we buy some goods and decline to buy others partly based on those different prices. It is true that when one spends money on goods, one is not saving, so that one can think about the interest rate foregone on savings not made as the "price" of consumption, but consumption itself has many possibilities. Nonetheless, built into models of aggregate demand management is the assumption that "the economy" goes bad because consumers are not demanding enough goods overall, and can in fact grow too fast (for reasons outlined later in this chapter) because consumers are demanding too many. Before getting into this in more detail, a few other terms about the overall trend of the economy must be defined.

When real GDP (not even real GDP per capita, note) is growing, this is known as an *expansion*. Expansion can be brisk—in the U.S., any growth rate of real GDP of about 4% probably qualifies—or it can be slow—anything between 0–2% is generally what people mean by slow growth. (Note that in other countries where recent economic growth has been much faster, such as China, even 4% would be disappointing.) When real GDP contracts for two consecutive quarters as measured by a private group, the National Bureau of Economic Research (NBER), the official term for this is *recession*. When real GDP contracts either by a large amount or for extended period of time, this is generally referred to as a *depression*, although not even the NBER has an official definition for where a recession stops and a depression begins.

Perhaps because economists are reluctant to admit that the toolkit they developed to manage the economy (described in upcoming sections) cannot prevent depressions, they have basically been unwilling to use the word since the Great Depression of the 1930s. But in my view, the period 2007–2012 (which includes, in addition to an officially certified recession, a recovery very weak by postwar standards) certainly qualified. In addition, fluctuations of the economy—its pattern of growing fast, growing slowly, and shrinking—also make up what is known as the *business cycle*. This is in truth an unhelpful term, because it suggests a regularity to the economy—it grows for four years, then declines for one, then grows for another four—that doesn't really exist. Economic growth is not like a sine wave, with an identical pattern of fluctuations around some basic growth rate. Rather, precisely because innovations, discovery of information, and entrepreneurial experimentation are mostly random, the economy could very easily grow for an extended period of time, have a brief recessionary interruption, grow for two years, and then have a severe recession. The economy, in other words, rises on average, but its short-term fluctuations are best thought of as random.

When the economy goes into recession, or certainly into depression, many businesses find that the information they had about future demand for their product was unjustifiably optimistic. Overall, the sellers of goods and services estimated that demand for what they produce would grow more than it in fact did. As noted earlier, it is urgent for them, if they want to stay in business, to cut costs. Cutting labor is an easy way to do that very quickly, especially if demand for that type of labor is relatively elastic, that is, if there is no overwhelming incentive to preserve a particular employee or kind of employee through bad times. In contrast, when the economy begins to recover or is in a sustained expansion, employers find that their expectations were too pessimistic (as do people who had thought about starting their own businesses but were worried about the risk in a bad economy), and so they begin to expand production or open new businesses. Thus, in the early stages of recession or depression unemployment goes up, just as it goes down in the early stages of an expansion. High unemployment as the economy adjusts more than usual often generates a great amount of political pressure to end the recession or depression. As already noted, even if economic fluctuations are partly or substantially random, this does not in and of itself mean that economic stabilization is a mistake, as long as the stabilization is effective and doesn't cost us growth in the long run. The government, in its attempts to stabilize, has two tools in its toolkit: monetary policy and fiscal policy.

Note Stabilization or aggregate demand management is about the short term only. Is it a good idea? That depends on its effectiveness and long-term cost.

Economic Stabilization—Monetary Policy

Monetary policy refers to *attempts by the government to influence the rate of "money" creation by private banks*. Its goal as an aggregate-demand-management or economic-stabilization tool is to keep the economy going on an even keel. In explaining monetary policy this way, remember that the dividing line among different kinds of wealth assets between "money" and non-"money" is arbitrary. But clearly among the most liquid assets are those that are known as demand deposits. The government can influence the rate at which banks are willing to make loans and thus influence the total value of demand deposits that exist at any time. The organization responsible for doing that is a government entity known as the Federal Reserve System, which is the U.S. central bank. Most countries have such a bank, and its primary tasks are to oversee the health of the banking system, to regulate banks, and to oversee the implementation of monetary policy. The system in the U.S., based on similar entities that already existed in several European countries, was born in the Federal Reserve Act of 1913. The modern Federal Reserve has evolved significantly since this act was passed. As currently structured, it is overseen by a Board of Governors, consisting of seven members, including one chair and one vice-chair. There are also 12 regional banks housed in various cities around the country. The regional banks do not have any direct control over monetary policy and will not be further considered. Each private bank in the country may choose whether or not to participate in the lending system that the Federal Reserve controls, which requires that they be subject to its rules. Most U.S. banks choose to do so.

But the Board of Governors is where monetary policy decisions are made. It must be noted that the structure of the Federal Reserve is different from that of much of the rest of the federal government. Typically, when we think of "federal agencies," what we are really thinking of are organizations partly or entirely under the direction of the executive branch. And those organizations come with a significant degree of political accountability. The secretary of agriculture, for example, must be named by the president and approved by the Senate, but the president may remove him at any time, and Cabinet secretaries can even be impeached and removed from office by Congress, although only one secretary has been so impeached in American history, and he was impeached after he had announced his resignation but before it had taken effect. (He was never tried.) It is taken for granted in the American system that the secretary of agriculture is an ordinary political officer. If the presidency changes hands, the secretary of agriculture may and probably will leave with the departing president, in particular if a new party takes over the White House. The terms of Cabinet secretaries, thus, seldom exceed those of the presidents who appointed them.

Federal Reserve governors are also appointed by the president and confirmed by the Senate and may also be impeached and removed, but the other elements of political accountability are not there. First, the president cannot simply dismiss a governor of the Federal Reserve Board the way he can a Cabinet secretary who no longer has his confidence. Second, five of the seven governors are appointed to serve 14-year terms, an extremely long term for any officer in the American constitutional system. (Only federal judges, with lifetime terms, serve longer.) Third, the other two members (the chair and vice-chair) serve four-year terms, but they are purposely set up to straddle presidential terms—each officer is appointed in the middle of one presidential term, and his term expires in the middle of the next. The Federal Reserve system has thus been built in a way that means that its members reach office in the same way that executive-branch officers do, but once they are in, they are supposed to be immune from the short-term political pressures we actually want the president and his secretary of agriculture to be subject to. This is because it is believed that making the central bank subject to these kinds of pressures will yield worse results because of the temptation to subordinate monetary-policy decision making to short-term electoral considerations, especially the temptation to take advantage of money illusion as described in Chapter 11. Monetary policy, in other words, is unlike other kinds of government decision making in that it should not be exposed to the vagaries of public opinion.

So what is it that the Federal Reserve Board of Governors does to merit this exemption? Recall from Chapter 11 that banks can create money by making loans. The Fed has a lot to do with how willing they are to do this. It may or may not make you uncomfortable (it shouldn't), but banks routinely in a sense run out of money. They would prefer not to keep deposits on hand, because they must pay interest on them. Instead, they want to lend that money out, so that they can earn interest. In the language of accounting, deposits are liabilities, loans are assets. The bank of course wishes to keep some "money" on hand—deposits that haven't been lent out—to be able to meet the daily desires of depositors to withdraw cash. Indeed, the Federal Reserve has a minimum *reserve requirement*—a rule that each member bank must keep a certain percentage of money on deposit, both as cash in the vault and with the Fed itself. The Fed can lower this requirement—say, from 5% to 4%—and then banks may lend at a faster rate. If the reserve requirement is raised, lending similarly slows down. However, because of the "money multiplier" mentioned in Chapter 11, one dollar in new lending by one bank creates other lending down the road—the reserve requirement is a relatively clumsy tool. If the reserve requirement is lowered from 6% to 5%, it means that for every dollar of every loan made, 95 cents instead of 94 cents is available for creating new lending, and that continues to be true as each loan moves through the banking system and creates more loans. It is thus powerful, but can easily result in a vast increase or decrease in lending. For this reason this tool is relatively seldom used.

The Fed also has direct control over two interest rates, which are known as the *Fed funds rate* and the *discount rate*. The former rate involves the rate the Federal Reserve requires be charged when member banks borrow from other member banks from funds the latter have on deposit at the Fed (hence the name *Fed funds*). These are short-term loans, often overnight, and are made because banks have liquidity constraints—that is, they fear they won't have, or may indeed not have, enough "money" on hand to fulfill their day-to-day obligations. These loans are perfectly normal. The other rate is the *discount rate*, the rate at which member banks borrow directly from the Fed itself. If the Fed raises either of these rates (and the Fed funds rate is the most often-used tool), banks become more reluctant lenders because the cost of having to borrow from another bank's Fed funds or from the Fed itself will be higher. Lending will go down. If the rates are lowered, lending will similarly go up as banks know that the consequences of having to engage in this short-term borrowing are lower. In addition, raising these two rates will cause banks to raise the rates they charge on their other loans, whereas lowering them also causes banks to pass on their lower costs to customers in the form of lower rates on home and business loans.

The final tool is known as *open-market operations*. To understand it, one needs to know first that the Department of Treasury of the United States (an ordinary political agency, distinct from the quasi-independent Fed by virtue of being a normal Cabinet department subject to the usual Congressional and Presidential controls) routinely borrows money on behalf of the government of the U.S. (because this government runs a deficit). The financial assets through which it borrows money are the Treasury bonds mentioned in Chapter 11. These bonds are freely bought and sold just like Microsoft stock or the futures contracts mentioned in Chapter 4. Many of those buying and selling these bonds are speculators working for financial trading firms, but some of them work for central banks and other government agencies around the world, who like to hold Treasury bonds because they are seen as very likely, compared to the bonds issued by governments of other countries or by private companies, to be paid back.

■ **Question 12.2** When people speculate on bonds, what are they speculating about, and what information do they generate for the rest of us?

The U.S. Federal Reserve is also a major buyer and seller of Treasury bonds. It buys and sells them as an instrument of monetary policy. The process can be illustrated through the simple model contained in Figures 12-3 and 12-4.

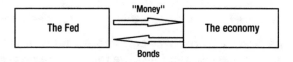

Figure 12-3. Expansionary open-market operations

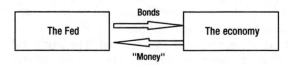

Figure 12-4. Contractionary open-market operations

The two boxes represent two separate worlds—the economy, where all of us live, engage in exchange, take risks and pursue our interests, and the coffers of the Fed, which hold large amounts of both cash (electronic) and bonds. Figure 12-1 depicts expansionary open-market operations, which are designed to increase economic activity by injecting "money" into the economy. In these operations, the Fed buys bonds from the public. Cash that it had held enters the economy, and bonds leave the economy to be held by the Fed until the direction of open-market operations turns. This means that bonds—a less-liquid asset—have been removed from the economy and replaced by a more-liquid asset. (Bonds are very liquid compared to, say, real estate, but there are many obligations they cannot be directly used to settle.) This means that, at least in the short term, people will be more likely to spend, because their wealth is now held in proportions that make spending easier. This is why the situation in Figure 12-3 is called *expansionary* open-market operations—because it is believed that the Federal Reserve swapping cash for bonds will cause spending and lending to increase and the economy thus to expand. It is worth noting that in response to the unusually severe economic downturn beginning in 2007, the Fed began years of unprecedented levels of bond buying. Whether it was effective in reviving the economy is a very open question.

In Figure 12-4, the direction is reversed. A more liquid asset, cash, is spent by the public to buy a less-liquid asset, bonds, from the Fed, because the Fed has decided to sell some of the bonds it holds. The overall liquidity of the nation's wealth goes down, and so do lending and spending. In other words, this policy contracts economic activity, so Figure 12-4 depicts contractionary open-market operations.

Interest rates can also be adjusted in an expansionary way, with the goal of increasing economic activity, or a contractionary way, decreasing economic activity. When the Fed lowers the rates it controls, this lowers the cost for banks to lend aggressively, thus banks lend more. This should result in more people taking out loans to buy homes and cars, and more people borrowing to expand or set up businesses. When interest rates are raised, economic activity should similarly slow down. Although (as noted) it is a fairly clumsy tool, reserve requirements also have an expansionary and contractionary side. To lower the reserve requirement is to give banks the ability to lend a greater fraction of every dollar they take in in deposits, and to raise reserve requirements is to require them to set aside a greater fraction of every dollar. Lowering the requirement is thus expansionary, and raising it is contractionary.

So when the economy is entering, threatening to enter, or stuck in a contraction (recession or depression), the Fed will lower interest rates and buy bonds from the public. Occasionally, it will lower the reserve requirement. When the economy is growing too fast, it raises rates, sells bonds to the public, and occasionally raises the reserve requirement. This is essentially how monetary policy works.

But a new question then arises. In Chapters 9 and 11, I argued that economic growth is a powerful force for bettering the human condition. Why would the Fed be worried about growth that is too fast? The reason is that there is a common belief among macroeconomists that growth in excess of the economy's underlying capacity will cause inflation, which we know from Chapter 11 is a bad result. The argument works through what is called the *wage-price spiral*. Suppose that the economy is going great guns, and businesses become so optimistic that they begin over-hiring. What does over-hiring mean? It means that, running short of labor, they hire workers to satisfy short-term demand even though the workers aren't any more productive, and they drive unemployment down below what is known as the *natural rate*—the rate of unemployment consistent with the normal flow of people leaving their jobs because of family reasons, because they have found something better, because they are fired for misconduct, and so on.

This natural rate of people transitioning between jobs, called *frictional unemployment*, is thought to be different from people losing jobs because the overall "economy" is bad. Even a rapidly growing economy ought to have some of this frictional unemployment, so that the efficient rate of unemployment is never zero. But when demand for labor becomes very high in very good times, wages begin to be bid up by employers desperate for workers despite the lack of higher productivity. When workers are paid more because they are more productive, higher wages need not translate as higher consumer prices. But if the labor market becomes cramped, workers may be hired in short-term desperation despite no advances in productivity. Now, higher wages *do* have to be passed on as higher prices for the goods the workers are making. But the workers, having the upper hand in the labor market because of artificially low unemployment (the opposite of Marx's argument of the "reserve army of labor,"[6] which is part of the overall Marxist doomsday argument outlined in Chapter 9), can simply demand, and get, higher wages to make up for higher prices of consumer goods, themselves caused by their original demands for higher wages, which are passed on to consumers. This means that prices go up yet again, and suddenly the inflationary spiral is on.

To prevent this, the Fed will begin to engage in contractionary policy not just at the first sight of incipient inflation, by which time many macroeconomists believe it is too late to prevent the spiral from kicking in, but merely at the onset of growth that is thought to be unsustainable. What is this level of growth? It surely is difficult to say. A former chairman of the Fed, Alan

---

[6]http://en.wikipedia.org/wiki/Reserve_army_of_labour

Greenspan, took a lot of criticism for his belief that the popularization of the Internet in the 1990s (which, he believed, raised productivity dramatically) meant that the sustainable growth rate of the economy was higher than in the past. While there was no outburst of high inflation during the period, the lack of sufficiently contractionary monetary policy, in the view of some, led not to unsustainable wage inflation but a bubble in the stock market, which popped ferociously after April 2000. The argument was that increased liquidity in the economy had to be invested somewhere, and one of the places it was invested was in the stock market, driving up stock prices unsustainably. (This interpretation, like much in macroeconomics, is disputed by some.)

But in any event, the fear is that an economy that grows in excess of its underlying capacity, which may lead to unemployment lower than its natural amount, will cause inflation. And so like all central banks, the Fed must walk a tightrope—on the one hand, keeping policy sufficiently contractionary to prevent inflation from developing, and on the other hand keeping policy sufficiently expansionary so as not to push the economy into recession. If inflation arises because monetary policy is unwisely loosened, then later on it will have to be dramatically tightened. In the 1970s, when oil prices surged on two occasions because of turmoil in the Middle East, it was reasonable to expect that this would cause a major economic slowdown—people had planned that oil would be much cheaper than it turned out to be. But in an effort to prevent that slowdown from happening, the Fed engaged in aggressive expansionary monetary policy. This did not solve the underlying problem of the need to adjust to a new world, a world in which oil was now much scarcer. So this meant those adjustments took place anyway, but with a lot more "money" sloshing around in the economy than before. The result was both recession and inflation, which necessitated a major episode of contractionary monetary policy after 1979 to wring money out of the economy by increasing interest rates (thus slowing down bank lending) and engaging in contractionary open-market operations, in order to bring inflation down. This result was achieved, but only at the cost of inciting what might once have been called a depression.

When a recession happens (assuming it is not intentionally brought about by the need to wring out inflation caused by excessive expansionary monetary policy), it is pretty obvious what should be done—expansionary monetary policy should occur to get the economy moving again. But when to *raise* interest rates to prevent inflation from taking hold because of the wage-price spiral is much harder to figure out. Some economists even believe that the wage-price spiral is nothing to worry about. If the labor market becomes excessively tight, we would expect business owners to figure out ways to substitute away from workers and towards other kinds of resources. When grocery workers become expensive in a tight labor market, self-checkout machines are introduced, causing demand for grocery clerks to go down. When drive-through clerks are hard to get, their jobs are outsourced to people taking orders hundreds or even thousands of miles away[7] over the Internet. Thus, in this view, higher wages unjustified by higher productivity should frequently induce a substitution of machines for workers (or cheaper workers, perhaps overseas, for more expensive ones), nipping the spiral in the bud. Although below-"natural" unemployment can indeed cause wages to go up once, perhaps even in excess of productivity, in this view the problem is temporary and self-solving.

The last thing to note with regard to monetary policy is that it is relied on much more than in the past. In the time before the creation of the Federal Reserve, the government had no instruments by which to conduct any sort of monetary policy, and recall that at that time, banks often issued their own currency notes. But monetary policy has in the postwar period been a, if not the, primary tool of economic stabilization. This has coincided with a general increase in the average rate of inflation, as documented in Figure 11-2. According to the data there, the CPI went up and down until almost exactly 1913, the year of the creation of the Fed. Since then, the index has gone up continuously, and hence the buying power of U.S. currency has declined continuously. As we saw in Chapters 9 and 11, standards of living in general and real GDP in particular have soared during this period, so it must be that compensation is going up faster. But if the problems of inflation noted in Chapter 11 hold at lower levels of inflation as well as under hyperinflation (and that is not clear), the era of modern central banking has brought us more stability (GDP fluctuations are probably lower than in the pre-Fed era), but has also increased these inflationary costs over the long term.

Economic Stabilization—Fiscal Policy

The toolbox for stabilizing the economy contains one other element besides monetary policy: fiscal policy, best defined as *the use of the government's taxing and spending powers for stabilization purposes*. Note that here "government" does not mean some quasi-independent organization like the Federal Reserve, but instead the ordinary executive and legislative branches of government, and the process by which they make tax policy and spend money.

The Coming of John Maynard Keynes

Fiscal policy as a stabilization tool is not as old as monetary policy. It made its appearance in a big way after World War II, but its genesis lies in the Great

---

[7]http://usatoday30.usatoday.com/money/companies/management/2007-05-14-drive-through_N.htm

Depression. This event was easily the worst in U.S. economic history. It is an instructive experience if you ever meet people with personal memories of the Depression to talk with them, although obviously there are fewer and fewer of them now.[8] It was a horrendous experience. Unemployment peaked at almost 25 percent, there was an explosion of soup kitchens and homeless encampments, the banking system almost fell apart between 1929 and 1932, and many Americans bewildered by the catastrophe flirted with fascism, socialism, and communism. Because the country itself was not nearly as wealthy as now, the Depression's impact on ordinary people's ability to survive day to day was dramatic, and the era produced some of our most compelling art describing these effects—the books of John Steinbeck and the photographs of Dorothea Lange, among others.

As an epidemic of bank failures tore through the nation because of a series of bank runs by panicky depositors, monetary policy became less and less relevant, and in any event, monetary policy was not well understood and was used poorly. Many economists of the time also had only one answer beyond monetary policy, and that was to do nothing. According to standard economic theory, if unemployment had skyrocketed, the thing to do was to wait for wages to come down until equilibrium had been restored in the labor market, just as the standard supply-demand model for labor suggests. And yet the Depression did not end. Part of this was due to the aggressive intervention of President Hoover, who used persuasion and the law to try to keep wages up and prevent jobs from being eliminated—two things the standard theory would suggest was something that had to happen for the economy to resume its normal growth path. History has painted Hoover as someone who believed in doing nothing and letting the market correct itself, but more recent history calls that depiction very seriously into question. He aggressively leaned on chief executive officers and union leaders to avoid layoffs and intervened dramatically in international markets by signing a massive increase in taxes on imported goods known as the Smoot-Hawley tariff. So the perception of him as some ideologue who wanted to wait for the Great Depression to fix itself is far from the mark.

The depth and length of the Depression cost Herbert Hoover his job, and it also prompted economists to think about why the economy continued not to get better. The smartest was an Englishman named John Maynard Keynes (rhymes with "gains"). He had become famous in the early 1920s by correctly

---

[8]A fascinating book came out a few years ago, which contained the discovered diary of a lawyer from Youngstown, who recounted his reaction to the unfolding economic catastrophe and to the government attempts to fix it. The book is called *The Great Depression: A Diary* (http://www.amazon.com/The-Great-Depression-A-Diary/dp/158648799X).

predicting that the Treaty of Versailles that ended World War I would impose impossible obligations on the defeated Germans, and indeed the Germans hyperinflated their way out of that debt (that is, printed so much currency that the value of the money they were using to pay back debts deteriorated to essentially nothing). But his most influential work was *The General Theory of Employment, Interest and Money*, which was published in 1936, nearly at the end of Franklin Roosevelt's mostly unsuccessful first term.

Keynes' diagnosis of the Depression was revolutionary. In his judgment, it was not like an ordinary economic breakdown. During such events, monetary policy could work just as the theory predicted it should. The Fed would engage in expansionary monetary policy, and under the greater liquidity and lower interest rates businesses would be more willing to take risks. (Consumer borrowing was a smaller phenomenon then than it is now, so monetary policy was thought mostly to influence business and not the consumer.) But after the Depression had been bad enough for long enough, people lost hope that the future would ever be better. They became permanently unwilling to spend money, and this made business correspondingly unwilling to build new plants or otherwise increase production, and so they also refused to hire workers. In other words, consumers weren't willing to spend because they had no job or feared losing the one they had, and businesses refused to hire because consumers weren't willing to spend. Under circumstances like this, simply lowering interest rates did no good, because there was no rate low enough to induce businesses to borrow money to expand.

When Interest Rates Hit Rock-Bottom—The Need for Fiscal Policy

Recall that interest rates reflect the rate at which wealth today trades for wealth in the future. People who are very optimistic about their future might be willing to pay high interest rates, people who are pessimistic will not. (Note that this is an argument about the demand for loans. Most of the examples in the earlier discussion of interest rates focused on things affecting the supply of loans.) So now Keynes's argument becomes a little clearer. After the Depression had gone on a few years, people began to adopt an attitude of permanent pessimism. There was no longer any reason for businesses to engage in any expansion or risk taking, because things were bad and likely to stay that way. Interest rates cannot go below zero, because anyone can earn zero interest just by taking cash and putting it in his mattress. So if I as a businessman am offered a chance to borrow $20,000 at a rate barely above zero, I am still unwilling to do it. No investment opportunity that I have will earn enough money to allow me to pay the loan back, and there is a significant chance that I will default because the economy is so bad. Interest rates therefore become completely impotent as an expansionary tool. The Fed can lower interest rates almost to zero (as it essentially did), but the economy will stay depressed.

But Keynes's great genius was to think about very low interest rates in a different way. As we just saw, very low rates indicate that there are not a lot of people standing in line to borrow money. People are so pessimistic that very few projects are seen as worth the risk. But this means that if the government charges in and borrows huge amounts of money, the social opportunity cost—investment projects that don't occur because the money is lent to the government instead—is minimal, close to zero in fact. This is thus the ideal time for the government to come in and borrow that money and use it to put people to work. Doing this will cause large numbers of people to start earning regular paychecks again. They will then spend this money on goods, which will give business the confidence it needs to begin investing in expansion again. Massive public spending of borrowed money, in other words, is a way to jump-start the economy. Those people could be hired to build valuable public infrastructure—roads, bridges, schools, hospitals, and so on—at substantially lower opportunity cost than if those projects were undertaken at a time of economic boom. However, Keynes went so far as to suggest that the goal was not to build infrastructure per se, but to end the economy's *coordination failure*—the fact that employers would hire if only they knew that there would be demand for their goods by the time their projects were finished, but workers would signal a willingness to buy products only if they knew that they would have jobs. Indeed Keynes famously said that it would be sufficient to hire people to do nothing more than bury cash in abandoned coal mines and then dig it up again. The main issue was not to invest in productive activities per se—if the results of public spending were productive, that would just be a bonus—but to break the iron grip of pessimism.

And so Keynes built an impressive intellectual foundation under an idea that had already existed, that the government should build public-works projects when times are really bad. In the past, this had been done sometimes merely to cultivate political support—to keep people from taking out their rage on the current politicians—as much as to revive the economy. But Keynes provided a powerful theoretical justification for doing this, and for doing it on a large scale. As noted, President Hoover had himself, contrary to conventional wisdom, engaged in very activist attempts to right the ship after the October 1929 stock market crash, urging businesses to keep wages up and engaging in numerous infrastructure projects. Once he took office in 1933, Franklin Delano Roosevelt did much the same, hiring people to manage the national parks, create art, build major electric-power projects in the Tennessee Valley and in rural America more generally, construct such urban projects as LaGuardia Airport, and to do many other tasks.

But of course the Depression lasted until close to the end of the 1930s, and many take that as evidence that the Keynes approach failed. Others contend, however, that the New Deal projects were too few and too small-scale to do what Keynes said needed to be done. Note that the same argument occurred over the gigantic economic-stimulus legislation passed in 2009, after the great financial-market crash of 2008. The fact that the economy failed to grow vigorously after this legislation passed is taken by many as an indictment of the whole Keynes approach, while others argue, just like before, that the main flaw was that the stimulus package was too small. This reminds us that macroeconomics, or at least the macroeconomics of economic stabilization, is considerably less well established than microeconomics.

Lost in Translation—How the Economics of Keynes Became Keynesian Economics

Keynes died in 1946, which means he did not live to see the movement of economic stabilization to the top of economists' (and politicians') priorities. Because the Depression was such a catastrophic event, attention naturally turned after the war to making sure that such a thing never happened again. Some people began to conceive of using fiscal policy not as a cure for an economy that had already fallen apart, but as prevention to keep a slowing economy, or an economy that had already entered into a recession, from falling into full-on depression. Once the economy began to slow, people could be hired by the government with borrowed money to do the same sorts of things that were done in the 1930s, and their paychecks would be spent at stores and elsewhere, and so businesses would see their incomes go up, and the recession would either never happen or quickly end. And to prevent overheating, when the economy was growing too fast, fiscal policy should be used just like monetary policy to slow it down. In other words, when a recession is imminent or has begun, the government should engage in *expansionary fiscal policy—increasing spending (or cutting taxes) to put money in people's pockets to restore economic growth to its normal level.* When the economy is growing faster than its underlying capacity, threatening inflation through the wage-price spiral, the government should engage in *contractionary fiscal policy—cutting spending or increasing taxes.* This aggressive use of fiscal policy came to be known as *Keynesian economics,* which in its aggressive, preemptive use of fiscal policy was a step beyond the crisis rationale that Keynes himself had offered.

The Depression had firmly cemented in the American mind the idea that it was the responsibility of government to fix "the economy" when it was broken, and so Keynesian economics fit comfortably with this belief. The rise of Keynesian economic theory after the war, which built mathematical models showing that government spending could promote stability, led to governments hiring large numbers of economists to build complicated macroeconomic models to predict where the economy was headed. By the early 1970s, when Republican President Richard Nixon told the country, "I am now a Keynesian in economics," this approach was nearly universally accepted as a means to prevent excessive economic volatility. The transformation of fiscal policy (and monetary policy too, for that matter) from cure to prevention supposed that every ordinary recession was just like (or could easily become like) the catastrophe of the 1930s.

Problem 1—Crowding Out

But in fact, the argument that garden-variety recessions were not the same thing as the Great Depression led to the first of three criticisms of Keynesian economics, the idea of *crowding out*. Remember that during the Depression, nominal interest rates fell to almost zero. The discussion of interest rates earlier in this chapter indicates that this meant the social opportunity cost of massive government borrowing was also nearly zero. But in an ordinary recession, businesses are still making long-term plans, and because of that, real interest rates, although lower than during an expansion, are still significantly above zero. In this environment, government borrowing to spend on public works is no longer a nearly free activity. Every dollar that the government borrows is bid away from some private-sector actor, an entrepreneur or a business who would've used it to take risks. Any workers hired to do the government projects built with borrowed money who were previously working creating something else for society, also have to count as crowding out. And there is no reason to think that public-sector employment comes primarily from workers who were unemployed before the project began. Indeed, to the extent that federal and state government work is carried out through unionized contractors, the workers who get those jobs may well be those who were highest on the union's priority list—who were precisely those who were most likely to be working before.

Of course, if the value of what the government spends the money on exceeds the value of what the private-sector actor would've spent it on, the borrowing can still be justified. However, the entire analysis of Chapter 5 indicates there are reasons to doubt this. If there is extensive waste or corruption in government spending, there will be a net social loss from having government spending crowd out private spending. If the government spends most of the money rewarding not the unemployed but the politically well-connected by building, in the colorful expression of the economist Gordon Tullock, "tunnels to nowhere," Keynesian fiscal policy during a recession has made us worse off.

Problem 2—Fiscal Policy Mechanics

The second problem is the actual mechanics of fiscal policy, as opposed to the mechanics of fiscal policy as described in a textbook or on a chalkboard. The U.S. Constitution is designed to make lawmaking difficult, and budget legislation is no different. (There are many years when the U.S. government fails, despite being legally obliged to, to officially pass a unified budget, instead opting for piecemeal agency-by-agency and department-by-department budgets.) Even if the orthodox process is followed, three quarters of a year may lapse between the time fiscal stimulus (that is, laws carrying out expansionary fiscal policy) is proposed and the time it is adopted. The time when the money actually arrives in the hands of those who were supposed to spend it is farther still in the future. This clumsiness is depicted in Table 12-1, which shows the official beginning and ending dates of postwar recessions as certified by the National Bureau of Economic Research (not including the great financial crash of 2008), along with the dates when fiscal stimulus was enacted.

Table 12-1. Beginning and Ending Dates of Recessions and Date of Enactment of Fiscal Stimulus

Beginning Date	End Date	Enactment of legislation
November 1948	October 1949	October, 1949
August 1957	April 1958	January, 1958; July, 1958
April 1960	February 1961	May, 1961; September, 1962
December 1969	November 1970	August 1971
November 1973	March 1975	March 1975; July 1976; May 1977
July 1981	November 1982	January 1983; March 1983
July 1990	March 1991	December 1991; April 1993
March 2001	November 2001	June 2001
December 2007	June 2009	February 2009; December 2010

In fairness, it must be said that the NBER only announces that recessions have begun and ended several months after the event or more, because the necessary data have to be compiled. Of course, looked at another way, this delay suggests that it is difficult to use fiscal policy in a timely way to address economic downturns. And late fiscal policy is worse than no fiscal policy at all, because once the recovery has begun, the opportunity cost of public borrowing in terms of private risk taking forgone is even higher than it was during the ordinary recession, that is, crowding out is worse. And this inefficiency of timing must be added on to the previously mentioned inefficiency of corruption and regulatory capture in determining how the money is spent.

Problem 3—Rational Expectations

The third cost involves people learning not to be surprised by fiscal policy, whose very effectiveness depends on surprise. This criticism, that people learn from the past when they try to predict the future, is known as the *rational expectations* problem. In the first recession after the creation of Keynesian fiscal policy, it may be that unemployed workers are put to work building roads, or Congress passes a big tax cut to put money in people's pockets, which they immediately spend. However, what is supposed to happen is that after the economy recovers, spending is supposed to be cut and/or taxes are supposed to be raised to retire the recently issued debt. People will learn about this pattern, and will start saving their tax cuts instead of spending them. Or, if they are businesses depending on the spending of the newly hired construction workers, they will quickly learn that this too was a flash in the pan, and so they should just put most of that money aside. Over time, in other words, fiscal policy will lose its effectiveness.

So does Keynesian fiscal policy work? The trouble with macroeconomic research is that it is possible to come up with statistical models with results that can confirm the belief that it does or that it doesn't; there was in fact a vigorous debate among very accomplished economists in the 1970s over this very question. (If one wishes to read more recent popular commentary from an advocate of Keynesian fiscal policy, Paul Krugman is one of its most consistent and vigorous advocates; he blogs here[9] and has also written books on this topic. For criticism, see this essay by Robert Higgs on the topic of "vulgar Keynesianism."[10]) It is a mistake, I think, to suppose that the question can ever be conclusively answered. It seems to be true that before the great crash of 2008, the postwar period had been marked by greater economic stability than before the war. Until this crash, the kinds of booms followed by severe downturns that took place in 1873, 1893, 1907, shortly after World War I, and in 1929 were not found after the war. That is an argument in favor of Keynesian macroeconomic management. But clearly very aggressive fiscal policy in the immediate aftermath of the 2008 crash, not just in the U.S. but in a number of countries around the world, conspicuously failed to get advanced economies, including that of the U.S., moving again. Then again, radical budget-cutting in the name of improving a country's fiscal situation (so-called "austerity), which is supposed to restore investor confidence, has also been argued by the financial writer Martin Wolf to be of little value.[11] Taken in total this suggests that macroeconomists may know little about the very things we want them to know the most about.

Keynes himself may have been right in his supposition that the macroeconomy can take care of itself until such time as it enters a severe depression, although even that is arguable in light of the recovery from the often very severe depressions before Keynes, when the only response was to do nothing.

---

[9] http://krugman.blogs.nytimes.com/
[10] http://www.independent.org/newsroom/article.asp?id=2448
[11] Martin Wolf, "The Impact of Fiscal Austerity in the Eurozone," *The Financial Times*, April 27, 2012.

But the post-2008 experience suggests that stimulus is not sufficient to end major downturns. Higgs argues[12] in a research paper presented for scholars of political economy that the politicized decision making of the Depression years actually increased investor uncertainty about what policies would come next and therefore decreased their willingness to invest. As we have seen, such politicization is an unavoidable part of Keynesian expansionary fiscal policy. But here the interested reader is best advised to go out and explore the issues himself.

Answers to In-Text Questions

12.1. The layoffs must occur according to the procedures specified in the contract. The contract will have been negotiated by representatives of the existing workers and will probably be designed to minimize management flexibility, if history is any guide. Layoff protection will thus tend to reward seniority and not past productivity. Indeed, collective bargaining can have the perverse effect of senior workers who will be the last to be laid off to support layoffs in lieu of reducing everyone's hours when demand for a firm's products declines. The article is older, but that unionized businesses tend to be more prone to laying workers off has been demonstrated in James L. Medoff, "Layoffs and Alternatives Under Trade Unions in U.S. Manufacturing," *American Economic Review* 69 (3) (June 1979): 380–395.

12.2. They are speculating that the rate of return, adjusted for such risks as the risk of nonrepayment, are higher for the bonds in question than for other investment options like other bonds, stocks, or directly investing in some local startup. Thus, when there is a crisis in, say, Cyprus, that may prompt investors to be eager to invest in bonds issued by the much stabler government of Germany. The government of Cyprus, in contrast, will, in order to persuade people to buy its bonds, have to agree to pay higher interest rates than before. When bond speculators drive the interest rate on bonds up or down, they are revealing what they think they know about how risky those investments are relative to the alternatives.

---

[12]http://www.independent.org/newsroom/article.asp?id=2448

Economics Out There

12.1. In an interview posted at the web site of *The Washington Post*,[13] the writer Michael Grunwald says that the fact that the economic stimulus of 2009–10 seems to have left us with nothing as clearly useful as the Golden Gate Bridge or La Guardia Airport (products of government spending in the 1930s) is not a problem, because the stimulus benefits "[are] often invisible. Even the stuff where you actually build big things—the world's largest wind farm, a half dozen of the world's largest solar farms—you'll still use your X-Box the same way. The energy is just coming from somewhere different." He also notes that the fact that the highest amount of job creation in years, which occurred after the stimulus passed but also after the worst episode of job destruction since the Great Depression, indicates that "[e]verything people think they know about the stimulus is wrong" (that is, that it worked much better than people thought).

Are the benefits of a more efficient energy system more "invisible" than the benefits of the X-Box? If so, what are those benefits? Is the fact that jobs fell sharply, the stimulus passed, then jobs grew really sharply an indication that the stimulus worked? What would a relatively slow rate of job creation in subsequent years indicate about its efficacy, and the reasons for it (or lack thereof)? Under what circumstances would you expect public perception of the benefits of economic stimulus to be at variance with the reality?

12.2. If you search the Internet for "Did the stimulus work?" you get a wide variety of pages with a wide variety of answers. One of the more cautious (although somewhat technical) attempts to answer this question is from Dylan Matthews here.[14] Surveying some research, he argues that the evidence is mixed but on balance positive.

---

[13]http://www.washingtonpost.com/blogs/wonkblog/wp/2012/09/09/everything-people-think-they-know-about-the-stimulus-is-wrong/
[14]http://www.washingtonpost.com/blogs/wonkblog/post/did-the-stimulus-work-a-review-of-the-nine-best-studies-on-the-subject/2011/08/16/gIQAThbibJ_blog.html

How does a car company that introduces a new engine design know that it "works"? How do we know that the theory of gravity "works"? How could we be confident about the claim (made in this book, among other places) that a low price ceiling on gasoline prices will often cause people to have to wait in line a long time to get it? What criteria should we use to decide whether the stimulus "worked," and how will we know whether those criteria have been met? Why do you suppose commentators and politicians are prone to having such strong views on the latter question? Are those views justified by the evidence? (Economics Out There question 5.4 may be of some help in thinking about macroeconomic systems and how precisely we can explain them.)

Macroeconomics

The Short and the Long Runs

Chapter 12 was devoted to the study of how government manages short-term economic fluctuations. This policy is not difficult to justify, at least on the surface. Economic downturns cause some people, often seemingly randomly and unfairly, to bear the costs of losing jobs. Sometimes downturns pass with little pain, sometimes (the 1930s, the years after 2007) they endure. Assuming the flow of technological innovation doesn't come to a permanent halt, which it never has before in human history (and especially since 1780), the economy will eventually right itself. But how long must we wait? Keynes himself famously dismissed the preoccupation with the tendency of the economy to *eventually* recover with a famous quote:

> *But this long run is a misleading guide to current affairs. In the long run we are all dead. Economists set themselves too easy, too useless a task if in tempestuous seasons they can only tell us that when the storm is long past the ocean is flat again.*[1]

Although Keynes was actually talking about economic problems after World War I, especially hyperinflation in Europe, the remark is often tied to his belief that when the economy is not growing—and in fact is in severe depression—it doesn't do any good to talk about its ultimate self-restorative powers. Instead, something must be done now. This is unquestionably short-term thinking, but is it wrong?

---

[1] John Maynard Keynes, *A Tract on Monetary Reform* (1923).

What Are We Aggregating?

First, remember that the government is like a low-magnification satellite trying to observe street-level details on a planet below. It is also an entity that has a very hard time making decisions. It is possible, therefore, that overly aggressive management—some call it micromanagement—of the economy does more harm than good, even discounting the effect (which we should not) of corruption on its decision making. But even apart from this, the core of the concept beloved by Keynes, and by his Keynesian followers after the war, deserves more scrutiny. That concept is *aggregate demand*, which Keynes felt declines during a depression and is then in need of revival by monetary and especially fiscal policy. When large numbers of people lack jobs, both those people and others become scared and stop spending their carefully hoarded savings on anything. Fiscal policy restores their confidence, and with it economic growth. Typically, Keynesians who want to model economic downturns refer to the concept of *aggregate demand* as completely chained to *aggregate supply*, which refers to the willingness of producers to supply more of some generic amount of everything as the price of this generic production changes. The standard supply-demand model of Chapters 2 and 3 is altered so that the supply of, for example, sofas becomes the aggregate supply of all goods and services, and the demand for sofas becomes the aggregate demand for everything. Figure 13-1 shows how this new model looks.

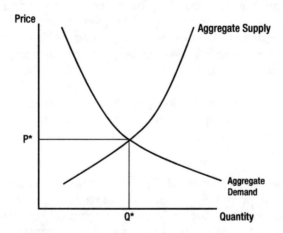

Figure 13-1. Aggregate supply and aggregate demand

This way of thinking about the economy has a certain surface explanatory power. When the stock market crashes, as it did in 1929 for example, people feel less wealthy. (Those who own assets such as stocks that decline in price *are* less wealthy.) Their demand for a wide variety of goods goes down, although demand for others—for example, low-cost substitutes for consumer goods or tomato seeds instead of fresh tomatoes—probably increases. In the Keynesian framework, it is simply demand for everything (aggregate demand) that has declined, and so the aggregate demand curve shifts left and the quantity of everything produced goes down, as does the overall price level (as measured, for example, by the consumer price index).

This seems to be a pretty good account of what happened during the Great Depression. People did start consuming a lot less, driven by the collapse in the values of their stocks, the massive wave of bank failures, and a terrifying deflation that took place during the first three or four years of the Depression. Fixing the economy is thus a simple matter of doing something to pump up aggregate demand, and massive government spending will, by shifting the aggregate demand curve to the right, seemingly do the trick. Thus the aggregate supply/aggregate demand model allows us to depict the idea of *economic stimulus* as a rightward shift in the aggregate demand curve—increased government demand for goods increases total social demand, because of the lack of crowding out during depression times owing to massive amounts of idle resources. The inability of the market (or really, of participants in all markets) to achieve this result without government prodding, because of the coordination failure between businesses and consumers, means that action is needed to revive the economy now—otherwise, the long-run growth we take for granted can't resume. This is Keynes's argument.

However, economics is all about making choices, and markets in particular are about making choices based on the price system among a near-infinite variety of *different* activities. Here is Robert Higgs, mentioned in Chapter 12, on the risks we take in engaging in this potential fallacy of composition, the treatment of "the economy" like a single market within it:

> This way of compressing diverse, wide transactions into single variables has the effect of suppressing recognition of the complex relationships and differences within each of the aggregates. Thus, in this framework, the effect of adding $1 million of investment spending for teddy-bear inventories is the same as the effect of adding one million dollars of investment spending for digging a new copper mine. Likewise, the effect of adding a million dollars of consumption spending for movie tickets is the same as the effect of adding $1 million of consumption spending for gasoline. Likewise, the effect of adding $1 million of government spending for children's inoculations against polio is the same as the effect of adding $1 million of government spending for 7.62 mm ammunition. It does not take much thought to conceive of ways in which the suppression of the differences within each of the aggregates might cause our thinking about the economy to go seriously awry.

> In fact, "the economy" does not produce an undifferentiated mass we call "output." Instead, the millions of producers who bring forth

"aggregate supply" provide an almost infinite variety of specific goods and services that differ in countless ways. Moreover, an immense amount of what goes on in a market economy consists of dealings among producers who supply no "final" goods and services at all, but instead supply raw materials, components, intermediate products, and services to one another. Because these producers are connected in an intricate pattern of relations, which must assume certain proportions if the entire arrangement is to work effectively, critical consequences turn on what in particular gets produced, when, where, and how.

These extraordinarily complex micro-relationships are what we are really referring to when we speak of "the economy." It is definitely not a single, simple process for producing a uniform, aggregate glop.[2]

So, if expansionary fiscal policy is targeted precisely at activities that need to shrink—because new alternatives for those activities have been found, or because the resources needed to carry out those activities now have better alternate uses, or are only in such high demand because their owners have unusual political power—throwing money at them will actually make the economy less able to use resources to meet people's conflicting needs in the most effective way. Higgs's analysis seems to suggest that we can think of fiscal policy as applied indiscriminately across a wide variety of activities, but there is some reason to think that it will be targeted not just at those with the best connections to the politicians dispensing the money (although that is a problem too) but to those activities that are in the most trouble—those activities, in other words, that the competitive process has most revealed to be in need of paring back. If Keynes is wrong about why depressions happen, aggregate demand management thus postpones the necessary reckoning.

▓ **Note**   If major economic downturns reveal that many people had beliefs that are now known to be mistaken, that major reallocation of resources needs to occur, then focusing on short-term revival of the economy by delaying these necessary liquidations will delay recovery.

In the Long Run, the Short-Run Bill Comes Due

In addition, Keynesian thinking is short-term thinking, as even Keynes himself would agree, but it faces a long-term constraint: the total sum of government spending from now until infinity cannot exceed the total amount the

---

[2]Robert Higgs, "Recession and Recovery: Six Fundamental Errors of the Current Orthodoxy," *The Independent Review* 14 (3) (2010): 466–467.

government takes in in revenue from now until infinity. The government can borrow money today, keep borrowing it tomorrow, and maybe even the day after that, but eventually that which has been borrowed has to be paid back, so that eventually we must pay out more than we spend for some period of time if we borrow today. (Unless we default, which will make it harder to borrow in the future.) Any individual managing his own finances knows this instinctively. And the analysis of Keynesian fiscal policy presented in Chapter 12 indicated that the original idea was that governments would run deficits when the economy was struggling, and it would run surpluses when it was doing very well—especially if it was in danger of overheating. So is that what actually has happened? Figure 13-2 suggests not. It shows the federal government's budget deficit (the annual amount by which federal spending exceeds taxes taken in) or surplus (the opposite circumstances) from 1930–2011. The chart is expressed as surplus or deficit as a percentage of GDP, with surpluses being greater than zero. This, rather than the absolute dollar amount of the surplus or deficit, is the best way to think about it.

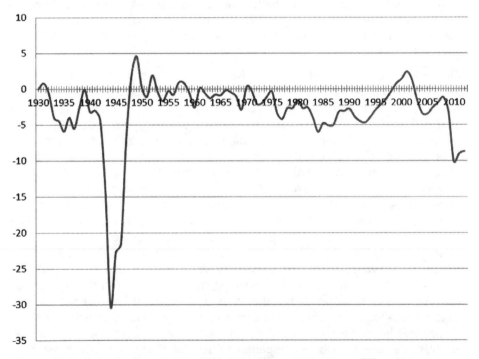

Figure 13-2. Federal budget deficits, 1930–2011. (*Source: White House Office of Management and Budget*)

Note first that there are several parts of the chart that deserve more explanation. The rapid rise in the budget deficit in the early 1930s (which means that net federal spending goes farther below the horizontal axis) was partly due to aggressive increases in federal spending to try to promote employment, but also to the collapse in tax revenues resulting from the Depression. The huge increase in the deficit during the World War II years was obviously to pay for the war; a huge amount of so-called war bonds were issued for precisely this purpose. And the elimination of the budget deficit for a short period in the late 1990s was significantly due to a booming stock market owing to the introduction of the Internet and other dramatic high-technology productivity improvements, which dramatically increased tax revenue. (This is a reminder of how important economic growth is in making things possible, in this case even government things.) But these anomalous periods aside, the chart suggests that the federal deficit on average has relentlessly increased as a percentage of GDP in the postwar period. The surpluses that are supposed to be run during good economic times never seem to arrive, while the average size of the deficit when times are bad seems to get relentlessly larger. The United States is not alone in this regard; many European countries and Japan have also seen the "normal" budget deficit expand in the postwar decades.

This may be because political incentives are heavily tilted toward the short term. Politicians serve a few terms, and then move on. Even a career politician will only be around 20 or 30 years. If the consequence of running a deficit now is that the politician who votes for the spending gets reelected, while the consequences in terms of debt obligation to future generations are some future politician's problem, the urge to vote to spend more is irresistible. But of course, if debt levels relative to the overall productive capacity of a society get large enough, people begin to doubt whether the economy whose government has issued that debt will generate enough economic growth in order to produce the taxes to pay it back. At this point, all the choices become bad. On the one hand, government spending must be cut significantly and/or taxes must go up significantly. To the extent the Keynesian model is correct, this will lead to significant economic difficulty. Alternatively, those who hold the debt of this government may decide to get rid of it, which will make it difficult to issue new debt at anything other than astronomical interest rates in the future. (Recall the discussion on interest rates. If lenders increase their belief that repeat borrowers won't pay money back, lenders start charging borrowers higher interest rates to compensate them for that higher perceived risk.) Or, the government that represents the people of the society may simply decide to repudiate the debt so as to avoid the hardest choices. It may do this by simply not paying interest that is due (perhaps negotiating with bondholders for partial repayment, but perhaps not), or by inflating the currency so badly that in real terms the bond payments are worth little.

▓ **Note**   Running fiscal deficits is politically easy. Running the surpluses needed to pay them back is politically hard.

People often do not realize it, but government debt is not certain in the same way that day following night is. Any government bond is only as safe as the willingness of future taxpayers in the society that has issued the bond to make the payments on it. The same argument applies to promised government payments for retirement. If future taxpayers are unwilling to shoulder these burdens, the debt becomes worthless. As I write this in 2013, several countries in Europe—Greece, Cyprus, and Spain especially—are going through precisely these horrible choices. If political incentives are short term enough, an economic policy focused on the short term may lead to a steadily deteriorating government financial profile. As noted earlier, this is a different kind of tragedy of the commons—everybody over-consumes government services now for short-term (that is, stabilization) benefit, because they won't be around to pay the bills.

Is Stabilization, in the End, the Primary Economic Objective?

For much of global economic history, economic instability was largely a nonissue. This was because the change that generates instability was slow and rare. It is change at whatever speed that generates both growth and contraction. The creation of a new technology, most obviously, presents new but uncertain opportunities, but it also brings with it a need to replace some existing ways of doing things. Because of decentralized, costly information, both the opportunities and what precisely they make obsolete take time to discover, and people may make mistakes in the course of applying the new breakthroughs. In ancient times, new technologies were rare, although new resources could be brought into use through discovery (new deposits of lead, say, which human ingenuity turns into a mine) or even through conquest. In Roman times, for example, there was constant pressure to obtain new resources, especially gold, other metals, and slaves, through conquest to preserve the standard of living of those already living in Roman territory. This ultimately contributed to struggles for power over the treasures that came with it, and thus to the breakdown of Roman law.

Rome was certainly not the only society to become great and then become ruthless in this way. In feudal times, after the Roman empire had fallen, the social structure kept everyone—from the king to the lowliest serf—in his place, and the nature of production was mostly agricultural and unchanging. Economic instability of the sort that we take for granted now was scarcely conceivable. There were few "booms" and "busts" unless there was a freak-ish event like the Black Death. It was only the creation of the modern tidal wave of innovation, which accompanied the stabilization of property rights and the industrialization it helped create, that ushered in the modern concept of expansions and depressions, of rising expectations, and of unemployment—layoffs in declining industries, for example. And even in the industrial era, the belief in the relevance of public policy toward economic stabilization—the idea that there was an "economy" that could and should be stabilized—did not exist until the early 20th century. It was just assumed that industries rose and industries fell, and it was the job of people to leave where the opportunity now wasn't and go to where it now was.

But now technological change (and the spread of the modern economic sys-tem to places full of potential innovators like China and India) is ubiquitous and not going away. The clamor for easing the pain when the costs, in terms of unemployment from liquidation, seemed at a particular moment to out-pace the beneficial effect of new innovations led to the modern theory and practice of stabilization. But a good argument can be made that stabilization is not really the most compelling economic problem, that by focusing only on the short term we are missing what is important. The French political and economic thinker Claude Frédéric Bastiat (1801–1850) told a story that came to be known as the *broken-windows fallacy*. Thinking ahead of his time about the weakness of economic stimulus and the mistake of focusing on short-term growth in GDP (although the concept of GDP would not itself be created until the mid-20th century), he argued if current additions to national income (that is, short-term GDP growth) are the only things to think about in terms of economic policy, then breaking a window actually makes society better off, by increasing the window repairman's income, and then the income of the stores where he spends his newly acquired money, and the income of the stores where those store owners spend their money, and so on down the line. But then, why stop there? Breaking all the windows will increase all repair-men's income, and hence GDP goes up that much more. And in a sense this claim might be right. *This year's* GDP might well go up, but over the long term the need to replace the windows draws resources away from activities that are more lucrative and exposes people unnecessarily, whether in the buildings in which they live or those in which they work, to disease and the weather. Breaking windows might increase income right now, but destroys some of the ability to use resources to produce wealth. (People in colder buildings are less productive.)

The key reason the fallacy fails to hold is the difference between *income* and *wealth*. As noted in Chapter 6, wealth includes all assets of value. At the national or global level, it includes things like oil in the ground, machinery, land, improvements to the land, and, most importantly, human capital—the accumulated human knowledge about how to combine the other resources better. The more wealth an individual—or any group of individuals, including a nation or the entire human race—has, the more things he or it can do, the greater the gains to trade, and the more human problems can be solved. Income, in contrast, is gains earned over some period of time as the result of bringing more existing wealth to the market—turning useless oil into valuable gasoline, a bad farmer selling his land to a better one, the invention of a new smartphone app. The creation of income—which is usually, recall, money paid to individuals in exchange for using the resources they control (especially their human capital) to help someone else create new wealth—will add more wealth to the extent it is not immediately consumed.

To use an example popular with economists, if we eat this year's seed corn, it is not available to create more corn next year. But if we avoid eating it, we have more corn to plan for next year, leading to even more corn then. But in the Bastiat example, there is the paradoxical problem of a destruction of wealth— the windows, whose elimination makes the buildings containing them less productive. It might well increase income earned right now, especially those of repairmen, for a few weeks, but the destructive effects of diverting resources to repair destroyed wealth instead of using that wealth to produce more new things soon outweighs that. (And recall that this assumes no political waste in how public stimulus money is spent.) As obvious as this seems, similar mistaken arguments exist today. Some economists, for example, argued that the horrible Japanese earthquake and tsunami of 2011, which killed thousands and wiped out many buildings in coastal areas near Sendai, could serve to stimulate an economy that had been growing slowly since the early 1990s. Apart from the sheer emotional horror of the event, it is clear that the Japanese people were worse off because of the awful destruction of so much human capital and infrastructure. Even if it could be guaranteed that no humans would be injured, the idea that Japan would prosper with an 8.9 earthquake every year is obviously preposterous.

To be sure, this reasoning, and the broken-windows fallacy, do not per se indict short-term economic stabilization, because the former two involve active destruction of wealth, and stabilization policy does not intrinsically do so. However, by diverting resources toward politically directed ends, such policies may lower future wealth creation. And either way, stabilization shares with these two examples the emphasis on short-term changes in economic activity as the primary economic problem. In fact, income earned in any given time period (in a year, say, which is the common measuring period for growth in real per-capita GDP) is a function of how much wealth exists to be deployed to produce that income. To the extent that short-term stabilization detracts from the long-term creation of wealth, either by using resources inefficiently or by consuming politicians' attention so that the production of such wealth is neglected, it damages a society's long-term growth prospects.

But does it? If aggregate-demand management (another term for stabilization policy, recall) targets economic stability as the main goal of government policy, rather than the need to encourage the creation of new technologies, it may actually increase the frictions that prevent adjustment. If the president calls union leaders and big-business CEOs into the Oval Office and urges that wages be propped up instead of being allowed to fall, in order to prevent an economic downturn from becoming worse, or if government regulations prevent prices from falling because it thinks "destructive competition" during a depression are the problem and not merely the messenger (both of which happened after the 1929 stock market crash), it is because he views the economy as a single entity, as a machine that when broken can be repaired by pushing the right button, and not the infinitely complex reconciling of the conflicting goals of hundreds of millions of people.

Inevitably, stabilization privileges some activities (by allowing them to earn or charge more than if prices were able to adjust freely, or by giving them access to taxpayer money) and therefore penalizes others by causing them to lose access to resources. Given the costly-information problem, there is reason to wonder whether viewing the economy as a lumpy "aggregate" does more harm than good. The short-term focus of economic stabilization, especially during a depression, means that it views the primary problem as jump-starting "the economy," rather than facilitating the movement of resources from where they mistakenly ended up (in the construction of too many houses, in the example of the 2007–08 housing crash) to where they ought to be. The latter task actually requires that liquidation and change happen faster while reviving a depressed economy. Stabilization policy—as opposed to government spending designed to achieve some other purpose, with recession-fighting as an alleged ancillary benefit—is really about preventing change. This is just as true if stabilization props up the construction industry by spending money on infrastructure, or by passing laws making homes easier to buy, or by trying to prevent workers' wages in some industries facing lower demand from falling.

There is a story about a Canadian politician named William Aberhart, who visited a public-works project at an airport in the 1930s and discovered that workers were being given "picks and shovels [instead of machinery] to lengthen the work," according to newspaper accounts. Machines get the job done faster, but shovels allow more people to draw paychecks, just as Keynes indicated was necessary. But Aberhart acerbically responded that if jobs were the goal, then if workers were given spoons and forks instead of shovels even *more* jobs could be created.[3] A very high-cost way of doing things shoved aside a lower-cost way. (Note that Keynes, who was willing to bury wealth

---

[3]This story is sometimes attributed to the economist Milton Friedman, who is said to have made the remarks to a government official while Friedman was visiting India. He may have said it, but the history of this story suggests that Aberhart was the original maker of the argument. For a history of this quote, see http://quoteinvestigator.com/2011/10/10/spoons-shovels/.

underground and dig it up again to create jobs, would have thought this perfectly acceptable.) If creating "jobs" is the primary objective of economic policy, other objectives—building airports that open on time and have lower (not higher) social cost, for example—don't get done. Short-term economic stabilization, thus, is not the only game in town and may require us to give up other things over the longer term.

■ **Note**   The sacrifice of some long-term economic growth may be the opportunity cost of fixation with short-term economic management.

Economic Policy for the Long Term

The preceding analysis suggests that the modern miracle outlined in Chapter 9 depends critically on giving people reasons to think for the long term, and the analysis in Chapter 4 and throughout the book suggests that an important task is the seeking out (or discovering) through competition of better ways to do things. One other school of macroeconomic thought, distinct from Keynesian economics, is often known as *supply-side economics*, which asserts that government taxes and regulation of economic activity destroy the incentive to take risks and engage in otherwise useful activities. If government focuses on enabling potentially profitable risk taking by enforcing property and contract rights and controlling market failures but otherwise refraining from taxing and regulating, then over the long haul entrepreneurs do their thing and progress happens as fast as it can. In the view of the modern supply-sider, taxes are always too high and regulation too extensive (and thus too expensive).

That taxes damage the incentive to do socially useful things (while perhaps being spent on other socially useful things) is almost beyond dispute. Supply and demand tell us that when the returns to activities are lower, people will engage in them less. If, say, the income tax goes up from 30 percent to 50 percent, many attempts to earn more income through entrepreneurial gambles (and many other attempts to earn more income through sure things, like working more hours) that make the cut at 30 percent will not seem worthwhile at 50 percent. This does not in and of itself make the increase in tax rates a bad thing; if the money is spent on economically useful things (public goods, especially) or people believe the forgone economic growth and wealth accumulation are worth the things they get from higher taxes, the taxes may be justified. Some of these things that higher taxes may accomplish—more uniform allotment of goods, such as health care, for example—are things that must be judged morally. Economics is of little help in making these calls, although it can help suggest to us the consequences of trying to achieve these goals.

Creating a more uniform allotment of goods this year (such as "improving income distribution"), by having the state assess high taxes and make sure that poorer people get more medical care and rich people less than they otherwise would, may decrease risk taking and innovation in the medical industries. Yet whereas today's poor do better, the poor *and* wealthy in the future, who aren't around yet to vote, get less than they otherwise would. This is an inevitable cost if progress is the fruit of constant entrepreneurial risk taking, and a decrease in such risk taking is the consequence when taxes go up, because risk taking has costs. This is nothing more than the implication of positively sloped supply curves. This in effect is also a lesson in the importance of thinking about the future, as well as of the weakness of democracy (people alive today vote, people born tomorrow don't) as a means for achieving economic efficiency. It is no surprise coming from this point of view that public debt and deficits in many democracies have increased for decades.

And while the supply-sider criticizes the destructive effects of high taxes, he is really, even if unknowingly, criticizing the extensive array of things modern governments spend money on. Much of this—in the U.S. context, the retirement program Social Security, the medical programs Medicare and Medicaid, the provision of income support to single mothers, and assorted other spending programs like subsidy of farming—has the effect of lowering much of the risk of modern life. No one, as long as Social Security is solvent, need worry that his retirement income will fall below a certain level. Of course, its solvency depends on the willingness of future generations to keep paying Social Security taxes, which in a climate of diminished economic growth might vanish. In that sense, there are no "entitlements," only claims on future resources that future taxpayers may or may not be willing to honor. And government spending must of course be funded either out of wealth creation by private individuals or else by enslavement of the population, the latter presumably not in the offing.

In that sense it is striking that by 2010 the average of government expenditure to GDP in the 27 countries of the European Union, according to the EU's statistical office Eurostat, had reached 50.3 percent, with Denmark leading the way at 58.2 percent and France in second at 56.2 percent.[4] (The comparable figure for the U.S. is about 40 percent for all levels of government, but it has risen almost continuously for over 100 years.[5]) The opportunities foregone

---

[4]Ireland actually led at 67.0 percent, but this figure was inflated by a gigantic bailout of failed banks. Source: http://epp.eurostat.ec.europa.eu/statistics_explained/index.php?title=File:Total_general_government_expenditure_by_country,_2005-2010_%28%25_of_GDP_and_millions_of_euro_and_in_2010%29.PNG&filetimestamp=20111006133248.
[5]http://www.usgovernmentspending.com/downchart_gs.php?year=1900_2010&units=p&title=Spending%20as%20percent%20of%20GDP#copypaste

because of massive government spending are unseen, as most opportunity costs are. But as the state has monopolized more and more problem solving, it is quite possible that those problems have been solved by political rather than economic competition, with all that entails, and that other problems have gone unsolved because higher taxes leave fewer resources for entrepreneurs to use in trying to solve them. One supposes (and indeed the evidence from Communist societies in the 20th century would seem to confirm) that there is only so much activity decided on the basis of markets that can be shoved aside by the state before the people become unable to effectively coordinate scarce-resource use, but I cannot say (no one can, in fact) whether modern societies such as the U.S. have reached that point.

On Government Budget Deficits and Your Children

The most common argument against restraint of taxation is that it causes budget deficits to go up. The supply-sider would reply that cutting taxes actually makes revenue go up, because the lower haul of each earned dollar taken as taxes encourages people to start and expand their businesses in great numbers. A smaller share of much more economic activity thus causes revenue to go up. At some level this effect is certainly true; at a tax rate of 100 percent no activity (outside the nontaxable black market) takes place, because all income-earning activity incurs some opportunity cost, and thus ceases to be rational. (People would resort to the black market to get that which they desired.) Cutting the rate to 90% cannot help but increase revenue. Cutting taxes from 90 to 10 percent would almost certainly also increase taxes taken in for this reason. But whether cutting taxes from where they are in the U.S. now to a modestly lower rate would achieve this is a deeply controversial issue, with a majority of economists dismissing this argument. (Google "The Laffer Curve" if you are interested.) But if too few taxes are collected relative to government expenditure, deficits are incurred, and it is often argued that tax cutting is damaging to society because of this increase in debt, which places obligations on future taxpayers.

Steven Landsburg has offered, in his book *The Armchair Economist* (Free Press, 2012) a provocative way of thinking about this problem. (The argument actually dates to the early 18th-century economist David Ricardo.) Suppose the government has decided to spend $1,000 per person on some Critical Task and must decide whether to borrow the money or raise it in current taxes. Suppose too that you as an individual have $5,000 that you want to set aside for your child to receive in 20 years. Suppose finally, for simplicity's sake, that there is only one interest rate paid on your savings and on government bonds, and it is the rate that causes one dollar saved today to become two dollars in

20 years.[6] (Assuming multiple interest rates complicates the problem without adding much to the analysis.)

The irresponsible thing to do, we are told, is to borrow the money. Doing that means that you put away the $5,000 for your child, which in 20 years becomes $5000 × 2 = $10,000, but when he gets it, he also inherits a $1,000 × 2 = $2,000 debt obligation. He thus is left with only $8,000, and not the $10,000 he would've otherwise received. So don't borrow from the children, in other words. Pay for things now. But, doing that (by funding the Critical Task through taxes levied now) leaves you only $4,000 to save for your child today, which thanks to the magic of interest in 20 years becomes $4,000 × 2 = ... $8,000! *Thus, the decision to tax or borrow is irrelevant, and the only thing that takes money away from your child is the decision by the government to spend $1,000 of your money today instead of allowing you to save it for your own children.*

So, the key question is not deficits or taxes, but whether to spend the money to begin with. How can we make this decision? Economic theory per se offers no conclusive guidance, but there is one distinction that sensible people make in their own lives that is useful. That distinction is between *consumption* and *investment*. The former, recall, is the act of using wealth right now so it is unavailable for future use, and the latter is using it to construct something that takes a while to finish in the hopes that it will yield greater opportunity to consume later. At the individual level, the act of investment, as the term is commonly used, is often indistinguishable from saving, although when businesses invest in factories instead of distributing profits to workers as higher wages or to stockholders as higher dividends, the definition becomes clearer. For the individual, spending money on a vacation is consumption, and putting it away in a retirement fund is investing.

When is it acceptable to borrow money? Sound financial practice generally requires that individuals limit their borrowing except to purchase assets that will provide extensive value and be used over a long period of time, and perhaps increase in value in the interim. A house can qualify on both grounds, and a car on the first (by enabling someone to drive to work). In each case, borrowing opens up doors to future opportunities to consume or earn income. As long as the increase in income allows a person to make his loan payments, the investment can be justified (depending on the interest rate, individual tastes for the good in question, and so on). Borrowing money for a vacation is clearly foolish, because that is momentary consumption today that produces nothing in the future and will limit consumption opportunities then, as opposed to an asset (like a house) that will provide consumption benefits *and*

---

[6]One can solve for this interest rate by noting that $1(1 + i)^{20} = $2, with *i* being the interest rate in question. Solving for it yields a rate of approximately 3.53%. (I am assuming no inflation, so this is a real interest rate.)

(probably) increased income or wealth in the future. For businesses, too, the distinction is clear. Borrowing money to build a new factory may be justifiable if the income from the factory allows loan payments to be made and profits still to increase. Borrowing money to rent the local NFL stadium for the office Christmas party or to make a gold-plated bathroom for the company president would be an exercise in self-indulgent consumption and might induce shareholders to fire the company president who made that decision.[7]

In private decision making, the lesson is that borrowing is defensible if you get something (get enough, actually) to repay down the line what you have borrowed, whereas borrowing for the here and now is foolish (as is borrowing to make investments that are foolish, such as a home that is too expensive). And it is the same with government decision making. It is perfectly justifiable for governments to borrow money to build projects that over the long term will allow citizens to trade more productively with one another and create more wealth. Public water and health systems, transportation and other infrastructure, and the construction of school buildings are examples of these kinds of investments, and governments routinely borrow money to make them. A road, if it enables enough wealth creation to generate at least enough tax revenue to pay the loans taken out to build it back, can be a justifiable investment, even if it means we go into debt right now. As we have seen, private entrepreneurs can provide many of these services once the basic infrastructure is built, but the record of increased wealth as a result of investments of this kind is impressive. People who live in nations with good transportation, communications, and public-health systems are, other things equal, more able to convert what they know and have into goods they can use by obtaining them through trade with others.

On the other hand, borrowing money to consume right now is just as foolish as a family borrowing money to go on vacation. Current expenses—defending the country right now, paying retirement benefits right now, subsidizing farmers right now to produce this year's crop—should be funded out of current taxes if the system is to be sustainable. Again, as a reminder, people who lend money to the government do not have an ironclad claim to future wealth. The security of a government bond is only as good as future taxpayers' willingness to pay the money the small print in the bonds says they owe, and those who have bought bonds issued in recent years by the country of Greece (as with many other countries before it; dozens of countries and numerous U.S. municipalities defaulted on their debt in the last century) have discovered just how shaky those promises are. So a good recipe for responsible government decision making, in addition to those mentioned earlier, is *to borrow money only to fund projects that will raise private productivity enough to justify the investment*. In that sense, the long-term deterioration in government deficits

---

[7] If the gold-plated bathroom allowed the company to get much better CEOs, then this would be an investment, and perhaps a justifiable one.

in the United States, which have grown in recent years to approach 10% of GDP, are worrisome, given that the fastest-growing and largest component of federal spending is entitlement spending,[8] much of which is the payment of cash for living expenses right now, rather than any investments that will make us wealthier in the future. (Spending that substantially improves the health of the poor, because it would improve the current generation of poor's human capital, might be an exception.)

■ **Note**   The alleged choice between borrowing and burdening our children or taxing now and burdening ourselves is usually a false one. The true choice is whether to take resources from people in the future or not, regardless of whether we take them now through taxation or later through repayment of public debt..

Note finally that the so-called supply-side perspective also includes the deterrent effect of regulations (in addition to taxation) on wealth creation. Just as with taxes, there is once again a trade-off. Taxes are essential to fund government, and government is essential to make private exchange possible. But excessive taxation, including in particular when it is imposed on people in the future, kills the golden goose, even as it has a certain appeal in democratic societies. So too with regulations. Regulations to control market failure clearly make people better off on balance. We are healthier when people are not allowed to pollute the air as the mood strikes them. The state's effective control of theft and violence (offset to some extent by its propensity to wage war against other states), something only thoroughly achieved in the last few centuries, has been an important human achievement.

But once the government is accepted as an arbiter of what kinds of trades may and may not happen, the regulatory-capture problem quickly surfaces. If regulations are used merely to keep foreign airlines from carrying passengers within the U.S., thus raising ticket prices, to keep workers who don't wish to join a union from coming on their own to an agreement with their employer, or to allow people who oppose real estate development to use wetlands regulation to prevent homebuilders from achieving their dream instead of bargaining with those homeowners over how to use the land through the market (and the market's value lies precisely in its ability to peacefully arbitrate these kinds of disputes), this impoverishes society as a whole. Just as public borrowing should be limited to true investments, regulations should be limited to those that control externalities that cannot properly be controlled

---

[8]http://fivethirtyeight.blogs.nytimes.com/2013/01/16/what-is-driving-growth-in-government-spending/

through the market, and to prevent true tragedy-of-the-commons problems. Remember that what economics has to say about whether public spending is a good thing or not is limited to talking about its costs. People may decide that using the government to insure themselves against life's setbacks is justified despite its cost, and the economist may help inform the public what the costs of doing so are likely to be.

If much of this chapter seems like a contradiction of the optimism of Chapter 9, remember that it is speculative. I am speculating that the appetite of those living today for the money of those yet to be born is very high, and that the diversion of resources needed to fund these appetites to government from private citizens trying to pursue their interests will cause the economy to grow too slowly to generate the taxes in the future needed to pay what has been promised today. As we have seen, speculation about the future is difficult, and pessimistic speculation is very likely to be wrong. What does differentiate the analysis here and the earlier analysis in Chapter 9 is that Chapter 9 takes comfort in the long history of entrepreneurs solving what were thought to be unsolvable problems, whereas this chapter takes caution from the history of government and what drives it, and its frequent hostility towards those entrepreneurs in particular. The incentives of those who govern and those who create are at odds from time to time. In a book on economics, perhaps that is as good a place to end as any.

Economics Out There

13.1. In 2011, CNN hosted a discussion between two economists of some renown[9] on how to get the economy moving again, three years after it crashed. They disagree on the wisdom of issuing a lot of new government debt to revive it. (Paul Krugman, who supports the debt, actually colorfully updates the Keynes metaphor by suggesting the government persuade the people that an attack from outer space is imminent, so that the defenses we build will jump-start the economy.) When the government borrows money, it spends scarce resources now. Borrowed wealth is spent now. Where is that wealth borrowed from? (Hint: the primary answer is not a place or activity but a time.) Under what circumstances would you be prepared to say that large-scale public borrowing, *for the primary purpose of stimulating the economy*, is worthwhile?

---

[9]http://globalpublicsquare.blogs.cnn.com/2011/08/18/what-do-we-need-to-fix-the-economy/

13.2.   In an influential piece called "The Burden of the Public Debt," (in Lloyd A. Metzler et al. (eds.), *Income, Employment and Public Policy, Essays in Honour of Alvin Hanson*, (New York, NY: W. W. Norton, 1948): 255–275, Abba P. Lerner made an argument that public debt is of no consequence per se because, in essence, "we owe the money to ourselves." In particular, he argued:

> A variant of the false analogy is the declaration that national debt puts an unfair burden on our children, who are thereby made to pay for our extravagances. Very few economists need to be reminded that if our children or grandchildren repay some of the national debt these payments will be made *to* our children or grandchildren and to nobody else. Taking them altogether they will no more be impoverished by making the repayments than they will be enriched by receiving them.

> In attempts to discredit the argument that we owe the national debt to ourselves it is often pointed out that the "we" does not consist of the same people as the "ourselves." The benefits from interest payments on the national debt do not accrue to every individual in exactly the same degree as the damage done to him by the additional taxes made necessary. That is why it is not possible to repudiate the whole national debt without hurting anybody. While this is undoubtedly true, all it means is that some people will be better off and some people will be worse off. Such a redistribution of wealth is involved in every significant happening in our closely interrelated economy, in every invention or discovery or act of enterprise. If there is some good general reason for incurring debt, the redistribution can be ignored because we have no more reason for supposing that the new distribution is worse than the old one than for assuming the opposite. That the distribution will be *different* is no more an argument against national debt than it is an argument in favor of it. (p. 256)

Suppose that "the money borrowed now" is given to "some people" whose last name starts with a letter drawn randomly from an urn, and the necessary taxes are later paid by other people whose last names start with a different random letter. Will this affect how "some people," other people, and the rest of us behave when it is possible to issue public debt? (Hint: think about the act of deciding how much to consume now and how much to invest in hopes of future rewards.) What if "some people" receive a check in the name of stimulating the economy because they currently do not work for pay, while other people later on are made to pay additional taxes because the companies they own happen to have a lot of cash to spare when it comes time to repay the debt?

Suppose we decide to cancel all homeowner mortgage debt in the U.S. because we know that while "some people" who held those mortgages and were expecting them to be paid off are worse off, other people who are paying off (or trying to pay off) those mortgages will be better off. Since the mortgages are just "money we owed ourselves," is the forgiveness costless? Is it something we should only evaluate on the basis of whether there is "a good general reason for it"? As a general rule, to what extent is public spending based on debt like or not like an "invention or discovery or act of enterprise"?

I

Index

Other Apress Business Titles You Will Find Useful

Deficit, 2nd Edition
Bussing-Burks
978-1-4302-4839-2

Health Care Reform Simplified, 2nd Edition
Parks
978-1-4302-4896-5

Broken Markets
Mellyn
978-1-4302-4221-5

Corporate Tax Reform
Sullivan
978-1-4302-3927-7

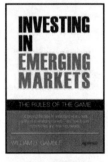

Investing in Emerging Markets
Gamble
978-1-4302-3825-6

Plan Your Own Estate
Wheatley-Liss
978-1-4302-4494-3

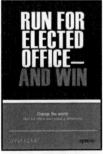

Run for Elected Office— and Win
Kemp
978-1-4302-3798-3

Tax Insight
Murdock
978-1-4302-4737-1

Healthcare, Insurance, and You
Zamosky
978-1-4302-4953-3

Available at www.apress.com

CPSIA information can be obtained at www.ICGtesting.com
Printed in the USA
LVOW10s2223100913

351906LV00005B/250/P

9 781430 259411